A·N·N·U·A·L E·D·I·T·I·O·N·S

Early Childhood Education 00/01

Twenty-First Edition

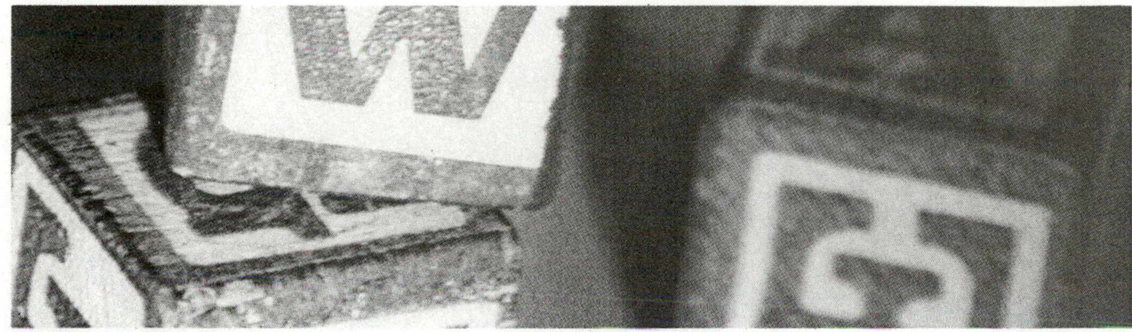

EDITORS

Karen Menke Paciorek
Eastern Michigan University

Karen Menke Paciorek is a professor of early childhood education at Eastern Michigan University. Her degrees in early childhood education include a B.A. from the University of Pittsburgh, an M.A. from George Washington University, and a Ph.D. from Peabody College of Vanderbilt University. She is the coeditor, with Joyce Huth Munro, of *Sources: Notable Selections in Early Childhood Education* (Dushkin/McGraw-Hill). She has served as president of the Michigan Association for the Education of Young Children and is the current chair of the Michigan Early Childhood Education Consortium. She presents at local, state, and national conferences on curriculum planning, guiding behavior, preparing the learning environment, and working with families.

Joyce Huth Munro
Joyce Huth Munro is an educational consultant and editor in early childhood education. She has been an administrator and professor at colleges in Kentucky, South Carolina, and New Jersey. Currently, she is researching and writing about leadership in child care administration. She is coeditor (with Karen Menke Paciorek) of *Sources: Notable Selections in Early Childhood Education* At regional and national conferences, she presents seminars on innovative methods of teacher education and curriculum design. Dr. Munro holds an M.Ed. from the University of South Carolina and a Ph.D. from Peabody College at Vanderbilt University.

Dushkin/McGraw-Hill
Sluice Dock, Guilford, Connecticut 06437

Visit us on the Internet
http://www.dushkin.com/annualeditions/

Credits

1. Perspectives
Unit photo—© 2000 by Cleo Freelance Photography.
2. Childhood Development and Families
Unit photo—Dushkin/McGraw-Hill photo by Adelaide Raucci.
3. Care and Educational Practices
Unit photo—© 2000 by Cleo Freelance Photography.
4. Guiding and Supporting Young Children
Unit photo—© 2000 by PhotoDisc, Inc.
5. Curricular Issues
Unit photo—© 2000 by Cleo Freelance Photography.
6. Trends
Unit photo—New York Times photo by John Sotomayor.

Copyright

Cataloging in Publication Data
Main entry under title: Annual Editions: Early Childhood Education. 2000/2001.
1. Education, Preschool—Periodicals. 2. Child development—Periodicals. 3. Child rearing—United States—Periodicals. I. Paciorek, Karen Menke, *comp.;* Munro, Joyce Huth, *comp.* II. Title: Early childhood education.
ISBN 0-07-236540-4   372.21'05   77-640114   ISSN: 0272-4456

Twenty-First Edition

Cover image © 2000 PhotoDisc, Inc.

Printed in the United States of America   234567890BAHBAH543210   Printed on Recycled Paper

Editors/Advisory Board Staff

Members of the Advisory Board are instrumental in the final selection of articles for each edition of ANNUAL EDITIONS. Their review of articles for content, level, currentness, and appropriateness provides critical direction to the editor and staff. We think that you will find their careful consideration well reflected in this volume.

To the Reader

In publishing ANNUAL EDITIONS we recognize the enormous role played by the magazines, newspapers, and journals of the public press in providing current, first-rate educational information in a broad spectrum of interest areas. Many of these articles are appropriate for students, researchers, and professionals seeking accurate, current material to help bridge the gap between principles and theories and the real world. These articles, however, become more useful for study when those of lasting value are carefully collected, organized, indexed, and reproduced in a low-cost format, which provides easy and permanent access when the material is needed. That is the role played by ANNUAL EDITIONS.

New to ANNUAL EDITIONS is the inclusion of related World Wide Web sites. These sites have been selected by our editorial staff to represent some of the best resources found on the World Wide Web today. Through our carefully developed topic guide, we have linked these Web resources to the articles covered in this ANNUAL EDITIONS reader. We think that you will find this volume useful, and we hope that you will take a moment to visit us on the Web at ***http://www.dushkin.com*** to tell us what you think.

Early childhood education is an interdisciplinary field that includes child development, family issues, educational practices, behavior guidance, and curriculum. *Annual Editions: Early Childhood Education 00/01* brings you the latest information in the field from a wide variety of recent journals, newspapers, and magazines. In selecting articles for this edition we were careful to provide you with a well-balanced look at the issues and concerns facing teachers, families, society, and children. There are four themes found in readings chosen for this twenty-first edition of *Annual Editions: Early Childhood Education.* They are: (1) the continued release of key findings on how the brain develops and how teachers can best meet the learning needs of young children, (2) the importance of professionals receiving specific academic preparation in early childhood or child development for quality early childhood education to occur, (3) appropriate, authentic curricula that supports children's desire to investigate issues most relevant to their lives, and (4) the evergrowing quest for excellence in early childhood education.

Continuing in this edition of *Annual Editions: Early Childhood Education* are selected *World Wide Web* sites that can be used to further explore topics addressed in the articles. These sites will be cross-referenced by number in the *topic guide.* We have chosen to include only a few high-quality sites.

Given the wide range of topics it includes, *Annual Editions: Early Childhood Education 00/01* may be used by several groups: undergraduate or graduate students studying early childhood education, professionals pursuing further development, parents seeking to improve their skills, or administrators new to early childhood education who want to develop an understanding of the critical issues in the field.

The selection of readings for this edition has been a cooperative effort between the two editors. We meet each year with members of our advisory board, who share with us in the selection process. The production and editorial staff of Dushkin/McGraw-Hill ably support and coordinate our efforts. This book is used at over 550 colleges and universities throughout the country. We realize that this is a tremendous responsibility—to provide a thorough review of the current literature—and one that we take seriously. Our job is to provide the reader with a snapshot of the critical issues facing professionals in early childhood education. We thank the members of the advisory board who contribute articles throughout the year. It takes many people making selections to develop a complete collection of current readings. We would also like to thank Eastern Michigan University early childhood graduate student Whitney Young for her efforts to obtain quality readings for this collection.

To the instructor or reader interested in the history of early childhood care and education programs throughout the years, we invite you to review our latest book, also published by Dushkin/McGraw-Hill. *Sources: Notable Selections in Early Childhood Education, 2nd edition* (1999) is a collection of numerous writings of enduring historical value by influential people in the field. All of the selections are primary sources that allow you to experience at first hand the thoughts and views of these important educators. The instructor interested in using both *Sources* and *Annual Editions* may contact the editors for a list of compatible readings from the two books.

We are grateful to readers who have corresponded with us about the selection and organization of previous editions. Your comments and articles sent for consideration are welcomed and will serve to modify future volumes. Take time to fill out and return the postage-paid article rating form on the last page. You may also contact either of us at karen.paciorek@emich.edu or jhmunro@aol.com.

We look forward to hearing from you.

Karen Menke Paciorek
Editor

Joyce Huth Munro
Editor

Contents

The concepts in bold italics are developed in the article. For further expansion please refer to the Topic Guide and the Index.

Child Development and Families

Six selections consider the effects of family life on the growing child and the importance of parent education.

The concepts in bold italics are developed in the article. For further expansion please refer to the Topic Guide and the Index.

UNIT 3

Care and Educational Practices

Eleven selections examine various educational programs, assess the effectiveness of some teaching methods, and consider some of the problems faced by students with special needs.

The concepts in bold italics are developed in the article. For further expansion please refer to the Topic Guide and the Index.

UNIT 4

Guiding and Supporting Young Children

Five selections examine the importance of establishing self-esteem and motivation in the child and consider the effects of stressors such as violence on behavior.

The concepts in bold italics are developed in the article. For further expansion please refer to the Topic Guide and the Index.

Curricular Issues

Eight selections consider various curricular choices. The areas covered include play, authentic learning, emergent literacy, motor development, technology, and conceptualizing curriculum.

The concepts in bold italics are developed in the article. For further expansion please refer to the Topic Guide and the Index.

Trends

Five selections consider the present and future of early childhood education.

The concepts in bold italics are developed in the article. For further expansion please refer to the Topic Guide and the Index.

The concepts in bold italics are developed in the article. For further expansion please refer to the Topic Guide and the Index.

Topic Guide

This topic guide suggests how the selections and World Wide Web sites found in the next section of this book relate to topics of traditional concern to students and professionals involved with early childhood education. It is useful for locating interrelated articles and Web sites for reading and research. The guide is arranged alphabetically according to topic.

The relevant Web sites, which are numbered and annotated on pages 4 and 5, are easily identified by the Web icon (◎) under the topic articles. By linking the articles and the Web sites by topic, this ANNUAL EDITIONS reader becomes a powerful learning and research tool.

TOPIC AREA	TREATED IN
Academics	16. Homework Doesn't Help 17. Make or Break 18. Playtime Is Cancelled 19. "But What's Wrong with Letter Grades?" 38. Why Students Lose When "Tougher Standards"Win 40. Early Learning, Later Success ◎ ***2, 3, 4, 5, 8, 15, 17, 24, 25***
Aggressive Behavior	10. Boys Will Be Boys 23. Why and Wherefore 25. Television Violence and Its Effects ◎ ***16, 18, 19, 21, 22, 23***
Assessment	15. Case for Developmental Continuity 19. "But What's Wrong with Letter Grades?" 32. Documenting Children's Learning 33. Challenging Movement Experiences 39. Achieving Excellence in Education ◎ ***11, 13, 17, 18, 27, 31, 35***
Brain Development	4. Mysteries of the Brain 5. Using Early Childhood Brain Development Research 7. Fetal Psychology 9. Baby Talk 27. Adverse Effects of Witnessing Violence 39. Achieving Excellence in Education ◎ ***14***
Child Care: Full Day/Half Day	3. Child Shall Lead Us 12. Petite Elite 26. Fostering Intrinsic Motivation 37. Almost a Million Children in School before Kindergarten 40. Early Learning, Later Success ◎ ***6, 7, 19***
Child Development	4. Mysteries of the Brain 5. Using Early Childhood Brain Development Research 7. Fetal Psychology 8. Children's Prenatal Exposure to Drugs 9. Baby Talk 10. Boys Will Be Boys 11. Education of Hispanics ◎ ***11, 14, 21, 23***
Collaboration	3. Child Shall Lead Us 22. Inclusion of Young Children with Special Needs 27. Adverse Effects of Witnessing Violence 37. Almost a Million Children in School before Kindergarten ◎ ***1, 19, 23***
Constructivist Practice	31. Productive Questions 32. Beginning to Implement the Reggio Philosophy 39. Achieving Excellence in Education ◎ ***20, 24, 26, 32, 34, 35***
Creativity	27. Play as Curriculum 31. Beginning to Implement the Reggio Philosophy ◎ ***24, 26, 28***
Curriculum	11. Petite Elite 28. Play As Curriculum 29. Why Curriculum Matters 30. Isn't That Cute? 31. Productive Questions 32. Beginning to Implement the Reggio Philosophy 34. Challenging Movement Experiences 39. Achieving Excellence in Education ◎ ***15, 17, 18, 20, 24, 25, 27, 29, 30***
Developmentally Appropriate Practice	1. Starting Early 13. Simply Sensational Spaces 15. Case for Developmental Continuity 17. Make or Break 20. From Philosophy to Practice 29. Why Curriculum Matters 34. Challenging Movement Experiences 35. What Role Should Technology Play . . . ? 38. Why Students Lose When "Tougher Standards" Win 39. Achieving Excellence in Education ◎ ***18, 19, 22, 34***
Discipline	23. Why and Wherefore 24. Teaching Peace Concepts 26. Fostering Intrinsic Motivation ◎ ***15, 17, 18, 19, 22***
Diversity	3. Child Shall Lead Us 11. Education of Hispanics 20. From Philosophy to Practice 38. Why Students Lose When "Tougher Standards" Win ◎ ***10, 13***
Emergent Literacy	9. Baby Talk 21. Emergent Literacy ◎ ***24***
Emotional Development	8. Children's Prenatal Exposure to Drugs 10. Boys Will Be Boys 13. Simply Sensational Spaces 14. Don't Shut Fathers Out 27. Adverse Effects of Witnessing Violence ◎ ***11, 14***
Families	3. Child Shall Lead Us 5. Using Early Childhood Brain Development Research 10. Boys Will Be Boys 14. Don't Shut Fathers Out 20. From Philosophy to Practice 22. Inclusion of Young Children with Special Needs 37. Almost a Million Children in School before Kindergarten 40. Early Learning, Later Success ◎ ***1, 10, 12, 23, 33***
Guiding Behavior	23. Why and Wherefore 24. Teaching Peace Concepts 25. Television Violence and Its Effects 26. Fostering Intrinsic Motivation 27. Adverse Effects of Witnessing Violence ◎ ***15, 17, 18, 19, 20***

TOPIC AREA	TREATED IN
Inclusion	20. From Philosophy to Practice 21. Emergent Literacy 22. Inclusion of Young Children with Special Needs ***10, 13***
Infants and Toddlers	4. Mysteries of the Brain 7. Fetal Psychology 8. Children's Prenatal Exposure to Drugs 9. Baby Talk 13. Simply Sensational Spaces 26. Fostering Intrinsic Motivation Classrooms ***7, 11***
Intervention	8. Children's Prenatal Exposure to Drugs 20. From Philosophy to Practice 22. Inclusion of Young Children with Special Needs 40. Early Learning, Later Success ***8, 11, 13***
Language Development	9. Baby Talk 13. Simple Sensational Spaces 40. Early Learning, Later Success ***7, 10, 11, 13, 14***
Learning	1. Starting Early 4. Mysteries of the Brain 13. Simply Sensational Spaces 15. Case for Developmental Continuity 16. Homework Doesn't Help 19. "But What's Wrong with Letter Grades?" 21. Emergent Literacy in an Early Childhood Classroom 29. Why Curriculum Matters 33. Documenting Children's Learning 35. What Role Should Technology Play . . . ? 36. Learning to Go with the Grain of the Brain 38. Why Students Lose When "Tougher Standards" Win 40. Early Learning, Later Success ***10, 11, 13, 14, 15, 24, 25, 26, 28***
Motor Development	7. Fetal Psychology 13. Simply Sensational Spaces 18. Playtime Is Cancelled 34. Challenging Movement Experiences ***22***
Multicultural	11. Education of Hispanics ***10, 13, 34, 35***
Play	12. Petite Elite 13. Simply Sensational Spaces 18. Playtime Is Cancelled 28. Play As Curriculum 29. Why Curriculum Matters ***15, 17, 18, 21, 28, 29***
Prenatal	7. Fetal Psychology 8. Children's Prenatal Exposure to Drugs 23. Why and Wherefore ***4, 14***
Preschool	1. Starting Early 14. Don't Shut Fathers Out 21. Emergent Literacy 25. Television Violence and Its Effects 29. Why Curriculum Matters 37. Almost a Million Children in School before Kindergarten ***6, 19***
Primary Grades	14. Don't Shut Fathers Out 16. Homework Doesn't Help 17. Make or Break 19. "But What's Wrong with Letter Grades?" 32. Documenting Children's Learning ***24, 25, 26, 27, 28, 29, 30***
Quality	1. Starting Early 12. Petite Elite 37. Almost a Million Children in School before Kindergarten 40. Early Learning, Later Success ***8, 35***
Research	5. Using Early Childhood Brain Development Research 7. Fetal Psychology 10. Boys Will Be Boys 16. Homework Doesn't Help 22. Inclusion of Young Children with Special Needs 37. Almost a Million Children in School before Kindergarten 40. Early Learning, Later Success ***4, 5, 7, 35***
Social Development	10. Boys Will Be Boys 22. Inclusion of Young Children with Special Needs 24. Teaching Peace Concepts ***11, 13***
Special Needs	20. From Philosophy to Practice 21. Emergent Literacy 22. Inclusion of Young Children with Special Needs ***5, 11, 18, 19, 21, 22, 23***
Teachers/ Training	1. Starting Early 2. What Makes Good Early Childhood Teachers? 4. Mysteries of the Brain 12. Petite Elite 16. Homework Doesn't Help 23. Why and Wherefore 24. Teaching Peace Concepts 26. Fostering Intrinsic Motivation 27. Adverse Effects of Witnessing Violence 29. Why Curriculum Matters 30. Isn't That Cute? 31. Productive Questions 32. Beginning to Implement the Reggio Philosophy 33. Documenting Children's Learning 39. Achieving Excellence in Education ***3, 10, 15, 17, 18, 22, 24, 25, 27, 28, 29, 30, 31, 32, 35***
Testing	18. Playtime Is Cancelled 19. "But What's Wrong with Letter Grades?" 38. Why Students Lose When "Tougher Standards" Win ***29, 34, 35***
Violence	3. Child Shall Lead Us 23. Why and Wherefore 25. Television Violence and Its Effects 27. Adverse Effects of Witnessing Violence ***21, 23***

World Wide Web Sites

DUSHKIN ONLINE

AE: Early Childhood Education

The following World Wide Web sites have been carefully researched and selected to support the articles found in this reader. If you are interested in learning more about specific topics found in this book, these Web sites are a good place to start. The sites are cross-referenced by number and appear in the topic guide on the previous two pages. Also, you can link to these Web sites through our DUSHKIN ONLINE support site at *http://www.dushkin.com/online/*.

The following sites were available at the time of publication. Visit our Web site—we update DUSHKIN ONLINE regularly to reflect any changes.

General Sources

1. Connect for Kids

http://www.connectforkids.org

This nonprofit site provides news and information on issues affecting children and families, with over 1,500 helpful links to national and local resources.

2. Eric Clearing House on Elementary and Early Childhood Education

http://www.ericeece.org

This invaluable site provides links to all ERIC system sites: clearinghouses, support components, and publishers of ERIC materials. You can search the massive ERIC database and find out what is new in early childhood education.

3. National Association for the Education of Young Children

http://www.naeyc.org

The NAEYC Web site is a valuable tool for anyone working with young children. Also see the National Education Association site: *http://www.nea.org*.

4. National Institute on Early Childhood Development and Education (ECI)

http://www.ed.gov/offices/OERI/ECI/

ECI was created by the U.S. Department of Education to provide programs of research, development, and dissemination to improve early childhood development and education. Access to grants, publications, presentations, on-line conferencing, and networking are available.

5. U.S. Department of Education

http://www.ed.gov/pubs/TeachersGuide/

Government goals, projects, grants, and other educational programs are listed here as well as many links to teacher services and resources.

Perspectives

6. Child Care Directory: Careguide

http://www.careguide.net

Find licensed/registered child care by state, city, region, or age of child at this site. Site contains providers' pages, parents' pages and many links.

7. Early Childhood Care and Development

http://ecdgroup.harvard.net

This site concerns international resources in support of children to age 8 and their families. It includes research and evaluation, policy matters, programming matters, and related Web sites.

8. Goals 2000: A Progress Report

http://www.ed.gov/pubs/goals/progrpt/index.html

Open this site to survey a progress report by the U.S. Department of Education on the Goals 2000 reform initiative. It provides a sense of educator's future goals.

Child Development and Families

9. Administration for Children and Families

http://www.acf.dhhs.gov

This site provides information on federally funded programs that promote the economic and social well-being of families, children, and communities.

10. Global SchoolNet Foundation

http://www.gsn.org

Access this site for multicultural education information. The site includes news for teachers, students, and parents as well as chat rooms, links to educational resources, programs, and contests and competitions.

11. The National Academy for Child Development

http://www.nacd.org

The NACD, an international organization, is dedicated to helping children and adults reach their full potential. Its home page presents links to various programs, research, and resources into such topics as learning disabilities, ADD/ADHD, brain injuries, autism, accelerated and gifted, and other similar topic areas.

12. National Parent Information Network/ERIC

http://npin.org

This clearinghouse of elementary, early childhood, and urban education data has information for parents and for people who work with parents.

13. World Education Exchange/Hamline University

http://www.hamline.edu/~kjmaier/

This site, which aims for "educational collaboration," takes you around the world to examine virtual classrooms, trends, policy, and infrastructure development. It leads to information about school reform, multiculturalism, technology in education, and much more.

14. Zero to Three

http://www.zerotothree.org

Find here developmental information on the first 3 years of life—an excellent site for both parents and professionals.

Care and Educational Practices

15. Canada's Schoolnet Staff Room

http://www.schoolnet.ca/home/e/

Here is a resource and link site for anyone involved in education, including special-needs educators, teachers, parents, volunteers, and administrators.

16. Children's Defense Fund

http://www.childrensdefense.org

The mission of the CDF is to advocate for children who are at risk and children with disabilities.

17. Classroom Connect

http://www.classroom.net

A major Web site for K–12 teachers and students, this site provides links to schools, teachers, and resources online. It includes discussion of the use of technology in the classroom.

18. ERIC Clearinghouse on Disabilities and Gifted Education

http://www.cec.sped.org/gifted/gt-faqs.htm

Information on identifying and teaching gifted children, attention deficit disorders, and other topics in disabilities and gifted education may be accessed at this site.

19. National Resource Center for Health and Safety in Child Care

http://nrc.uchsc.edu

Search through this site's extensive links to find information on health and safety in child care. Health and safety tips are provided, as are other child-care information resources.

20. Online Innovation Institute

http://oii.org

A collaborative project among Internet-using educators, proponents of systemic reform, content-area experts, and teachers who desire professional growth, this site provides a learning environment for integrating the Internet into educators' individual teaching styles.

Guiding and Supporting Young Children

21. Child Welfare League of America (CWLA)

http://www.cwla.org

The CWLA is the United States' oldest and largest organization devoted entirely to the well-being of vulnerable children and their families. Its Web site provides links to information about issues related to morality and values in education.

22. Early Intervention Solutions (EIS)

http://www.earlyintervention.com

EIS presents this site to address concerns about child stress and reinforcement. It suggests ways to deal with negative behaviors that may result from stress and anxiety among children.

23. National Network for Family Resiliency

http://www.nnfr.org

This organization's home page will lead you to a number of resource areas of interest in learning about resiliency, including General Family Resiliency, Violence Prevention, and Family Economics.

Curricular Issues

24. California Reading Initiative

http://www.sdcoe.k12.ca.us/score/promising/prreading/prreadin.html

The California Reading Initiative site provides valuable insight into topics related to emergent literacy. Many resources for teachers and staff developers are provided.

25. Early Childhood Education Online

http://www.ume.maine.edu/cofed/eceol/welcome.shtml

This site gives information on developmental guidelines, presents issues in the field, gives tips for observation and assessment, and information on advocacy.

26. Kathy Schrock's Guide for Educators

http://www.discoveryschool.com/schrockguide/

This is a classified list of sites on the Internet found to be useful for enhancing curriculum and teacher professional growth. It is updated daily.

27. Phi Delta Kappa

http://www.pdkintl.org

This important organization publishes articles about all facets of education. By clicking on the links in this site, for example, you can check out the journal's online archive, which has resources such as articles having to do with assessment.

28. Reggio Emilia

http://ericps.ed.uiuc.edu/eece/reggio.html

Through ERIC, you can link to publications related to the Reggio Emilia Approach and to resources, videos, and contact information.

29. Teachers Helping Teachers

http://www.pacificnet.net/~mandel/

Basic teaching tips, new teaching methodology ideas, and forums for teachers to share their experiences are provided on this Web site. Download software and participate in chat sessions. It features educational resources on the Web, with new ones added each week.

30. Tech Learning

http://www.techlearning.com

An award-winning K–12 educational technology resource, this site offers thousands of classroom and administrative tools, case studies, curricular resources, and solutions.

Trends

31. Awesome Library for Teachers

http://www.neat-schoolhouse.org/teacher.html

Open this page for links and access to teacher information on everything from educational assessment to general child development topics.

32. EdWeb/Andy Carvin

http://edweb.cnidr.org

The purpose of EdWeb is to explore the worlds of educational reform and information technology. Access educational resources around the world, learn about trends in education policy and information infrastructure development, and examine success stories of computers in the classroom.

33. Future of Children

http://www.futureofchildren.org

Produced by the David and Lucille Packard Foundation, the primary purpose of this page is to disseminate timely information on major issues related to children's well-being.

34. National Institute on the Education of At-Risk Students

http://www.ed.gov/offices/OERI/At-Risk/

The At-Risk Institute supports a range of research and development activities designed to improve the education of students at risk of educational failure due to limited English proficiency, race, geographic location, or economic disadvantage. Access numerous links and summaries of the Institute's work at this site.

35. Prospects: The Congressionally Mandated Study of Educational Growth and Opportunity

http://www.ed.gov/pubs/Prospects/index.html

This report analyzes cross-sectional data on language-minority and LEP students in the United States and outlines what actions are needed to improve their educational performance. Family and economic situations are addressed. Information on related reports and sites is provided.

We highly recommend that you review our Web site for expanded information and our other product lines. We are continually updating and adding links to our Web site in order to offer you the most usable and useful information that will support and expand the value of your Annual Editions. You can reach us at: *http://www.dushkin.com/annualeditions/*.

Unit 1

Unit Selections

1. **Starting Early: The Why and How of Preschool Education,** Rebecca Jones
2. **What Makes Good Early Childhood Teachers?** Sally Cartwright
3. **A Child Shall Lead Us,** Marian Wright Edelman
4. **Mysteries of the Brain,** Robert R. Bimonte
5. **Using Early Chilhood Brain Development Research,** Nina Sazer O'Donnell

Key Points to Consider

❖ How can quality preschool programs benefit children?

❖ What are the qualities of a competent early childhood educator?

❖ What steps should be taken to ensure that all children have a fair start for a lifetime of learning?

❖ What are the components of a strong early childhood program that would support future learning?

❖ How can partnerships be formed between families, teachers, and members of the community to support young children's brain development?

Links

www.dushkin.com/online/

6. **Child Care Directory: Careguide**
   http://www.careguide.net
7. **Early Childhood Care and Development**
   http://ecdgroup.harvard.net
8. **Goals 2000: A Progress Report**
   http://www.ed.gov/pubs/goals/progrpt/index.html

These sites are annotated on pages 4 and 5.

Perspectives

Just as a corporate executive looks at an advertising campaign and hopes it will encourage people to buy a product, those of us in the early childhood field hope the recent attention paid to children's issues will encourage the public to realize the importance of what we do. The message in the press has been consistent. Quality early childhood programs are so very important.

We have chosen for this twenty-first edition of *Annual Editions: Early Childhood Education* a lead article aimed at school board members. These individuals are elected citizens from a local community often with little or no preparation in the education field. The article, written by Rebecca Jones, senior editor of the *American School Board Journal,* outlines for school board members the importance of early childhood education in their community. The message presented is clear: If early childhood programs are being considered, only if they are of sufficient quality to actually affect the future learning abilities of children should they be done. These programs should also only be staffed by individuals with a background in early childhood education. Staff with preparation solely in elementary education are not prepared to address the issues in a developmentally appropriate early childhood program. A good strong early foundation will enable the children in school districts to continue to learn and develop as they make their way through the system.

Following the plea of the National School Boards Association to staff programs with well-prepared early childhood teachers is Sally Cartwright's article, "What Makes Good Early Childhood Teachers?" Unlike secondary teachers, where knowledge of subject matter is a key component in the preparation of teachers, successful teachers of young children need to possess the qualities that Cartwright outlines. As stated in the article, "The important thing is not what they study, but how they learn. Good teachers know the value of a child's innate curiosity and deep satisfaction in the learning process." We need teachers who are well grounded in child development principles, have warmth and respect for young children, and serve as role models for these young learners. If an individual doesn't consider these qualities as part of his or her repertoire, then a different profession should be considered.

The article "Mysteries of the Brain" continues to bring to the forefront the importance of teachers being aware of the recent research on brain development. Enriched environments that are compatible to the learning styles of young children will foster continued growth and development. Children who are provided with the opportunity to make meaningful choices and have sufficient time to formulate thoughtful questions, investigate, and come to conclusions will develop skills that will enable them to be successful learners. There are individuals like John T. Bruer, president of the James S. McDonnell Foundation in St. Louis, who caution us to proceed very slowly with the introduction of new educational practices into the schools. Bruer admits that eventually we may be certain of the impact brain science has on education, but we must proceed with caution and not abandon all educational practices while we are still gathering information. The technology now available for viewing brains in action, positron emission tomography (PET) has allowed us access to medical information never before available. Teachers can read about the research with interest, and make informed decisions about appropriate changes to current teaching methods based on the findings.

Marian Wright Edelman keeps moving more and more of us to action each time she writes or speaks. She feels passionate about what our country does and does not guarantee children. Children living in the United States are not guaranteed medical care, child care, or a quality education. What they are guaranteed is a prison cell after they get into trouble. She wants this to change. We lead the world in military technology and military expenditures, but we have children who can't walk to school safely because of violence in their communities. Every day in the United States, 12 children die as a result of guns. The Children's Defense Fund is working on issuing report cards for each state related to how that state serves and cares for its youngest children.

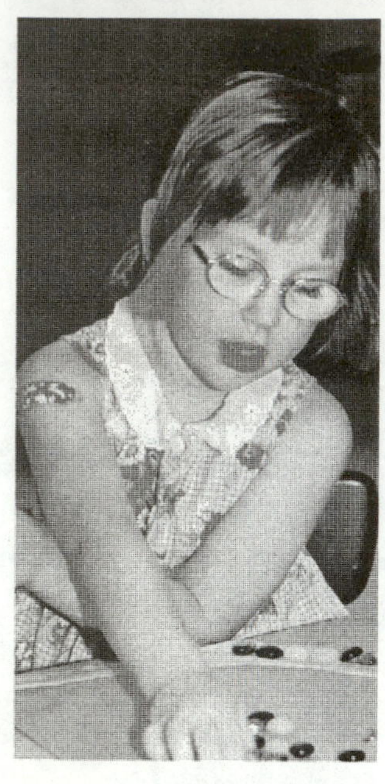

Starting Early

The why and how of preschool education

BY REBECCA JONES

Some pregnant women eat broccoli, listen to Mozart, and read Shakespeare to their bellies. Others smoke pot, watch Jerry Springer, and curse the dog. If the disparity continues after birth, it shows up in your classrooms five or six years later, with some kids ready to conjugate French verbs and others who don't know what state they live in.

Teachers can spot the kids who've been earmarked for failure. They're the ones who can't sit still, can't listen, can't concentrate, and can't follow directions. They don't know colors, can't name seasons, and hold picture books upside down.

Some of these children never catch up, even after years of expensive intervention and special education. "There are some kids who by age 4 already have severe problems that make the next 12 years of public education a nightmare for everyone involved," says Dr. Jeff W. Lichtman, a neuroscientist at the Washington University School of Medicine who is the father of two school-age children and an adviser to the Parents As Teachers National Center in St. Louis.

Can anything be done to prevent the nightmare?

Many neuroscientists say Yes. Their research indicates that intensive intervention in the early years can make a dramatic difference, especially for at-risk children. The brain is not fully developed at birth, they say, with vital neural connections yet to be made in the first few years of life. But if these connections aren't made soon enough, some windows of opportunity slam shut.

Inspired by such research, state legislatures and school districts around the country are racing to save kids—and special education costs—by creating and expanding early childhood education programs. Dozens of studies—including the legendary High/Scope Perry Preschool Project that began tracking preschoolers in the 1960s and continues to follow those same "kids," now in their 40s—show that effective preschool programs produce everything from higher IQs and fewer special education referrals to bigger paychecks and lower divorce rates.

These programs are expensive, but their payoff is impressive: R. Clay Shouse, director of educational programs at High/Scope Educational Research Foundation in Ypsilanti, Mich., says every dollar spent on the original Perry Preschoolers has saved $7 in special programs and services later in life.

But guess what? Only top-quality programs produce such stunning results. And most preschool programs just aren't that good.

Research indicates only 14 percent of early childhood education programs are high quality, says Edward Zigler, the Yale University professor sometimes called the father of Head Start. The rest range from mediocre to poor programs that actually do harm. "We see more and more children, probably numbering in the millions, who are in settings that compromise their growth and develop-

Rebecca Jones is a senior editor of The American School Board Journal.

The children photographed for this story are students at the Center for Young Children, College Park, Md. Photographs by Sally Foster.

ment," says Zigler, now director of Yale's Bush Center in Child Development and Social Policy.

Researchers know what needs to be done. They've compiled clear, convincing evidence of what works in early childhood education, with little or none of the hedging that accompanies research on class size, educational technology, and other megabuck strategies aimed at improving student achievement. But the studies have concentrated on at-risk children. Do the same principles and strategies apply with ordinary kids, too?

"My sense is that they do," says Fran Favretto, director of the research-oriented Center for Young Children, which serves the offspring of faculty, staff, and students at the University of Maryland-College Park. "Children need to be in environments with instructional integrity." Here's what researchers say you should do to create such environments:

1 Decide—and design—what you need. For this, you'll need the advice of specialists in early childhood education. And no, researchers say, a background in elementary education is not enough. "Four-year-olds are not miniature 8-year-olds," says Barbara Willer of the National Association for the Education of Young Children (NAEYC) in Washington, D.C. "Simply assigning your staff who may have been trained in other elements of elementary education is not appropriate. You've got to make sure people really understand early childhood and really understand early childhood education."

Early childhood education—or ECE, as insiders call it—is indeed a different animal from elementary education. It focuses on active, developmentally appropriate, hands-on learning and balances reasonable expectations with a child's need to play. Some people trained in elementary education can make the switch almost effortlessly, but many can't.

Dick Clifford, president of NAEYC and investigator at the Frank Porter Graham Child Development Center at the University of North Carolina at Chapel Hill, remembers one elementary school principal who forbade blocks in a pre-K classroom. "This is a school, not a playground," the principal said, evidently unaware of research that shows the importance of blocks in helping children develop, among other things, an understanding of spatial relationships.

"This principal didn't get it," Clifford says. "He didn't understand that very young children learn through somewhat different methodologies."

But before buying blocks or anything else for pre-K classrooms, your early childhood specialists should take a thoughtful look at the preschools already in your community—and at state laws. Of the 35 states that now provide funding for ECE programs, 27 allow districts to contract out at least some of the programs, says Anne Mitchell, founder of Early Childhood Policy Research near Albany, N.Y.

Mitchell suggests dangling the possibility of a contract with the district as an incentive for private ECE centers to improve the quality of their programs. (A good form of quality control is requiring NAEYC accreditation—something now held by only 10 percent of ECE programs in the country.) But even if you decide not to establish a business relationship with existing preschools (or can't, because of state laws), Mitchell suggests sharing the district's health, diagnostic, and other services with them.

This sounds reasonable to Lichtman, in light of his own and other neuroscientists' studies of the irreversible effects of deprivation on animal brain development: "Would [schools] rather spend money on special education classes, or on preventing kids from ever needing special education classes? It seems to me obvious. It's vastly cheaper and ultimately better to deal with [a problem] right off the bat." Researchers also ask you to make ECE accessible to those who need it most by offering wrap-around programs that combine good-quality day care with a preschool experience. "If you create really wonderful two-and-a-half-hour-a-day programs," Mitchell says, "lots and lots of kids are not going to be able to take advantage of them because the parents aren't available to come and get them."

2 Hire qualified teachers, and give them opportunities to grow. The biggest problem in pre-K education, say researchers, is unqualified teachers. Some states require nothing more than a high school diploma, and some will even settle for anyone who is, as Favretto puts it, "16 and warm-blooded." Whether hired as "teachers" or teaching assistants, these underqualified people often earn close to minimum wage and switch jobs frequently, resulting in staff turnover that disturbs both the continuity of the curriculum and the psyches of young students.

The most important thing you can do for kids in pre-K classes, researchers say, is to hire real teachers, trained and experienced in ECE. (Again, a background in elementary education isn't enough.) "Even if some other factors aren't met, a good teacher can make a program work," says Ellen Freve, a developmental psychologist and professor at the College of New Jersey who has studied the characteristics of effective preschool programs.

Assistant teachers also need training in ECE. An assistant "really has to be an instructional staff person," Freve says, "not just there to take care of the menial chores or the toileting. Otherwise, you're diluting the intensity" of the program. The most effective teaching in an ECE classroom is one-on-one. "You sit down on the floor and have a genuine conversation between a big person and a little person, rather than having an adult ask a lot of questions that have right or wrong answers," says High/Scope's Shouse.

Research shows that the most effective teachers draw kids into "school-like discourse patterns" by asking questions, Freve says—not "What letter is this?" or "What do you want to have for lunch?" but thought-provoking questions like, "Which of these objects do you think will float?" Such questions are good preparation for school, she says: "Research shows children are genuinely puzzled by this type of question if they're not used to it. [They wonder] 'Why is this adult asking me a question she obviously knows the answer to?' "

Both teachers and assistants need time to reflect on their teaching and to pursue more training opportunities. They also need thoughtful supervision—again by someone expert in ECE. "How do you know you're doing it right unless you're getting feedback from someone else?" asks W. Steven Barnett, a Rutgers University professor and coauthor of *Early Care and Education for Children in Poverty* (State University of New York Press, 1998). "Typically, quality suffers not because of indifference but because people think they're doing it well when they're not."

3 Keep classes small. "The ideal is one-on-one tutoring," Barnett says, "and the question is, how small does your class have to be for children to get enough one-on-one time?" The answer, according to his meta-analysis of 38 ECE research studies, is 15, with a certified teacher and a trained assistant in the classroom. This is in line with NAEYC's recommendations, which advocate different staffing patterns according to the children's ages.

"If you want to intervene [with at-risk children], then you need a more intensive program," Freve explains, "and a more intensive program means smaller class size."

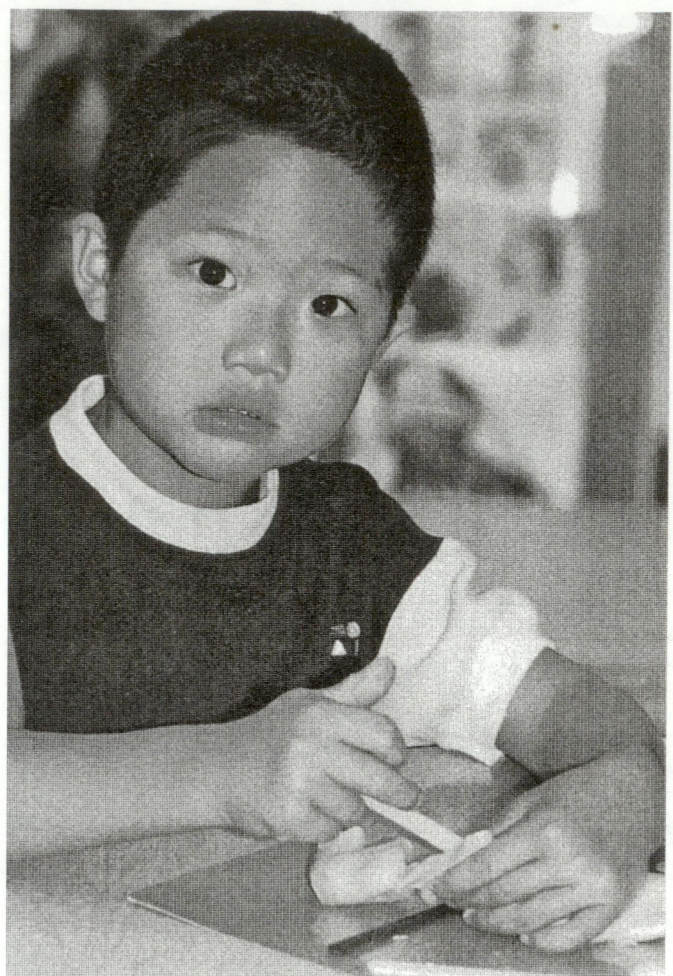

4 Engage kids in learning. A generation ago, Swiss psychologist Jean Piaget taught that children learn best when they construct meaning out of their environment. In ECE today, that translates to finding lessons where children live ("If you're teaching in Alaska, you wouldn't be talking about deserts," says the University of Maryland's Favretto) and engaging in hands-on activities initiated by kids and guided by teachers. It also translates to an absolute horror of worksheets, despite the yearnings of many parents.

"It's difficult to explain that when you make a bug out of an egg crate, you are learning to cut and count," says Barbara Wasik, principal researcher at the Center for the Social Organization of Schools at Johns Hopkins University. "But for some reason, if you send home a worksheet that shows [a child] colored all the bears blue, that seems to say to parents, 'Yes, something was happening academically.' "

At a Head Start research conference in Washington, D.C., last summer, a teacher described how parents kept asking why their children weren't bringing home worksheets. The teacher said she decided to demonstrate the benefits of hands-on, active learning at a parents' meeting by dividing the parents into two groups, one with worksheets and one with hands-on projects. At the end

of the evening, the parents agreed hands-on learning was better, even for adults. But a couple of weeks after the meeting, they started asking about worksheets again. "I gave up," the teacher said. "I started giving kids one worksheet every day, just to keep parents happy."

Another teacher at the conference suggested that the parents might have been looking for evidence that their children were working on a curriculum. If so, they had the right idea—even though worksheets weren't the way to go about it. Research shows "it seems to matter that you have content in your curriculum, not just that you let [kids] come in and play every day," says Freve. In the most effective schools, "the children have something they're investigating and learning about."

High/Scope studies show that the best learning occurs when a teacher follows the children's lead in deciding what they'll investigate. Also important: beginning with a concrete fact and moving on to an abstract idea. Shouse criticizes most preschools for doing the opposite: "They'll tell you that children learn best from concrete to abstract, but what they're doing is starting with the abstract—the books, videos, stories about a fire station—rather than starting with [a visit to] the fire station itself."

Some subjects beg to be covered in an ECE curriculum. Ongoing studies at the University of California-Irvine and the University of Wisconsin-Oshkosh indicate that music training improves kids' spatial-temporal reasoning—the kind of reasoning used in proportional math, fractions, and geometry. After six months of piano keyboard lessons, 3-year-olds in a Los Angeles school performed 34 percent better on standardized tests that measured such reasoning than children who hadn't had the lessons, says Gordon Shaw, professor emeritus at Irvine and president of M.I.N.D. (Music Intelligence Neural Development) Institute in Orange County.

"If you're looking for long-term benefits, I think we don't have all the answers yet," says Shaw, "but all the indications are that music is really helping to hardwire the brain to improve what we call spatial-temporal reasoning."

5 **Make room to grow.** "A good teacher can make almost any space work," Freve says, but NAEYC recommends at least 35 square feet of usable play space indoors per child, and your state probably has minimum requirements as well. Ideally, an ECE center should also have low sinks and small toilets, preferably in the classroom.

But kids need more than square footage and good plumbing. When Indiana licensing consultant Bob Mills enters an ECE classroom, he says he immediately looks for signs of an effective program: "Is a sand/water area open and in use? Is an art easel open and available? Does the room have a good supply of unit blocks? Is the teacher actively involved in play with the children?"

Based on her research, Freve looks for a logical, somewhat tidy arrangement of interest areas ("In the Art Area, you have only art materials—you don't have small manipulatives"); unstructured materials such as blocks, Legos, and art supplies ("There have to be plenty of them; children shouldn't be fighting over them"); and a large selection of books, papers, pens, and other literacy-related materials. A computer is OK, she says, but "if you're just starting up a program or if you don't have a lot of money, that's not where I would put my money. It's a luxury."

Outdoors, NAEYC recommends at least 75 square feet of play space per child. (If you don't have enough space, you can take fewer kids outside at a time.) For safety's sake, preschoolers need a separate playground, with equipment specifically designed for 2- to 5-year-olds, says Donna Thompson, director of the National Program for Playground Safety at the University of Northern Iowa: "I wouldn't allow them to be on the school-age equipment at all. Ever."

But you might not need traditional playground equipment. Opportunities to build things out of sand, water, and other materials are probably more important. Thompson also recommends "a tricycle path so [kids] can ride around, not just in a circle, but maybe in a figure 8 or at least something not totally predictable."

6 **Take care of teeth, toes, and tummies.** Effective, research-backed ECE programs usually provide dental, medical, and diagnostic services or referrals. And food.

Small, growing children need to eat more frequently than big people do—which makes snacks important, says Suzanne Rigby, a nutritionist at the American School

Food Services Association in Alexandria, Va. "Their little tummies can't sit and eat all the calories they need" in three meals, she says. "They simply can't do it."

Because fat is important in the formation of brain cells, very young children shouldn't limit their fat intake, either. Rigby, known for her cut-the-fat advice for older kids, recommends going beyond the federal dietary guidelines (which advise not restricting fat for children under the age of 2) and allowing more fat for 3- and 4-year-olds, as well. She advises gradually tapering down until kids reach the recommended guidelines (limiting fat to 30 percent of the caloric intake) by age 5.

"Offer things in moderation," she advises. "Train those little tastebuds to like fruits and vegetables and to like foods that aren't really fatty, but don't be so concerned if there is some fat in the diet."

7 Test gently. Many researchers are understandably nervous about testing preschoolers, even for school readiness. Most such tests have not been good predictors of children's performance in the early grades. "The question is, should we test young children?" asks Samuel Meisels, an ECE assessments researcher at the University of Michigan. "I answer it with both a Yes and a No. The No is if we're going to use group-administered, standardized achievement tests." In addition to tripping kids up with multistep directions, such tests "don't give us a true picture of what kids know," he says, "and they tend to focus on things out of context."

Meisels says Yes to individually administered tests designed to identify kids suspected of needing special help. Waiting until kindergarten or first grade means waiting to "start a special ed referral, which can take a long, long time," he says. "The problems just get concretized."

Be aware that testing preschoolers is a touchy subject. "We don't want children to be tiered and classified at the preschool age," says Evelyn Moore, president of the Black Child Development Institute in Washington, D.C. Meisels agrees and has designed the respected Work Sampling System, a performance assessment tool that depends on ECE teachers' observations over a school year to determine school readiness.

8 Don't forget parents. Educators have long known that the surest indicator of children's success in school is the involvement of their parents or guardians. And the best time to hook parents is in the early years. In fact, some experts attribute the notorious "fade-out" of many Head Start students—their failure to keep pace in the early grades, after leaving Head Start—to the fact that their parents are no longer as deeply involved as they were during their kids' Head Start years.

Research shows that the most effective ECE programs, especially for at-risk students, include home visits where teachers get to know families better and share information about stages of child development. The Perry Preschool provides just half-day sessions for kids, so teachers can devote their afternoons to visiting homes—enabling each family to receive a 90-minute visit every week.

Many successful programs bring parents into the classroom. Training and paying parents as teaching assistants can also help the staff achieve an ethnic and racial mix representative of the community, provide role models for children, and keep the community informed about what's going on at the school—not bad goals for all schools, says Moore. "I think if we had had community oversight of our public schools," she says, "we would not have the deterioration that came from so many years of neglect and people not knowing how bad things were."

Some states and school districts are trying to reach and involve parents even before preschool. Georgia sends each new mother home from the hospital with a classical music CD or tape, for instance, and Parents as Teachers (PAT) representatives from Missouri school districts prowl hospital maternity wards, seeking recruits for the enrichment program that has been endorsed by neuroscientists.

PAT offers personal visits by trained parent educators, weekly meetings with other parents, medical referrals, and other resources. By the time PAT children leave the program at age 3, their language skills are significantly more developed than those of other children their age. And the comparative advantage continues through at least fourth grade, says Mildred Winter, executive director of PAT.

The fact that the program is available to families at all income levels makes PAT "more politically palatable," says Winter; it also recognizes that a parent's income and educational level aren't the only factors that can place a child at risk. And seeing doctors, lawyers, and teachers sign up for PAT, she says, makes "other people say, 'That's a program for winners.' Parents won't come in if it's seen as a program for losers."

Almost every parent and every school district would like to think of their children as winners. A top-flight ECE program can help make them so, but such programs are not cheap. If your district decides—or is required by law—to offer an ECE program, researchers beg you to commit yourself to excellence. "Don't try to do it on the cheap," says Rutgers' Barnett.

Researcher Mitchell agrees: "We know that bad programs actually hurt children, and mediocre programs don't do them any good. It's the quality programs that make a difference."

But even the best programs can't inoculate kids against poverty, poor parenting, and ineffective schools. More than 30 years after he helped launch Head Start for low-income children, Zigler continues to ask: "What can you realistically expect from a one-year program? We should expect better school readiness, . . . but that's not the end of the line."

RESOURCES

The Internet offers information aplenty about early childhood education. Here are some good places to start:

Early Childhood Initiatives, National Educational Goals Panel, Washington, D.C.; *www.negp.gov/webpg310.htm*

ERIC Clearinghouse on Elementary and Early Childhood Education, University of Illinois at Urbana-Champaign; *http://ericeece.org.*

Frank Porter Graham Child Development Center, University of North Carolina at Chapel Hill; *www.fpg.unc.edu.*

Head Start Bureau, U.S. Department of Health and Human Services, Washington, D.C.; *www.acf.dhhs.gov/programs/hsb*

High/Scope Educational Research Foundation, Ypsilanti, Mich.; *www.highscope.org.*

MuSICA: The Music and Science Information Computer Archive, University of California at Irvine; *www.musica.uci.edu*

National Black Child Development Institute, Washington, D.C.; *www.nbcdi.org*

National Association for the Education of Young Children, Washington, D.C.; *www.naeye.org.*

National Head Start Association, Alexandria, Va.; *www.nhsa.org.*

National Institute on Early Childhood Development and Education, Office of Educational Research and Improvement, U.S. Department of Education, Washington, D.C.; *www.ed.gov/offices/OERI/ECI.*

Parents as Teachers National Center, St. Louis, Mo.; *www.patnc.org.*

What Makes Good Early Childhood Teachers?

Sally Cartwright

I spent a remarkable month in New Zealand, where I visited, among other things, five kindergartens. When I mentioned the National Association for the Education of Young Children, teachers in Invercargill, Christchurch, and Wellington said in effect, "Oh, yes! Lillian Katz! A great help to us!" Was I pleased! And I knew at once we'd speak the same language. I felt at home in any case, for their kindergartens—children, space, equipment, materials, and programs—are much like ours, with the same delight and challenge we have in the States.

One challenge that New Zealand schools share with ours is finding first-rate teachers. As I talked with teachers and friends, we agreed it's more than love for children, more than training and experience that make a good teacher. We felt a teacher's maturity and deeply held values are of major importance, and the most important values are kindness, courage, and integrity, in that order.

©Nancy P. Alexander

We decided kindness means *heart,* in helping others to help themselves; courage means working through whatever odds for what you most care about; and integrity means a well-knit personality combined with honesty in all you do. It means, as Polonius told his son, "To thine own self be true, and it must follow as the night the day, thou canst not then be false to any man" (*Hamlet,* 1.3).

❊ ❊ ❊

To live by values requires maturity. This includes, first of all, inner security, self-awareness, and integrity.

Inner security. Barbara Biber wrote 50 years ago, "A teacher needs to be a person so secure within herself that she can function with principles rather than prescriptions, that she can exert authority without requiring submission, that she can work experimentally but not at random, and that she can admit mistakes without feeling humiliated" (Biber & Snyder 1948). One discerns these qualities in a teacher neither by résumé nor interview, but by observing her at work with children. Particularly watch for the qualities Biber mentions. And watch how the teacher encourages the children. When and how do they come to her? Are the children deeply involved in their play and work? How do they cooperate with each other? Is there a sense of warmth and humor as well as purpose among the children? Questions are endless. Keen obser-

---

__Sally Cartwright__ attended the famous City and Country School in New York City, taught at it, and sent her children there. She has a master's from Bank Street College of Education and for many years had her own state-of-the-art nursery school in Maine.

From *Young Children,* July 1999, pp. 4-7. © 1999 by the National Association for the Education of Young Children (NAEYC). Reprinted by permission.

vation requires attentive experience. Clear and consistent evidence of a teacher's inner security is truly important for good teaching.

Self-awareness. Because of its major importance, I began with the need for personal integration, or inner security, and shall come around to it again when I mention *detachment*. However, as teachers develop self-awareness, they improve in each quality mentioned as well as in self-evaluation. Teachers can help each other gain self-awareness through constructive criticism, with mutual trust and respect. Quiet reflection and professional counseling often help as well. A truly fine teacher knows what's at work inside her. She will have searched and brought to light salient, unconscious factors in herself. She's aware of their influence in the classroom and controls them as needed.

Integrity. My New Zealand friends and the quote from *Hamlet* speak well to integrity as meant here. Moreover, integrity is implicit in the educational philosophy of child growth through developmental interaction; it is implicit in NAEYC's position statement on developmentally appropriate practice (Bredekamp & Copple 1997, 3). Honesty and fairness when dealing with children is paramount. And in our present society, perhaps it is a quality worthy of attention before it becomes an endangered species.

A theoretical ground. Good teaching presupposes a conceptual framework in which to see children. I incline toward the developmental-interaction point of view put forward by Bank Street College of Education in *Education Before Five* (Boegehold et al. 1977). I feel it is the most useful foundation and guide for helping youngsters learn at their best in and for a democratic society. The word *development* suggests a continuing, complex process of growth and learning, while *interaction* occurs between the child's emotional, physical, and cognitive growth and between the child and his expanding physical and social environment. The stress is on *integrative* action by the children. Developmental-interaction is clearly aligned with NAEYC's developmentally appropriate practice.

General knowledge with an emphasis on environmental science, community, and young children's books. A good teacher of children younger than first grade should have the ability to impart the information needed for responsible citizenship in a democratic community. This includes having at least a college graduate's general knowledge, or its equivalent, and effective access to the media, libraries, and the Internet. Young children learn social and academic skills through daily classroom experience. And teachers today must also steer young children toward a caring respect for our physical environment. Further, the teacher's understanding of community is essential for developing cooperative learning in her classroom. It is through cooperative learning experience that children come to understand the benefits and responsibilities of a democratic community.

Good teachers know that, aside from their attainment of needed skills, young children do not require proficiency in traditional academic subjects. The important thing is not *what* they study, but *how* they learn. Good teachers know the value of a child's innate curiosity and deep satisfaction in the learning process. Let no school dampen a child's interest and joy in learning! And children soon know the value of firsthand experience. Einstein said, "Learning is experience. The rest is information." "Spot on!" as they say in New Zealand, meaning, "just so!"

The teacher's able selection of picture books and her daily reading aloud to the children are essential parts of the reading-readiness program for four- and five-year-olds. (Fours, as well as fives, attend New Zealand kindergartens.)

Warmth and respect for the child. Good teachers show unfailing warmth, respect, and courtesy to children as a group and to each child as a unique and unrepeatable human being. Helping a child to make constructive, independent choices toward self-disciplined creativity depends very much on our genuine, total, and caring respect for that child and her way of working, her way of learning. Such respect cannot be accomplished without a teacher having a very real knowledge of child development as well as the qualities of inner security, self-awareness, and integrity.

Integrity and respect invite discretion. For a teacher to have good rapport with a child and her parents, she must keep their concerns confidential. If a specific problem requires professional discussion, the teacher explains this to the parents as well as to the child, in terms the child can understand. Respect for the privacy of the child and her family is essential to gain their trust.

Trust in the child. An outstanding characteristic of the good teacher is her ability to trust each child to find his own way toward personal integrity, acceptable behavior, and good learning purpose and ultimately to realize his unique potential. Genuine trust in a child depends on fundamental knowledge of child development and keen observation of the individual child. It depends on a teacher understanding the importance of carefully chosen structure for the learning environment. And it depends on an intuitive knowledge of the child in the learning situation.

Trust and respect for the child go hand in hand. Both demand a keen perception of the child's capacities and limits.

Unconditional caring. A good teacher cares about a child not because she needs to care for someone but because she knows intuitively that this child at this moment requires warm and close concern. She seeks nothing but the child's hopeful development in return.

Good teachers are approachable and friendly. They listen well, give warm support as needed, and share in laughter with, not *at*, the children.

Good teachers are keenly aware of emotional and physical safety for each child. Care is shown in constructing the environment for learning by the careful choice of equipment, materials, and spatial arrangements and a consistent, predictable program.

Children need unconditional approval: deep, steady, warm approval. A good teacher may condemn a child's words or actions, but not the child herself. While sometimes critical of *behavior*, a good teacher backs the *child* with her heart, *and the child knows it.*

Intuition. Contrary to strictly linear thinking, which Western science has insisted upon since Isaac Newton's *Principia* in 1687, intuition, a nonreasoning, often sudden, gut approach to thinking, is now gaining credence even among scientists. For many of us it often sways our thinking. Why? Mainly because it *feels* right and it works. A well-balanced, mature, and keenly observant teacher *knows in her bones* how to be with a child. Later she may defend her actions with reason. Einstein said, "Imagination is more important than knowledge," and imagination lives with intuition.

Detachment. Professional detachment allows respect, trust, and unconditional love to come through to the child. On the surface, detachment and love may seem a paradox, but precisely the opposite is true. A teacher with inner security and mature self-awareness, a teacher at ease and fulfilled by her own adult development, does not impose her personal needs onto her relationships with children. A teacher's detachment allows her to feel empathy without projection; she does not naively attribute her own unconscious, negative feelings to the children. Detachment gives children psychological space. It deters sarcasm and contempt, which are crushing to a child. Detachment helps a teacher test and use her knowledge of child development with a degree of wisdom.

Laughter. One sign of detachment is often delightful humor, and humor in the classroom is important. It signals enjoyment. It invites friendship. It often opens the way for cooperative learning. While shared humor lights the morning, laughing at a child's expense should be nipped at once. Affectionate laughter is an indispensable quality in good teaching.

A model for children. Teachers, like it or not, are models of emotion, thought, and behavior for the children in their care. A substantial part of a child's learning is modeling, copying, and trying to think, feel, and be like persons consistently close at hand and dear to the child. To the degree that a teacher fills a child's needs and is loved by him, she will personify values and behavior that touch him deeply, often throughout his life. The personality of a teacher, her instinctive kindness, her deep integrity, her lively interest in life and learning, will all affect the children. It's a sobering responsibility, an inspiring challenge.

❊ ❊ ❊

Whether in our country or halfway around the world in New Zealand, we do need good teachers. And, as Barbara Biber has said, "Good teaching requires a fine blend of strength and delicacy" (Biber and Snyder 1948). Besides love for children, besides training and experience, a teacher's respect for and trust in each child support that fundamental, child initiative, which is crucial for good learning. A teacher's inner security and self-awareness, mutually beneficial, form a foundation for caring and detachment.

Teaching young children should be grounded in developmental learning theory; humor is best woven throughout; and the teacher, particularly as a model for children, must somehow unite all these qualities within herself. They form a good mix—with my New Zealand friends' values of kindness, courage, and integrity—to promote child learning at its best. One need only add the teacher's joy and frustration, her patience, sensitivity, perseverance, wisdom, and immeasurably important for young children, her humility.

References

Biber, B., & A. Snyder. 1948. How do we know a good teacher? *Childhood Education* 24 (6): 281–85.

Boegehold, B. D., H. K. Cuffaro, W. H. Hooks, & G. J. Klopf, eds. 1977. *Education before five,* 45–52. New York: Teachers College Press.

Bredekamp, S., & C. Copple, eds. 1997. *Developmentally appropriate practice in early childhood programs.* Rev. ed. Washington, DC: NAEYC.

For further reading

Biber, B., E. Shapiro, & D. Wickens. 1971. *Promoting cognitive growth from a developmental-interaction point of view.* Washington, DC: NAEYC.

Katz, L. G., & D. E. McClellan. 1997. *Fostering children's social competence: The teacher's role.* Washington, DC: NAEYC.

Shapiro, E., & B. Biber. 1972. The education of young children: A developmental-interaction approach. *Teachers College Record* 74 (1).

A Child Shall Lead Us

America is great because America is good, and if America ever ceases to be good, America will cease to be great.

Alexis de Tocqueville

Capitalism forgets that life is social, and the kingdom of brotherhood is found neither in the thesis of communism nor the antithesis of capitalism but in a higher synthesis. It is found in a higher synthesis that combines the truth of both. . . . It means ultimately coming to see that the problem of racism, the problem of economic exploitation, and the problem of war are all tied together! These are the triple evils that are interrelated."

Dr. Martin Luther King Jr.
Where Do We Go from Here: Chaos or Community?

You shall not pervert the justice due to your poor.

Exodus 23:6

Marian Wright Edelman
President, Children's Defense Fund

America appears to be riding high on the cusp of the 21st century and third millennium. Wall Street is booming. Excess, Russell Baker says, has become a way of life for the very rich. In what may be the ultimate in corporate hubris, Miller Brewing Company has applied for a trademark or been recently registered as the "official sponsor of the Millennium" according to *Harper's Magazine.* Corporate CEOs, who earned 41 times as much as their workers made in 1960, made 185 times as much as their workers in 1995. The average CEO in 1995 earned more every two days than the average worker earned in a whole year. Fortune 500 CEOs averaged $7.8 million each in total compensation. This exceeds the average salaries of 226 school teachers a year.

The rosy view of American prosperity at the top hides deep and dangerous moral, economic, age, and racial fault lines lurking beneath the surface. Unless we heed and correct them, they will destroy America's fundamental ideals of justice and equal opportunity, family and community stability, economic productivity, and moral legitimacy as the democratic standard bearer in the next era.

In the 25 years since the Children's Defense Fund began, great progress has been made in improving children's lives in many areas. Millions of children with disabilities have a right to education; millions of poor children have received a Head Start, health care, immunizations, better child care, and permanent adoptive homes. But shamefully high child poverty rates persist, and children are the poorest group of Americans. The gap between America's poor and rich has grown into a chasm, the wages of young families with children have eroded, and many middle class families are treading economic water.

Since 1989 the poorest fifth of families have lost $587 each and the richest 5 percent have gained $29,533 each. We have five times more billionaires but 4 million more poor children. While millions of stock options helped quintuple the earnings of corporate CEOs between 1980 and 1995, those same employers threw millions of children out of health insurance plans at their parents' workplaces, and parental wages stagnated.

More than 11 million children are uninsured, 90 percent of whom have working parents. More parents worked longer hours and more families

From *The State of America's Children Yearbook, 1998,* pp. xi-xix.

sent a second or only parent into the labor force to meet family necessities. But for millions of families, work did not pay a family-supporting wage, and a minimum wage no longer prevents poverty. Sixty-nine percent of poor children live in working families. Ending welfare as we know it will not help them. Ending poverty as we know it will. Sustained economic investment in rebuilding our communities and in stable jobs with decent wages, quality affordable child care, and health insurance must become top American priorities.

Six years of economic expansion with low inflation and a soaring stock market have not filtered down to 36.5 million poor people, including 14.5 million children. In 1996 the number of *very* poor people who live below half the poverty line (a mere $8,018 for a family of four) increased, while the current income of households in the top 5 percent increased by $12,500. Today more than one in five children is growing up poor and one in 11 is growing up extremely poor. This is shameful and unnecessary.

If we are truly concerned about preventing welfare, teen pregnancy, youth violence, school dropouts, and crime, then we need to start first by preventing child poverty and ensuring every child a fair start in life. The moral, human, and economic costs of permitting 14.5 million children to be poor are too high.

- A baby born poor is less likely to survive to its first birthday than a baby born to an unwed mother, a high school dropout, or a mother who smoked during pregnancy.
- Poverty is a greater risk to children's overall health status than is living in a single-parent family.
- Poor children face greater risk of stunted growth, anemia, repeated years of schooling, lower test scores, and less education, as well as lower wages and lower earnings in their adult years.
- Poverty puts children at a greater risk of falling behind in school than does living in a single-parent home or being born to teenage parents.

Dr. Laura D'Andrea Tyson, former chair of the President's Council of Economic Advisors, says, "Policies to reduce the poverty rate among children—which typically remains higher in the United States than in any other advanced industrial countries—must be a fundamental part of our efforts to build a healthy economy for the 21st century." Nobel laureate in economics Robert M. Solow of the Massachusetts Institute of Technology states, "In optimistic moments, I like to believe that most Americans would want to lift children out of poverty even if it cost something. It is hard to blame little children for the problems that surround them now and will damage their future health, ability, and learning capacity. Doing nothing about it seems both immoral and unintelligent."

All segments of society pay the costs of child poverty and would share the gains if child poverty were eliminated. America's labor force is projected to lose as much as $130 billion in future productive capacity for every year 14.5 million American children continue to live in poverty. These costs will spill over to employers and consumers, making it harder for businesses to expand technology, train workers, or produce a full range of high-quality products. Additional costs will be borne by schools, hospitals, and taxpayers and by our criminal justice system. Poor children held back in school require special education and tutoring, experience a lifetime of heightened medical problems and reliance on social service, and fail to earn and contribute as much in taxes.*

When legitimate avenues of employment are closed, poor youths and adults turn to illegitimate ones, especially the lethal underground economy of drugs and crime fueled by out-of-control gun trafficking. Since 1970 America's prison population has increased more than fivefold at an annual taxpayer tab exceeding $20 billion. Almost one in three young Black and one in 15 young White males between ages 20 to 29 are under some type of correctional control (incarceration, probation, or parole). Two-thirds of state prison inmates in 1991 had not completed high school and one-third had annual incomes under $5,000. Joseph Califano, head of Columbia University's National Center on Addiction and Substance Abuse, reports that if present trends persist, one of every 20 Americans born in 1997 will spend some time in jail, including one of every 11 men and one of every four Black men.

Is this America's dream for its children and itself? Can an $8.7 trillion American economy not afford decent jobs, quality child care, education, and health care for all its children?

---

* These and other findings are detailed in a CDF report by Arloc Sherman, *Poverty Matters: The Cost of Child Poverty in America.*

What Kind of Ancestors Will We Be? What Is America's Legacy?

It is time for every American to see and excise the moral tumors of child neglect, violence, poverty, and racism eating away the core of our national soul. What kind of billboard are we for democracy or capitalism—in a world where more than 3 billion people live on less than $2 per day and 200 million children suffer malnutrition every year—when millions of American children are hungry, homeless, neglected, abused, and dying from diseases we have the money and power but not the decency to prevent?

How will we lead a world where 5 of 6 billion citizens are not White, when young Black and Latino males see no jobs, hope, or future choices beyond prison and death? How do we fill our privileged children—who, like many poor children, are longing for a sense of purpose things cannot meet—with spiritual anchors and worthwhile goals? Will our children have something besides drugs and booze and cigarettes and rollicking good times to turn to when life's rough seas batter their souls?

How will they remember us as parents and leaders? Will they remember the jets, second mansions, and multiple nannies, or will they remember how often we watched their games and plays and concerts and were home to soothe over a bad nightmare? Will their memory books be chock-full of expensive toys and designer clothes, or of regular mealtimes, shared conversation, family games, prayer, and worship? Are they able to get our attention in the small daily ways that matter and say I love you, or only through desperate screams of violence, gangs, guns, sexual promiscuity, and substance abuse?

Does what we do every day really matter for anyone besides ourselves and our immediate family? Is our example one we would like our children to emulate and pass on to our grandchildren and the children of the world? Will we leave them a country and Earth more just, virtuous, and safe than we inherited? What messages do our lives convey about the brotherhood and sisterhood of humanity?

How will each of us add to or subtract from America's moral bank account when the God of the universe asks for an accounting? Will God care how many times our excessive nuclear stockpiles can blow up humankind? Will God be proud that we sell more weapons to other nations than any other country, which

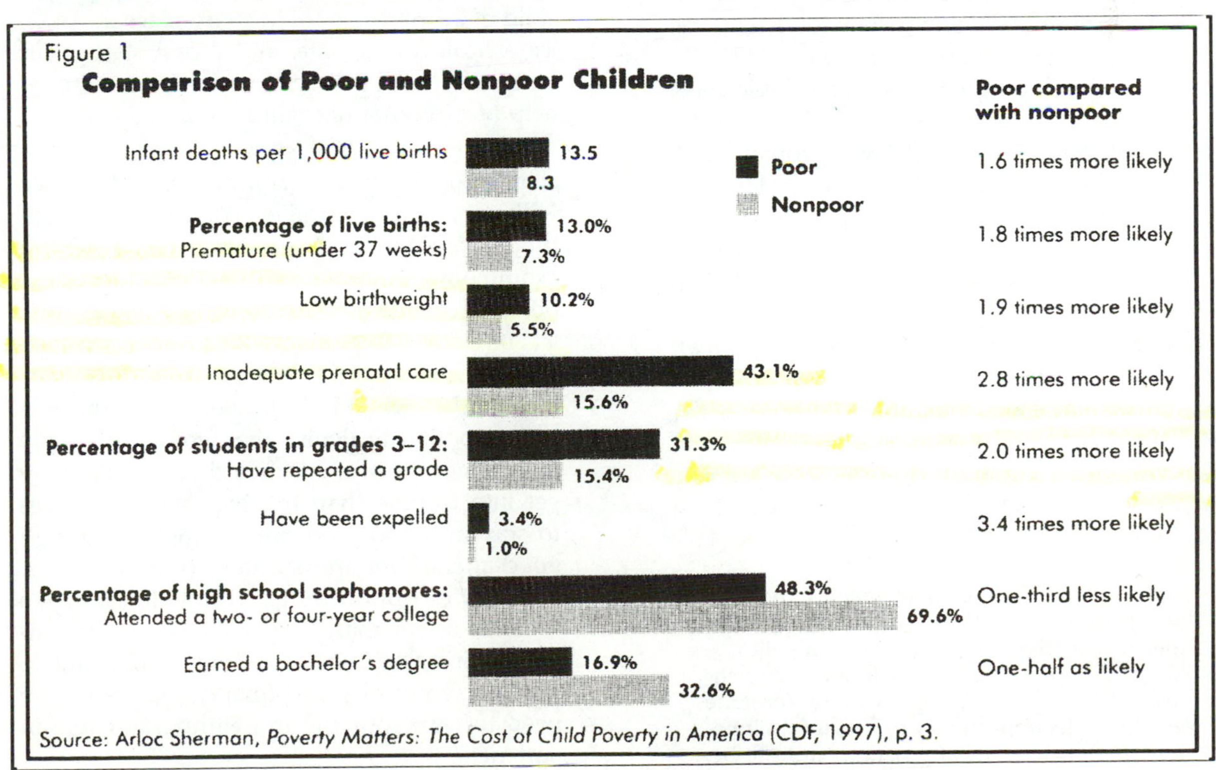

Source: Arloc Sherman, *Poverty Matters: The Cost of Child Poverty in America* (CDF, 1997), p. 3.

Table 1 **Poor Outcomes for Poor Children**

Outcome	Poor children's higher risk relative to nonpoor children
Health	
Death in childhood	1.5 to 3 times more likely
Stunted growth	2.7 times more likely
Iron deficiency in preschool years	3 to 4 times more likely
Partial or complete deafness	1.5 to 2 times more likely
Partial or complete blindness	1.2 to 1.8 times more likely
Serious physical or mental disabilities	About 2 times more likely
Fatal accidental injuries	2 to 3 times more likely
Pneumonia	1.6 times more likely
Education	
Average IQ score at age 5	9 points lower
Average achievement scores at age 3 and above	11 to 25 percentiles lower
Learning disabilities	1.3 times more likely
Placement in special education	2 or 3 percentage points more likely
Below-usual grade for child's age	2 percentage points more likely for each year of childhood spent in poverty
Dropping out between ages 16 and 24	2 times more likely than middle-income youths; 11 times more likely than wealthy youths

Source: Arloc Sherman, *Poverty Matters: The Cost of Child Poverty in America* (CDF, 1997), p. 4.

fuel wars all over the globe that kill mostly women and children? Will God ask how many billionaires and millionaires we created with the land and water and talents God blessed us with and praise us for developing the cleverest ads to sell tobacco's deadly poisons to our children? Will God agree that a child's life in Bangladesh is less precious than one in Bangor, Maine, as America's tobacco industry markets its deadly wares to developing nations? Or will God ask did we feed the hungry, heal the sick, visit the prisoner, protect the widow, orphan, and stranger? How will America answer? How will you and I answer? How will we teach our children to answer as citizens of the richest nation on earth blessed with the opportunity to abolish want and disease?

America's children will make or break America's greatness and future. One in four current Americans is a child. Children are the future tense of our humanity. Its quality will depend largely upon our present-tense care of them. The Rev. Dr. Gardner Taylor, the dean of American preachers,says:

> If we do not bequeath to them something worth calling life, then we cannot expect of them any lives that are worthwhile. . . . Might it be that this land with all of its richness, with all of its opportunity for true greatness, its opportunity to present itself before the world as what a nation ought to be, might now be sowing the seeds of its very destruction in abandonment of its children?

I believe so. That is why the Children's Defense Fund has been struggling for 25 years to plant seeds for a massive moral movement to Leave No Child Behind and to ensure every child of every race born in every place in America a healthy, fair, safe, and moral start in life and a successful passage to adulthood, with the help of caring families and communities.

Children are life, power, hope, and the chance for renewal and immortality. Children will carry on our families, communities, institutions, and values. How then do we honestly examine and transform the values and priorities of the wealthiest nation in history, which lets its children be the poorest group of Americans and lets a child be killed by guns every hour and a half? How do we reverse the prevailing political calculus that would rather pay three times more to lock children up *after* they get into trouble than to give them incentives to stay in school and out of trouble, through good afterschool and summer programs, jobs, and service opportunities? How do we make it easier rather than harder for parents to balance work and family responsibilities and to get the community and financial support they need to carry out the most important role in America?

Key Facts About American Children

1 in 2	preschoolers has a mother in the labor force.
1 in 2	will live in a single-parent family at some point in childhood.
1 in 2	never completes a single year of college.
1 in 3	is born to unmarried parents.
1 in 3	will be poor at some point in childhood.
1 in 3	is a year or more behind in school.
1 in 4	is born poor.
1 in 4	is born to a mother who did not graduate from high school.
1 in 4	lives with only one parent.
1 in 5	is poor now.
1 in 5	lives in a family receiving food stamps.
1 in 5	is born to a mother who received no prenatal care in the first three months of pregnancy.
1 in 6	has a foreign-born mother.
1 in 7	has no health insurance.
1 in 7	lives with a working relative but is poor nonetheless.
1 in 8	never graduates from high school.
1 in 8	is born to a teenage mother.
1 in 11	lives at less than half the poverty level.
1 in 12	has a disability.
1 in 13	is born at low birthweight.
1 in 24	is born to a mother who received late or no prenatal care.
1 in 25	lives with neither parent.
1 in 132	dies before age 1.
1 in 680	is killed by gunfire before age 20.

Five Questions All American Citizens Should Ask Ourselves and Our Political Leaders About National Priorities

As a Democrat, as a Christian, as a southern Baptist, as someone who fundamentally believes in the words of the Bible . . . I [do not] believe that God's response to the poor is to treat them as though they are the least priority, almost as though they are a nuisance to be dealt with. . . . With all due respect to the Christian Coalition, where does it say in the Scriptures that the character of God is to give more to those who have and less to those who have not? . . . If there is one thing evident in the Scriptures, it is that God gives priority to the poor.

U.S. Representative Glenn Poshard
Democrat, Illinois 19th district
Speech to the House of Representatives

No one may claim the name Christian and be comfortable in the face of hunger, hopelessness, insecurity, and the injustice found in this country and around the world. . . . Every economic decision and institution must be judged in light of whether it protects or undermines the dignity of the human person.

National Conference of Catholic Bishops
Pastoral Letter on the Economy

The time has come for an all-out world war against poverty. The rich nations must use their vast resources of wealth to develop the underdeveloped, school the unschooled and feed the unfed. The well-off and the secure have too often become indifferent and oblivious to the poverty and deprivation in their midst. The poor in our countries have been shut out of our minds, and driven from the mainstream of our societies, because we have allowed them to become invisible. Ultimately, a great nation is a compassionate nation. No individual or nation can be great if it does not have a concern for "the least of these."

Dr. Martin Luther King Jr.
Where Do We Go from Here:
Chaos or Community?

1. **Why is our nation continuing to spend $265 billion a year, $5.1 billion a week, $727 million a day, and $30 million an hour on "National Defense" in a post-Cold War era with no towering external enemies?** Our military budget exceeds the total military expenditures of the 12 next-largest spenders—including Russia, France, Great Britain, Germany, and China—combined. Congress gave the Pentagon $9 billion more than it requested in 1996, while cutting $54 billion from child nutrition programs for poor and legal immigrant children and families. The military plans to purchase three new tactical fighter systems that will cost $355 billion—systems the U.S. General Accounting Office says we don't need and can't afford—at a time when millions of struggling parents left behind in the global economy need better-paying jobs and millions of children need health care, quality child care, education, and housing.

As President Dwight Eisenhower reminded us in 1953, "Every gun that is made, every warship launched, every rocket fired signifies . . . a theft from those who hunger and are not fed, those who are cold and not clothed. This world in arms is not spending money alone. It is spending the sweat of its laborers, the genius of its scientists, and the hopes of its children."

- Every 14 hours we spend more on the military than we do annually on programs to prevent and treat child abuse.
- Every 29 hours we spend more on the military than we do annually on summer jobs for unemployed youths.
- Every six days we spend more on the military than we do annually on the Child Care and Development Block Grant for child care for low-income working parents.
- Every six days we spend more on the military than we do annually on Head Start, which still serves only one in three eligible children.
- Every 11 days we spend more on the military than we do annually on Title I compensatory education for disadvantaged children.

It takes only a few nuclear weapons to blow up humankind. America spends tens of billions of dollars to maintain a nuclear overkill "advantage" at a time when irresponsible leaders and gangsters seek access to inadequately secured nuclear weapon stockpiles and a cheap computer chip can accidentally launch a nuclear war. "Can't we do better than condone a world in which nuclear weapons are accepted as commonplace?" asks retired General George Lee Butler, former head of the Strategic Air Command. "The elimination of nuclear weapons," Butler states, "is called utopia by people who forget that for so many decades the end of the Cold War was considered utopia."

Key Facts About Poor Children

3 in 5	are White.
1 in 3	lives in suburban America.
1 in 3	lives in a family with married parents.
2 in 3	live in a working family.

As we near the close of a 20th century marked by dazzling scientific and technological progress, but also the bloodiest century in history, we all need to reassess the meaning of power and of life. More than 109 million human beings lost their lives in wars during this century, and far more civilians than soldiers died due to military conflicts. We must heed General Omar Bradley's warning on Armistice Day in 1948:

> We have grasped the mystery of the atom and rejected the Sermon on the Mount. . . . Ours is a world of nuclear giants and ethical infants. We know more about war than we know about peace, more about killing than we know about living. The way to win an atomic war is to make certain it never starts. And the way to make sure it never starts is to abolish the dangerous costly nuclear stockpiles which imprison humankind.

2. **Why, with over 200 million guns in circulation already killing a child every hour and a half, does our country manufacture or import a new gun every eight seconds?** American children under age 15 are 12 times more likely to die from gunfire than children in 25 other industrialized nations combined. Virtually all violent youth crime is gun-driven. Yet many politicians seek to return to the barbaric practice of locking up children (the majority of whom are neither violent nor repeat offenders) in adult jails instead of locking up the adults who sold or gave them the guns. Why seek to protect guns rather than protect children from guns?

When the polio virus killed 2,700 children and adults in its peak year—seven a day—we declared a national emergency. Why don't we declare a national emergency to stop the deadly gun virus that kills almost twice as many children—5,285 a year, 14 a day—in their homes,

Moments in America for Children

Every 9 seconds	a child drops out of school
Every 10 seconds	a child is reported abused or neglected.
Every 15 seconds	a child is arrested.
Every 25 seconds	a child is born to an unmarried mother.
Every 32 seconds	a child sees his or her parents divorce.
Every 36 seconds	a child is born into poverty.
Every 36 seconds	a child is born to a mother who did not graduate from high school.
Every minute	a child is born to a teen mother.
Every 2 minutes	a child is born at low birthweight.
Every 3 minutes	a child is born to a mother who received late or no prenatal care.
Every 3 minutes	a child is arrested for drug abuse.
Every 4 minutes	a child is arrested for an alcohol-related offense.
Every 5 minutes	a child is arrested for a violent crime.
Every 18 minutes	an infant dies.
Every 23 minutes	a child is wounded by gunfire.
Every 100 minutes	a child is killed by gunfire.
Every 4 hours	a child commits suicide.

neighborhoods, schools, and parks? It is ironic that the world's leading military power stands by as White militia gangs and Black, Latino, Asian, and White street gangs stockpile arsenals that endanger all citizens.

3. **How much do we truly value children and families when we don't put our money and our respect behind our words?** Is a child care worker who earns $6.12 an hour, $12,058 a year, and receives no benefits 182 times less valuable to America's future than the average professional basketball player who earns $2.2 million a year, or 162 times less valuable than the average HMO head who made $1.95 million in 1996? Is she only one-fourth as important to America's well-being as an advertising manager for a tobacco brand who makes $23.32 an hour? Most states require 1,500 hours of training to become a manicurist or hair stylist, but more than 30 states do not require a single hour of training for child care workers.

What family values dictate a public policy in many states that pays more to nonrelatives than to relatives to care for children whose parents cannot nurture and protect them? Why are we willing to spend $10,000 a year to place a child in a foster home and much more to place a child in an institution *after* the family fails but refuse to invest $4,500 in job creation, child care, and income supplements for poor parents? Why does an average welfare payment of $365 a month to a poor family undermine personal responsibility when billions in "subsidies and incentives"—euphemisms for government welfare for the nonpoor and powerful—do not?

4. **Why should every 66-year-old in the United States be guaranteed health coverage and not every 6-year-old or 16-year-old?** Is one life more valuable than the other? Why should a child in one state have a chance to live and grow up healthy and not a child in another state? Why should our leaders decide it is acceptable to provide health insurance to *every other child?* And why are some of our political leaders and powerful lawyers so eager to protect a tobacco industry that saps 420,000 lives a year, $50 billion in direct health costs, and entices nearly 2 million children to smoke and shorten their lives? Former Surgeon General C. Everett Koop and former Food and Drug Administration head David Kessler propose a $2 a pack tobacco tax to deter teen smoking. That money not only could save millions of young lives by preventing them from smoking but also fund millions of children's hopes and dreams. A $2 tobacco tax would yield more than $100 billion dollars. That is enough to end childhood poverty, fund child care for working families, and ensure every child the healthy start that the tobacco industry has done so much to destroy.

5. **Why is the United States, save Somalia (which lacks a legally constituted government to act), alone among nations in failing to ratify the Convention on the Rights of the Child?** All the other nations of the world are willing to commit to the convention's goals of ending illegal child labor, sexual exploitation, violent abuse of, and capital punishment for children. Why do we refuse to pledge to make reasonable efforts to give all of our nation's children the adequate health care, food, shelter, and education that should be every child's birthright? . . .

Mysteries OF THE BRAIN

Students thrive in a brain-compatible learning environment.

ROBERT R. BIMONTE

It would be virtually impossible not to have read or heard some bit of research in the past few years about the human brain. Every magazine, newspaper and educational journal regularly features articles that highlight some new finding. Indeed, there seems to be an explosion of interest in this incredible source of our intelligence, but we have only just begun to understand its mysteries.

One significant finding that has clearly emerged is the importance of creating a brain-compatible learning environment. . . . It is a significant determinant in the learning process, and in many ways, the key factor to the success of . . . students. It is also something we often take for granted.

In order for young people to thrive and succeed to the best of their abilities, it is essential that our classrooms reflect the following eight components of a brain-compatible learning environment.

Absence of threat

Much of current brain research speaks about a "triune" brain (figure 1). According to this research, there are three major areas of the human brain. Each has a distinct function, but all three operate simultaneously, and for the most part, harmoniously. These three areas are the reptilian brain or brain stem, the paleomammalian brain or limbic system and the neomammalian brain or cerebral cortex.

Positron Emission Tomography (PET) scans have allowed us to view the brain's electrical activity and see how it is distributed throughout the brain. Various circumstances and stimuli determine which of the brain's three areas receives the most energy.

For example, when someone experiences fear or senses a threat or danger, the electrical energy is concentrated in the reptilian brain or brain stem. When this purely instinctual area receives the majority of the brain's energy, the body becomes tense and rigid, the heart starts beating faster and our basic survival re-

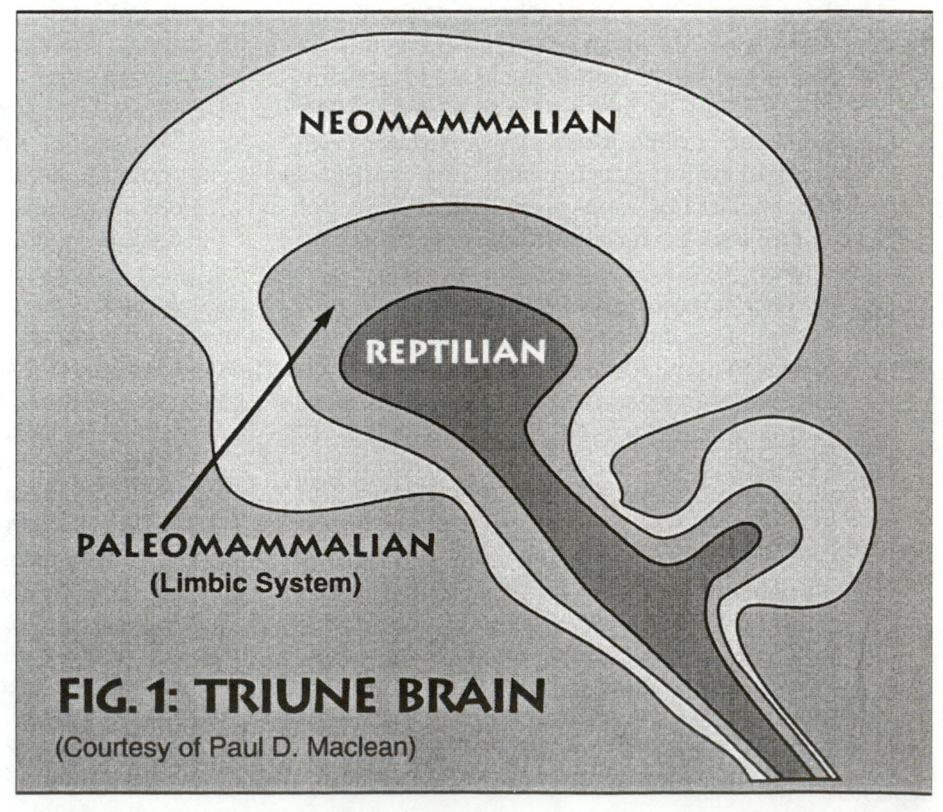

FIG. 1: TRIUNE BRAIN
(Courtesy of Paul D. Maclean)

Brother Robert Bimonte, FSC, is the superintendent of Catholic Education in Buffalo, New York.

From *Momentum*, the official journal of the National Catholic Educational Association, October/November 1998, pp. 16-18. © 1998 by the NCEA. Reprinted by permission.

sponse of "fight or flight" is engaged. The problem is that when the brain's energy is concentrated here, it means that less energy is directed to the cerebral cortex, which is the part of the brain responsible for thinking, language and learning.

This is why it is so important that students feel safe in the school environment. If they feel threatened, the energy in their brains will be directed to the reptilian brain, and as a result, the amount of learning is diminished.

Absence of threat also means creating a learning environment where mistakes are regarded as part of the learning process.

Meaningful content

The key to all learning is experience. It is experience that creates dendrites—the hair-like extensions that grow from neurons and create the neural pathways necessary for learning. The very best dendrites are grown from real world experience.

Far too often, we presume levels of experience that students today simply do not have. As a result, many are labelled as "learning disabled" when they are actually "experientially deprived." They simply have not had the experiences to grow the dendrites that create the neural networks necessary for learning.

Teachers, therefore, must try to provide as many real world experiences as possible. Helping students see connections between what they are studying and real life is absolutely essential.

Choices

One of the most important findings in modern educational theory is that we all learn differently. Some of us are visual learners; others respond best to auditory stimulation. Still others are kinesthetic and learn best through "hands-on" experience. Howard Gardner's work on multiple intelligences—musical, linguistic, logical/mathematical, bodily/kinesthetic, spatial, naturalist, interpersonal and intrapersonal—has opened new vistas

FAR TOO OFTEN WE PRESUME LEVELS OF EXPERIENCE THAT STUDENTS TODAY SIMPLY DO NOT HAVE.

on how teaching and learning should be structured.

While some students may respond well to traditional methods of reading and lecture, and do well on written assessments, others will be able to better express their learning through singing, drawing a picture or acting out a role in a play.

It is important to give students choices for both learning and assessment, but it is equally important to monitor those choices so that students develop and use all eight intelligences.

Adequate time

Learning does not take place in forty-minute periods. We know from our own experience that when we are actively involved or emotionally engaged in what we are doing, we do not even notice the passing of time. Students need to be actively involved and emotionally engaged in the learning process.

While the entire brain is involved in the process of memory, it is the paleomammalian brain or limbic system that is central to remembering. Eighty percent of the brain's memory circuits are located in the limbic system, and those neurons are stimulated primarily by adrenaline. Adrenaline is produced in the brain stem when we are excited, interested or actively engaged. Adrenaline is not produced when students are sitting passively. Many schools are exploring block scheduling to provide the time students need to get involved in projects and activities that will enhance the learning process.

Enriched environment

All of us are influenced by our surroundings far more than we realize. Walt Whitman said: "We become what we behold"[1] and there is tremendous truth in that statement.

Classrooms must be beautiful. They must also reflect the fact that they are centers for learning. Natural lighting, plants, soft music and anything else we can use to add a touch of beauty to our classrooms will have a positive effect on students. Clutter and too many things hanging on the walls or objects on display can, in reality, be distracting.

We also need to have a variety of resource materials available. Students must understand that textbooks are only one resource among many. The use of multiple resources must become natural.

Collaboration

In the past 20 years, a great deal of research has focused on collaborative learning, and a variety of models and styles have been developed. Collaborative learning works best with clear procedures and guidelines. Students working together can often accomplish far more than working alone. Collaboration also engenders excitement, which we have already noted is essential to stimulating the memory centers of the limbic system.

Above and beyond the benefits of using a collaborative learning methodology, collaboration is an essential skill that we must cultivate in our classrooms. As we become a global society, it is imperative that we teach students not only the benefits of working together but the skills to do so. The job market of today and tomorrow is looking for people who know how to be team players, and if we do not equip our students with the appropriate skills, we will diminish their potential. . . .

Immediate feedback

The brain is a pattern-seeking device. Patterns that are repeated over time become programs. We have patterns and programs for so many of the things we do, say and think that we are not even aware of them. We have complex patterns for relating to people and simple patterns for performing daily routines. Every pattern we have ever learned since the time we were in our mother's womb is stored in our brain.

Sometimes in learning new patterns or expanding upon already established ones, the brain picks up "mismemes" or incorrect cues. If these are not corrected as soon as possible with the substitution of the right cue, the brain develops incorrect or inappropriate patterns. Those patterns repeated over time become increasingly difficult to change.

In learning new patterns, or trying to change old or incorrect ones, there are three approaches to which the brain responds best: creativity and usefulness and emotional connection.

Creativity. Stimulating students' creativity is one of the best ways to ensure that learning takes place. Here again, Howard Gardner's work on multiple intelligences can be very helpful. Teaching to a variety of learning styles is beneficial for everyone, as is real world experience.

Usefulness. The value of what is being taught is determined by the individual learner in the here and now. Telling students that they need some piece of information or a particular skill for the future only provides sufficient motivation if students already know their career choice. If medicine is their chosen career, studying biology is then seen as useful. All too often, students do not have a sense of what they want to do, so teachers need to show them the usefulness of the material they are studying in the present moment.

Emotional connection. Making a positive connection with another person is probably the most powerful motivator of all. In his book *Pygmalion in the Classroom,* Robert Rosenthal concluded that the best predictor of student achievement is an affirmative response to the question "Does the teacher like me?"[2]

Responding positively to the people we care about and who care about us is the most normal of human reactions. When students know that their teachers care about them, they respond in kind.

TEACHERS HAVE THE ABILITY TO MAKE CHILDREN LOVE LEARNING OR HATE THE ENTIRE SCHOOL EXPERIENCE.

Mastery

Education is preparation for life. It is not simply a matter of knowing and repeating facts. In this age of information, students must also learn how to learn. With access to the Internet, they can find information throughout the world with the click of a mouse button. We must teach them how to critically analyze information with a clear moral and ethical sense, and simultaneously, synthesize it in new and creative ways.

Students must also develop an appropriate set of life skills like initiative, perseverance, patience, curiosity and caring. Teachers must consistently recognize and affirm these behaviors and reward students' efforts in the learning process.

Our goal must be to have each of our students become life-long learners who are on fire with a passion and thirst for knowledge, understanding and wisdom.

Teachers are among the most important people in the world today—they exert a powerful influence in the determination of the future. What each teacher says, does and creates in the classroom has immediate and long-term effects on the lives of every student. Teachers have the ability to make children love learning or hate the entire school experience. All of our attitudes and world views have been influenced by the teachers in our lives.

As we look to the future, it is more crucial than ever that we do not underestimate the power we have. We must commit ourselves to providing the best possible school experience for all of the students whose lives we touch.

Notes

1. Walt Whitman, "Behavior," New York, NY, Washington Square Press.
2. Robert Rosenthal, *Pygmalion in the Classroom,* New York, NY, Holt, Rinehart and Winston, 1986.

Resources

Caine, Geoffrey and Renate, Making *Connections: Teaching and the Human Brain,* Virginia, ASCD, 1991.

Caine, Geoffrey and Renate, *Education on the Edge of Possibility,* Virginia, ASCD, 1997.

Hart, Leslie, *Human Brain and Human Learning*, Washington, Books for Educators, 1983.

Kovalik, Susan, *Integrated Thematic Instruction: The Model,* Arizona, Susan Kovalik and Associates, 1993.

Using Early Childhood Brain Development Research

by Nina Sazer O'Donnell

In recent years, there has been increasing public interest in early childhood brain development. This is due, in part, to new technologies that allow neuroscientists to actually see inside the human brain and to share images of what they see. It is also due to the work of many national, state, and local organizations and individuals through The Reiner Foundation's *I Am Your Child Campaign* and the Families and Work Institute's national *Early Childhood Public Engagement Campaign.* These two coordinated efforts have helped galvanize public attention on how critical children's earliest years are to their future school, work, and life success.

These two efforts are carried out through a nationwide Early Childhood Public Engagement Network—105 diverse state and local coalitions and 150 national organizations that work together to:

- raise public awareness about the importance of early childhood;
- link families with young children with information, programs, and resources that help them raise healthy and successful children; and
- increase public will and action to support such programs and resources.

Throughout the country, families, early childhood programs and practitioners, educators, policy makers, employers, governors, mayors, county commissioners, legislators, faith communities, law enforcement and other state and community leaders are working together to build systems of early childhood education and care. And they are finding that the availability of information about early childhood brain research is very helpful.

Nina Sazer O'Donnell, M. Ed., is director of the Families and Communities Program at Families and Work Institute. She has a diverse background in early childhood policy and practice, philanthropy, communications, community mobilization and outreach at the local, state, and national levels, and directs several FWI projects on early childhood public engagement and community mobilization.

What Early Childhood Brain Development Research Tells Us

Recent elections demonstrated that Americans care deeply about the education that their children receive. Early childhood brain development research helps us to re-frame the definition of education to include a variety of programs and services that support families with young children, including:

- providing information and parenting support to all families with young children;
- linking families with young children to health care and other critical services, such as housing and employment assistance;
- expanding and improving the quality of early care and education; and
- enabling communities to mobilize their resources to systematically expand and improve early childhood programs and services.

But this is not new, you say, we've known this for years. And you're right. Much of what the new brain research explains has been learned through a rich history of research in developmental and behavioral psychology, education, medicine, and other disciplines. Although there are exciting new lessons from neurosci-

From *Child Care Information Exchange,* March 1999, pp. 58-62. © 1999 by Exchange Press, Inc. Reprinted by permission.

ence, such as the concept of sensitive periods (prime times for specific types of learning as the brain wires itself) or the fact that in adolescence the brain prunes away brain cells and pathways that are not used or needed, many lessons from the new research underscore what early childhood professionals have long known: the importance of secure, attached, and loving relationships (consistency of care); the importance of reading and responding to a child's cues and clues (developmentally appropriate practice); the importance of language rich, healthy, and safe environments; the importance of play and many other elements of good quality early childhood education and care. So what *is* new?

➤ Brain Research As Communications Tool

In addition to new knowledge about how human beings grow, learn, and develop, this research provides us with powerful new ways to explain what occurs in early childhood. It gives us a new language that is compelling to the many business, policy, and other leaders who do not resonate to the jargon of *child development-ese.*

Most audiences perceive the new brain development research as concrete, as hard science. We can see pictures of brains, neurons, and natural pathways developing, and these pictures speak powerfully for themselves. As audiences learn about early brain development, they tend to think about their own early childhoods and their own families.

This information makes it easier to explain why the quality of child care and early education matters; why well-qualified, well-compensated, and consistent staff are needed; and why investments in early childhood programs and services are wise public policy. As early childhood public engagement leaders throughout the country present this information to business, media, community leaders, elected officials, policy makers, and others, they are typically met with a consistent response: "I get it, what do you want me to do?"

It is essential for early childhood programs and professions to be prepared to answer this question. What is it you would like your staff, your program, your families, your board, area employers, your community, and your state to do to give the young children in your care the best possible foundation for school, work, and life?

➤ Using Early Childhood Brain Development Research in Early Childhood Programs

There are many ways that early childhood program directors, staff, volunteers, and others can use early childhood brain development information.

1. IMPROVING THE QUALITY OF EARLY CHILDHOOD PROGRAMS

Early childhood programs can use this information in several ways to improve program quality, including:

- Adapting or adopting early childhood brain development information into existing and future preservice and in-service training and education activities.

There are now several efforts underway throughout the country to integrate the latest brain development information into teacher preparation, education, and training programs that translate into better care for our nation's young children.

For example, Families and Work Institute is currently partnering with the American Business Collaboration for Quality Dependent Care, the American Academy of Pediatrics, the Erikson Institute, and Zero to Three to develop curricular modules, including hands-on strategies, trainer guidance, video segments, activities, and handouts that translate the brain development information into training and educational information for teachers, directors, and community early childhood educators who work across disciplines.

- Inviting a brain development expert or trainer to talk to your staff and begin a discussion about what this information means for your program.
- Sending your staff to a conference or workshop on early childhood brain development and asking them to translate what they've learned into action.
- Inviting a child development expert to facilitate a staff effort to integrate the latest brain development research into daily practice with children.

2. SUPPORT PARENTS AND FAMILIES BY SHARING INFORMATION ABOUT EARLY CHILDHOOD DEVELOPMENT.

Early childhood programs can:

- Distribute existing materials and information with parents and families in your program.

The national *I Am Your Child Campaign* created free videotapes and booklets for new parents on child development and choosing child care, available for the cost of shipping and handling from The Reiner Foundation (see contact information at the end of this article). Other national organizations also provide valuable resources that can be shared with families. For more information about obtaining materials to share with families, contact the organizations listed at the end of this article.

- Adapt information from the *I Am Your Child Campaign* and other sources into your program's infor-

Ten Tips for Families and Caregivers

1. **Be warm, loving, and responsive.** When children receive warm, responsive care, they are more likely to feel safe and secure with the adults who take care of them.

2. **Respond to the child's cues and clues.** Recognizing and responding to the sounds, movements, and expressions that a child makes will help build secure attachments.

3. **Talk, sing, and read to children.** All of these interactions help the child's brain make the connections it needs for growth and later learning.

4. **Establish rituals and routines.** Teach young children to know when its time for bed by developing routines such as singing a song and pulling the curtains. Daily routines and rituals then become associated with pleasurable feelings and are reassuring to children.

5. **Encourage safe exploration and play.** As infants grow, they begin to explore the world beyond their caregivers. Parents should encourage this exploration. While many of us think of learning as simply acquiring facts, children actually learn through playing.

6. **Make television watching selective.** Watch television with the child, and talk about what is being seen. Don't use TV as a baby-sitter.

7. **Use discipline as an opportunity to teach.** In addition to consistent and loving adult supervision, teach children limits. Never hit or shake a child.

8. **Recognize that each child is unique.** Children grow at different rates. Their ideas and feelings about themselves reflect, in large measure, parents' and caregivers' attitudes towards them.

9. **Choose quality child care and stay involved.** Frequently visit child care providers and seek someone who responds warmly and responsively to each baby's needs.

10. **Caregivers need to take care of themselves.** They need nurturing, too. When parents and caregivers are exhausted, irritable, depressed, or overwhelmed, they may have a harder time meeting the needs of young children.

These tips were created based on a review of the research and interviews with child development experts throughout the country for the *I Am Your Child Campaign.* They are available in a booklet for parents and caregivers entitled *The First Years Last Forever* from The Reiner Foundation (contact information listed in box, "How to Get More Information"). These tips can also be copied, reproduced, and posted in classrooms as long as appropriate credits are included.

mation and materials, such as newsletters, bulletin boards, or printed on bookmarks or magnets.

- Use information about early childhood brain development as discussion topics at parent gatherings.
- Host parent information and education programs to share information with parents and families, including fathers, grandparents, and others.
- Provide parents and families with lists of other family and parent support organizations in your community.
- Help parents and families learn how to tell their family stories to elected officials and the media.
- Partner with other organizations that help parents and families with young children to inform parents about early childhood brain development.

3. INCREASE PUBLIC AND PRIVATE SUPPORT FOR EARLY CHILDHOOD PROGRAMS.

The economics of running high quality early childhood programs make many kinds of support necessary, from zoning approvals to in-kind and cash donations from area businesses to public-private partnerships that result in increasing and improving early childhood programs and services in a neighborhood, community, or state. Early childhood brain development research can help make a strong case for why high quality early childhood programs matter; and it can be used in a variety of ways, such as:

- Including early childhood brain development facts in brochures, promotional materials, and funding proposals.

Rethinking the Brain: New Insights Into Early Development

To help make information about early childhood brain development accessible to a wide variety of audiences and to suggest ways that individuals and organizations can help improve early childhood programs, Families and Work Institute has created a variety of tools, including:

- ***Rethinking the Brain: New Insights into Early Development***—which was reviewed by approximately 30 neuroscientists and distributed by the National Association for the Education of Young Children to its comprehensive members and by the Academy of Pediatrics to its 60,000 members—summarizes the new brain research.
- ***A PowerPoint Presentation based on Rethinking The Brain***—a tool that makes it easy to present accurate information about early brain development to a wide variety of audiences.
- ***Early Childhood Action Tips***—a set of suggested actions for a wide variety of stakeholders. To order these and other resources, visit the FWI website: www.familiesandwork.org.

Get Involved!

- Early Childhood Public Engagement Network (EC-PEN) member organizations and coalitions are listed on the I Am Your Child website: www.yourchild.yahoo.com. Contact these groups to get involved in your area.
- The EC-PEN LISTSERV is a free electronic network sponsored by Families and Work Institute (FWI). Members share information and ideas and are notified about publications, technical assistance, and other resources, such as monthly conference calls on hot early childhood topics. To join, e-mail: jboose@familiesandwork.org.

How to Get More Information

These organizations provide information, publications, experts, technical assistance, and other resources related to early childhood brain development. Contacting them as you explore ways to use early childhood brain development in your early childhood program may help you do it right and avoid reinventing the wheel.

I Am Your Child Campaign
For materials to distribute:
I AM YOUR CHILD
PO Box 15605
Beverly Hills, CA 90209
(888) 447-3400
For information about the campaign:
www.yourchild.yahoo.com

Families and Work Institute
330 7th Avenue
New York, NY 10001
(212) 465-2044 www.familiesandwork.org>

Children's Defense Fund
25 E Street NW
Washington, DC 20001
(202) 628-8787 www.childrensdefense.org>

Fight Crime, Invest in Kids
1334 G Street NW, Suite B
Washington, DC 20005-3107
(202) 638-0690 www.fightcrime.org>

National Association for the Education of Young Children
1509 16th Street NW
Washington, DC 20036-1426
(800) 424-2460 www.naeyc.org>

National Conference of State Legislatures
1560 Broadway, Suite 700
Denver, CO 80202
(303) 830-2200 www.ncsl.org>

National Child Care Information Center
301 Maple Avenue West, Suite 602
Vienna, VA 22180
(800) 616-2242 www.nccic.org>

National Governors' Association
444 North Capitol Street, Hall of States
Washington, DC 20001-1512
(202) 624-5300 www.nga.org>

Zero to Three

National Center for Infants, Toddlers, and Families
734 15th Street NW, Suite 1000
Washington, DC 20005
(202) 638-1144 www.zerotothree.org>

- Using visual presentations on early childhood brain development to educate funders, the media, and policy makers.
- Publishing short fact sheets for policy and decision makers, using materials from the resource organizations listed at the end of this article.
- Referring to early childhood brain development in op eds, letters to the editor, and media appearances.
- Building community, regional, and statement partnerships and collaborations that result in increasing and improving the quality of care available to families with young children, using early childhood brain development information to engage prospective partners.

➤ Cautions in Interpreting The Brain Research

Finally, it is critical that we not misuse or overstate the research. This could detract from the credibility of accurate information and might even cause harm. The following cautions, provide some guidance for how and how not to use this powerful information.

- *This research should not be used to market toys and materials to build bigger and better brains.* Children grow and learn through emotional connections to other adults. Reading, singing, talking, and responding to young children's cues and clues is what is important.
- *This research does not indicate that it's all over after the child's early years. It is never too late.* The brain's plasticity is one of the remarkable features of brain development. Studies simply indicate that it's easier to give our young children the best start we can—and continue this as they grow.
- *This research should not be used to increase parental anxiety.* Being a parent means we all make mistakes and learn from them. There is no such thing as a perfect parent—parenting is a process of problem solving.
- *This research does not mean that funding spent on older children should be diverted to early childhood programs.* Investments in early childhood will take many years to mature and pay off. In the meantime, essential services for older children—from out of school time activities to remedial education and crime prevention—must continue to be available to those children and youth who need them.
- *The research must be presented accurately.* If in doubt, check with one of the organizations listed for advice and information.

Unit 2

Unit Selections

6. **Do Working Parents Make the Grade?** Ellen Galinsky
7. **Fetal Psychology,** Janet L. Hopson
8. **Children's Prenatal Exposure to Drugs: Implications for Early Childhood Educators,** Phyllis K. Mayfield and J. Keith Chapman
9. **Baby Talk,** Shannon Brownlee
10. **Boys Will Be Boys,** Barbara Kantrowitz and Claudia Kalb
11. **The Education of Hispanics in Early Childhood: Of Roots and Wings,** Eugene E. Garcia

Key Points to Consider

❖ What do children wish they could change about their parents?

❖ What are some of the negative effects of prenatal drug exposure on an infant? How can parents and teachers minimize these conditions?

❖ Describe some of the behavioral characteristics that are unique to boys. What positive qualities exist as a result of boys' behaviors?

Links

www.dushkin.com/online/

9. **Administration for Children and Families**
   http://www.acf.dhhs.gov
10. **Global SchoolNet Foundation**
    http://www.gsn.org
11. **The National Academy for Child Development**
    http://www.nacd.org
12. **National Parent Information Network/ERIC**
    http://npin.org
13. **World Education Exchange/Hamline University**
    http://www.hamline.edu/~kjmaier/
14. **Zero to Three**
    http://www.zerotothree.org

These sites are annotated on pages 4 and 5.

Child Development and Families

School children receive report cards as do school districts and individual schools within a district. Ellen Galinsky takes this one step further and grades parents in her new book, *Ask the Children*. Galinsky directed her questions at children of working parents, but all parents could ask themselves the hard questions related to providing emotional support, establishing routines and rituals, involvement in their children's education, and acceptance of the child. One wonders how the distribution of parent report cards would affect the education reform taking place in many school districts. Teachers, school administrators, and the local community cannot be expected to make all the changes.

Teachers should not accept the full criticism aimed at education when only a handful of their parents attend parent conferences or open houses. It will take the school staff, families, and the local community to participate in school improvement.

Juggling work and family duties can cause tension in anyone's life. Successful families communicate frequently about responsibilities as well as build in relaxed time for children to develop lasting relationships with both parents. The debate is no longer centered on the working parent issue but has moved to the way parental employment affects parenting. Some parents are better able to handle the stress of working and parenting. This day-to-day stress is clearly observed by the children. Their wish for their parents is for them to be less stressed in their lives. Slow down, spend a few relaxed moments with your children each day, and cherish the days they are still with you.

The startling information about brain development has brought on a flurry of speculation about the best ways to prepare children for a lifetime of learning. The information indicates that the types of experiences that children have before the age of 10 can affect their future capacity to learn. Early experiences, once thought to be useless, now have been found to help support the developing neurons in a child's brain. These neurons, which make successful and complete connections when a child is young, will be used in the future to work complicated mathematical problems, learn a second language, or play a musical instrument.

Early childhood educators are often the first professionals to interact with children who were exposed to drugs before birth. Phyllis Mayfield and Keith Chapman provide specific guidelines for those educators as well as suggestions for family-centered intervention programs in their article, "Children's Prenatal Exposure to Drugs: Implications for Early Childhood Educators."

The very beginning stages of learning one's language are both fascinating and exciting to observe as emphasized by Shannon Brownlee in "Baby Talk." Participating in a game of mousie, an adult walked her fingers up 18-month-old Margaret's legs and trunk and tickled her under her chin while saying, "mousie, mousie, mousie," etc. Margaret walked around the room for a few minutes, then found 10-year-old Clay lying on the floor. She went over to him and moved her hand up his body while saying, "mou, mou, mou." Adults who are active participants in the language-learning process can be key supports to children in this challenging task.

Parents of boys have long been told that their boys are more aggressive and not as easy to control as girls are. In "Boys Will Be Boys," authors Barbara Kantrowitz and Claudia Kalb provide guidance to parents and teachers. Parents of young boys and their teachers have noticed an alarming trend in education. Little boys are increasingly unable to conform to the restrictive learning environment in many elementary classrooms. With the push for academics permeating many schools, little boys find their active bodies are in direct conflict with the quiet paper and pencil task-oriented environment in which they find themselves. Some even call schools antiboy. Dan Kindlon, coauthor of "Raising Cain: Protecting the Emotional Life of Boys" noted that "young boys are typically more rambunctious than girls, . . . yet grade school teachers, overwhelmingly women, confine them to chairs for long periods and punish them for activity. As a result, some boys develop a negative notion of education as controlling and prohibitive." Psychologists have noted that first and second grades are especially difficult for many boys. They are not developmentally ready to sit and concentrate. They are more apt to learn through activity. The philosophy of "hands on, minds on" should be adopted by all teachers of young children. The day-to-day challenges of raising boys can be draining for many parents and teachers. One parent reported that she is worried that her years of telling her son to "keep yourself in check, C.B.," or to "calm down," will greatly curtail his energy, creativity, and zest for life and learning that have been such a major part of who he is as a person. Just what is the best way to handle all of that energy? Parents and teachers can ensure that all children, but especially boys, have an adequate amount of playtime that offers active child-initiated learning in a safe yet challenging setting.

Book Excerpt: In the debates over quality time and how to balance work and family, kids are rarely heard. A new 'Ask the Children' study reveals how kids rate their moms and dads—and what children really want. BY ELLEN GALINSKY

Do Working Parents Make The Grade?

WHENEVER I MENTION THAT I AM STUDYing how kids see their working parents, the response is electric. People are fascinated. Parents want to know what I have found, but inevitably they are nervous, too. Sometimes they say, "I wonder what other people's children would say. I'm not sure that I'm ready to hear what mine have to say!"

Why has a comprehensive, in-depth study of this question never been conducted? Because we have been afraid to ask, afraid to know. But now I feel the time is right. The answers of children are illuminating, not frightening. They help us see that our assumptions about children's ideas are often at odds with reality. Ultimately, this information will help us be better parents—and better employees, too. In fact, adding children's voices to our national conversation about work and family life will change the way we think about them forever.

Many of the debates we've been having about work and family miss the mark. For example, we have been locked in a longstanding argument about whether it is "good or bad" for children if their mothers work. Numerous observational studies have found that having a working mother doesn't harm children, yet the debate still rages. Another way to assess this issue is to see whether children of mothers who are not employed and children of working mothers differ in the way they feel they are being parented. In our "Ask the Children" study, we had a representative group of more than 1,000 children in grades three through 12 to evaluate their parents in 12 areas strongly linked to children's healthy development, school readiness and school success. In their responses—rendered in actual letter grades—having a mother who worked was never once predictive of how children assess their mothers' parenting skills. We also found that while the amount of time children and parents spend together is very important, most children don't want more time with their parents. Instead, they give their mothers and fathers higher grades if the time they do spend together is not rushed but focused and rich in shared activities.

It may seem surprising that children whose mothers are at home caring for them full time fail to see them as more supportive. But a mother who is employed can be there for her child or not, just as mothers who are not employed can be. Indeed, children of nonworking fathers see their dads less positively when it comes to making them feel important and loved and to participating in important events in the children's lives. Fathers who work part time are less likely to be seen as encouraging their children's learning. Perhaps fathers who work less than

Family Values

56% of parents think their kids want more time together; only 10% of kids want more time with Mom, 15.5% with Dad. Most kids, however, feel they have enough time.
62.5% of parents say they like their work a lot. Only 41% of children say Dad enjoys his job, and 42% says the same about Mom.
44.5% of kids say time with Mom is rushed, 37% say so with Dad. Only 33% of parents think time with their kids is rushed.
23% of kids want their parents to earn more; 14% of parents think kids want this.

From *Newsweek,* August 30, 1999, pp. 52-56. Excerpted from *Ask the Children* by Ellen Galinsky (Morrow, 1999).

Grading Dad

He instills good values, but doesn't always know what 'really' goes on

SUBJECT	A	B	C	D	F
Raising me with good values	69%	18%	8%	4%	2%
Appreciating me for who I am	58	21	11	8	2
Encouraging me to enjoy learning	57.5	24	12	4	2
Making me feel important and loved	57	22	13	6	2
Being able to go to important events	55	22	13	5	5.5
Being there for me when I am sick	51.5	20	16	8	4
Spending time talking with me	43	24	19	10	4
Establishing traditions with me	41	26	15	11	7
Being involved in school life	38	24	19	12	7
Being someone to go to when upset	38	22	15	12	13
Controlling his temper	31	27	20	10	12
Knowing what goes on with me	31	30	17	12.5	10

NOTE: GRADES GIVEN BY CHILDREN IN SEVENTH THROUGH 12TH GRADES

full time or who are unemployed are feeling financial and role strain, which could affect how they interact with their children.

That children can appreciate the efforts of working parents is clear. Said one 12-year-old son of working parents: "If parents wish to provide some of the better things in life, both parents need to work and share the home and children responsibilities." A 15-year-old girl whose father works full time and whose mother does not said: "Your children may not like you working now, but it will pay off later on."

The problem isn't that mothers (and fathers) work: it is how we work and how work affects our parenting. For example, we asked the children in this study, "If you were granted one wish to change the way that your mother's or your father's work affects your life, what would that wish be?" We also asked more than 600 parents to guess what their child's response would be. Taken together, 56 percent of parents assume that their children would wish for more time together and less parental time at work. And 50 percent of parents with children up to 18 years old say they feel that they have too little time with their child—fathers (56 percent) even more so than mothers (44 percent).

But only 10 percent of children wish that their mothers would spend more time with them, and 15.5 percent say the same thing about their fathers. And surprisingly, children with employed mothers and those with mothers at home do not differ on whether they feel they have too little time with Mom.

What the largest proportion of children (23 percent) say that they want is for their mothers and their fathers to make more money. I suspect that money is seen as a stress-reducer, given children's other answers. The total number of children who wish that their parents would be less stressed or less tired by work is even larger: 34 percent make this wish for their mothers and 27.5 percent for their fathers. Sympathy for working parents comes through loud and clear: "I would like to thank the parents of America for working so hard to earn money," says one 15-year-old girl. "I know that a working parent goes through so much for their children."

The study also reveals what children learn from their parents about the world of work. Only about two in five children think their parents like their work a lot, compared with 62.5 percent of parents who say they do. That's probably because many of us have said to our kids, "I have to go to work." Or "I wish I didn't have to leave." We seem to talk around children rather than with them about our jobs. And our reluctance to talk to our children about our work has meant that young people are getting haphazard rather than intentional information, sometimes blaming themselves for distress we pick up on the job, and not fully appreciating the potential of their own future careers.

As a result, many children play detective to figure out what is going on in our jobs that upsets or elates us. They study our moods at the end of the workday. One of our young subjects says you can tell if your parents are in a bad mood "because you get a short and simple answer. If they had a bad day, they won't talk. Or they will just go off by themselves."

What makes a good parent? Through our interviews with parents and children, eight critical parenting skills emerged. We then asked the children in our national survey to grade their own mothers and dads on those criteria. They are:

1. Making the child feel important and loved
2. Responding to the child's cues and clues
3. Accepting the child for who he or she is, but expecting success
4. Promoting strong values
5. Using constructive discipline
6. Providing routines and rituals to make life predictable and create positive neural patterns in developing brains
7. Being involved in the child's education
8. Being there for the child

Which of these skills earned parents the highest—and lowest—grades? Among children in the seventh through the 12th grades, mothers are given the highest grades for being there when the child is sick (81 percent gave their mothers an A) and for raising their children with good values (75 percent). They receive the lowest grades for controlling their tempers

Time spent in shared activities wins parents high marks—but not if it feels hurried or rushed

when their children make them angry (only 29 percent gave their mothers an A) and for knowing what is really going on in their children's lives (35 percent). The age of the child makes a difference. Younger children consistently rate their parents more favorably than older ones, which no doubt reflects the way teenagers separate emotionally from their parents.

Money also matters. In analysis after analysis, the children's perception of their families' economic health is strongly linked to how they rate their moms' and dads' parenting skills. Although the public often views the problems of children as primarily moral in nature, our analyses show that families that do not have to worry about putting bread on the table may have more to give to their children emotionally. They also may be able to raise their children in more positive, cohesive communities.

These findings illustrate why it is so important to ask the children rather than to rely on our own assumptions. The issue of time with children has typically been framed in the public debate as a mothers' issue. But when we ask the children, we see that fathers need to be front and center in this discussion, as well.

Children in the seventh through the 12th grades judge their fathers less favorably than their mothers in some important respects, such as making their child feel important and loved and being someone whom the child can go to if upset. Teenagers are more likely than their younger counterparts to want more time with their fathers. Thirty-nine percent of children 13 through 18 years old feel they have too little time with their fathers, compared with 29 percent of children 8 through 12 years old.

We found that the quantity of time with mothers and fathers does matter a great deal. Children who spend more time with their mothers and fathers on workdays and nonworkdays see their parents more positively, feel that their parents are more successful at managing work and family responsibilities, and see their parents as putting their families first. "I think that if the parents spend more time with their children, they will become better people in life," says a 12-year-old boy whose father works part time while his mom stays home.

But to move beyond simply cataloging the number of hours children and parents spend together, we looked at what parents and children do while they are together, such as eating a meal, playing a game or sport or exercising, doing homework (together) and watching TV. For all these activities, the same pattern holds: the more frequently parents and children engaged in them together, the more positive the assessment parents got from their children.

But spending time together isn't enough. Many children said their interactions with parents feel rushed and hurried, and they gave their mothers and fathers lower marks as a result. More than two in five (44.5 percent) children feel that their time with their mother is rushed, while 37 percent feel their time with their father is rushed. Some mentioned mornings as particularly hectic times for their families. One 12-year-old girl said of her mother: "She's rushing and telling me to rush . . . And my backpack weighs a ton, so if she walks me to school, it's like running down the street. I'm like, 'wait up . . .' "

Predictably, children are more likely to see their parents positively if their time together is calmer. For example: of children 8 through 18 years of age who rate their time with their mothers as very calm, 86 percent give their mothers an A for making them feel important and loved, compared with 63 percent of those who rate their time with their mothers as very rushed. And 80 percent of children who feel their time with their fathers is very calm give them an A for "appreciating me for who I am," compared with only 50.5 percent of those who rate their time with their fathers as very rushed.

The flip side of feeling rushed and distracted with children is concentration and focus. In one-on-one interviews, we asked parents to describe moments when they felt particularly successful at home. Over and over, we heard the word "focus." The mother of a 12-year-old says: "It's the time you spend with your children [when] you are really focused on them that's good; not a distracted time."

Of children in the seventh through 12th grades, 62 percent say that mothers find it "very easy" and 52 percent say that fathers find it very easy to focus on them when they are to-

Grading Mom

She's there during illness, but sometimes loses her temper

SUBJECT	A	B	C	D	F
Being there for me when I am sick	81%	11%	5%	2%	1%
Raising me with good values	75	15	6	3	2
Making me feel important and loved	64	20	10	5	1
Being able to go to important events	64	20	10	3	3.5
Appreciating me for who I am	64	18	8	6	5
Encouraging me to enjoy learning	59	23	11.5	3	3
Being involved in school life	46	25	14	10	6
Being someone to go to when upset	46	22	14	8	9
Spending time talking with me	43	33	14	6	4
Establishing traditions with me	38	29	17	10	6
Knowing what goes on with me	35	31	15	10	9
Controlling her temper	29	27.5	20.5	12	11

Kids who think their families are financially secure feel more positive about Mom and Dad

gether. And children are very attuned to the times when their parents are truly focused on them: "They're not just saying normal things like 'uh huh . . . uh hmmm.' They seem to be very intent on what I'm saying, they're not just looking away," said a 10-year-old boy. Some children even have "tests" of whether their parent is focusing on them. For example, one 13-year-old boy throws nonsense statements — like "a goldfish on the grass"—into the middle of a sentence to check out whether his parents are really listening to him.

Every analysis we conducted revealed that when children feel that their mothers and fathers can focus on them, they are much more likely to feel that their parents manage their work and family responsibilities more successfully and put their families before their work. And they give their parents much higher marks for all of the parenting skills we examined.

So, is it quantity time or quality time? Clearly, the words we're using to describe time within the family are wrong. To change the debate, we need new words. Since "focus" is the word that parents use to describe the quality of time they treasure most, I suggest we use it. And since parents and children highly value the quantity of time they spend being together, whether sharing a meal or just being around each other in a nonrushed way, we need a phrase for that, too. Children need focused times and hang-around times.

I hope that, as a result of this book, the conversations around work and family will change. When parents and children talk together about these issues, reasonable changes can be made. Children will tell us how some things could be better. Yes, they will still try to push our guilt buttons. Yes, they will still read our moods and plead their case for what they want because kids will be kids. But we are the adults, and we set the tone for our relationships with our children.

I repeat the wisdom of a 12-year-old child: "Listen. Listen to what your kids say, because you know, sometimes it's very important. And sometimes a kid can have a great idea and it could even affect you." So let's ask the children.

FETAL PSYCHOLOGY

Behaviorally speaking, there's little difference between a newborn baby and a 32-week-old fetus. A new wave of research suggests that the fetus can feel, dream, even enjoy *The Cat in the Hat*. The abortion debate may never be the same.

By Janet L. Hopson

The scene never fails to give goose bumps: the baby, just seconds old and still dewy from the womb, is lifted into the arms of its exhausted but blissful parents. They gaze adoringly as their new child stretches and squirms, scrunches its mouth and opens its eyes. To anyone watching this tender vignette, the message is unmistakable. Birth is the beginning of it all, ground zero, the moment from which the clock starts ticking. Not so, declares Janet DiPietro. Birth may be a grand occasion, says the Johns Hopkins University psychologist, but "it is a trivial event in development. Nothing neurologically interesting happens."

Armed with highly sensitive and sophisticated monitoring gear, DiPietro and other researchers today are discovering that the real action starts weeks earlier. At 32 weeks of gestation—two months before a baby is considered fully prepared for the world, or "at term"—a fetus is behaving almost exactly as a newborn. And it continues to do so for the next 12 weeks.

As if overturning the common conception of infancy weren't enough, scientists are creating a startling new picture of intelligent life in the womb. Among the revelations:

- By nine weeks, a developing fetus can hiccup and react to loud noises. By the end of the second trimester it can hear.
- Just as adults do, the fetus experiences the rapid eye movement (REM) sleep of dreams.
- The fetus savors its mother's meals, first picking up the food tastes of a culture in the womb.

A fetus spends hours in the rapid eye movement sleep of dreams.

• Among other mental feats, the fetus can distinguish between the voice of Mom and that of a stranger, and respond to a familiar story read to it.

• Even a premature baby is aware, feels, responds, and adapts to its environment.

• Just because the fetus is responsive to certain stimuli doesn't mean that it should be the target of efforts to enhance development. Sensory stimulation of the fetus can in fact lead to bizarre patterns of adaptation later on.

The roots of human behavior, researchers now know, begin to develop early—just weeks after conception, in fact. Well before a woman typically knows she is pregnant, her embryo's brain has already begun to bulge. By five weeks, the organ that looks like a lumpy inchworm has already embarked on the most spectacular feat of human development: the creation of the deeply creased and convoluted cerebral cortex, the part of the brain that will eventually allow the growing person to move, think, speak, plan, and create in a human way.

At nine weeks, the embryo's ballooning brain allows it to bend its body, hiccup, and react to loud sounds. At week ten, it moves its arms, "breathes" amniotic fluid in and out, opens its jaw, and stretches. Before the first trimester is over, it yawns, sucks, and swallows as well as feels and smells. By the end of the second trimester, it can hear; toward the end of pregnancy, it can see.

FETAL ALERTNESS

Scientists who follow the fetus' daily life find that it spends most of its time not exercising these new abilities but sleeping. At 32 weeks, it drowses 90 to 95% of the day. Some of these hours are spent in deep sleep, some in REM sleep, and some in an indeterminate state, a product of the fetus' immature brain that is different from sleep in a baby, child, or adult. During REM sleep, the fetus' eyes move back and forth just as an adult's eyes do, and many researchers believe that it is dreaming. DiPietro speculates that fetuses dream about what they know—the sensations they feel in the womb.

Closer to birth, the fetus sleeps 85 to 90% of the time, the same as a newborn. Between its frequent naps, the fetus seems to have "something like an awake alert period," according to developmental psychologist William Fifer, Ph.D., who with his Columbia University colleagues is monitoring these sleep and wakefulness cycles in order to identify patterns of normal and abnormal brain development, including potential predictors of sudden infant death syndrome. Says Fifer, "We are, in effect, asking the fetus: 'Are you paying attention? Is your nervous system behaving in the appropriate way?' "

FETAL MOVEMENT

Awake or asleep, the human fetus moves 50 times or more each hour, flexing and extending its body, moving its head, face, and limbs and exploring its warm wet compartment by touch. Heidelise Als, Ph.D., a developmental psychologist at Harvard Medical School, is fascinated by the amount of tactile stimulation a fetus gives itself. "It touches a hand to the face, one hand to the other hand, clasps its feet, touches its foot to its leg, its hand to its umbilical cord," she reports.

Als believes there is a mismatch between the environment given to preemies in hospitals and the environment they would have had in the womb. She has been working for years to change the care given to preemies so that they can curl up, bring their knees together, and touch things with their hands as they would have for weeks in the womb.

Along with such common movements, DiPietro has also noted some odder fetal activities, including "licking the uterine wall and literally walking around the womb by pushing off with its feet." Laterborns may have more room in the womb for such maneuvers than first babies. After the initial pregnancy, a woman's uterus is bigger and the umbilical cord longer, allowing more freedom of movement. "Second and subsequent children may develop more motor experience in utero and so may become more active infants," DiPietro speculates.

Fetuses react sharply to their mother's actions. "When we're watching the fetus on ultrasound and the mother starts to laugh, we can see the fetus, floating upside down in the womb, bounce up and down on its head, bum-bum-bum, like it's bouncing on a trampoline," says DiPietro. "When mothers watch this on the screen, they laugh harder, and the fetus goes up and down even faster. We've wondered whether this is why people grow up liking roller coasters."

FETAL TASTE

Why people grow up liking hot chilies or spicy curries may also have something to do with the fetal environment. By 13 to 15 weeks a fetus' taste buds already look like a mature adult's, and doctors know that the amniotic fluid that surrounds it can smell strongly of curry, cumin,

By 15 weeks, a fetus has an adult's taste buds and may be able to savor its mother's meals.

What's the Impact on Abortion?

Though research in fetal psychology focuses on the last trimester, when most abortions are illegal, the thought of a fetus dreaming, listening and responding to its mother's voice is sure to add new complexity to the debate. The new findings undoubtedly will strengthen the convictions of right-to-lifers—and they may shake the certainty of pro-choice proponents who believe that mental life begins at birth.

Many of the scientists engaged in studying the fetus, however, remain detached from the abortion controversy, insisting that their work is completely irrelevant to the debate.

"I don't think that fetal research informs the issue at all," contends psychologist Janet DiPietro of Johns Hopkins University. "The essence of the abortion debate is: When does life begin? Some people believe it begins at conception, the other extreme believes that it begins after the baby is born, and there's a group in the middle that believes it begins at around 24 or 25 weeks, when a fetus can live outside of the womb, though it needs a lot of help to do so.

"Up to about 25 weeks, whether or not it's sucking its thumb or has personality or all that, the fetus cannot survive outside of its mother. So is that life, or not? That is a moral, ethical, and religious question, not one for science. Things can behave and not be alive. Right-to-lifers may say that this research proves that a fetus is alive, but it does not. It cannot."

"Fetal research only changes the abortion debate for people who think that life starts at some magical point," maintains Heidelise Als, a psychologist at Harvard University. "If you believe that life begins at conception, then you don't need the proof of fetal behavior." For others, however, abortion is a very complex issue and involves far more than whether research shows that a fetus hiccups. "Your circumstances and personal beliefs have much more impact on the decision," she observes.

Like DiPietro, Als realizes that "people may use this research as an emotional way to draw people to the pro-life side, but it should not be used by belligerent activists." Instead, she believes, it should be applied to helping mothers have the healthiest pregnancy possible and preparing them to best parent their child. Columbia University psychologist William Fifer, Ph.D., agrees. "The research is much more relevant for issues regarding viable fetuses—preemies."

Simply put, say the three, their work is intended to help the babies that live—not to decide whether fetuses should.—*Camille Chatterjee*

garlic, onion and other essences from a mother's diet. Whether fetuses can taste these flavors isn't yet known, but scientists have found that a 33-week-old preemie will suck harder on a sweetened nipple than on a plain rubber one.

"During the last trimester, the fetus is swallowing up to a liter a day" of amniotic fluid, notes Julie Mennella, Ph.D., a biopsychologist at the Monell Chemical Senses Center in Philadelphia. She thinks the fluid may act as a "flavor bridge" to breast milk, which also carries food flavors from the mother's diet.

FETAL HEARING

Whether or not a fetus can taste, there's little question that it can hear. A very premature baby entering the world at 24 to 25 weeks responds to the sounds around it, observes Als, so its auditory apparatus must already have been functioning in the womb. Many pregnant women report a fetal jerk or sudden kick just after a door slams or a car backfires.

Even without such intrusions, the womb is not a silent place. Researchers who have inserted a hydrophone into the uterus of a pregnant woman have picked up a noise level "akin to the background noise in an apartment," according to DiPietro. Sounds include the whooshing of blood in the mother's vessels, the gurgling and rumbling of her stomach and intestines, as well as the tones of her voice filtered through tissues, bones, and fluid, and the voices of other people coming through the amniotic wall. Fifer has found that fetal heart rate slows when the mother is speaking, suggesting that the fetus not only hears and recognizes the sound, but is calmed by it.

FETAL VISION

Vision is the last sense to develop. A very premature infant can see light and shape; researchers presume that a fetus has the same ability. Just as the womb isn't completely quiet, it isn't utterly dark, either. Says Fifer: "There may be just enough visual stimulation filtered through the mother's tissues that a fetus can respond when the mother is in bright light," such as when she is sunbathing.

Japanese scientists have even reported a distinct fetal reaction to flashes of light shined on the mother's belly. However, other researchers warn that exposing fetuses (or premature infants) to bright light before they are ready can be dangerous. In fact, Harvard's Als believes that retinal damage in premature infants, which has long been ascribed to high concentrations of oxygen, may actually be due to overexposure to light at the wrong time in development.

A six-month fetus, born about 14 weeks too early, has a brain that is neither prepared for nor expecting signals from the eyes to be transmitted into the brain's visual cortex, and from there into the executive-branch frontal lobes, where information is integrated. When the fetus

A fetus prefers hearing Mom's voice over a stranger's—speaking in her native, not a foreign tongue—and being read aloud familiar tales rather than new stories.

is forced to see too much too soon, says Als, the accelerated stimulation may lead to aberrations of brain development.

FETAL LEARNING

Along with the ability to feel, see, and hear comes the capacity to learn and remember. These activities can be rudimentary, automatic, even biochemical. For example, a fetus, after an initial reaction of alarm, eventually stops responding to a repeated loud noise. The fetus displays the same kind of primitive learning, known as habituation, in response to its mother's voice, Fifer has found.

But the fetus has shown itself capable of far more. In the 1980s, psychology professor Anthony James DeCasper, Ph.D., and colleagues at the University of North Carolina at Greensboro, devised a feeding contraption that allows a baby to suck faster to hear one set of sounds through headphones and to suck slower to hear a different set. With this technique, DeCasper discovered that within hours of birth, a baby already prefers its mother's voice to a stranger's, suggesting it must have learned and remembered the voice, albeit not necessarily consciously, from its last months in the womb. More recently, he's found that a newborn prefers a story read to it repeatedly in the womb—in this case, *The Cat in the Hat*—over a new story introduced soon after birth.

DeCasper and others have uncovered more mental feats. Newborns can not only distinguish their mother from a stranger speaking, but would rather hear Mom's voice, especially the way it sounds filtered through amniotic fluid rather than through air. They're xenophobes, too: they prefer to hear Mom speaking in her native language than to hear her or someone else speaking in a foreign tongue.

By monitoring changes in fetal heart rate, psychologist Jean-Pierre Lecanuet, Ph.D., and his colleagues in Paris have found that fetuses can even tell strangers' voices apart. They also seem to like certain stories more than others. The fetal heartbeat will slow down when a familiar French fairy tale such as *"La Poulette"* ("The Chick") or *"Le Petit Crapaud"* ("The Little Toad"), is read near the mother's belly. When the same reader delivers another unfamiliar story, the fetal heartbeat stays steady.

The fetus is likely responding to the cadence of voices and stories, not their actual words, observes Fifer, but the conclusion is the same: the fetus can listen, learn, and remember at some level, and, as with most babies and children, it likes the comfort and reassurance of the familiar.

FETAL PERSONALITY

It's no secret that babies are born with distinct differences and patterns of activity that suggest individual temperament. Just when and how the behavioral traits originate in the womb is now the subject of intense scrutiny.

In the first formal study of fetal temperament in 1996, DiPietro and her colleagues recorded the heart rate and movements of 31 fetuses six times before birth and compared them to readings taken twice after birth. (They've since extended their study to include 100 more fetuses.) Their findings: fetuses that are very active in the womb tend to be more irritable infants. Those with irregular sleep/wake patterns in the womb sleep more poorly as young infants. And fetuses with high heart rates become unpredictable, inactive babies.

"Behavior doesn't begin at birth," declares DiPietro. "It begins before and develops in predictable ways." One of the most important influences on development is the fetal environment. As Harvard's Als observes, "The fetus gets an enormous amount of 'hormonal bathing' through the mother, so its chronobiological rhythms are influenced by the mother's sleep/wake cycles, her eating patterns, her movements."

The hormones a mother puts out in response to stress also appear critical. DiPietro finds that highly pressured mothers-to-be tend to have more active fetuses—and more irritable infants. "The most stressed are working pregnant women," says DiPietro. "These days, women tend to work up to the day they deliver, even though the implications for pregnancy aren't entirely clear yet. That's our cultural norm, but I think it's insane."

Als agrees that working can be an enormous stress, but emphasizes that pregnancy hormones help to buffer both mother and fetus. Individual reactions to stress also matter. "The pregnant woman who chooses to work is a different woman already from the one who chooses not to work," she explains.

She's also different from the woman who has no choice but to work. DiPietro's studies show that the fetuses of poor women are distinct neurobehaviorally—less active, with a less variable heart rate—from the fetuses of middle-class women. Yet "poor women rate themselves as less stressed than do working middle-class women," she notes. DiPietro suspects that inadequate nutrition and exposure to pollutants may significantly affect the fetuses of poor women.

Stress, diet, and toxins may combine to have a harmful effect on intelligence. A recent study by biostatistician Bernie Devlin, Ph.D., of the University of Pittsburgh, suggests that genes may have less impact on IQ than previously thought and that the environment of the womb may account for much more. "Our old notion of nature influencing the fetus before birth and nurture after birth needs an update," DiPietro insists. "There is an antenatal environment, too, that is provided by the mother."

Parents-to-be who want to further their unborn child's mental development should start by assuring that the antenatal environment is well-nourished, low-stress, drug-free. Various authors and "experts" also have suggested poking the fetus at regular intervals, speaking to it through a paper tube or "pregaphone," piping in classical music, even flashing lights at the mother's abdomen.

Does such stimulation work? More importantly: Is it safe? Some who use these methods swear their children are smarter, more verbally and musically inclined, more physically coordinated and socially adept than average. Scientists, however, are skeptical.

"There has been no defended research anywhere that shows any enduring effect from these stimulations," asserts Fifer. "Since no one can even say for certain when a fetus is awake, poking them or sticking speakers on the mother's abdomen may be changing their natural sleep patterns. No one would consider poking or prodding a newborn baby in her bassinet or putting a speaker next to her ear, so why would you do such a thing with a fetus?"

Als is more emphatic: "My bet is that poking, shaking, or otherwise deliberately stimulating the fetus might alter its developmental sequence, and anything that affects the development of the brain comes at a cost."

Gently talking to the fetus, however, seems to pose little risk. Fifer suggests that this kind of activity may help parents as much as the fetus. "Thinking about your fetus, talking to it, having your spouse talk to it, will all help prepare you for this new creature that's going to jump into your life and turn it upside down," he says—once it finally makes its anti-climactic entrance.

How does substance abuse by pregnant women affect their children? Knowing about the impact of children's prenatal exposure to drugs can help caregivers work more effectively with children and their families.

Children's Prenatal Exposure to Drugs: Implications for Early Childhood Educators

Phyllis K. Mayfield and J. Keith Chapman

Pregnant women who use or abuse alcohol, tobacco, and illicit substances endanger not only their own lives and well-being, but their unborn children as well. The dramatic increase in the use of cigarettes by teenagers and the abuse of illicit substances such as crack-cocaine by pregnant women in the United States are among the issues that remain of public concern.

Women who use drugs rarely use only one. Illegal substances such as cocaine and marijuana are typically combined with cigarettes and/or alcohol. Polydrug use makes it difficult to determine the extent, duration, or the direct effects of a specific type of substance on fetal development (Kronstadt, 1991). Along with the effects of continued use of well-known drugs and addictive narcotics, such as phencyclidine (PCP) and heroin, educators and related professionals must address the needs of these families and their children as they develop from infancy into adulthood.

Effects of Drug Use During Pregnancy

Early Impact on Development

Research findings on the potential harmful impact of legal drugs such as cigarettes and alcohol on the fetus are relatively consistent. Isolating the specific and unique effects of common illicit drugs has proven to be more difficult. Although cocaine, crack-cocaine, marijuana, and heroin are the most common illicit substances used by childbearing women (Feig, 1990; GAO, 1990), no drug-specific syndrome or distinct developmental profile correlated with illicit substance exposure has been identified. There are however, several indicators of the effects of these substances on unborn and newborn children.

The unique needs of families with children who were exposed prenatally to drugs necessitate a comprehensive, interdisciplinary family-centered approach.

Phyllis K. Mayfield, Ph.D., is Early Childhood Program Specialist at Shelby County Public Schools, Alabaster, Alabama.

J. Keith Chapman, Ph.D., is Assistant Professor, College of Education, programs in Special Education, at The University of Alabama, Tuscaloosa.

From *Dimensions of Early Childhood,* Summer/Fall 1998, pp. 20-22. © 1998 by the Southern Early Childhood Association (SECA), Little Rock, AR. Reprinted by permission.

What Is the Extent of Women's Drug Use?

- Each year, between 100,000 to 375,000 women in the United States give birth to infants prenatally exposed to drugs (GAO, 1990).
- Approximately 15% of women from 15 to 44 years of age use illicit drugs (National Institute on Drug Abuse [NIDA], 1991).
- Overall, the prevalence of cocaine use in this country is declining, but women of childbearing age continue to use cocaine at high rates (NIDA, 1991).
- An estimated 4.8 million women of childbearing age use some form of illicit substance(s) during any given month (Khalsa & Gfroerer, 1991).
- Each year, approximately 10 to 45% of women giving birth use cocaine during their pregnancy (Mentis & Lundgren, 1995).
- About 15% of women use alcohol or some type of drug(s) during pregnancy, and these patterns of substance abuse cross all socio-economic boundaries (Chasnoff, Landress, & Barrett, 1990).
- An increase in the number of infants exposed to drugs is anticipated (Office of the Inspector General, 1990).
- One conservative estimate is that each year 11% of all live births in this country are prenatally exposed to some form(s) of legalized and/or illicit substances (Tyler, 1992).
- Approximately 34 million women of childbearing age consume alcoholic beverages. More than 18 million are cigarette smokers. More than 6 million use an illicit drug, of which 44% have tried marijuana, and 14% have tried cocaine at least once (NIDA, 1991).

Drugs such as cocaine, marijuana, and PCP may cause a reduction in the flow of blood and vital nutrients to the developing infant, resulting in intrauterine growth retardation. This can lead to spontaneous abortion, abruptio placentae, premature labor, fetal cerebral infraction, and stillbirth (Feig, 1990).

Medical researchers have documented a high incidence of premature birth, low birth weight and shorter length, abnormal head circumference, intracranial hemorrhage, heart rate abnormalities, and occasional congenital anomalies (Chasnoff, Griffith, Freier, & Murray, 1992; Lutiger, Graham, Einarson, & Koren, 1991; van de Bor, Walthes, & Sims, 1990). By the time infants are 6 months old, their brain measurements are similar to those of infants who were not exposed to drugs in utero, but concerns remain as to the drugs' effects on mental functioning, such as memory in later childhood.

Furthermore, drug-exposed infants may exhibit initial abnormal behavioral patterns such as extreme irritability, irregular sleep and wake cycles, tremors, gaze aversion, limited coping skills during child and caregiver separation, and poor feeding routines (Eisen et al., 1991; Neuspiel & Hamel, 1991; Odom-Winn & Dunagan, 1991).

Effects on Later Development

Researchers are also interested in the relationships among prenatal drug exposure, postnatal development, and long-term outcomes (Chasnoff, Griffith, Freier, & Murray, 1992; Hawley, Halle, Drasin, & Thomas, 1995; Phelps & Cox, 1993). The imprint of prenatal substance exposure may persist into toddlerhood and beyond.

Knowledge about short- and long-term effects of exposure to crack-cocaine is only beginning to emerge. Most children who have experienced substance exposure have normal intellectual abilities but less capacity to modulate and control their own behavior and less task persistence than nonexposed peers (Griffith, 1992).

Many children who are drug-exposed exhibit behavior difficulty, impulsivity, and moodiness which may be directly related to central nervous system damage (Odom-Winn & Dunagan, 1991). This damage may lead to learning difficulties as the child matures (Tyler, 1992; Wright, 1994).

The GAO (1990) predicted that between 42 to 52% of children prenatally exposed to drugs will require special education. The report also found that 25% of children prenatally exposed to drugs exhibit some type of developmental delay, and that 40% experienced neurologic dysfunction that may affect their ability to relate to others in the classroom setting.

Among the findings about prenatal drug exposure that persist into childhood are these:

- Young children may exhibit delays in cognition, language (especially in the decoding of receptive information), adaptive behavior, and fine motor development, which may extend into diverse long-

Table 1. Teachers may find these behavioral and learning characteristics in children prenatally exposed to drugs

Behavioral Characteristics	Learning Characteristics
Behavioral extremes	Inconsistent problem-solving
Difficulty with relationships	Language delays
Easily overstimulated	Lack of concentration
Increased testing of limits	Fine motor difficulty
Difficulty with transitions	Reduced visual attention
Adverse to touch	Random and less imaginative play
Little remorse for hurting others	Memory difficulty
Less sense of a conscience	Difficulty with visual cues
Excessive fidgeting	Less understanding of cause and effect

term learning and behavior problems (GAO, 1990; Griffith, 1992; Trad, 1992; Williams & Howard, 1993; Wright, 1994).

- Children's communication skills may be affected (Angelilli et al., 1994; Griffith, Azuma, & Chasnoff, 1994; Johnson, Seikel, Madison, Foose, & Rinard, 1997).
- Children showed significant delays in verbal reasoning skills over time (Griffith et al., 1994).
- Children with histories of prenatal polydrug exposure were at risk for language delays and deficits (Johnson et al., 1997).
- In a follow-up study from 1995, children with polydrug exposure that included cocaine were at risk for speech-language, cognitive, and behavioral deficits (Rivers & Hedrick, 1998).
- Abnormal behavioral features in social interaction, organizing play, achievement of goals, and following through with task to successful completion have been observed (Rivers & Hedrick, 1998).

Table 1 summarizes behavioral and learning characteristics identified through research (Chasnoff et al., 1992; GAO, 1990; Trad, 1992; Tyler, 1992).

Guidelines for Early Childhood Educators

Current knowledge about the long-term effects of substance exposure on children's school performance is limited. However, the projected increase in the numbers of children prenatally exposed to drugs makes it clear that effective interventions for these children and their families will require a coordinated effort by many different disciplines and agencies.

Screenings, and thorough assessments as indicated, are essential to assure that children's placements are appropriate and that the best education practices are implemented to address each child's strengths and special needs (Wolery, Strain, & Bailey, 1992). Some children may be eligible for special services to assist them in compensating for their developmental difficulties. Many are likely to benefit from enrollment in inclusive environments.

Classroom Recommendations

The most effective teaching strategies, such as those considered here, demonstrate respect for children's cultures and individual learning styles, and incorporate the most recent knowledge about how to support children's learning. In general, the fields o[f] early children and special education are moving away from rigid, behavioristic approaches, and toward more integrated, responsive teaching methods (see Thompson, 1998).

Among the early proposals for working with children who have been exposed prenatally to drugs was Bellisimo's (1990) classroom teaching model. This model

General intervention guidelines for early childhood settings that include children with prenatal drug exposure

Structure the learning environment

- Establish supportive home-school relationships and encourage family participation whenever possible
- Set up small designated learning areas rather than a large open area
- Organize the environment and define boundaries
- Use area signs or drawings to help children associate specific behaviors, activities, and materials with a particular space
- Rotate materials; do not put everything out at once
- Limit the number of classroom rules, and keep them positive
- Make daily routines as predictable as possible, and limit interruptions
- Keep adult-child ratios low

Encourage teacher-child interactions

- Address children by name and make eye contact or touch children before making a verbal request if these are appropriate in their cultures
- Focus children's attention by limiting distractions and providing engaging activities
- Praise verbally and specifically rather than with just hugs or smiles
- Encourage decision making by providing daily opportunities for choices, and talk about consequences of choices
- Structure and limit the number and length of transitions, prepare children for transitions with verbal cues and role playing
- Encourage attachments and respect
- Provide role models and direct instruction if needed for appropriate classroom behaviors such as sharing, greeting, and thanking
- Encourage communication, and respond to all attempts to verbalize
- Urge children to verbally express their wants and needs

Plan engaging activities

- Structure, model, and guide appropriate play activities; provide individual instruction to support play behaviors, such as how to join a group or welcome another child
- Initiate opportunities for children to engage in parallel and small-group play
- Implement a developmentally appropriate, integrated curriculum
- Promote active participation in group activities

Infants exposed to drugs prenatally are at greatest risk when other environmental risk factors are present.

recommended environments that are predictable, with established routines; are characterized by self-directed exploration; are sensitive to transitional periods; and have a small teacher-pupil ratio designed to enhance positive attachments to caregivers.

Most children are not likely to need a separate curriculum or methodology (Shores, 1991; Kinnison, Sluder, & Cates, 1995). Instead, these authors suggest that children who were exposed to drugs prenatally will benefit from the use of professional educational practices, with emphasis placed on long-term expectations and predictable routines, individualized teaching strategies, reteaching of concepts, concrete activities, and modeling.

Family-Centered Intervention

Education and social service agencies must be well prepared to work with families and children who were, and may still be, abusing drugs. Most research studies show that infants exposed to drugs prenatally are at greatest risk when other environmental risk factors are present, such as:

- poverty
- parents or caregivers who have not completed high school
- one-parent households
- multiple foster-care placements of children or their teen parents
- more than four people in a family
- discrimination due to ethnicity or language

The unique needs of families with children who were exposed prenatally to drugs necessitate a comprehensive, interdisciplinary family-centered approach which sees the family in holistic terms as a diverse and heterogeneous group who are at increased risk for an array of developmental, behavioral, and societal challenges (Chapman, Mayfield, Cook, & Chissom, 1995). Service providers can assist these families in identifying their concerns, priorities, and resources.

The GAO (1990) found that tremendous diversity exists among county, state, and federal agencies in attempting to identify and serve these children and families. Families with children who were exposed to drugs prenatally are most likely to realize their full potential when allied professionals develop and implement a formal referral and assessment process, offer family-centered educational programs, provide consistent and coordinated multiple agency involvement, and increase public awareness about the opportunities and challenges in working with these young children.

Key elements of family-centered services

- Services must fit the family rather than making the family fit the services
- Families are usually the constant in children's lives, while professionals come and go
- Parent-professional collaboration is essential in all decision making
- Unbiased information about child and family care must be shared with families
- Policies must meet the emotional and financial needs of families
- Family individuality must be respected
- Parent-to-parent support must be facilitated
- Services must be flexible and accessible

(adapted from Bailey, Buysse, Edmondson, & Smith, 1992)

References

Angelilli, M. L., Fischer, H., Delaney-Black, V., Rubinstein, M., Ager, J. W., & Sokol, R. J. (1994). History of in-utero cocaine exposure in language-delayed children. *Clinical Pediatrics, 33*(9), 514–516.

Bailey, D. B., Buysse, V., Edmondson. R., & Smith, T. M. (1992). Creating family-centered services in early intervention: Perceptions of professionals in four states. *Exceptional Children, 58,* 298–309.

Bellisimo, Y. (1990, January). Crack babies: The school's new high-risk students. *Thrust,* pp. 23–26.

Chapman, J. K., Mayfield, P. K., Cook, M. J., & Chissom, B. S. (1995). Service patterns and educational experiences among two groups who work with young children prenatally exposed to cocaine: A study across four states. *Infant-Toddler Intervention: The Transdisciplinary Journal, 5,* 31–50.

Chasnoff, I. J., Griffith, D. R., Freier, C., & Murray, J. (1992). Cocaine/polydrug use in pregnancy: Two-year follow-up. *Pediatrics, 89,* 284–289.

Chasnoff, I. J., Landress, H. J., & Barrett, M. E. (1990). The prevalence of illicit drug or alcohol use during pregnancy and discrepancies in mandatory reporting in Pinellas County, Florida. *The New England Journal of Medicine, 322*(17), 1202–1206.

Eisen, L. M., Field, T. M., Bandstra, E. S., Roberts, J., Morrow, C., Larson, S., & Steele, B. M. (1991). Perinatal cocaine effects on neonatal stress behavior and performance on the Brazelton Scale. *Pediatrics, 88,* 477–480.

Feig, L. (1990). *Drug-exposed infants and children: Service needs and policy questions.* Washington, DC: U.S. Department of Health and Human Services. Office of Social Services, Division of Children and Youth Policy.

General Accounting Office (GAO). (1990). *Drug-exposed infants: A generation at risk.* Washington, DC: U.S. Department of Health and Human Services.

Griffith, D. R. (1992, September). Prenatal exposure to cocaine and other drugs: Developmental and educational prognoses. *Phi Delta Kappan,* 30–34.

Griffith, D. R., Azuma, S. D., & Chasnoff, I. J. (1994). Three-year outcome of children exposed prenatally to drugs. *Journal of the American Academy of Child and Adolescent Psychiatry, 33*(1), 20–27.

Hawley, T. L., Halle, T. G., Drasin, R. E., & Thomas, N. G. (1995). Children of addicted mothers: Effects of the "crack epidemic" on the caregiving environment and the development of preschoolers. *American Journal of Orthopsychiatry, 65*(3), 364–379.

Johnson, J. M., Seikel, J. A., Madison, C., Foose, S. M., & Rinard, K. D. (1997). Standardized test performance of children with a history of prenatal exposure to multiple drugs/cocaine. *Journal of Communication Disorders, 30,* 45–73.

Khalsa, J. H., & Gfroerer, J. (1991). Epidemiology and health consequences of drug abuse among pregnant women. *Seminars in Perinatology, 15,* 265–270.

Kinnison, L. R., Sluder, L. C., & Cates, D. (1995). Prenatal drug exposure: Implications for teachers of young children. *Day Care and Early Education,* 22(30), 35–37.

Kronstadt, D. (1991, Spring). Complex developmental issues of prenatal drug exposure. *The Future of Children,* 36–49.

Lutiger, B., Graham, K., Einarson, T., & Koren, G. (1991). Relationship between gestational cocaine use and pregnancy outcome: A meta-analysis. *Teratology, 44,* 405–414.

Mentis, M., & Lundgren, K. (1995). Effects of prenatal exposure to cocaine and associated risk factors on language development. *Journal of Speech and Hearing Research, 38,* 1303–1318.

National Institute on Drug Abuse (NIDA). (1991). *National household survey of drug abuse for 1990.* Bethesda, MD: Author.

Neuspiel, D. R., & Hamel, S. C. (1991). Cocaine and infant behavior. *Developmental and Behavioral Pediatrics, 12,* 55–64.

Odom-Winn, D., & Dunagan, D. (1991). *Crack kids in school: What to do and how to do it.* Freeport, NY: Educational Activities.

Office of the Inspector General. (1990). *Crack babies.* Washington, DC: U. S. Department of Health and Human Services.

Phelps, L., & Cox, D. (1993). Children with prenatal cocaine exposure: Resilient or handicapped? *School Psychology Review,* 22(4), 710–724.

Rivers, K. O., & Hedrick, D. L. (1998). A follow-up study of language and behavioral concerns of children prenatally exposed to drugs. *Infant Toddler Intervention: The Trans-disciplinary Journal, 8*(1), 29–51.

Shores, E. F. (1991). *Prenatal cocaine exposure: The South looks for answers.* Little Rock, AR: Southern Early Childhood Association.

Thompson, S. H. (1998, January). Working with children of substance-abusing parents. *Young Children, 53*(1), 34–37.

Trad, P. V. (1992). Toddlers with prenatal cocaine exposure: Diagnostic peer groups Part II. *Infant-Toddler Intervention: The Transdisciplinary Journal, 2,* 285–305.

Tyler, R. (1992). Prenatal drug exposure: An overview of associated problems and intervention strategies. *Phi Delta Kappan,* 705–708.

Van de Bor, M., Walthes, F. J., & Sims, M. E. (1990). Increased cerebral bloodflow velocity in infants of mothers who abuse cocaine. *Pediatrics, 85,* 733–736.

Williams, B. F., & Howard, V. F. (1993). Children exposed to cocaine: Characteristics and implications for research and intervention. *Journal of Early Intervention, 17,* 61–72.

Wolery, M., Strain, P.S., & Bailey, D. B., Jr. (1992). Reaching potentials of children with special needs. In S. Bredekamp & T. Rosegrant (Eds.), *Reaching potentials: Appropriate curriculum and assessment for young children, Vol. 1.* Washington, DC: National Association for the Education of Young Children.

Wright, R. (1994). Drugged out. *Texas Monthly, 20*(11), 150–154.

Learning language, researchers are finding, is an astonishing act of brain computation—and it's performed by people too young to tie their shoes

BY SHANNON BROWNLEE

Inside a small, dark booth, 18-month-old Karly Horn sits on her mother Terry's lap. Karly's brown curls bounce each time she turns her head to listen to a woman's recorded voice coming from one side of the booth or the other. "At the bakery, workers will be baking bread," says the voice. Karly turns to her left and listens, her face intent. "On Tuesday morning, the people have going to work," says the voice. Karly turns her head away even before the statement is finished. The lights come on as graduate student Ruth Tincoff opens the door to the booth. She gives the child's curls a pat and says, "Nice work."

Karly and her mother are taking part in an experiment at Johns Hopkins University in Baltimore, run by psycholinguist Peter Jusczyk, who has spent 25 years probing the linguistic skills of children who have not yet begun to talk. Like most toddlers her age, Karly can utter a few dozen words at most and can string together the occasional two-word sentence, like "More juice" and "Up, Mommy." Yet as Jusczyk and his colleagues have found, she can already recognize that a sentence like "the people have going to work" is ungrammatical. By 18 months of age, most toddlers have somehow learned the rule requiring that any verb ending in *-ing* must be preceded by the verb *to be*. "If you had asked me 10 years ago if kids this young could do this," says Jusczyk, "I would have said that's crazy."

Linguists these days are reconsidering a lot of ideas they once considered crazy. Recent findings like Jusczyk's are reshaping the prevailing model of how children acquire language. The dominant theory, put forth by Noam Chomsky, has been that children cannot possibly learn the full rules and structure of languages strictly by imitating what they hear. Instead, nature gives children a head start, wiring them from birth with the ability to acquire their parents native tongue by fitting what they hear into a preexisting template for the basic structure shared by all languages. (Similarly, kittens are thought to be hard-wired to learn how to hunt.) Language, writes Massachusetts Institute of Technology linguist Steven Pinker, "is a distinct piece of the biological makeup of our brains." Chomsky, a prominent linguist at MIT, hypothesized in the 1950s that children are endowed from birth with "universal grammar," the fundamental rules that are common to all languages, and the ability to apply these rules to the raw material of the speech they hear—without awareness of their underlying logic.

The average preschooler can't tell time, but he has already accumulated a vocabulary of thousands of words—plus (as Pinker writes in his book, *The Language Instinct*) "a tacit knowledge of grammar more sophisticated than the thickest style manual." Within a few months of birth, children have already begun memorizing words without knowing their meaning. The question that has absorbed—and sometimes divided—linguists is whether children need a special language faculty to do this or instead can infer the abstract rules of grammar from the sentences they hear, using the same mental skills that allow them to recognize faces or master arithmetic.

The debate over how much of language is already vested in a child at birth is far from settled, but new linguistic research already is transforming traditional views of how the human brain works and how language evolved. "This debate has completely changed the way we view the brain," says Elissa Newport, a psycholinguist at the University of Rochester in New York. Far from being an orderly, computer-like machine that methodically calculates step by step, the brain is now seen as working more like a beehive, its swarm of interconnected neurons sending signals back and forth at lightning speed. An infant's brain, it turns out, is capable of taking in enormous amounts of information and finding the regular patterns contained within it. Geneticists and linguists recently have begun to challenge the common-sense assumption that intelligence and language are inextricably linked, through research on a rare genetic disorder called Williams syndrome, which can seriously impair cognition while leaving language nearly intact (box, Rare Disorder Reveals Split between Language and Thought). Increasingly sophisticated technologies such as magnetic resonance imaging are allowing researchers to watch the brain in action, revealing that language literally sculpts and reorganizes the connections within it as a child grows.

The path leading to language begins even before birth, when a developing fetus is bathed in the muffled sound of its mother's voice in the womb. Newborn babies prefer their mothers' voices over those of their fathers or other women, and researchers recently have found that when very young babies hear a recording of their mothers' native language, they will suck more vigorously on a pacifier than when they hear a recording of another tongue.

At first, infants respond only to the prosody—the cadence, rhythm, and pitch—of their mothers' speech, not the words. But soon enough they home in on the actual sounds that are typical of their parents' language. Every language uses a different assortment of sounds, called phonemes, which combine to make syllables. (In English, for example, the consonant sound "b" and the vowel sound "a" are both phonemes, which combine for the syllable *ba*, as in *banana.*) To an adult, simply perceiving, much less pronouncing, the phonemes of a foreign language can seem impossible. In English, the p of *pat* is "aspirated," or produced with a puff of air; the p of *spot* or *tap* is unaspirated. In English, the two p's are considered the same; therefore it is hard for English speakers to recognize that in many other languages the two p's are two different phonemes. Japanese speakers have trouble distinguishing between the "l" and "r" sounds of English, since in Japanese they don't count as separate sounds.

Polyglot tots. Infants can perceive the entire range of phonemes, according to Janet Werker and Richard Tees, psychologists at the University of British Columbia in Canada. Werker and Tees found that the brains of 4-month-old babies respond to every phoneme uttered in languages as diverse as Hindi and Nthlakampx, a Northwest American Indian language containing numerous consonant combinations that can sound to a nonnative speaker like a drop of water hitting an empty bucket. By the time babies are 10 months to a year old, however, they have begun to focus on the distinctions among phonemes of their native language and to ignore the differences among foreign sounds. Children don't lose the ability to distinguish the sounds of a foreign language; they simply don't pay attention to them. This allows them to learn more quickly the syllables and words of their native tongue.

An infant's next step is learning to fish out individual words from the nonstop stream of sound that makes up ordinary speech. Finding the boundaries between words is a daunting task, because people don't pause . . . between . . . words . . . when . . . they speak. Yet children begin to note word boundaries by the time they are 8 months old, even though they have no concept of what most words mean. Last year, Jusczyk and his colleagues reported results of an experiment in which they let 8-month-old babies listen at home to recorded stories filled with unusual words, like *hornbill* and *python.* Two weeks later, the researchers tested the babies with two lists of words, one composed of words they had already heard in the stories, the other of new unusual words that weren't in the stories. The infants listened, on average, to the familiar list for a second longer than to the list of novel words.

The cadence of language is a baby's first clue to word boundaries. In most English words, the first syllable is accented. This is especially noticeable in words known in poetry as trochees—two-syllable words stressed on the first syllable—which parents repeat to young children (BA-by, DOG-gie, MOM-my). At 6 months, American babies pay equal amounts of attention to words with different stress patterns, like gi-RAFFE or TI-ger. By 9 months, however, they have heard enough of the typical first-syllable-stress pattern of English to prefer listening to trochees, a predilection that will show up later, when they start uttering their first words and mispronouncing giraffe as *raff* and banana as *nana*. At 30 months, children can easily repeat the phrase "TOM-my KISS-ed the MON-key," because it preserves the typical English pattern, but they will leave out the *the* when asked to repeat "Tommy patted the monkey." Researchers are now testing whether French babies prefer words with a second-syllable stress—words like *be-RET* or *ma-MAN*.

Decoding patterns. Most adults could not imagine making speedy progress toward memorizing words in a foreign language just by listening to somebody talk on the telephone. That is basically what 8-month-old babies can do, according to a provocative study published in 1996 by the University of Rochester's Newport and her colleagues, Jenny Saffran and Richard Aslin. They reported that babies can remember words by listening for patterns of syllables that occur together with statistical regularity.

The researchers created a miniature artificial language, which consisted of a handful of three-syllable nonsense words constructed from 11 different syllables. The babies heard a computer-generated voice repeating these words in random order in a monotone for two minutes. What they heard went something like "bidakupadotigolabubidaku." *Bidaku*, in this case, is a word. With no cadence or pauses, the only way the babies could learn individual words was by remembering how often certain syllables were uttered together. When the researchers tested the babies a few minutes later, they found that the infants recognized pairs of syllables that had occurred together consistently on the recording, such as *bida*. They did not recognize a pair like *kupa*, which was a rarer combination that crossed the boundaries of two words. In the past, psychologists never imagined that young infants had the mental capacity to make these sorts of inferences. "We were pretty surprised we could get this result with babies, and with only brief exposure," says Newport. "Real language, of course, is much more complicated, but the exposure is vast."

Learning words is one thing; learning the abstract rules of grammar is another. When Noam Chomsky first voiced his idea that language is hardwired in the brain, he didn't have the benefit of the current revolution in cognitive science, which has begun to pry open the human mind with sophisticated psychological experiments and new computer models. Until recently, linguists could only parse languages and marvel at how quickly children master their abstract rules, which give every human being who can speak (or sign) the power to express an infinite number of ideas from a finite number of words.

There also are a finite number of ways that languages construct sentences. As Chomsky once put it, from a Martian's-eye view, everybody on Earth speaks a single tongue that has thousands of mutually unintelligible dialects. For instance, all people make sentences from noun phrases, like "The quick brown fox," and verb phrases, like "jumped over the fence." And virtually all of the world's 6,000 or so languages allow phrases to be moved around in a sentence to form questions, relative clauses, and passive constructions.

Statistical wizards. Chomsky posited that children were born knowing these and a handful of other basic laws of language and that they learn their parents' native tongue with the help of a "language acquisition device," preprogrammed circuits in the brain. Findings like Newport's are suggesting to some researchers that perhaps children can use statistical regularities to extract not only individual words from what they hear but also the rules for cobbling words together into sentences.

This idea is shared by computational linguists, who have designed computer models called artificial neural networks that are very simplified versions of the brain and that can "learn" some aspects of language. Artificial neural networks mimic the way that nerve cells, or neurons, inside a brain are hooked up. The result is a device that shares some basic properties with the brain and that can accomplish some linguistic feats that real children perform. For example, a neural network can make general categories out of a jumble of words coming in, just as a child learns that certain kinds of words refer to objects while others refer to actions. Nobody has to teach kids that words like *dog* and *telephone* are nouns, while *go* and *jump* are verbs; the way they use such words in sentences demonstrates that they know the difference. Neural networks also can learn some aspects of the meaning of words, and they can infer some rules of syntax, or word order. Therefore, a computer that was fed English sentences would be able to produce a phrase like "Johnny ate fish," rather than "Johnny fish ate," which is correct in Japanese. These computer models even make some of the same mistakes that real children do, says Mark Seidenberg, a computational linguist at the University of Southern California. A neural network designed by a student of Seidenberg's to learn to conjugate verbs sometimes issued sentences like "He jumped me the ball," which any parent will recognize as the kind of error that could have come from the mouths of babes.

But neural networks have yet to come close to the computation power of a toddler. Ninety percent of the sentences uttered by the average 3-year-old are grammatically correct. The mistakes they do make are rarely random but rather the result of following the rules of grammar with excessive zeal. There is no logical reason for being able to say "I batted the ball" but not "I holded the rabbit," except that about 180 of the most commonly used English verbs are conjugated irregularly.

Yet for all of grammar's seeming illogic, toddlers' brains may be able to spot clues in the sentences they hear that help them learn grammatical rules, just as they use statistical regularities to find word boundaries. One such clue is the little bits of language called grammatical morphemes, which among other things tell a listener whether a word is being used as noun or as a verb. *The,* for instance, signals that a noun will soon follow, while the suffix *ion* also identifies a word as a noun, as in vibration. Psycholinguist LouAnn Gerken of the University of Arizona recently reported that toddlers know what grammatical morphemes signify before they actually use them. She tested this by asking 2-year-olds a series of questions in which the grammatical morphemes were replaced with other words. When asked to "Find the dog for me," for example, 85 percent of children in her study could point to the right animal in a picture. But when the question was "Find *was* dog for me," they pointed to the dog 55 percent of the time. "Find *gub* dog for me," and it dropped to 40 percent.

Fast mapping. Children may be noticing grammatical morphemes when they are as young as 10 months and have just begun making connections between words and their definitions. Gerken recently found that infants' brain waves change when they are listening to stories in which grammatical morphemes are replaced with other words, suggesting they begin picking up grammar even before they know what sentences mean.

Such linguistic leaps come as a baby's brain is humming with activity. Within the first few months of life, a baby's neurons will forge 1,000 trillion connections, an increase of 20-fold from birth. Neurobiologists once assumed that the wiring in a baby's brain was set at birth. After that, the brain, like legs and noses, just grew bigger. That view has been demolished, says Anne Fernald, a psycholinguist at Stanford University, "now that we can eavesdrop on the brain." Images made using the brain-scanning technique positron emission tomography have revealed, for instance, that when a baby is 8 or 9 months old, the part of the brain that stores and indexes many kinds of memory becomes fully functional. This is precisely when babies appear to be able to attach meaning to words.

Other leaps in a child's linguistic prowess also coincide with remarkable changes in the brain. For instance, an adult listener can recognize *eleph* as *elephant* within about 400 milliseconds, an ability called "fast mapping" that demands that the brain process speech sounds with phenomenal speed. "To understand strings of words, you have to identify individual words rapidly," says Fernald. She and her colleagues have found that around 15 months of age, a child needs more than a second to recognize even a familiar word, like *baby.* At 18 months, the child can get the picture slightly before the word is ending. At 24 months, she knows the word in a mere 600 milliseconds, as soon as the syllable *bay* has been uttered.

Fast mapping takes off at the same moment as a dramatic reorganization of the child's brain, in which language-related operations, particularly grammar, shift from both sides of the brain into the left hemisphere. Most adult brains are lopsided when it comes to language, processing grammar almost entirely in the left temporal lobe, just over the left ear. Infants and toddlers, however, treat language in both hemispheres, according to Debra Mills, at the University of California–San Diego, and Helen Neville, at the University of Oregon. Mills and Neville stuck electrodes to toddlers' heads to find that processing of words that serve special grammatical functions, such as prepositions, conjunctions, and articles, begins to shift into the left side around the end of the third year.

From then on, the two hemispheres assume different job descriptions. The right temporal lobe continues to perform spatial tasks, such as following the trajectory of a baseball and predicting where it will land. It also pays attention to the emotional information contained in the cadence and pitch of speech. Both hemispheres know the meanings of many words, but the left temporal lobe holds the key to grammar.

This division is maintained even when the language is signed, not spoken. Ursula Bellugi and Edward Klima, a wife and husband team at the Salk Institute for Biological Studies in La Jolla, Calif., recently demonstrated this fact by studying deaf people who were lifelong signers of American Sign Language and who also had suffered a stroke in specific areas of the brain. The researchers found, predictably, that signers with damage to the right hemisphere had great difficulty with tasks involving spatial perception, such as copying a drawing of a geometric pattern. What was surprising was that right hemisphere damage did not hinder their fluency in ASL, which relies on movements of the hands and body in space. It was signers with damage to the left hemisphere who found they could no longer express themselves in ASL or understand it. Some had trouble producing the specific facial expressions that convey grammatical information in ASL. It is not just speech that's being processed in the left hemisphere, says MIT's Pinker, or movements of the mouth, but abstract language.

Nobody knows why the left hemisphere got the job of processing language, but linguists are beginning to surmise that languages are constructed the way they are in part because the human brain is not infinitely capable of all kinds of computation. "We are starting to see how the universals among languages could arise out of constraints on how the brain computes and how children learn," says Johns Hopkins linguist Paul Smolensky. For instance, the vast majority of the world's languages favor syllables that end in a vowel, though English is an exception. (Think of a native Italian speaking English and adding vowels where there are none.) That's because it is easier for the auditory centers of the brain to perceive differences between consonants when they come before a vowel than when they come after. Human brains can easily recognize *pad, bad,* and *dad* as three different words; it is much harder to distinguish *tab, tap,* and *tad.* As languages around the world were evolving, they were pulled along paths that minimize ambiguity among sounds.

Birth of a language. Linguists have never had the chance to study a spoken language as it is being constructed, but they have been given the opportunity to observe a new sign language in the making in Nicaragua. When the Sandinistas came to power in 1979, they established schools where deaf people came together for the first time. Many of the pupils had never met another deaf person, and their only means of communication at first was the expressive but largely unstructured pantomime each had invented at home with their hearing families. Soon the pupils began to pool their makeshift gestures into a system that is similar to spoken pidgin, the form of communication that springs up in places where people speaking mutually unintelligible tongues come together. The next generation of deaf Nicaraguan children, says Judy Kegl, a psycholinguist at Rutgers University, in Newark, N.J., has done it one better, transforming the pidgin sign into a full-blown language complete with regular grammar. The birth of Nicaraguan sign, many linguists believe, mirrors the evolution of all languages. Without conscious effort, deaf Nicaraguan children have created a sign that is now fluid and compact, and which contains standardized rules that allow them to express abstract ideas without circumlocutions. It can indicate past and future, denote whether an action was performed once or repeatedly, and show who did what to whom, allowing its users to joke, recite poetry, and tell their life stories.

Linguists have a long road ahead of them before they can say exactly how a child goes from babbling to banter, or what the very first languages might have been like, or how the brain transforms vague thoughts into concrete words that sometimes fly out of our mouths before we can stop them. But already, some practical conclusions are falling out of the new research. For example, two recent studies show that the size of toddlers' vocabularies depends in large measure on how much their mothers talk to them. At 20 months, according to a study by Janellen Huttenlocher of the University of Chicago, the children of talkative mothers had 131 more words in their vocabularies than children whose mothers were more taciturn. By age 2, the gap had widened to 295 words.

In other words, children need input and they need it early, says Newport. Parking a toddler in front of the television won't improve vocabulary, probably because kids need real human interaction to attach meaning to words. Hearing more than one language in infancy makes it easier for a child to hear the distinctions between phonemes of more than one language later on.

Newport and other linguists have discovered in recent years that the window of opportunity for acquiring language begins to close around age 6, and the gap narrows with each additional candle on the birthday cake. Children who do not learn a language by puberty will never be fluent in any tongue. That means that profoundly deaf children should be exposed to sign language as early as possible, says Newport. If their parents are hearing, they should learn to sign. And schools might rethink the practice of waiting to teach foreign languages until kids are nearly grown and the window on native command of a second language is almost shut.

Linguists don't yet know how much of grammar children are able to absorb simply by listening. And they have only begun to parse the genes or accidents of brain wiring that might give rise, as Pinker puts it, to the poet, the raconteur, or an Alexander Haig, a Mrs. Malaprop. What is certain is that language is one of the great wonders of the natural world, and linguists are still being astonished by its complexity and its power to shape the brain. Human beings, says Kegl, "show an incredible enthusiasm for discourse." Maybe what is most innate about language is the passion to communicate.

Boys will be Boys

Developmental research has been focused on girls; now it's their brothers' turn. Boys need help, too, but first they need to be understood.

BY BARBARA KANTROWITZ AND CLAUDIA KALB

IT WAS A CLASSIC MARS-VENUS ENCOUNTER. Only in this case, the woman was from Harvard and the man—well, boy—was a 4-year-old at a suburban Boston nursery school. Graduate student Judy Chu was in his classroom last fall to gather observations for her doctoral dissertation on human development. His greeting was startling: he held up his finger as if it were a gun and pretended to shoot her. "I felt bad," Chu recalls. "I felt as if he didn't like me." Months later and much more boy-savvy, Chu has a different interpretation: the gunplay wasn't hostile—it was just a way for him to say hello. "They don't mean it to have harsh consequences. It's a way for them to connect."

Researchers like Chu are discovering new meaning in lots of things boys have done for ages. In fact, they're dissecting just about every aspect of the developing male psyche and creating a hot new field of inquiry: the study of boys. They're also producing a slew of books with titles like "Real Boys: Rescuing Our Sons From the Myths of Boyhood" and "Raising Cain: Protecting the Emotional Life of Boys" that will hit the stores in the next few months.

What some researchers are finding is that boys and girls really are from two different planets. But since the two sexes have to live together here on Earth, they should be raised with special consideration for their distinct needs. Boys and girls have different "crisis points," experts say, stages in their emotional and social development where things can go very wrong. Until recently, girls got all the attention. But boys need help, too. They're much more likely than girls to have discipline problems at school and to be diagnosed with attention deficit disorder (ADD). Boys far outnumber girls in special-education classes. They're also more likely to commit violent crimes and end up in jail. Consider the headlines: Jonesboro, Ark.; Paducah, Ky.; Pearl, Miss. In all these school shootings, the perpetrators were young adolescent boys.

Even normal boy behavior has come to be considered pathological in the wake of the feminist movement. An abundance of physical energy and the urge to conquer—these are normal male characteristics, and in an earlier age they were good things, even essential to survival. "If Huck Finn or Tom Sawyer were alive today," says Michael Gurian, author of "The Wonder of Boys," "we'd say they had ADD or a conduct disorder." He says one of the new insights we're gaining about boys is a very old one: boys will be boys. "They are who they are," says Gurian, "and we need to love them for who they are. Let's not try to rewire them."

Indirectly, boys are benefiting from all the research done on girls, especially the landmark work by Harvard University's Carol Gilligan. Her 1982 book, "In a Different Voice: Psychological Theory and Women's Development," inspired Take Our Daughters to Work Day, along with best-selling spinoffs like Mary Pipher's "Reviving Ophelia." The traditional, unisex way of looking at child development was profoundly flawed, Gilligan says: "It was like having a one-dimensional perspective on a two-dimensional scene." At Harvard, where she chairs the gender-studies department, Gilligan is now supervising work on males, including Chu's project. Other researchers are studying mental illness and violence in boys.

While girls' horizons have been expanding, boys' have narrowed, confined to rigid ideas of acceptable male behavior no matter how hard their parents tried to avoid stereotypes. The macho ideal still rules. "We gave boys dolls and they used them as guns," says Gurian. "For 15 years, all we heard was that [gender differences] were all about socialization. Parents who raised their kids through that period said in the end, 'That's not true. Boys and girls can be awfully different.' I think we're awakening to the biological realities and the sociological realities."

But what exactly is the essential nature of boys? Even as infants, boys and girls behave differently. A recent study at Children's Hospital in Boston found that boy babies are more emotionally expressive; girls are more reflective. (That means boy babies tend to cry when they're unhappy; girl babies suck their thumbs.) This could indicate that girls are innately more able to control their emotions. Boys have higher levels of testosterone and lower levels of the neurotransmitter serotonin, which inhibits aggression and impulsivity. That may help explain why more males than females carry through with suicide, become alcoholics and are diagnosed with ADD.

The developmental research on the impact of these physiological differences is still in the embryonic stage, but psychologists are drawing some interesting comparisons between girls and boys (chart). For girls, the first crisis point often comes in early adolescence. Until then, Gilligan and others found, girls have an enormous capacity for establishing relationships and interpreting

From *Newsweek*, May 11, 1998, pp. 54-60.

Some Tips for Parents

• **Common sense helps.** So does a sense of humor. Most of all, boys need to know that the two most important people in their lives, their parents, are there for them.

• **Boys need hugs, too.** Don't try to turn him into Clint Eastwood at the age of 4. You're not coddling him by showing tenderness; you're developing emotional solidarity with your son and teaching him empathy.

• **Don't sweat the gun issue.** Even if you ban all guns, chances are your son will find a way to play at fighting: fingers or carrots work equally well. There's no evidence that this kind of play will turn your boy into a killer any more than playing with trucks will make him a truckdriver.

• **It's OK to get mad.** When he's at an appropriate age, you can help him understand the difference between legitimate feelings of anger and expressing it by hitting, kicking or screaming.

• **Stay in touch.** As they get older, boys still need their parents. Look for opportunities to communicate, like picking him up at school. He'll be strapped in a seat belt, so you know he can't get away.

emotions. But in their early teens, girls clamp down, squash their emotions, blunt their insight. Their self-esteem plummets. The first crisis point for boys comes much earlier, researchers now say. "There's an outbreak of symptoms at age 5, 6, 7, just like you see in girls at 11, 12, 13," says Gilligan. Problems at this age include bed-wetting and separation anxiety. "They don't have the language or experience" to articulate it fully, she says, "but the feelings are no less intense." That's why Gilligan's student Chu is studying preschoolers. For girls at this age, Chu says, hugging a parent goodbye "is almost a nonissue." But little boys, who display a great deal of tenderness, soon begin to bury it with "big boy" behavior to avoid being called sissies. "When their parents drop them off, they want to be close and want to be held, but not in front of other people," says Chu. "Even as early as 4, they're already aware of those masculine stereotypes and are negotiating their way around them."

It's a phenomenon that parents, especially mothers, know well. One morning last month, Lori Dube, a 37-year-old mother of three from Evanston, Ill., visited her oldest son, Abe, almost 5, at his nursery school, where he was having lunch with his friends. She kissed him, prompting another boy to comment scornfully: "Do you know what your mom just did? She kissed you!" Dube acknowledges, with some sadness, that she'll have to be more sensitive to Abe's new reactions to future public displays of affection. "Even if he loves it, he's getting these messages that it's not good."

There's a struggle—a desire and need for warmth on the one hand and a pull toward independence on the other. Boys like Abe are going through what psychologists long ago declared an integral part of growing up: individualization and disconnection from parents, especially mothers. But now some researchers think that process is too abrupt. When boys repress normal feelings like love because of social pressure, says William Pollack, head of the Center for Men at Boston's McLean Hospital and author of the forthcoming "Real Boys," "they've lost contact with the genuine nature of who they are and what they feel. Boys are in a silent crisis. The only time we notice it is when they pull the trigger."

No one is saying that acting like Rambo in nursery school leads directly to tragedies like Jonesboro. But researchers do think that boys who are forced to shut down positive emotions are left with only one socially acceptable outlet: anger. The cultural ideals boys are exposed to in movies and on TV still emphasize traditional masculine roles—warrior, rogue, adventurer—with heavy doses of violence. For every Mr. Mom, there are a dozen Terminators. "The feminist movement has done a great job of convincing people that a woman can be nurturing and a mother and a tough trial lawyer at the same time," says Dan Kindlon, an assistant professor of psychiatry at Harvard Medical School. "But we haven't done that as much with men. We're afraid that if they're too soft, that's all they can be."

And the demands placed on boys in the early years of elementary school can increase their overall stress levels. Scientists have known for years that boys and girls develop physically and intellectually at very different rates (time-line). Boys' fine motor skills—the ability to hold a pencil, for example—are usually considerably behind girls. They often learn to read later. At the same time, they're much more active—not the best combination for academic advancement. "Boys feel like school is a game rigged against them," says Michael Thompson, coauthor with Kindlon of "Raising Cain." "The things at which they excel—gross motor skills, visual and spatial skills, their exuberance—do not find as good a reception in school" as the things girls excel at. Boys (and girls) are also in academic programs at much younger ages than they used to be, increasing the chances that males will be forced to sit still before they are ready. The result, for many boys, is frustration, says Thompson: "By fourth grade, they're saying the teachers like girls better."

A second crisis point for boys occurs around the same time their sisters are stumbling, in early adolescence. By then, say Thompson and Kindlon, boys go one step further in their drive to be "real guys." They partake in a "culture of cruelty," enforcing male stereotypes on one another. "Anything tender, anything compassionate or too artis-

The Wonder (and Worry) Years

There may be no such thing as *child* development anymore. Instead, researchers are now studying each gender's development separately and discovering that boys and girls face very different sorts of challenges. Here is a rough guide to the major phases in their development.

Boys

0–3 years At birth, boys have brains that are 5% larger than girls' (size doesn't affect intelligence) and proportionately larger bodies—disparities that increase with age.

4–6 years The start of school is a tough time as boys must curb aggressive impulses. They lag behind girls in reading skills, and hyperactivity may be a problem.

Age 1 | 2 | 3 | 4 | 5 | 6 | 7

Girls

0–3 years Girls are born with a higher proportion of nerve cells to process information. More brain regions are involved in language production and recognition.

4–6 years Girls are well suited to school. They are calm, get along with others, pick up on social cues, and reading and writing come easily to them.

Trouble Spots: Where Boys Run Into Problems

Not all boys are the same, of course, but most rebel in predictable patterns and with predictable weapons: underachievement, aggression and drug and alcohol use. While taking chances is an important aspect of the growth process, it can lead to real trouble.

When Johnny Can't Read

Girls have reading disorders nearly as often as boys, but are able to overcome them. Disability rates, as identified by:

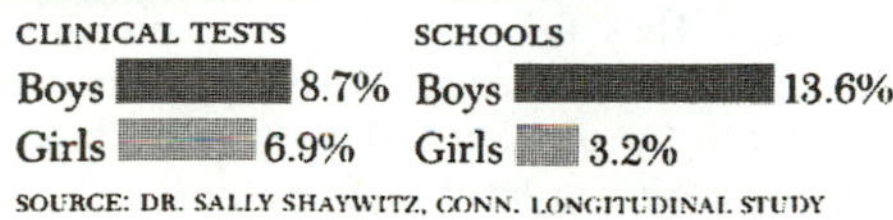

SOURCE: DR. SALLY SHAYWITZ, CONN. LONGITUDINAL STUDY

Suicidal Impulses

While girls are much more likely to try to kill themselves, boys are likelier to die from their attempts.

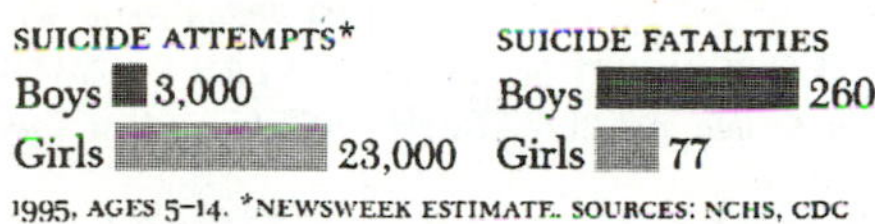

1995, AGES 5–14. *NEWSWEEK ESTIMATE. SOURCES: NCHS, CDC

Binge Drinking

Boys binge more on alcohol. Those who had five or more drinks in a row in the last two weeks:

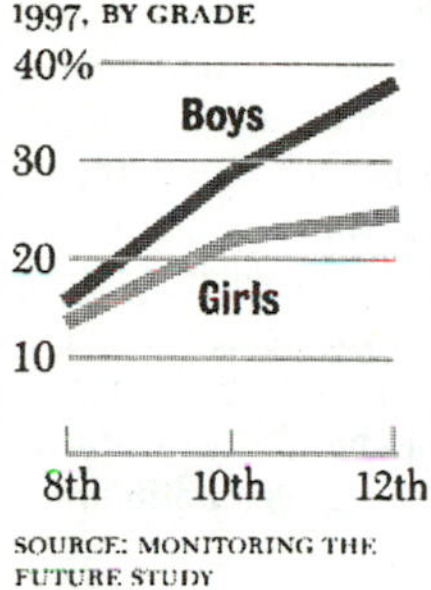

SOURCE: MONITORING THE FUTURE STUDY

Aggression That Turns to Violence

Boys get arrested three times as often as girls, but for some nonviolent crimes the numbers are surprisingly even.

Arrests of 10- to 17-year-olds: ■ Boys ■ Girls

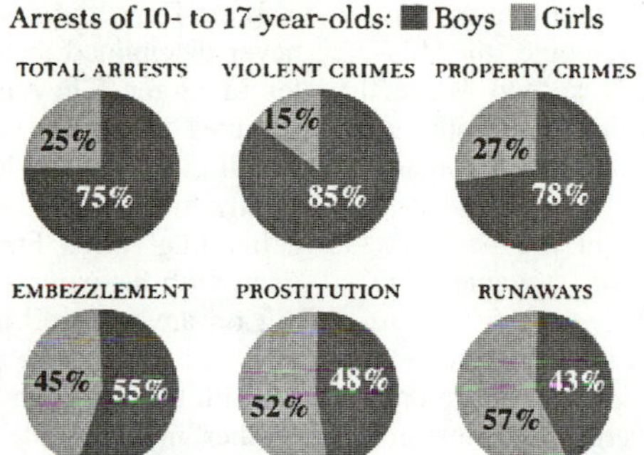

ESTIMATES, 1996. SOURCE: NAT'L CENTER FOR JUVENILE JUSTICE

Eating Disorders

Boys can also have eating disorders. Kids who used laxatives or vomited to lose weight:

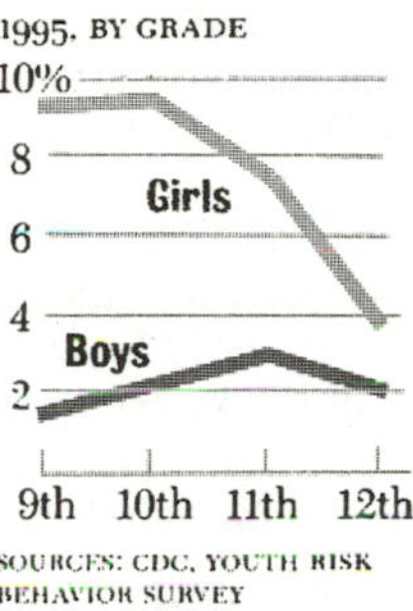

SOURCES: CDC, YOUTH RISK BEHAVIOR SURVEY

tic is labeled gay," says Thompson. "The homophobia of boys in the 11, 12, 13 range is a stronger force than gravity."

Boys who refuse to fit the mold suffer. Glo Wellman of the California Parenting Institute in Santa Rosa has three sons, 22, 19 and 12. One of her boys, she says, is a "nontypical boy: he's very sensitive and caring and creative and artistic." Not surprisingly, he had the most difficulty growing up, she says. "We've got a long way to go to help boys . . . to have a sense that they can be anything they want to be."

In later adolescence, the once affectionate toddler has been replaced by a sulky stranger who often acts as though torture would be preferable to a brief exchange of words with Mom or Dad. Parents have to try even harder to keep in touch. Boys want and need the attention, but often just don't know how to ask for it. In a recent national poll, teenagers named their parents as their No. 1 heroes. Researchers say a strong parental bond is the most important protection against everything from smoking to suicide.

For San Francisco Chronicle columnist Adnir Lara, that message sank in when she was traveling to New York a few years ago with her son, then 15. She sat next to a woman who told her that until recently she would have had to change seats because she would not have been able to bear the pain of seeing a teenage son and mother together. The woman's son was 17 when his girlfriend dumped him; he went into the garage and killed himself. "This story made me aware that with a boy especially, you have to keep talking because they don't come and talk to you," she says. Lara's son is now 17; she also has a 19-year-old daughter. "My daughter stalked me. She followed me from room to room. She was yelling, but she was in touch. Boys don't do that. They leave the room and you don't know what they're feeling." Her son is now 6 feet 3. "He's a man. There are barriers. You have to reach through that and remember to ruffle his hair."

With the high rate of divorce, many boys are growing up without any adult men in their lives at all. Don Elium, coauthor of the best-selling 1992 book "Raising a Son," says that with troubled boys, there's often a common theme: distant, uninvolved fathers, and mothers who have taken on more responsibility to fill the gap. That was the case with Raymundo Infante Jr., a 16-year-old high-school junior, who lives with his mother, Mildred, 38, a hospital administrative assistant in Chicago, and his sister, Vanessa, 19. His parents divorced when he was a baby and he had little contact with his father until a year ago. The hurt built up—in sixth grade, Raymundo was so depressed that he told a classmate he wanted to kill himself. The classmate told the teacher, who told a counselor, and Raymundo saw a psychiatrist for a year. "I felt that I just wasn't good enough, or he just didn't want me," Raymundo says. Last year Raymundo finally confronted his dad, who works two jobs—in an office and on a construction crew—and accused him of caring more about work than about his son. Now the two spend time together on weekends and sometimes go shopping, but there is still a huge gap of lost years.

7–10 years While good at gross motor skills, boys trail girls in finer control. Many of the best students but also nearly all of the poorest ones are boys.

11–13 years A mixed bag. Dropout rates begin to climb, but good students start pulling ahead of girls in math skills and catching up some in verbal ones.

14–16 years Entering adolescence, boys hit another rough patch. Indulging in drugs, alcohol and aggressive behavior are common forms of rebellion.

8	9	10	11	12	13	14	15	16

7–10 years Very good years for girls. On average, they outperform boys at school, excelling in verbal skills while holding their own in math.

11–13 years The start of puberty and girls' most vulnerable time. Many experience depression; as many as 15% may try to kill themselves.

14–16 years Eating disorders are a major concern. Although anorexia can manifest itself as early as 8, it typically afflicts girls starting at 11 or 12; bulimia at 15.

SOURCES: DR. MICHAEL THOMPSON, BARNEY BRAWER. RESEARCH BY BILL VOURVOULIAS—NEWSWEEK

Black boys are especially vulnerable, since they are more likely than whites to grow up in homes without fathers. They're often on their own much sooner than whites. Black leaders are looking for alternatives. In Atlanta, the Rev. Tim McDonald's First Iconium Baptist Church just chartered a Boy Scout troop. "Gangs are so prevalent because guys want to belong to something," says McDonald. "We've got to give them something positive to belong to." Black educators like Chicagoan Jawanza Kunjufu think mentoring programs will overcome the bias against academic success as "too white." Some cities are also experimenting with all-boy classrooms in predominantly black schools.

Researchers hope that in the next few years, they'll come up with strategies that will help boys the way the work of Gilligan and others helped girls. In the meantime, experts say, there are some guidelines. Parents can channel their sons' energy into constructive activities, like team sports. They should also look for "teachable moments" to encourage qualities such as empathy. When Diane Fisher, a Cincinnati-area psychologist, hears her 8- and 10-year-old boys talking about "finishing somebody," she knows she has mistakenly rented a violent videogame. She pulls the plug and tells them: "In our house, killing people is not entertainment, even if it's just pretend."

Parents can also teach by example. New Yorkers Dana and Frank Minaya say they've never disciplined their 16-year-old son Walter in anger. They insist on resolving all disputes calmly and reasonably, without yelling. If there is a problem, they call an official family meeting "and we never leave without a big hug," says Frank. Walter tries to be open with his parents. "I don't want to miss out on any advice," he says.

Most of all, wise parents of boys should go with the flow. Cindy Lang, 36, a full-time mother in Woodside, Calif., is continually amazed by the relentless energy of her sons, Roger Lloyd, 12, and Chris, 9. "You accept the fact that they're going to involve themselves in risky behavior, like skateboarding down a flight of stairs. As a girl, I certainly wasn't skateboarding down a flight of stairs." Just last week, she got a phone call from school telling her that Roger Lloyd was in the emergency room because he had fallen backward while playing basketball and school officials thought he might have a concussion. He's fine now, but she's prepared for the next emergency: "I have a cell phone so I can be on alert." Boys will be boys. And we have to let them.

With KAREN SPRINGEN *in Chicago,*
PATRICIA KING *in San Francisco,*
PAT WINGERT *in Washington,* VERN E. SMITH
in Atlanta and ELIZABETH ANGELL *in New York*

Research in Review

The Education of Hispanics in Early Childhood: Of Roots and Wings

Eugene E. Garcia

As director of the Office of Bilingual Education and Minority Languages Affairs in the U.S. Department of Education, I sought to engage my *professional* experience and expertise as an educational researcher and my *personal* cultural and linguistic experience to address national education policy. The professional in me has been nurtured at some of the best educational institutions in the United States, while the nonprofessional has been nurtured in a large, rural, Mexican American family. Born in the United States and speaking Spanish as our first language for generations, our family included 10 children—four high school graduates and one college graduate.

Bringing these *personas* (Spanish for "persons") together was not as difficult as I had expected and the mixture was quite helpful to the wide variety of people I interacted with in my national role. Bringing together these personas, I communicated with individuals in ways not possible had I spoken only with one voice or separate voices.

This article presents my intersecting but distinct voices to help further our understanding of life in a diverse society—particularly of Hispanics growing up in the United States during their early childhood years. The historical pattern of the education of Hispanics in the United States is a continuous story of underachievement. It need not continue to be that way.

The three voices here address issues of the past, present, and future. They recognize the multiple selves that not only make up my own persona but those that are a reality for all of us. It is useful to recognize that we walk in varied and diverse cultures. There is great diversity within each individual, just as there is diversity among individuals and the many cultures they belong to or represent. We all live with diversity, some of us more than others. No one escapes this challenge or its advantages and disadvantages.

While English First, an organization committed to English as the official U.S. language, is passionately concerned that multilingualism will produce divisiveness and significant conflict, indigenous people whose roots in the Americas outdistance the "White man's" presence

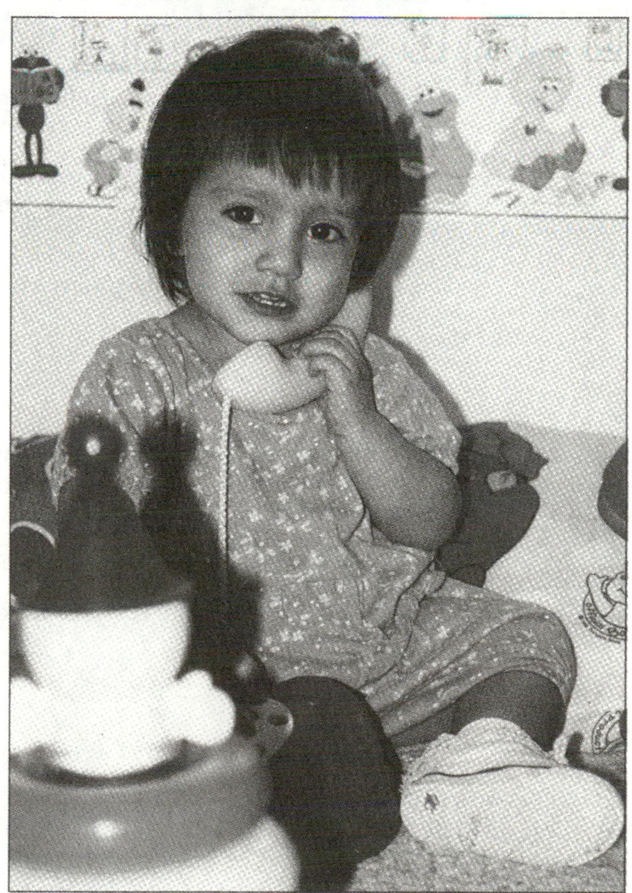

© Subjects and Predicates

Eugene E. Garcia, Ph.D., is professor and dean of the Graduate School of Education at the University of California in Berkeley He continues to do research in areas related to language, culture, and schooling. He served as director of the Office of Bilingual Education and Minority Language Affairs in the U.S. Department of Education, 1993–95.

This is one of a regular series of Research in Review columns. The column in this issue was invited by ***Carol Seefeldt,*** *Ph.D., professor at the University of Maryland, College Park.*

The Voices

Eugene.

This voice often represents my intellectual upbringing and is recognized primarily by my academic credentials—degrees received and where and when, how successful I was in those environments, academic positions I have held and their status in the academic world, the empirical research I have done, my teaching, and, of course, the articles and books I have written. This set of experiences and accomplishments, at its core, attempts to expand in critical and strategic ways our broader understanding of language acquisition, teaching, learning, and schooling, and the specific relevance of these to language-minority populations—learners who come to the educational enterprise not knowing the language of that formal enterprise and particularly for students like me who are classified as Hispanic in the present jargon of educators and demographers. I did not begin my academic pursuits with this specific population in mind but have naturally gravitated toward using my professional skills to address issues of relevance to it, but not *only* to it.

Gene.

Other parts of me are more rooted in the nonacademic world, my social and cultural realities. I am a son, brother, husband, father, and so on. In such social and cultural roles, I have experienced a wonderful family environment, learning much from my father and mother—neither of whom ever had the opportunity to attend school. They taught me to respect them, my elders, my brothers and sisters, and others who were not members of my family—such as my teachers—or not like me, and, most of all, to respect myself. They never gave me a formal lesson about these things; they just lived them, in the harsh realities of poverty and the hard work any migrant or sharecropping family understands. This teaching and learning included experiences of outright racism and subtle institutional racism in which our language, color, and heritage were not always met with either individual or group respect. From these experiences and teachers emerged the voice of Gene (a name used most often by my family and friends).

This persona agreed to work as an undergraduate in the migrant camps, tutoring adults in English and related subjects so that they could earn the GED (general equivalency diploma). This persona realized early that he was different. I spoke primarily Spanish, my peers only English. I and my family worked in the fields; my peers and their families hired us to work in their fields. My peers enjoyed a much higher standard of living—I recall being embarrassed that my family did not take summer vacations or have running water and inside toilets. Quite honestly, most of the time, these differences did not weigh heavy on my mind or affect my behavior—I had lots of friends, some like me and others quite different from me.

It was likely more Gene than Eugene who accepted the invitation to join the Clinton administration and Secretary of Education Richard Riley in the Department of Education. In political/policy roles like this one, I realized that policymakers and practitioners of education do not always act based on the best theory, proven educational practices, or even promising educational innovations. They act mostly out of political interests. I realized the importance of the politics of education. Gene's voice is often dominated by these lessons, although Eugene is not totally unaffected by them.

mourn just as passionately the loss of their languages and cultures. As this country and the world shrinks communicatively, economically, socially, and intellectually, diversity is becoming harder to hide, but it has always been there. In the following pages, I address issues related to the education of Hispanics in early childhood with the varied voices within me.

The "Hispanic" debate

Eugene, Gene, and Gino realize that their voices are not alone nor are their views held by all Hispanics in the United States. Most critical of such views of the interactive relationship of "roots and wings" for Hispanics are two well-regarded and influential Hispanic authors, each in her or his own way refuting the importance of roots and the relationship of those roots to the educational development of Hispanics.

Linda Chavez, an adviser in the Reagan White House, journalist, commentator, and author of *Out of the Barrio: Toward a New Politics of Hispanic Assimilation,* suggests that

> Every previous group—Germans, Irish, Italians, Greeks, Jews, Poles—struggled to be accepted fully into the social, political and economic mainstream, sometimes against the opposition of a hostile majority. They learned the language, acquired education and skills, and adapted their own customs and traditions to fit an American context. (1991, 2)

The key for Hispanic success in America, Chavez argues, is minimizing the public/governmental recogni-

Gino.

Another voice within me is identified best by the endearing name that my mother used for me—Gino. In my large, quite Catholic family, to baptize a child is a distinct honor and, in recognition of that honor, *los padrinos,* the godparents, are given the authority to name the child. At my birth my parents selected my eldest sister and her husband to serve as my padrinos, and my sister was enchanted with the name Eugene. That is how I came to have a Greek name in a cohort of brothers and sisters named Antonio, Emelio, Cecelia, Caprianita, Abel, Federico, Tiburcio, and Christina, and born of parents named Lorenzo and Juanita. My mother could not pronounce *Eugene,* so to her and my immediate family I became Gino.

Gino carries a distinct sense of cultural "Hispanic-ness," "Chicanismo," "Latino-ness," or "Raza-ness." These concepts reflect a deep regard for the linguistic and cultural roots that foster identity—best exemplified by a lesson from my father:

> For farmworkers and sharecroppers, winter was a time to prepare for work—there was not much work during this period. One winter in the high plains of Colorado where I was born and raised, my father pointed to an *árbol*—a cottonwood tree. He asked, *Por qué puede vivir ese árbol en el frio del invierno y en el calor del varano?* (How can that tree survive the bitter cold winter and the harsh heat of summer?) My father was a man of few words—relatives often characterized him as quiet and shy—but when he spoke we all listened very carefully. I rambled on about how big and strong the tree was and how its limbs and trunk were like the strong arms and bodies of my elder brothers. Then he kindly provided a different perspective by referring to a common Spanish *dicho/consejo* (proverb): *El árbol fuerte tienen raices maduros* (A strong tree has mature/strong roots).

In articulating this significant piece of the analysis that was absent from my youthful thoughts, my father made clear that without strong roots, strong trees are impossible—and we don't even see the roots! The roots of many Hispanics in this country have either been ignored or stripped away in the name of growing strong. Many have been directed to stop speaking Spanish, to perceive their culture as a "less-than" one, and to assimilate as quickly as possible so they can succeed in American society (Chavez 1991). Unfortunately, many have suffered the fate of the rootless tree—they have fallen socially, economically, academically, and culturally.

However, to Gino, my mother made it very clear: roots and their concomitant integrity and self-respect were not enough. She wanted the very best for all her children, certainly not the long and painful fieldwork that she had endured for a lifetime. She wanted us *bien educados*—to have a set of formal and marketable skills. She made very clear that children needed wings, like the wings she insisted we children grew every night upon falling asleep, so as to fly to heaven to be with God. "All children," she said, "are angels." In recent stories by Chicano author Victor Villaseñor, his mother elaborates further on this notion (Villaseñor 1991). She says that the children fly to God each night and station themselves as stars in His heaven. Both our mothers expressed a special regard for the sanctity of childhood and required children to have wings to perform their related roles. My mother emphasized that she could not provide the kind of wings that God and a good education could provide. She knew that the teachers and schools would have to take me further than she could personally. Education would need to provide the strong and elaborate wings for me to succeed where she often felt she had failed: "Go to school—strong wings like those of an eagle are also what you need in this world to raise your family and provide for them all that we have been unable to provide for you."

For Hispanics in this country, the emphasis on building wings in school has strategically focused on teaching English language skills: "Teach them English well and then they will succeed." Yet all educators realize that in today's information age, education must provide broad and strong intellectual wings related to fundamental linguistic, mathematical, scientific, and technological literacies. English literacy is important, but it is not enough. Gino feels that Hispanics, such as those he and his family represent, have been educationally shortchanged.

tion of Hispanic roots and the individual and governmental promotion of assimilation. She chides the federal government, particularly federal bilingual education programs, and Hispanic leaders for promoting permanent victim status and vying with Black Americans for the distinction of being the poorest, most segregated, and least educated minority, thereby entitling them to government handouts. These actions in turn, her conclusion advances, encourage Hispanics to maintain their language and culture and their specific identity in return for rewards handed out through affirmative action and federal, state, and local educational policies that thwart assimilation. This does not sound like my father's concern for the importance of roots or my mother's emphasis on wings.

Yet another Hispanic author, Richard Rodriguez, is very eloquent in his description of his upbringing in a Mexican home and a Catholic school where the English-speaking nuns literally beat the Spanish language and the "Hispanic-ness" out of him. His book *Hunger of Memory* (1982) describes this forced assimilation, painful as it was, that propelled him to new heights of educational achievement. Although he himself never articulates the conclusion, he leaves open the suggestion that such treatment of Hispanics is exactly what they need to get over their "problems." Eugene, Gene, and Gino reach a very different conclusion in this discussion. But you should know that the debate exists.

The following discussion indirectly addresses this debate but includes an expanded research-related discussion of vulnerability factors both within and outside the education arena along with data related to the "effective" treatment of this growing population of young children and families. The discussion addresses the following:

1. An overall demographic assessment of factors related to the schooling of culturally diverse populations, including issues of poverty, family stability, and immigrant status;

2. A particular analysis of the challenges associated with the growing number of language-minority students who are Hispanic—children who come to school with limited or no proficiency in English; and

3. A presentation of conceptual and empirical perspectives that sets the stage for a more informed approach to the education of Hispanics in early childhood.

The research

The demographic picture

The Census Bureau in its attempts to provide clarifying demographic information never fails in confusing us. In documenting the racial and ethnic heterogeneity of our country's population, it has arrived at a set of highly confusing terms that place individuals in separate exclusionary categories: White, White non-Hispanic, Black, Hispanic (with some five subcategories of Hispanics). Unfortunately, outside of the census meaning of these terms, they are for the most part highly ambiguous and nonrepresentative of the true heterogeneity which the Census Bureau diligently seeks to document. Therefore, it is important to note at the outset of this discussion that these categories are useful only as the most superficial reflection of our nation's true diversity. I do not know many census-identified "Whites," "Blacks," or "Hispanics" who believe they are "White," "Black," and so on, but given the forced-choice responses allowed them in census questionnaires, they are constrained by these choices.

Having consented to this significant restriction regarding efforts to document population diversity in this country, I still must conclude that an examination of the available data provides a fuzzy but useful portrait of our society and the specific circumstances of various groups within our nation's boundaries. That sketch is one of consummate vulnerability for non-White and Hispanic (usually referred to as "minority") families, children, and students. On almost every indicator, non-White and Hispanic families, children, and "at-risk" students are likely to fall into the lowest quartile on indicators of "well-being": family stability, family violence, family income, child health and development, and educational achievement. Yet this population has grown significantly in the last two decades and will grow substantially in the decades to come. The table ("Hispanic Demographics") summarizes these factors for census-derived information on Hispanics.

The demographic transformation that has become more evident in the last decade was easily foreseen at least that long ago. Our schools' future student profile is as predictable: in a mere 40 years, White students will be a minority in every category of public education as we know it today. Unfortunately, the emerging student majority of ethnic and racial background continues to be at risk in today's social institutions. The National Center for Children in Poverty (1995) provided a clear and alarming demographic window on these at-risk populations. Of the 21.9 million children under six years of age in 1990 who will move slowly through society's institutions—family, schools, the workplace—five million (25%) were living in poverty. Although less than 30% of all children under six years of age were non-White, more than 50% of the children in poverty were non-White. In addition, these children continued to live in racial/ethnic isolation. Some 56% lived in racially isolated neighborhoods in 1966; 72% resided in such neighborhoods in 1994; 61% of children in poverty live in concentrations of poverty where 20% of the population is poor.

High school or equivalent completion rates are alarming for these emerging majority student populations. In 1994 the high school completion rate for the U.S. population was 81.1% for 19-year-olds, 86.5% for 24-year-olds, and a very respectable 86% for 29-year-olds. For Blacks and Hispanics the rate of completion in all age groups was close to 60% (U.S. Department of Commerce 1990). With regard to academic achievement, in 1994, 30% of 13-year-old students were one grade level below the norm on standardized achievement measures. However, this differed significantly for emerging majority and White students: 27% for White students, 40% for Hispanic students, and 46% for Black students.

While English First, an organization committed to English as the official U.S. language, is passionately concerned that multilingualism will produce divisiveness and significant conflict, indigenous people whose roots in the Americas outdistance the "White man's" presence mourn just as passionately the loss of their languages and cultures.

The qualitative description of education presented above is further affirmed for Hispanics by other quantitative descriptions. A recent study reported by de Leon Siantz (1996) uses descriptive data from the Hispanic Health and Nutrition Examination Survey, a national effort sampling stratified populations of Mexican American, Puerto Rican, and Cuban American families in three U.S. regions (southwest, northeast, and

Hispanic Demographics

General demographic character

- Of the approximately 22.7 million Hispanics in the continental United States, the following information characterizes the population's ethnic diversity.

Country/area of origin	*Number (in millions)*	*%*
Mexico	14.6	64.3
Puerto Rico	2.4	10.6
Central/South America	3.0	13.4
Cuba	1.1	4.7
Other Hispanic countries	1.6	7.0

- 89.5% of the total Hispanic population in the United States is concentrated in three states: California (26%), Texas (25.5%), and New Mexico (38%). Other states with significant Hispanic populations are Arizona (19%), Colorado (13%), Florida (12%), and New York (12%).
- Average age of the Hispanic population in 1993 was 26.7 years.
- 200,000 Hispanics immigrate legally to the United States annually; Hispanics are 40% of all legal immigrants. (An estimated 200,000 Hispanics immigrate illegally.)
- The Hispanic population grew by 53% from 1980 to 1990, compared to the 9.8% growth in the general U.S. population.
- 17 million Hispanics report speaking Spanish in the home.
- 90% of Hispanics live in metropolitan areas; 52% in central cities.

Indices of "vulnerability"

- Median family income has fluctuated for Hispanics (1982—$23,814; 1991—$24,614; 1992—$23,912), remaining below that of non-Hispanics (1982—$35,075; 1991—$38,127; 1992—$38,015).
- In 1992, 26.2% of Hispanic families lived below the poverty line, compared to 27.2% in 1982. (In 1992, 10.4% of non-Hispanic White families lived below the poverty line.)
- In 1993, 1,239,094 Hispanic families (23.3%) were maintained by a female head-of-household (an increase of .5% from 1983 when it was 22.8% or 827,184); 48.8% of these households lived below the poverty line.
- 72.9% of Hispanics hold unskilled and semiskilled jobs, compared to 50.8% of non-Hispanics.

Education

- Approximately 50% of Hispanics leave school prior to graduation (70% by 10th grade).
- 38% of Hispanics are held back at least one grade.
- 50% of Hispanics are overage at grade 12.
- 90% of Hispanic students are in urban districts.
- 82% of Hispanic students attend segregated schools.
- Hispanics are significantly below national norms on academic achievement tests of reading, math, science, social science, and writing at grades 3, 7, and 11, generally averaging one to two grade levels below the norm. At grade 11, Hispanics average a grade 8 achievement level on these tests.
- Hispanics are placed in special education services six times more often than the general student population.

Sources: U.S. Bureau of the Census, *The Hispanic Population in the United States: March 1993* (Washington DC: U.S. Government Printing Office, 1993); U.S. Bureau of the Census, *Social and Economic Characteristics in the US: 1990 Census of the Population* (Washington DC: GPO, 1990); M.A. Reddy, *Statistical Record of Hispanic Americans* (Michigan: Gale Research, Inc., 1993); and U.S. Immigration and Naturalization Service, *Statistical Yearbook of the Immigration and Naturalization, 1993* (Washington DC: GPO, 1994).

southeast). This study reports very small differences in family well-being and child well-being indicators across these groups and regions. The Hispanic population was described as growing, youthful, poor, lacking parental care, and at high risk for AIDS.

Moreover, recent national Head Start data (Phillips & Cabrera 1996) indicate that only one-third of the programs had an enrollment characterized by a single language, with a range of 1 to 32 languages represented in programs, while 72% of programs had enrollments of between 2 and 3 languages. The predominant languages represented in these programs were Spanish and English.

Combined with the contemporary educational zeitgeist that embraces excellence and equity for all students, attention to the Hispanic children, families, and students has been significant. Following this theme are recent analyses and recommendations: the California State Department of Education efforts to better train infant and toddler caregivers in state-supported programs (California State Department of Education 1992), the U.S. Department of Education reforms for federally funded education programs (Garcia & Gonzales 1995), the National Academy of Education discussion of standards-based reform (McLaughlin & Shepard 1995), the National

Research Council's Roundtable on Head Start Research efforts to provide an issue analysis of research needed to produce a thriving future for Head Start for a highly diverse population of children and families (Phillips & Cabrera 1996), the National Council of Teachers of English and the International Reading Association's treatment of language arts standards (NCTE/ IRA 1996), and NAEYC's position statement on linguistic and cultural diversity (NAEYC 1996). All of these publications have attended to the vulnerabilities of Hispanics and have addressed issues of language and culture in light of this country's past treatment of this population and the present conceptual and empirical understanding of the need for institutions to be more responsive. Much of this thinking about policy and practice is based on the issues and research findings that follow.

Part of the current push for excellence and equity for all students has been increased attention to Hispanic children.

Our past approach: Americanization

Historically, Americanization has been a prime institutional education objective for Hispanic young children and their families (Elam 1972; Gonzales 1990; Garcia 1994). Schooling practices were adapted whenever the Hispanic student population rose to significant numbers in a community. This adaptation resulted in special programs applied to both children and adults in urban and rural schools and communities. The desired effect of Americanizing was to socialize and acculturate the targeted diverse community. In essence, if public efforts could teach these children and families English and American values, then social, economic, and educational failure could be averted. Ironically, social economists have argued that this effort was coupled with systematic efforts to maintain disparate conditions between Anglos and minority populations. Indeed, more than anything else, past attempts at addressing the Black, Hispanic, Indian, Asian, etc., "educational problem" have actually preserved the political and economic subordination of these communities (Spencer 1988). Coming from a sociological theory of assimilation, Americanization has traditionally been recognized as a solution to the problem of immigrants and ethnicity in the modern industrialized United States. Linda Chavez (1991) continues to champion this solution for Hispanics.

The Americanization solution has not worked. Moreover, it depends on the flawed notion of group culture. The Americanization solution presumes that culturally different children are, as a group, culturally flawed. To fix them individually, we must act on the individual as a member of a cultural group. By changing the values, language, and so forth of the group, we will have the solution to the educational underachievement of students representing these groups. The challenge facing educators regarding Hispanic students is not to Americanize them but to understand them and act responsively to the specific diversity they bring and the educational goal of academic success for all students.

Early childhood practices that meet the challenge

The debate regarding early childhood education of Hispanic students in the United States has centered on the role of cultural and developmental appropriateness of curriculum and pedagogy, along with Spanish language use and the development of English in these early childhood settings. Discussion of this issue has included cross-disciplinary dialogues involving psychology, linguistics, sociology, politics, and education. (For a more thorough discussion of these issues, see Cummins 1979, Troike 1981, Baker and deKanter 1983, Garcia 1983, Willig 1985, Rossell and Ross 1986, Hakuta and Gould 1987, August and Garcia 1988, Crawford 1989, Baker 1990, Kagan and Garcia 1991, Garcia 1994, Cole 1995, Garcia and Gonzalez 1995, and Rossell and Baker 1996.) The central theme of these discussions relates to the specific role of the native language.

Supporters of culturally sensitive and native language instruction are at one end in this debate. Proponents of this specially designed instructional strategy recommend the utilization of the child's native language and mastery of that language prior to the introduction of an English, more mainstream curriculum. This approach (Cardenas 1986; Fishman 1989) suggests that the competencies in the native culture and language, particularly about academic learning, provide important cognitive and social foundations for second-language learning and academic learning in general—you really only learn to read once. At the other end in this debate, introduction to the English curriculum is recommended at the onset of the student's schooling experience, with minimal use of the native language. This specially designed approach calls for English language "leveling" by instructional staff (to facilitate the understanding on behalf of the student with limited English proficiency) combined with an English-as-a-second-language component. In essence, the earlier the student confronts English and the more times he or she is confronted, the greater the English linguistic advantage (Rossell 1992; Rossell & Baker 1996).

The native language debate has ignored the contributions of Friere (1970), Bernstein (1971), Cummins (1979, 1986), Heath (1986), Ogbu (1986), Trueba (1987), Levin (1988), Tharp (1989), Rose (1989), Moll (1991), Garcia (1995), and Krashen (1996), who have suggested that the schooling vulnerability of such students must be understood within the broader contexts of this society's treatment of these students and their families in and out of educational institutions. That is, no quick fix is likely under social and early education conditions that mark the Hispanic-language minority student for special treatment of his or her language difference without consideration for the psychological and social-cultural circumstances in which that student resides. This is not to suggest that the linguistic character of this student is insignificant. Instead, it warns us against the isolation of this single attribute as the only variable of importance. This more comprehensive view of the education, particularly early childhood education, includes an understanding of the relationship between home and school, the sociocultural incongruities between the two, and the resulting effects on learning and achievement (Kagan & Garcia 1991; Garcia 1994).

Recent research findings have redefined the nature of the educational vulnerability of Hispanic children, destroyed common stereotypes and myths, and laid a foundation on which to reconceptualize present educational practices and launch new initiatives. This foundation recognizes the homogeneity and heterogeneity within and between diverse student populations. No one set of descriptions or prescriptions will suffice; however, a set of commonalties deserves particular attention.

Research focusing on early childhood classrooms, teachers, administrators, and parents revealed an interesting set of perspectives on the treatment of children (Hakuta & Gould 1987; Rose 1989; Garcia 1991; Moll 1991; Ramirez et al. 1991; Wong Fillmore 1991; Garcia 1994; Cole 1995). Classroom teachers were highly committed to the educational success of their students; perceived themselves as instructional innovators utilizing "new" learning theories and instructional philosophies to guide their practice; continued to be involved in professional development activities, including participation in small-group support networks; had a strong, demonstrated commitment to student-home communication (several teachers were utilizing a weekly parent interaction format); and felt they had the autonomy to create or change the instruction and curriculum in their classrooms even if it did not meet the district guidelines exactly. Significantly, these teachers "adopted" their students. They had high academic expectations for all their students ("Everyone will learn to read in my classroom") and also served as advocates for their students. They rejected any conclusion that their students were intellectually or academically disadvantaged.

Parents expressed a high level of satisfaction and appreciation regarding their children's educational experience in these classrooms. All indicated or implied that academic success was tied to their children's future economic success. Anglo and Hispanic parents were both quite involved in the formal parent-supported activities of the schools. However, Anglo parents' attitudes were much more in line with a child advocacy view—somewhat distrustful of the school's specific interest in doing what was right for their child. Conversely, Hispanic parents expressed a high level of trust for the teaching and administrative staff.

This recent research addresses some significant practice questions regarding effective academic environments for Hispanic children:

1. *What role did native language instruction play?*

Teachers considered native language use in daily instruction as key. They implemented an articulated native language and literacy effort that recognized language as a tool for learning and not as a learning objective.

2. *Who were the key players in this effective schooling drama?*

Administrators and parents played important roles. However, teachers were the key players. They achieved the educational confidence of their peers and supervisors. They worked to organize instruction, create new instructional environments, assess effectiveness, and advocate for their students. They were proud of their students, reassuring but consistently demanding. They rejected any notion of linguistic, cultural, or intellectual inferiority regarding their students. They were child advocates.

Be an advocate for our linguistically and culturally diverse children and families by nurturing, celebrating, and challenging them. They do not need our pity for what they do not have; they, like any individual and family, require our respect and the use of what they bring as a resource.

Imbedded in the activities of these educational enterprises for Hispanic students was the understanding that language, culture, and their accompanying values are acquired in the home and community environment; that children come to school with some knowledge about what language is, how it works, and what it is used for; that children learn higher-level metacognitive and metalinguistic skills as they engage in socially meaningful activities; and that children's development and learning are best understood in the interaction of linguistic, sociocultural, and cognitive knowledge and experiences. In particular for students who did not speak English, their native language was perceived as a resource instead of a problem. **In general terms, this research *suggests* moving away from a needs assessment and non-English-proficiency-as-a-problem approach to an asset inventory and native-language-as-a-resource approach.**

Conclusion

Effective early education curriculum, instructional strategies, and teaching staffs recognize that development and learning have their roots in sharing expertise and experiences through multiple avenues of communication. Further, effective early childhood education for linguistically and culturally diverse children encourages them to take risks, construct meaning, and seek reinterpretation of knowledge within the compatible social contexts. Within this nurturing environment, skills are tools for acquiring knowledge, not ends in themselves, and the language of the child is an incredible resource. The curriculum recognizes that any attempt to address the needs of these students in a deficit or subtractive mode is counterproductive. Instead, this knowledge base recognizes, conceptually, that educators must be additive in an approach to these students.

Recent statements about these challenges reinforce this charge. The National Council of Teachers of English and the International Reading Association (NCTE/IRA) in their enunciation of standards for English language arts recognize that

> Students develop an understanding of and respect for diversity in language use, patterns, and dialects across cultures, ethnic groups, geographic regions, and social roles.
>
> Students whose first language is not English make use of their first language to develop competency in the English language arts and to develop understanding of content across the curriculum.
>
> Celebrating our shared beliefs and traditions are not enough; we also need to honor that which is distinctive in the many groups that make up our nation. (1996, 3)

NAEYC echoes these same concerns in its position statement related to educational practices regarding linguistic and cultural diversity in early childhood:

> Early childhood educators can best help linguistically and culturally diverse children and their families by acknowledging and responding to the importance of the child's home language and culture. Administrative support for bilingualism as a goal is necessary within the educational setting. Educational practices should focus on educating children toward the "school culture" while preserving and respecting the diversity of the home language and culture that each child brings to the early learning setting. (1996, 12)

In the present era, this challenge must be met within the context of philosophical, ideological, and political debates surrounding our professional efforts to do things right and to do the right things for all children and families. Eugene, Gene, and Gino encourage you in these efforts, particularly for Hispanics, recognizing the significance of your role and regard for their roots and wings. Here are five practical applications that teachers can use to meet this challenge:

1. Know the linguistic and cultural diversity of your students. Like an ethnographer, be very observant and seek information regarding the languages and cultures represented by the children, families, and communities you serve. Learn to pronounce your student's name as the family pronounces it. For each student write down linguistic and cultural information so it becomes as important as the other things you write down.

2. Take on the new challenge of serving linguistic and culturally diverse children with resolve, commitment, and *ganas* (high motivation). Children and families will appreciate your willingness to learn their language—even small phrases of their language. They will also recognize paternalistic attitudes—attitudes that convey the notion that their children should negate their native language and culture.

3. Be up to date on the new knowledge base. We know so much more now about how better to deal with diversity. Most of us grew up or received our formal training in eras when diversity was not an issue. Incorporate personal and formal stories, games, songs, and poems from various cultures and languages into the curriculum.

4. Share the knowledge with the educational and noneducational community. There is so much strong feeling among educators and the general public that diversity is a problem and must be eliminated. Be clear about how you deal with diversity in ways that respect the need for common culture, shared culture, and individual integrity.

5. Above all else, care about and be an advocate for our linguistically and culturally diverse children and families by nurturing, celebrating, and challenging them. They do not need our pity or remorse for what they do not have; they, like any individual and family, require our respect and the use of what they bring as a resource.

References

August, D., & E. Garcia. 1988. *Language minority education in the United States: Research, policy and practice.* Chicago: Charles C. Thomas.

Baker, K.A. 1990. Bilingual education's 20-year failure to provide rights protection for language-minority students. In *Children at risk: Poverty, minority status and other issues in educational equity,* eds. A. Barona & E. Garcia, 29–52. Washington, DC: National Association of School Psychologists.

Baker, K.A., & A.A. deKanter. 1983. An answer from research on bilingual education. *American Education* 56: 157–69.

Bernstein, B. 1971. A sociolinguistic approach to socialization with some reference to educability. In *Class, codes and control: Theoretical studies towards a sociology of language,* ed. B. Bernstein, 146–71. London: Routledge & Kegan Paul.

California State Department of Education. 1992. *The program for infant/toddler caregivers: A guide to language development and communication.* Sacramento: Author.

Cardenas, J. 1986. The role of native-language instruction in bilingual education. *Phi Delta Kappan* 67: 359–63.

Chavez, L. 1991. *Out of the barrio: Toward a new politics of Hispanic assimilation.* New York: Basic.

Cole, R.W. 1995. *Educating everybody's children: What research and practice say about improving achievement.* Alexandria, VA: Association for Supervision and Curriculum Development.

Crawford, J. 1989. *Bilingual education: History, politics, theory, and practice.* Trenton, NJ: Crane.

Cummins, J. 1979. Linguistic independence and the educational development of bilingual children. *Review of Educational Research* 19: 222–51.

Cummins, J. 1986. Empowering minority students: A framework for intervention. *Harvard Educational Review* 56 (1): 18–35.

de Leon Siantz, M. 1996. Profile of the Hispanic child. In *Hispanic voices: Hispanic health educators speak out,* ed. S. Torres, 134–49. New York: NLN Press.

Elam, S. 1972. Acculturation and learning problems of Puerto Rican children. In *The Puerto Rican community and its children on the mainland,* eds. F. Corradasco & E. Bucchini, 116–38. Metuchen, NJ: Scarecrow.

Fishman, J. 1989. Bias and anti-intellectualism: The frenzied fiction of "English only." In *Language and ethnicity in minority sociolinguistic perspective,* ed. Multilingual Matters, 214–37. London: Multilingual Matters.

Friere, P. 1970. *Pedagogy of the oppressed.* New York: Seabury.

Garcia, E. 1983. *Bilingualism in early childhood.* Albuquerque: University of New Mexico Press.

Garcia, E. 1991. *Education of linguistically and culturally diverse students: Effective instructional practices. Education Report #1.* Washington, DC: Center of Applied Linguistics and the National Center for Research on Cultural Diversity and Second Language Learning.

Garcia, E. 1993. Language, culture and education. In *Review of research in education,* ed. L. Darling-Hammond, 51–97. Washington, DC: American Educational Research Association.

Garcia, E. 1994. *Understanding and meeting the challenge of student diversity.* Boston: Houghton Mifflin.

Garcia, E. 1995. Educating Mexican American students: Past treatments and recent developments in theory, research, policy, and practice. In *Handbook of research on multicultural education,* eds. J. Banks & C.A. McGee Banks, 372–426. New York: Macmillan.

Garcia, E., & R. Gonzalez. 1995. Issues in systemic reform for culturally and linguistically diverse students. *College Record* 96(3): 418-31.

Gonzalez, R. 1990. *Chicano education in the segregation era: 1915–1945.* Philadelphia: Balch Institute.

Hakuta, K., & L.J. Gould. 1987. Synthesis of research on bilingual education. *Educational Leadership* 44 (6): 39–45.

Heath, S.B. 1986. Sociocultural contexts of language development. In *Beyond language: Social and cultural factors in schooling language minority students,* ed. California Department of Education, 143–86. Los Angeles: Evaluation, Dissemination, and Assessment Center, California State University.

Kagan, S.L., & E. Garcia. 1991. Educating culturally and linguistically diverse preschoolers: moving the agenda. *Early Childhood Research Quarterly* 6: 427–43.

Krashen, S. 1996. *Under attack: The case against bilingual education.* Culver City, CA: Language Education Associates.

Levin, I. 1988. *Accelerated schools for at-risk students.* CPRE Research Report Series RR-010. New Brunswick, NJ: Rutgers University Center for Policy Research in Education.

McLaughlin, M.W., & L.A. Shepard. 1995. *Improving education through standard-based reform: A report by the national academy of education panel of standards-based education reform.* Stanford, CA: National Academy of Education.

Moll, L. 1991. *Funds of knowledge for change: Developing mediating connections between homes and classrooms.* Paper presented at the conference on "Literacy, Identity and Mind," University of Michigan, Ann Arbor.

NAEYC. 1996. NAEYC position statement: Responding to linguistic and cultural diversity—recommendations for effective early childhood education. *Young Children* 51 (2): 4-12.

National Center for Children in Poverty. 1995. *Welfare reform seen from a children's perspective.* New York: Columbia University School of Public Health.

NCTE/IRA (National Council of Teachers of English and International Reading Association). 1996. *Standards for the English language arts.* Urbana, IL: NCTE.

Ogbu, J. 1986. The consequences of the American caste system. In *The school achievement of minority children: New perspectives,* ed. U. Neisser, 73–114. Hillsdale, NJ: Erlbaum.

Phillips, D.A., & N.J. Cabrera. 1996. *Beyond the blueprint: Directions for research on Head Start's families.* Washington, DC: National Academy Press.

Ramirez, J.D., S.D. Yuen, D.R. Ramey, & D.J. Pasta. 1991. *Final Report: Longitudinal study of structured English immersion strategy, early-exit and late-exit transitional bilingual education programs for language-minority children.* San Mateo, CA: Aguirre International.

Rodriguez, R. 1982. *Hunger of memory.* New York: Bantam.

Rose, M. 1989. *Lives on the boundary.* New York: Free Press.

Rossell, C. 1992. Nothing matters? A critique of the Ramirez, et al. longitudinal study of instructional programs for language minority children. *Journal of the National Association for Bilingual Education* 16 (1–2): 159–86.

Rossell, C., & K. Baker. 1996. The education effectiveness of bilingual education. *Research in the Teaching of English* 30: 7–74.

Rossell, C., & J.M. Ross. 1986. *The social science evidence on bilingual education.* Boston: Boston University.

Spencer, D. 1988. Transitional bilingual education and the socialization of immigrants. *Harvard Educational Review* 58 (2): 133-53.

Tharp, R.G. 1989. *Challenging cultural minds.* London: Cambridge University Press.

Troike, R.C. 1981. Synthesis of research in bilingual education. *Educational Leadership* 38: 498-504.

Trueba, H.T. 1987. *Success or failure? Learning and the language minority student.* Scranton, PA: Harper & Row.

U.S. Department of Commerce. 1990. *The Hispanic population in the United States: March 1989.* Washington, DC: GPO.

Villaseñor, V. 1991. *Rain of gold.* New York: Delta.

Willig, A.C. 1985. A meta-analysis of selected studies on effectiveness of bilingual education. *Review of Educational Research* 55 (33): 269–317.

Wong Fillmore, L. 1991. When learning a second language means losing a first. *Early Childhood Research Quarterly* 6 (3): 323–46.

Unit 3

Unit Selections

Key Points to Consider

- What do you consider to be the essential elements of high-quality educational practice?
- Describe the play and relaxation time that children in grades 1 through 3 need.
- Comment on the idea that homework for primary grade children does not necessarily help them to learn.
- What does "inclusion" mean?
- Brainstorm three activities in a preschool classroom for children with limited motor abilities.

Links

www.dushkin.com/online/

15. **Canada's Schoolnet Staff Room**
    http://www.schoolnet.ca/home/e/
16. **Children's Defense Fund**
    http://www.childrensdefense.org
17. **Classroom Connect**
    http://www.classroom.net
18. **ERIC Clearinghouse on Disabilities and Gifted Education**
    http://www.cec.sped.org/gifted/gt-faqs.htm
19. **National Resource Center for Health and Safety in Child Care**
    http://nrc.uchsc.edu
20. **Online Innovation Institute**
    http://oii.org

These sites are annotated on pages 4 and 5.

Care and Educational Practices

Educational practices with young children seem to be always changing, yet always the same. The notion of what is good practice in early childhood education varies between two extremes. One approach is traditional, with an emphasis on skill and drill methods, segmented curriculum, and accuracy in work. The other approach, which includes curricular integration and an emphasis on play, is more constructive. These two approaches coexist in early childhood but are based in very different philosophies of how teaching and learning occur. So the dilemma is to determine which educational practice is most appropriate for children.

Our lead article describes high-quality, high-cost educational practice of child care centers in some well-to-do areas of the country. These centers believe that they are changing the way child care is perceived by providing luxurious educational features and paying higher salaries to teachers. This upscale approach to educational practice is a new phenomenon in the field of early childhood education.

An intriguing finding from research is that one educational practice may not be as effective as we have traditionally thought. That practice is dreaded homework. The effect of homework on young learners may be particularly damaging to future learning, especially if the work is "busywork" and doesn't reinforce new concepts. The result of bad homework is a decrease in motivation to learn and an increase in poor study habits. Sharon Begley gives us something to ponder in "Homework Doesn't Help," a brief article from a popular news magazine.

Two articles in this unit focus on the increasing pressure on schools to raise test scores of young children. In order to spend more time on academics in preparation for testing, children are being deprived of play and relaxation time. The results can be detrimental to development, as Kelly Alexander describes in "Playtime Is Cancelled." Parents are also caught in the bind of escalating academics. Since they are familiar with letter grades, they expect to see their children's learning reported in that format. " 'But What's Wrong with Letter Grades?' " Responding to Parents' Questions about Alternative Assessment" provides help for teachers when they have conferences with parents of primary grade children.

Good practice means teaching children, not curriculum. "From Philosophy to Practice in Inclusive Early Childhood Programs" is a description of a conceptual framework for combining developmentally appropriate practices with early childhood special education in order to teach all children well. The authors are careful to define inclusion as "all children attending the same program, all of the time." No child is pulled out for special programs; instead, each child is given the appropriate support for success in the setting. Effective inclusion practices begin with functional goals that are designed with families. The services provided for the child are multidisciplinary. The article ends with a helpful example of how to merge developmentally appropriate practice with special education practices.

The research article for this unit is "Inclusion of Young Children with Special Needs in Early Childhood Education: The Research Base." It was chosen for its comprehensive review of recent literature on inclusion at the early childhood level. The authors use an "ecological systems" approach for examining the perspectives of family, social policy, community, and culture. Each of these systems affects the way inclusion occurs in actual practice. For instance, some factors in the community may act as barriers to inclusion of young children in programs. It is important to discover whether policies and community practices help facilitate or hinder the development of children with special needs.

Good practice, appropriate for children's development and based on active play, has no shortcuts and cannot be trivialized. It takes careful thought and planning, using the latest knowledge of early childhood education, to make curriculum and practice choices. By working out specifics of routines and procedures, curriculum, and assessment suitable for young children, the early childhood professional strengthens skills in decision making. These are crucial tasks for a teacher interested in developmentally appropriate practice.

Child care is going upscale in some well-to-do areas of the country, and centers like Crème de la Crème—that pamper for a price—are designed to appeal to both parents and wee ones.

The Petite Elite

BY MICHELLE GALLEY

Denver

In a brown-brick building here, around the corner from a Circuit City and across the street from a Sam's Club warehouse store, sits what some say is a paradise for the sandbox set.

Just past sunrise, parents begin to pull up in Mercedes sport-utility vehicles and Toyota minivans. They walk their children past an off-duty police officer and step into a glass-enclosed foyer. Here, they use a touch-screen computer to enter the personal code assigned to their child. This registers the child for the day at Crème de la Crème and clicks open the front door. Inside, a receptionist sits ensconced in a burgundy leather swivel chair behind an ornate desk. Along one wall of the reception area, 20 color monitors display images captured by videocameras placed in nearly every room of the center.

A nearby gas fireplace is lit in the fall and winter "more for ambience than heat," says Cathy Clark, the executive director at this southern Denver child-care center. A love seat, chair, and ottoman form a cozy seating area in front of the fireplace. Framed photographs of children and the center's staff sit on an end table and on the mantle, which is held up by two white ceramic teddy bears.

Walking into a Crème de la Crème is more like walking into an upscale hotel than a day-care center. And that's OK with Bruce Karpas, the president and chief executive officer of Denver-based Crème de la Crème Inc. He doesn't even like the term "day care." "That's like calling college 'student care,' " he says.

In fact, tuition at the center rivals the cost of a private college. Full-time infant care is $1,190 a month, or $14,280 a year, falling just a few hundred dollars shy of the average yearly cost of a private, four-year college.

Photos by Benjamin Tice Smith

Zoe Zelesak spends some time on the Oriental rug in the infant room. The center accepts children as young as 6 weeks.

Toddler care is $100 less a month. Crème charges $890 a month for 3- to 5-year- olds. In the Denver area, the average yearly cost of center care for a 12-month-old is just under $5,100 a year, according to a December 1998 Children's Defense Fund report.

The Crème center here and others like it are part of a trend toward pricey day-care centers—so-called Ivy League preschools—that are opening in well-to-do suburban areas nationwide. Karpas says such centers are exactly what parents are looking for. He maintains that in addition to high-end amenities that appeal to busy parents, Crème is providing high-quality care. And, he says, parents are more than willing to pay the price.

•

Take Sylvia Palms, for example. The single African-American mother is a vice president at US West, a telecommunications company in nearby Englewood, Colo. She writes out hefty checks each month to Crème and says the cost is well worth it. "I was looking for a level of professionalism," she says of her search for care for her 22-month-old daughter, Royal. "I went and toured [the facility], and Royal was in and registered the next day."

Palms says she was taken with the center's attention to diversity, pointing out that dolls at Crème have varying skin tones and that she noticed an African-American woman on the cover of one of the books children use.

"It's the mind-set—meaning that these people are thinking out of the

Reprinted with permission from *Education Week*, Vol. 19, No. 3, September 22, 1999, pp. 24-29. © 1999 by Editorial Projects in Education. Reprinted by permission.

box," she says, adding that other centers she looked at "had not incorporated diversity of cultures, and that was disturbing."

The extras at Crème make up for the center's higher price, Palms says. "I have [to provide] no materials or supplies. That alone is a $200-a-month savings." In addition to supplying diapers, wipes, snacks, and meals, Crème washes the sheets and blankets the children use at nap time rather than sending them home to be cleaned.

And the center parks a cart filled with healthful foods near the door so that children can grab a snack for the ride home. "Every parent in America knows that when you pick up your child, your child is hungry," Palms says. "My quality time with my daughter has increased because of that traffic treat."

In the roughly three months since she moved Royal from a Montessori school to Crème, Palms says, her daughter has changed dramatically. "I thought I had a reclusive daughter," she says, but "she's socializing. She's laughing. She's very joyful. She's a different person."

At the Crème centers, children move to a new activity, ranging from French and math to computer use and dance, every 30 minutes throughout the day.

Palms is so taken with the program that she's willing to fork over money to send her future niece or nephew to Crème. "My sister moved to Chicago and is having a baby. I told her I would send her the money to send her child to the Crème there."

But the Crème centers are not without their critics. The centers' curriculum is based on the controversial idea that children should move from activity to activity every 30 minutes to encourage stimulation and prevent boredom. The children also regularly use computers and an interactive television studio, features that some education experts say are unnecessary and even harmful.

The centers themselves have a bit of a Disney feel with constant music

Alexa Hamilton tries out one of the center's computers.

in the hallways and Victorian-style facades on specialty classrooms.

Karpas says he's giving parents what they want and points out that his centers all have waiting lists. In recent years, he says, parents have become increasingly savvy about the earliest education of their children. They've all read about the numerous recent studies that point to the first five years of a child's life as the critical ones for intellectual development, he says.

Roger Neugebauer, the publisher of *Childcare Information Exchange*, a magazine focusing on the child-care industry, agrees that Karpas and Crème have a potential market in every metropolitan area. The current trend, Neugebauer says, is "for parents universally to be much more focused on the quality of care their child receives. Parents are aware that the education aspect is just as important as the caring."

Crème centers offer a lot to dazzle children as well as parents. Just beyond the reception area, a jungle-theme mural lines the path to the Coconut Theater, an area for children's performances. The walls are covered in faux bamboo, and oversized stuffed jungle animals hang from the rafters. Alongside the theater runs an indoor stream—stocked with koi goldfish—that trickles past silk greenery and fake trees.

Over the stream, through the woods, and under a skylight 32 feet above the floor sits a series of specialty classrooms that resemble a miniature Victorian town. A train runs through the eaves over the computer lab, and a wooden cat lazes on top of the sign for the foreign-language classroom—or, in Crème-speak, the *bibliothèque*—where children 3 and older get French lessons.

In keeping with the center's French theme, the phones are answered with a perky "Bonjour, Crème de la Crème," the after-school class is named "après school," and a storage closet is labeled "objets trouvés."

The Victorian villagescape includes the center's store, T. Bear & Co., which sells toys, games, and the uniforms that children wear while at the center. Staff members will also pick out and wrap gifts for parents. "Just tell them how much you want to spend, and it will be ready for you to pick up at the end of the day," Clark says. Across the hall is Victoria's Shortcuts, where children can get their hair cut for $15 during the day.

Next door is the math room, adjacent to the interactive-television studio. Inside, Steve Crankshaw is videotaping 4-year-old Carly, who is wearing a navy-blue cotton knit Crème de la Crème jumper. The children, from the toddlers on up, wear uniforms Monday through Thursday, with Friday being designated as a casual day of sorts. Most of the center's staff members also wear uniforms.

In the studio, Carly sits at a pint-sized replica of a news studio and talks about a stuffed fish she is holding. "He lives in the water," she says, looking into the camera. But the children watching, each of whom will have a turn in front of the camera, are quick to lose interest. One little girl asks if she can go play; she gives a big yawn when her request is denied. Two boys start wrestling, and Crankshaw gently reminds them to show their manners.

The words generosity, loyalty, patience, honesty, courage, and respect are painted on the wall bordering the ceiling in the adjoining classroom. When it's time to watch their tape, the children stare, rapt at their own images in the color monitors above the seating area. One little boy says to Carly, "I like your laugh." Carly thanks him, grinning broadly.

One of the most luxurious aspects of the center is a scaled-down water park fashioned after an old mine. Children slide down the gully washer or run under the sprinklers on treated material that resembles wood but won't cause splinters, and they can use the park every day, weather permitting, for 30 minutes.

In the dance studio, Scott Liebler's enthusiasm and an "Adventurerobics" cassette tape lead a class of six 3-year-olds down an imaginary ski slope. One straggler, wearing a red top and navy-blue sweatpants emblazoned with "I'm a Crème Kid" on the rear, stops to check her look in one of the mirrored walls behind the ballet barre, then runs back to the join the class. By then, the children have turned into a pack of foxes. When the tape prompts, they all land flat on their backs on a tumbling mat laid out on the hardwood floor, put their feet up in the air, and pretend to fly with their legs.

The exercises, though disguised in pretend play, work specific muscles and are not unlike those found in a typical adult workout. At the end of the 30-minute session, the sound of the class chanting, "I love myself and you, too," grows louder and louder until the youngsters are gleefully shouting.

Behind the 22,000-square-foot facility, enclosed in an 8-foot-high stockade fence, is a scaled-down soccer field, a basketball court, a biking track complete with a tricycle garage, a picnic pavilion, a little theater, and an enormous plastic pirate ship. There is also a separate outdoor playground for toddlers and even one for infants, where large padded blocks can be arranged as obstacles for adventurous crawlers to conquer.

Infants in the center, beginning as young as 6 weeks, are divided according to developmental level: those who cannot yet sit on their own; those who can sit but not crawl; those who can crawl or move about by holding onto furniture and other objects; and those who can walk on their own. At 23 months, infants move into the 2-year-old room.

Scott Liebler's movement class provides children with exercises disguised as play.

•

The first Crème de la Crème was built by husband and wife Don and Roberta Babb in Houston 18 years ago. Two years later, a group in Atlanta bought franchise rights and has since opened five centers in that area.

In 1996, Bob Russell, a Denver real estate developer, made a deal with the Babbs to take the concept nationwide.

While eye-grabbing extras like the water park may appeal to parents and children, the education experts say such elaborate amenities are not necessary.

While seeking investment money, he approached Karpas, a New York City-bred corporate lawyer and a founder and former president of Pay Per View Television. "I took one look at the concept and said, 'Bob, I don't want to invest in this, I want to run it,'" Karpas says.

"What I was enamored with was how different this was, and that I really could say . . . that we are making a difference, that we are changing the way child care is perceived, that we are changing children's lives," Karpas says.

Since he jumped on board in early 1997, Crème centers have popped up in Plano, Texas; Denver; Chicago; and most recently, Leewood, Kan., a suburb of Kansas City. Another is scheduled to open in the Dallas suburb of Colleyville early next year.

The company is in negotiations to raise the $25 million it would take to build five more centers next year. And Karpas is sure it will make a profit. "The competition isn't meeting the demand," he says. "I am a firm believer in something really simple called value. Customers pay for value."

Those customers primarily come in two forms, says Jillian Pitt, the director of marketing for Crème de la Crème Inc. One is the stay-at-home mother "looking for socialization and enrichment outside the home," and the other is the dual-income professional couple "looking for an option other than typical child care or preschool," she says. And if Crème can raise the bar for the quality of child care available to all parents, Pitt argues, then the whole field will benefit.

"It's nice to see that someone is out there challenging others about what we might do to meet the needs of the children," says Richard Clifford, a co-director of the National Center for Early Development and Learning at the University of North Carolina at Chapel Hill. And, he says, "it's not unreasonable to think that it is going to cost as much to provide high-quality infant and child care as it does to provide for higher education, but right now we're not spending anywhere near that amount of money." Clifford suggests that more government aid is needed to help with the costs of child care, similar to the resources available for higher education.

But he stresses the importance of how the money is spent. "The higher the proportion of money you spend on staff, the higher your quality is likely to be," Clifford says.

Crème starts its full-time teachers at between $10 and $12 an hour, depending on education and experience, Clark says.

While still above the norm of just under $7 an hour, Clifford maintains that the teacher compensation Crème offers is still far below what it should be. "Those salaries are still quite low, and if we compare it to teacher salaries in public schools," he says, "$20,000 [a year] is less than a beginning teacher makes for working less than 10 months a year for fewer hours a day."

And Clifford says he has concerns about the class-rotation program on which Crème's curriculum is founded. "You can't run children like an assembly line," he warns. "You want children to have a lot of control and opportunity to make choices themselves."

Jane M. Healy, an educational psychologist and consultant and the author of the books *Failure to Connect* and *Your Child's Growing Mind*, agrees. She says that sometimes 3-year-olds will pour the same sand in the same cup over and over. "There is something about that activity that the brain needs to learn that day," she says.

Healy believes that such activity could be teaching principles that underlie science, physics, and even calculus. "If you interrupt and drag her out of the sandbox and take her to French, you are closing off that brain's opportunity to learn. Maybe French lessons are not the most appropriate thing for that child at that time," she says.

Healy adds that some of the eye-catching features offered by Crème are unnecessary: "[Young children] don't need computers. They don't need a water park. They need blocks and sand and loving people who talk to them in a relaxed and unpressured setting, and it doesn't need to cost that much."

Among the factors essential to high-quality child care is the way the adults in a child's life relate to each other and to the child, says Mark Ginsberg, the executive director of the National Association for the Education of Young Children, based in Washington.

"The essence of the interaction between the adult teacher and caregiver and the child frames the nature of the quality," he says.

The NAEYC uses 10 criteria, among them staff qualifications, administration, and physical environment, in accrediting child-care centers.

But Ginsberg cautions that not all programs and centers are alike. "The fact that one program may look different from another doesn't necessarily mean that one is of poor quality or one is of better quality," he says.

•

Though some may criticize the cost of attending a Crème center, its curriculum, or even the centers' somewhat flashy appearance, Karpas stands firm behind the company.

"We are providing what should be provided, and we are charging what it costs to provide it, and not every parent can afford it," he says. "But you know what? Not every parent can afford Harvard."

Karpas says that eventually the company would like to offer scholarships for lower-income familes and even build a chain of scaled-down centers. "I don't need to put a tennis court and water park in every Crème, and I can still do better [than what is currently available]," he says. "There is a 'Crème Lite' out there which will be more affordable, and we will do it."

Karpas says his centers offer the best early education in part because his staff is better equipped to teach.

Generally, a day-care center is set up so that teachers are responsible for chores such as cleaning up after the children and setting up for lunch. "Who is interacting with the children? The teacher can't do that if they are expected to be doing housekeeping chores all day," Karpas says. "What do we do? We have a full-time housekeeping staff that does all those chores so the teachers can teach."

Crème employs a chef and an assistant to work in the kitchen preparing children's meals and snacks and delivering them to the classrooms. Around the corner from the kitchen is a lounge where teachers can spend their lunch breaks while aides watch over their classes.

Karpas adds that too many expectations are piled onto preschool teachers. "And we wonder why we have teacher turnover in this country. It's absurd."

For now, the 4-year-olds in Loma Anderson's class aren't really concerned with teacher turnover, high expectations, or tuition costs. They are more concerned with playing dress up and chasing each other around the room.

Kristin playfully pushes Christina, who then runs into a wall and falls over in perfectly exaggerated 4-year-old style. Kristin falls on top of her, and in a fit of giggles and a mess of sheer blue cotton and white lace, they roll over the oriental rug that adorns their classroom floor.

Simply Sensational Spaces: A Multi-"S" Approach to Toddler Environments

Linda H. Lowman and Linda H. Ruhmann

"Different strokes for different folks" takes on new meaning when planning room arrangements for toddlers in group care settings. With a basic understanding of the special developmental needs of toddlers, caregivers can provide physical environments that help these children feel relaxed and successful throughout the day.

Our visits to a variety of toddler rooms over the last few years reveal a trend to treat toddlers as smaller preschoolers. Toddlers often are the victims of the "push-down" movement so common in many other educational settings. Most child care programs provide toddlers with environments, equipment, and activities that are similar to those found in classrooms for three- to five-year-olds. Several authors (for example, Greenman 1988; Dodge, Dombro, & Koralik 1991) have reported on this trend.

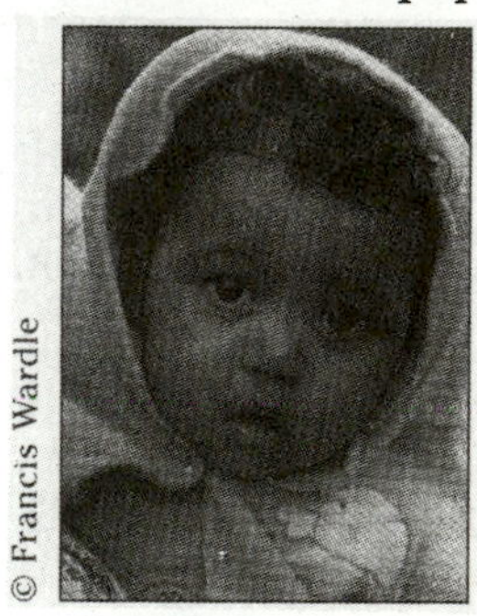
© Francis Wardle

Greenman notes,

> Toddlers are child care's equivalent of junior high school students. They often appear to be more mature than they are, and the frequent result in toddler programs is the tendency to treat them as proto-preschoolers—smaller and less competent. (1988, 52)

Developmentally Appropriate Practice in Early Childhood Programs Serving Children from Birth through Age 8 clearly states, however, that **"Good programs for children from birth to age 3 are distinctly different from all other types of programs—they are *not* a scaled down version of a good program for preschool children"** (Bredekamp 1987, 29).

One area in which this push-down is particularly apparent is the arrangement of the physical environment. Many toddler rooms we have visited are simpler versions of preschool classrooms complete with seven or eight traditional learning centers and the same kinds of toys and materials. This type of physical environment frequently proves frustrating to both children and adults because it does not meet the unique developmental needs of this particular age group.

Between the ages of one and three, children move from babyhood into the larger world of early childhood. During these two years important development is occurring that will greatly in-

Linda H. Lowman, M.Ed., is an associate professor in the Child Development Department at San Antonio College in Texas. She is a former toddler teacher and infant/toddler CDA instructor.

Linda H. Ruhmann, M.Ed., is a professor in the Child Development Department at San Antonio College in Texas. Linda serves as the infant-toddler coordinator for the college's Child Development Center and has advised many infant/toddler CDA students.

fluence later growth and learning. Toddlers are in a different stage of cognitive development than their preschool counterparts. Many are still in what Piaget calls the sensorimotor period, where their learning style involves processing information primarily through sensory and motor input. That's why toddlers must have environments that allow them to move around easily and explore materials thoroughly.

Toddlers are also working on two important psychosocial tasks, the mastery of which is essential if they are to move confidently into the preschool years: development of a sense of trust and development of a sense of autonomy (Erikson 1956). Therefore, one- and two-year-olds need both interpersonal and physical environments that provide a sense of security (building trust) and allow opportunities to make choices and experience mastery (encouraging autonomy).

Accommodating toddlers' physical needs in a flexible way helps them feel secure. Younger toddlers in particular need schedules and spaces that allow them to eat and nap as their own body rhythms dictate. As toddlers begin to push for autonomy, the environment should encourage appropriate choices and opportunities for mastering self-help skills. Low shelves with a modest number of clearly displayed materials and step-ups to sinks, cubbies, and windows encourage independence. In addition, most of the day should be spent in free-choice activities either inside or out rather than in teacher-directed activities.

Based on toddlers' developmental needs, there are special environmental requirements for toddler rooms. These may be addressed in terms of a multi-S environment. These Ss—simplicity, seclusion, softness, senses, stimulation, stability, safety, and sanitation—are outlined in the accompanying boxes. They serve as guidelines for developing physical environments for toddlers that foster their unique growth and help facilitate the transition between babyhood and early childhood.

The multi-S approach to toddler environments is designed to provide flexible guidelines within which teachers can work to meet the needs of their individual group of toddlers and the needs of individual children *within* the group. Careful observation and purposeful adjustments are essential to meet the changing needs of these unique learners. Our goal should always be to provide warm, stable relationships, especially one primary caregiver for each toddler, and simply sensational spaces in which toddlers can feel both comfortable and competent.

References

Berk, L. E., & A. Winsler. 1995. *Scaffolding children's learning: Vygotsky and early childhood education.* Washington, DC: NAEYC.

Bredekamp, S., ed. 1987. *Developmentally appropriate practice in early childhood programs serving children from birth through age 8.* Exp. ed. Washington, DC: NAEYC.

Cataldo, C. Z. 1983. *Infant and toddler programs: A guide to very early childhood education.* Reading, MA: Addison-Wesley.

Dempsey, J. D., & J. L. Frost. 1993. Play environments in early childhood education. In *Handbook of research on the education of young children,* ed. B. Spodek, 306–21. New York: Macmillan.

Dodge, D. 1992. Making classrooms work for children and adults. *Child Care Information Exchange* (January): 21–23.

Dodge, D. T., A. L. Dombro, & D. G. Koralek. 1991. *Caring for infants and toddlers.* Vol. 1. Washington, DC: Teaching Strategies.

Erikson, E. 1956. *Childhood and society.* New York: Norton.

Gonzalez-Mena, J., & D. Eyer. 1997. *Infants, toddlers, and caregivers.* Mountain View, CA: Mayfield.

Greenman, J. 1988. *Caring spaces, learning places: Children's environments that work.* Redmond, WA: Exchange Press.

Harris, A. C. 1986. *Child development.* New York: West.

Piaget, J. 1962. *Play, dreams and imitation in childhood.* New York: Norton.

For further reading

Balaban, N. 1992. The role of the child care professional in caring for infants, toddlers, and their families. *Young Children* 47 (5): 66–71.

Bredekamp, S., & C. Copple, eds. 1997. Part 3, Developmentally appropriate practice for infants and toddlers. In *Developmentally appropriate practice for early childhood programs,* rev. ed., 55–94. Washington, DC: NAEYC.

Bronson, M. B. 1995. *The right stuff for children birth to 8: Selecting play materials to support development.* Washington, DC: NAEYC.

Carnegie Task Force on Meeting the Needs of Young Children. 1994. *Starting points: Meeting the needs of our youngest children.* New York: Carnegie Corporation. (Available through NAEYC.)

Caruso, D. A. 1988. Research in review. Play and learning in infancy: Research and implications. *Young Children* 43 (6): 63–70.

Daniel, J. E. 1993. Infants to toddlers: Qualities of effective transitions. *Young Children* 48 (6): 16–21.

Da Ros, D., & A. Wong. 1994. Naptime: A transition with ease. *Young Children* 50 (1): 69.

Dittmann, L. L., ed. 1984. *The infants we care for.* Washington, DC: NAEYC.

Dittmann, L. L. 1986. Finding the best care for your infant or toddler. *Young Children* 41 (3): 43–46.

French, L. 1996. "I told you all about it, so don't tell me you don't know": Two-year-olds and learning through language. *Young Children* 51 (2): 17–20.

Gonzalez-Mena, J. 1992. Taking a culturally sensitive approach in infant-toddler programs. *Young Children* 47 (2): 4–9.

Greenberg, P. 1987. Ideas that work with young children. What is curriculum for infants in family day care (or elsewhere)? *Young Children* 42 (5): 58–62.

Greenberg, P. 1991. *Character development: Encouraging self-esteem and self-discipline in infants, toddlers, and 2-year-olds.* Washington, DC: NAEYC.

Greenman, J., & A. Stonehouse. 1996. *Prime times: A handbook for excellence in infant and toddler programs.* St. Paul: Redleaf.

Gullo, D. F., C. B. Burton-Maxwell, & S. J. Bruk. 1995. Milwaukee Early Schooling Initiative: Making it happen for young children. *Young Children* 50 (6): 12–17.

Hignett, W. F. 1988. Food for thought. Infant/toddler day care, yes; but we'd better make it good. *Young Children* 44 (1): 32–33.

Honig, A. S. 1985. High quality infant/toddler care: Issues and dilemmas. *Young Children* 41 (1): 40–46.

Honig, A. S. 1989. Quality infant/toddler caregiving: Are there magic recipes? *Young Children* 44 (4): 4–10.

Honig, A. S. 1993. Mental health for babies: What do theory and research tell us? *Young Children* 48 (3): 69–76.

Honig, A. S. 1995. Singing with infants and toddlers. *Young Children* 50 (5): 72–78.

Howes, C. 1989. Research in review. Infant child care. *Young Children* 44 (6): 24–28.

Hrneir, E. J. 1985. Infant play: A window to motivational competence. In *When children play: Proceedings from the International Conference on Play and Play Environments,* eds. F. L. Frost & S. Sunderlin, 339–42. Washington, DC: Association for Childhood Education International.

Hughes, F. P., J. Elicker, & L. C. Veen. 1995. A program of play for infants and their caregivers. *Young Children* 50 (2): 52–58.

Kendrick, A. S., R. Kaufmann, & K. P. Messenger. 1995. *Healthy young children: A manual for programs.* Washington, DC: NAEYC.

Koralek, D. G., L. S. Colker, & D. T. Dodge. 1995. Toddlers. In *The what, why, and how of high-quality early childhood education: A guide for on-site supervision, rev. ed.,* 41–65. Washington, DC: NAEYC.

Kupetz, B. N., & E. J. Green. 1997. Sharing books with infants and toddlers: Facing the challenges. *Young Children* 52 (2): 22–27.

Lowe, M. 1975. Trends in the development of representational play in infants from one to three years—An observational study. *Journal of Child Psychology, Child Psychiatry, & Allied Disciplines* 16: 33–47.

Meyerhoff, M. K. 1992. Viewpoint. Infant/toddler day care versus reality. *Young Children* 47 (6): 44–45.

Meyerhoff, M. K. 1994. Of baseball and babies: Are you unconsciously discouraging father involvement in infant care? *Young Children* 49 (4): 17–19.

Morris, S. L. 1995. Supporting the breast-feeding relationship during child care: Why is it important? *Young Children* 50 (2): 59–62.

Mueller, E., & J. Bergstrom. 1982. Fostering peer relations in normal and handicapped young children. In *The social life of children in a changing society*, ed. K. M. Borman. 191–215. Hillsdale, NJ: Erlbaum.

Raikes, H. 1996. A secure base for babies: Applying attachment concepts to the infant care setting. *Young Children* 51 (5): 59–67.

Reinsberg, J. 1995. Reflections on quality infant care. *Young Children* 50 (6): 23–25.

San Fernando Valley Child Care Consortium, A. Godwin & L. Schrag, cochairs. 1996. *Setting up for infant/toddler care: Guidelines for centers and family child care homes.* Rev. ed. Washington, DC: NAEYC.

Schreiber, M. E. 1996. Lighting alternatives: Considerations for child care centers. *Young Children* 51 (4): 11–13.

Shore, R. 1997. *Rethinking the brain: New insights into early development.* New York: Families and Work Institute.

Weissbourd, B., & J. S. Musick, eds. 1981. *Infants: Their social environments.* Washington, DC: NAEYC.

Zeavin, C. 1997. Toddlers at play: Environments at work. *Young Children* 52 (3): 72–77.

Simplicity

A **simplified** room arrangement provides toddlers a variety of appropriate experiences in a way that accommodates their unique movement patterns. We have found that four basic activity zones in a toddler room allow for ease of movement in and between areas and offer the kinds of materials that toddlers enjoy bringing together.

The four activity areas are a large-motor zone, a dramatic-play zone, a messy zone, and a quiet zone. These are normally placed in a modified peripheral arrangement and separated by low, sturdy dividers. A simplified arrangement also works well for mixed-age groups of which toddlers often are a part. In traditional preschool classrooms the zones are often subdivided into more elaborate learning centers.

1. A large-motor zone is essential in a toddler room. Considerable space allows children to work on rapidly developing gross-motor skills. Children at this age need many opportunities to challenge their growing ability to make their bodies work for them. If not provided with these challenges, they will find them by climbing on tables and shelves and pushing chairs around the room.

The large-motor zone can include various large-motor structures (climbers, slides, tunnels) as well as large lightweight blocks, push-and-pull toys, and riding toys. A CD or tape player and props encourage dancing and movement to music.

Courtesy of the authors

The large-motor zone should provide a variety of large-motor challenges.

This is different from the preschool classroom in which there is often a separate area for blocks, music, and perhaps gross-motor activities.

2. The dramatic-play zone is particularly conducive to pretend play. One sign of toddlers' increasing cognitive maturity is the advent of pretend play (Piaget 1962). At this age children are most interested in imitating familiar adults in familiar settings, so a variety of realistic home props, including large dolls, are the most satisfying.

Home-center equipment (stoves, sinks, refrigerators) should be open rather than closed to avoid pinched fingers and to accommodate the toddlers' still somewhat vague concept of object permanence (things out of sight still exist).

Dress-up clothes should be safe and simple enough for the child to use without assistance. Hats, purses, vests, and the slip-on shoes of older children are favorite items.

Objects that can be moved, such as strollers, shopping carts, and vacuum cleaners, also get frequent use, as do doll beds big and strong enough to hold toddler bodies.

Placing the dramatic-play area close to the large-motor zone allows for easy movement between these two popular spaces.

While preschoolers enjoy a variety of changing themes in the dramatic-play area, toddlers prefer the stability of the "home" setting.

3. The messy zone is that area of the room where children are encouraged to "mess around" with a variety of fluid materials (sand, water, paint, paste, etc.) and make discoveries about both the natural and physical sci-

Courtesy of the authors

Spaces to be alone in allow children retreats as well as spots from which to view others.

Courtesy of the authors

The quiet zone includes books, manipulatives, and discovery materials.

Courtesy of the authors

The messy zone is easy to clean so children can explore many art and sensory materials.

ences. The messy area should be close to a water source and have a washable floor covering. Tables for art experiences and eating can be in this area, as well as sensory tubs or tables, sturdy easels (at least two), and shelves for discovery items, art supplies (appropriate for the age), and perhaps an animal. Chairs can be put up during activity times since many toddlers prefer to stand when working with art and sensory materials and often see chairs as a large-motor challenge rather than a place to sit.

In a preschool room this area is often divided into three more complex centers—discovery, sensory, and art.

4. Every toddler room needs a haven where children can unwind, kick back, chill out, sink in, and just relax. The quiet zone provides such a spot. Here toddlers can enjoy cuddling with an adult, looking at books, working with manipulatives, or just doing nothing. As the softest and most inviting area of the classroom, the quiet zone includes books on a low shelf, stuffed animals and soft toys, manipulatives (which this age still prefers to play with on the floor), and additional discovery items. Terrariums and aquariums add interest. A comfortable chair or love seat that can accommodate an adult and one or two children should be included here.

Preschool children still need a quiet spot, which is often the library center. They prefer sitting at tables to use most manipulatives, so a separate table games center is often added.

Seclusion

Because toddlers frequently engage in onlooker and solitary play and can become easily overwhelmed in group settings, spaces that invite *seclusion* are very important in their environments (Cataldo 1983; Greenman 1988; Dodge 1992). An inviting alone space should be a part of each activity zone. Sturdy cardboard boxes or china barrels can serve this purpose.

Courtesy of the authors

The dramatic-play zone should be toddler size and contain realistic items for pretend play.

Softness

Many toddlers spend long hours away from home in a variety of child care settings. For such children it is essential that the environment be as homelike as possible. **Softness** in the environment helps a classroom seem more homey. Soft items, such as carpet fabric wall hangings, upholstered furniture, and stuffed toys, also help to absorb noise. Toddlers are attracted to soft spots for their sensory appeal as well as their comfort.

Remember, however, that the most inviting soft spots to toddlers are the arms and laps of favorite caregivers. Frequent touching gives toddlers confidence for further exploration. It is essential that each toddler receive appropriate cuddling throughout the day when *he* initiates or sends signals that he

(Continued on next page)

Courtesy of the authors

The environment should include a variety of things to see, hear, and touch without being overwhelmed.

needs it. Some caregivers only cuddle their favorites or impose cuddling on children. The best caregivers give *all* children good care and observe and respond to individuals.

The Senses

Because toddlers are sensorimotor learners, an environment rich in sensory appeal is important for encouraging optimal development. *Care must be taken, however, to avoid sensory overload.*

The toddler environment should appeal to all of the senses. There should be a variety of interesting things for children to look at, including the children's scribbles, pictures of real people and objects hung at the children's eye level, mirrors in standard and surprising places, and, if possible, opportunities to look outside. Bright-colored wind socks or streamers add visual interest as well. Because the figure-ground discrimination of this age is not yet well developed, it is important to surround both pictures and materials stored on shelves with space (Harris 1986). As we've said, keep it simple.

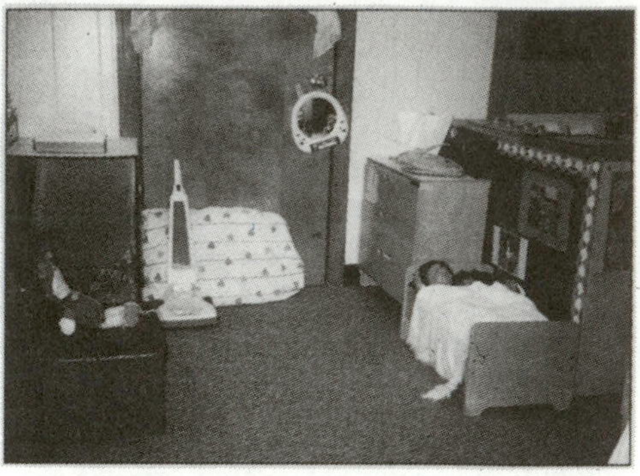

Courtesy of the authors

Softness helps create a more homelike atmosphere and encourages children to relax.

Toddlers enjoy listening to wind chimes, music boxes, an occasional

Stimulation

Environments for toddlers also need to be **stimulating,** providing a variety of appropriate challenges to meet growing skill levels. Skilled parents, family child care providers, and center-based caregivers observe individuals carefully and sense what would be a good "next step," a challenge, not a frustration (Berk & Winsler 1995).

Gonzalez-Mena and Eyer (1997) discuss the importance of the caregiver determining each child's level of optimum stress and providing activities accordingly. According to Cataldo (1983), materials that are open ended enough to be used by several age groups can provide realistic challenges for young children. Appropriate novelty and complexity of materials also maintain toddler interest (Dempsey & Frost 1993). Examples of such interesting, open-ended materials include a variety of common household objects, such as plastic butter tubs, jars, and makeup containers; dump-and-fill containers that can be carried; and different sizes and shapes of soft blocks. As toddlers near age three, introduce wooden blocks.

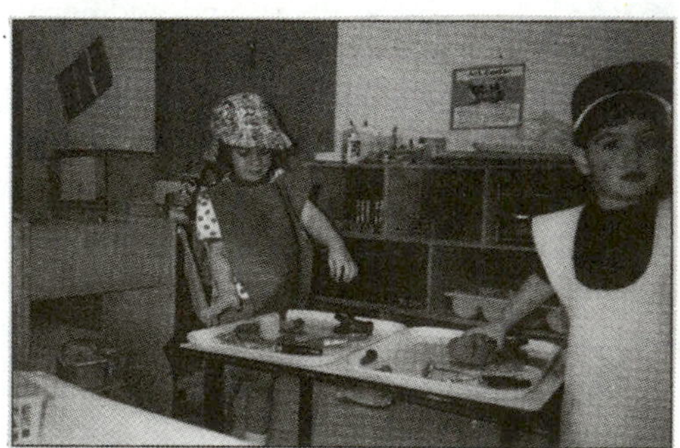

Courtesy of the authors

The environment needs to include materials that not only allow children to feel successful but also provide challenges.

Open-ended art materials appropriate for toddlers include larger crayons and chalk, paper for tearing, flour-and-water paste, and paint (initially colored water and then nontoxic varieties for older toddlers).

The quantity of materials should be carefully monitored. Too many choices of materials all at once overwhelm toddlers and lead to random exploration rather than more focused play. And we all know that many small loose toys frequently lead to social difficulties (possession problems) in toddler rooms, whereas larger pieces of gross-motor equipment (such as multifunction climber) lead to more positive social interactions because they allow children to be in close proximity yet not invading upon each other's space.

tape or radio music, toys with built-in sounds, and tape recordings of their own voices or voices of loved adults.

Provide pleasant smells with scented water and playdough, fresh flowers, herb collages, smelling bottles, and an electric potpourri pot (placed out of the children's reach).

A variety of textures also should be included throughout the room. Toddlers love to feel things and learn about the properties of objects through their fingertips. Bubble wrap and contact paper (sticky side up) taped to the floor fascinate children as they explore with fingers and feet.

Safety

Toddlers are avid explorers with little sense of danger and little impulse control, so **safety** must be a primary consideration in their environments. Close supervision is essential.

Furniture and outdoor equipment should be sturdy enough to be climbed on and scaled to toddler size to lessen the danger of falls. All objects in the classroom should be too big to be swallowed since many toddlers still mouth objects. The room must be carefully inspected daily for any potential hazards, and a choke tube should be standard equipment in every toddler room.

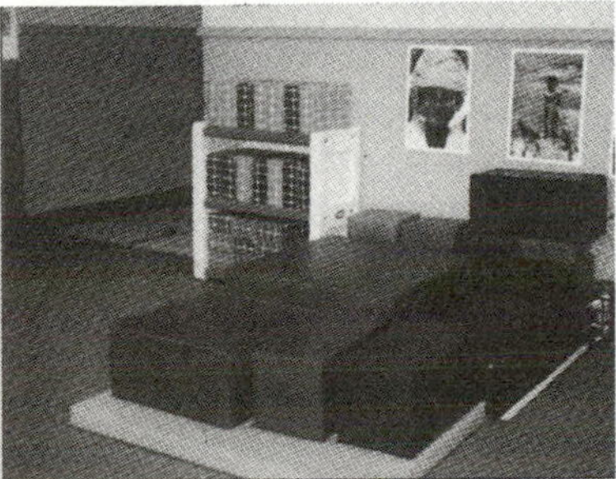

Courtesy of the authors

Easily accessible water, soap, and cleaning supplies help make keeping the room sanitary much easier.

Stability

Toddler environments need to remain relatively **stable.** The world is so confusing if you've only been in it a year or two. Toddlers feel more secure and more in control when they know on a daily basis what to expect and where to find things. Schedules and room arrangements should stay consistent. Toddlers have a strong need for repetition and ritual and for opportunities to thoroughly practice emerging skills before moving on. They need to know that favorite books, dolls, toys, and their special "loveys" (blankets, pacifiers) will remain in the environment as long as they are interested in them.

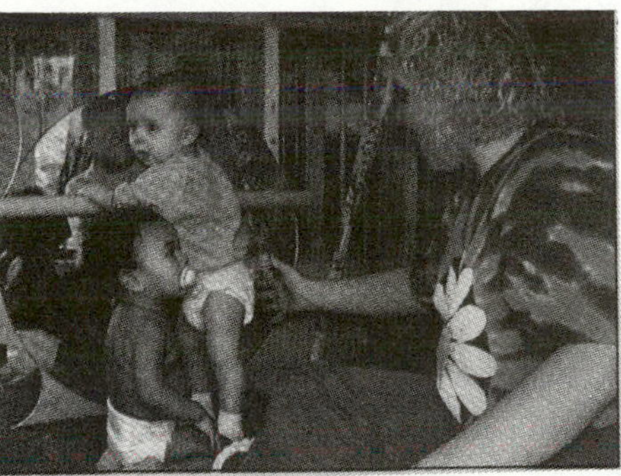

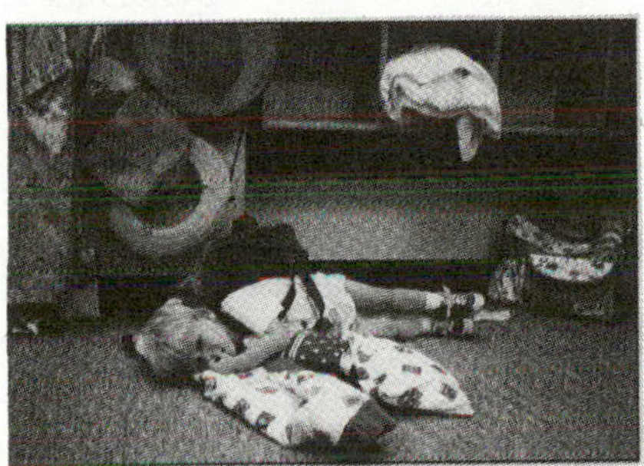

Courtesy of the authors

Equipment needs to be carefully selected and arranged so children can explore freely and safely.

Materials in toddler rooms should be rotated slowly and with careful attention to current interests and skills. Do not change all materials at once. Add new manipulatives, books, dramatic-play props, and large-motor challenges as children lose interest in what is available rather than change many things on a weekly basis to go along with a new unit of study (as is often done in preschool classrooms). As the children become more mature, the environment should change and grow more complex with them, but it still needs to remain stable enough to meet their security needs.

Sanitation

Last but by no means least—in fact, it should be a top priority in developing appropriate toddler environments—is good **sanitation**. Such essential toddler routines as diapering, toileting, feeding, and napping require careful attention to keep children healthy.

Courtesy of the authors

A stable environment helps children feel more secure at an age where transitions are often difficult.

Because toddlers still frequently prefer to play on the floor, floors must be well maintained. And since mouthing of toys does occur, all materials need to be washed daily in the dishwasher or by hand (first with detergent and water, then sprayed with a mix of one tablespoon of bleach to one quart of water). Convenient, adult-accessible storage of cleaning materials makes maintenance of sanitary environments much easier.

Working with Families

Don't Shut Fathers Out

Eugenia Hepworth Berger, Department Editor

INTRODUCTION

For those of you who were fortunate enough to have a nurturing father—model, encourager, guide, protector, care provider, breadwinner, teacher, story teller, play partner, and standard setter—you know how important a father can be. But did you know that as educators and child care providers you can make a difference in children's lives by encouraging fathers to get involved? If you provide a father friendly environment where fathers or father substitutes can participate, and if you model attitudes and activities that allow them to support their children, they will recognize their importance and the manner in which they can provide a human touch to children. Encourage participation and provide opportunities for men to become all that they can be to their children.

HISTORY

In past years, fathers in the United States have been viewed primarily as providers (breadwinners) even though there have always been other roles that fathers perform. At the turn of the twentieth century, fathers were viewed as the head of the family, the breadwinner, and standard setter. The philosophy for child care emphasized love and affection in the formation of character with the father participating as the standard setter and the mother providing the love. "The period of 1890 to 1910 stressed love and freedom, the period of 1910 to 1920 emphasized strict scheduling and discipline, and self-regulation appeared in the late 1920s and 1940s" (Berger, 1995, p. 60). "By the 1920s fathers were seeking information on everything . . . and in the ensuing years the new 'fatherhood' began to makes its cultural march as it became part of the experts' discourse on family life, personality development and psychological well-being" (Griswold, 1993, p. 6).

Children's Bureau. Interest in the welfare of families resulted in the establishment of the Children's Bureau in 1912 with the publication of *Infant Care* in 1914. The book's intention was to help mothers and fathers take care of their babies, but the focus was on the mother's role. In the 1942 issue of *Infant Care,* there was a shift in attitude and the father become a part of the parenting team. "Until this time, only women's identities were presumed to be tied to parenthood. Now it was possible for men's identities to be tied to parenthood too" (LaRossa, 1997, p. 55).

Responses in the 1940s. When young men were recruited for service in World War II, their examinations revealed that many young men had deficient mental health and physical development. Responses to these findings were illustrated by Dr. Benjamin Spock's book, *The Common Sense Book of Baby and Child Care* in which he urged parents to enjoy their children, thus influencing the rearing practices of many families, and Erik Erikson's book, *Childhood and Society.* Erikson looked at the child through bio-socio-psycho lenses, and recognized that the child's genetic being was also impacted by the child's world. A neo-Freudian, he described eight stages of growth, which continue to have relevance in human growth and development.

The 1950s. In the 1950s, the war was over, many women, who had worked or grown up during the war effort, married and began families; others welcomed their husband back from the war and returned to a two-parent

From *Early Childhood Education Journal,* Vol. 26, No. 1, Fall 1998, pp. 57-61. © 1998 by Plenum Publishing Corporation. Reprinted by permission.

family. The emphasis of parenting was on the mother with the father supporting her efforts and providing the breadwinner and standard-setting roles.

Diminishing Role of Fathers. Some who have studied fatherhood believe that fathers began to lose their dominant roles during the 1960s, continuing into the 1970s. It was suggested that children could be raised as well without fathers as with them. "The retreat from fatherhood began in the 1960s, gained momentum in the 1970s, and hit full stride in the 1980s. . . . It became relatively easy to argue fathers were not really necessary to the 'modern' family" (Horn, 1977, pp. 24–25).

During the second half of the twentieth century, changes in the father's role can be seen to be influenced by social changes and the varying beliefs in what was best for child development. One example of change was in the study of attachment. Initially, mother and infant attachment was studied and recognized as essential and the responsibility of the mother to care for the child. Later, it was recognized that attachment to fathers and significant others was valid as well.

Mothers in the Labor Force. The single greatest impact on change in family life came when women with young children joined the workforce. No longer is there a picture of a mother and children at home with the father going off to work each morning. In 1996, 78% of married women with children under the age of 18 were working; 38% of these women worked full time, year-round. Sixty-eight percent of women with children under the age of six worked with 31% working full time, year round. This compares with 44% working and 10% working full time, year round in 1970 (Bianchi & Spain, 1996, p. 21).

Single Parent Families. The second impact on families and fathers is the increase in single parent families. Unmarried women had nearly one in three births in 1995 compared to one in ten in 1970. The highest rate of births to unwed mothers was for the women in their early 20s (72 per 1000); second were women in their late 20s (59 per 1000). These were followed by teenagers with 46 per 1000 births (Bianchi & Spain, 1996, pp. 8, 9).

Single parents need support in providing their children with others that are significant to them including fathers, grandparents, relatives, and others who can help provide the love and caring children need. In order to paint a picture of the child's needs let us use Erikson's stages. The times suggested were not given by Erikson, are approximate, and each stage may carry back and over into another.

ERIKSON'S FIRST FIVE STAGES OF GROWTH

Trust vs. Mistrust (0–18 months)

During the first stage, the infant develops trust in his or her caregivers. Fathers, mothers, as well as other caregivers can begin the development of attachment with the infant. During the first 3 months, routine is important, infants are totally self-absorbed. But by the seventh or eighth month, the child identifies those that the child knows and shows separation anxiety toward others. "Consistency, continuity, and sameness of experience provide a rudimentary sense of ego identity" (Erikson, 1963, p. 147).

Traditionally, mothers have been recognized as the important person in attachment, with fathers supporting her, but fathers are also important attachment figures. "Researchers have gathered substantial evidence that infants form the attachment to both mothers and fathers at about the same period during the first year of life, although most infants develop a preference for the primary care providers" (Lamb, 1997, p. 15). Fathers can provide a loving, stable, predictable environment for the child. The child begins to recognize the world is a safe and stable place and they will be taken care of (LaCrosse, 1997). We know from recent studies that the brain is developing its connections and does this at a rapid rate during the first 3 years, so interaction with both parents increases the opportunity for the child to have the necessary brain development.

Autonomy vs. Shame and Doubt (18 months–3 years)

Toddlers are developing a sense of self. "If denied the gradual and well-guided experience of the autonomy of free choice, . . . the child turns against himself all his urge to discriminate and to manipulate. . . . From a sense of self control without loss of self-esteem comes a lasting sense of good will and pride" (Erikson, 1963, pp. 252, 254). Research shows that although fathers and mothers influence the children in similar rather than dissimilar ways, fathers are more apt to play with their young children with physically stimulating, unpredictable play and noncontaining interactions (Lamb, 1997, pp. 112, 113). Fathers can add to the children's development of selves during the period of autonomy as well as the next stage of initiative. "Young children need lots of verbal stimulation for developing the language centers of their brains, hence dads' style of parenting help children develop self regulation, while that of moms helps children acquire language skills" (Horn, 1997, p. 27).

Initiative vs. Guilt (3–5)

"Initiative adds to autonomy the quality of undertaking, planning and 'attacking' a task for the sake of being active and on the move" (Erikson, 1963, p. 255). Sex role identification, begun in the autonomy stage becomes stronger in the initiative vs. guilt stage. Father becomes important in role identity for both boys and girls.

The child's world widens and children begin to turn to other children through participation in preschool. Words become increasingly important for communication with other children. Mothers and teachers rely on words for guidance and self-control.

Industry vs. Inferiority (6–12)

The danger of this period of life, the elementary school days, is the feeling of inferiority. Children need to be supported and able to accomplish the challenges of education.

By the age of 12, the moral foundation is laid, and children are affected by the behavior of their parents. So the moral behavior of both parents is very important. Children develop their social skills and their beliefs in morality during this time. Most important to this development is the way the father and mother interact. Fathers teach their sons and daughters through modeling how women should be treated. If dads relate to their daughters in nonsexual ways, they make the daughters feel that they are important for who they are, not for their bodies. Girls with active and loving fathers do not need to use their bodies to relate to men (LaCrosse, 1997). Boys 6–12 are interested in many activities in which they and their fathers can participate together. During this period, it is important that both boys and girls have strong male models to help them in their development.

Identity vs. Role Confusion (12–18)

By this time, it is important that the moral rules of the family are internalized by the children so that they think about consequences before they act. It is again important for both father and mother to model the type of behavior that they want their children to have. Boundaries and expectations have been set and children now begin to set their own limits. Fathers can be extremely important if they will listen to and communicate with their children. Fathers continue to be important to both boys and girls. Fathers can help daughters know that love and sex are not synonymous (LaCrosse, 1997). If fathers continue to recognize their children's accomplishments, they will be able to handle the social issues of drugs and sex, and also able to function better as adults. Opportunities to work and play with their fathers allow fathers to have great influence on their sons's ability to handle the pressures of young adulthood.

WHY INVOLVE FATHERS?

Issues that make the need for encouraging fathers to be involved with their children include (1) the increase in single-parent families, (2) the need for children to have significant others who are men, and (3) the development of standards and morals.

Increase in Single Parent Families

In the two decades between 1970 and 1996, the number of children not living with their biological fathers almost tripled. In looking at family groups rather than total population, the numbers rose from 3 million, 480,000 single-parent mother family groups (11.5%) in 1970 to 9 million, 600,000 single-parent mothers (26.6%) in 1996. There were also more single-parent fathers in family groups going from 380,000 (1.3%) in 1970 to 1 million, 900,000 (5%) in 1996 (Bianchi & Spain, 1996, p. 14). The data makes it clear that resources to support both fathers and mothers in their roles as parents are necessary.

Outcomes Resulting from Fathers' Involvement

Research (Byrne, 1997, pp. 2, 3; Horn, 1997, p. 27; Levine, Murphy, & Wilson, 1997) indicates that children without fathers fail in school three times more often than those in two parent families. They are apt to have more emotional problems that need treatment. They have more behavioral problems and lower reading and mathematical ability. Suicide is three times higher for single-parent adolescents. The children are five times more likely to be in poverty. On the other hand, studies show that children of fathers who are involved in school activities complete more school and have greater incomes than those whose parents were not involved. And fathers who are positively involved with their children support their intellectual and emotional development (Byrne, 1997; Engle & Breaux, 1998; Lamb, 1997; Levine, Murphy, & Wilson, 1997).

Changes in Behavior

As boys get older, undesirable behavior increases. In a study by Harris and Associates (1995), conducted for the Boy Scouts of America, it was revealed that younger boys have higher moral standards than older boys. This study included boys in two-parent families as well as single-parent families, and they were asked "During the past year, I have . . ." Only 20% of the young group (7–10 years) cheated on tests or homework, while 76% of the 14–19 year old students had. In the 7–10-year-old group, only 7% had shoplifted; but in the older group, 33% had (p. 7). Eighty-three percent of young children thought spending time with their families was important, but only 41% of the older group thought so (p. 18). This suggests that caring and guidance needs to be established early in a child's life and that it needs to continue until adulthood.

INVOLVING FATHERS IN PROGRAMS

Fathers are an asset to a child's development, and communities can become an asset to a father's development. Here are a few strategies for an effective fatherhood program:

- Promote partnerships between fathers. Match up new dads with current participants and form peer support groups.
- Provide fathers with information on child development. Teach them techniques for raising sons and daughters of all ages.
- Make it easy for fathers to attend. Have flexible schedules, provide or pay for transportation, and offer child care.
- Offer life skills training. Teach classes on parenting, relationships, anger management, and leadership.
- Help identify the abilities and needs of fathers. Provide literacy, job training, and employment opportunities, information, and referrals.
- Have men in leadership roles of the program.
- Promote tolerance. Encourage cultural diversity and acknowledge the important roles of mothers.
- Teach standards and accountability for fatherhood. Let dads know there are rights, responsibilities, resources, and rewards ("4 Rs of Fatherhood") to being a good father.
- Listen and learn from fathers. Survey men for their ideas and interests, and let them know you value their opinions.
- Recognize all kinds of fathers. From teen dads, to men who serve as father-figures, to incarcerated fathers, remember that all dads need support (Governor Romer's Responsible Fatherhood Initiative, 1997, used with permission).

This list emphasizes the ways programs can get help from fathers and, at the same time, help them perfect their roles as fathers. They can also be helped in their development of skills needed for good employment opportunities, thus reducing unemployment and poverty and improving their self-esteem and ability to be the man they want to be.

MAKING INVOLVEMENT HAPPEN IN CENTERS AND SCHOOLS

When involving fathers, include any male who is serving as a friend or father substitute. "The stereotype that women alone should care for children—or that they alone are capable of caring for children—limits the opportunities and talents of both sexes" (Levine, Murphy, & Wilson 1997, p. 10). The term, father, includes father substitutes.

Father-Friendly Atmosphere

1. Create an atmosphere where men as well as women are expected to be involved.
2. Decorate bulletin boards so parents know they are welcome.
   a. Include displays of fathers, mothers and children.

b. Have children make posters that include men.
c. Include all ethnic groups with parents and children.
d. See if the children can bring photographs of their father or father substitute when he was young. Make a poster for the bulletin board.

3. Appoint a child to be a welcoming person (perhaps the V.I.P.—very important person of the day). Let them share a class notebook with the visitor. (Photographs will have to be taken. Include a father in one of the pictures).
4. Have nonthreatening activities with children that visitors can do when they first visit.
5. Make a special effort to help fathers with special needs children get involved with programs and other fathers (Davis & May, 1991).
6. Last, but not least, encourage all fathers to visit.

Communication

There are many opportunities to communicate and more can be planned.

1. During daily drop-off and pick-up, talk with fathers as well as mothers. If uncles, grandfathers, and others stand outside waiting for their children to come, find someone to watch the room and go out and talk with them. Always give them an opportunity to talk half of the time.
2. Encourage fathers to come early and participate with the children.
3. In newsletters include a picture and article about a father. As stated above, a father substitute, uncle, or friend will do. Send newsletters to both custodial and noncustodial parents unless the courts have found that the noncustodial parent should not be contacted. Parents who hear about their children continue to be involved.
4. Have parent teacher conferences at a time when both parents or single parents can attend. Have the noncustodial parent attend, too. You can have them at separate times if they prefer.
5. Make home visits. Try to visit when both parents can be present.
6. Advertise special days at convenient times for parents where fathers and mothers can share ideas and help prepare the center (complied from Berger, 1995, 1996; Levine, Murphy, & Wilson, 1993).

Activities

Special days can encourage parents to come. The following are just samples. Get the fathers together and let them think of more ideas.

1. Paint the pumpkin. Get pumpkins from a store or have fathers bring a pumpkin. Let the children classify the pumpkins according to size. Make graphs of the pumpkin sizes. Enlist the father to help with the action. Paint the pumpkin faces together.
2. Plan physical activities stations. The children rotate around the activity centers. Try centers such as a balance beam, jump rope, jump over the pretend stream, play catch, bean bags, and hop scotch. Let fathers supervise each center.
3. Go on field trips. Plan some exciting field trips that fathers would enjoy participating in. The zoo, farm, or history museum would be excellent choices (ideas compiled from Berger, 1995, Levine, 1997.)

Recruit

Getting Men Involved: Strategies for Early Childhood Programs. (Levine, Murphy, & Wilson, 1993): If you are having trouble recruiting, get a copy of this book; it is filled with suggestions. One that stands out is the use of bus drivers (pp. 74–75). Parents in Community Action from Indianapolis redefined the role of the bus driver and successfully used their 54 bus drivers to be part of the program and to also recruit other fathers. The drivers attend all educational staff meetings and also work 1 hour in the classroom. Some end up working longer periods of time in the centers. Drivers meet the parents because they pick up the children. They also need parent volunteer riders to ride with them in the bus. Through these contacts, they are able to recruit others to become involved in their Head Start centers.

CONCLUSIONS

If personnel in centers and schools recognize the importance of fathers in the lives of their children, they can respond by including men in their work. Each center and school will have to develop their own directions for involving fathers. They will examine where they are and how they can respond to fathers, where they want to be, and how they can get there. Action is next. Plans are only effective if they are put into action.

REFERENCES

Bianchi, S. M., & Spain, D. (December, 1996). Women, work and family in America. In *Population Bulletin, 51*(3). Washington, DC: Population Reference Bureau.

Berger, E. H. (1995). *Parents as partners in education: Families and schools working together.* Englewood Cliffs, NJ: Prentice Hall.

Berger, E. H. (1996). Don't leave them standing on the sidewalk. *Early Childhood Education, 24*(2), 131–133.

Byrne, G. (October 1997) Father may not know best, but what does he know? *Population Today, 25*(10), 1–3.

Davis, P. B., & May, J. F. (1991). Involving fathers in early intervention and family support programs: Issues and strategies. *Children's Health Center, 20*(2), 87–92.

Engle, P. L., & Breaux, C. (1998). Fathers' involvement with children: Perspectives from developing countries. In *Social policy report, 12*(1). Ann Arbor, MI: Society for Research in Child Development.

Erikson, E. H. (1963). *Childhood and Society* (2nd ed.). New York: W. W. Norton.

Governor Romer's Responsible Fatherhood Initiative (1997). *Colorado fathers' resource guide.* Denver, CO: Author.

Griswold, R. L. (1993). *Fatherhood in America.* New York: Basic Books.

Horn, W. F. (July, August 1997). You've come a long way, daddy. *Policy Review, 84,* 24–30.

Lamb, M. E. (Ed.) (1997). *The role of the father in child development* (3rd ed.). New York: Wiley.

LaCrosse, R. (October 1997) Stages of Development. Paper presented at Colorado Summit on Fatherhood, Denver, CO.

LaRossa, R. (1997). *The modernization of fatherhood: A social and political history.* Chicago: The University of Chicago Press.

Levine, J. A., Murphy, D. T., & Wilson, S. (1993). *Getting men involved: Strategies for early childhood programs.* New York: Scholastics.

A Case for Developmental Continuity in a Bilingual K–2 Setting

Yazmin E. Kuball

When I began my career as a kindergarten teacher, I had been a preschool teacher for five years. I was the morning kindergarten teacher for 30 Spanish-speaking children, and my room partner was the afternoon kindergarten teacher for a modified bilingual classroom. We shared a classroom in a teacher-controlled environment.

With my room partner's help and the administrators' support, we reorganized the classroom.

Kindergartners, first-graders, and second-graders work side by side at their own developmental levels. They help, encourage, and guide each other.

First, we created an appropriate kindergarten

We referred back to the developmentally appropriate environment (Bredekamp 1987) at the preschool, and we also did some research to create a more child-centered environment and curriculum.

Yazmin E. Kuball, M. A., has been teaching for 13 years. She has presented workshops in California and published several articles on attempting to implement developmentally appropriate practices. Photographs courtesy of the author.

We established learning centers

We created many activity centers for children to choose from: dramatic-play area, writing center, reading center, sand table, rug game center, art center, computer center, science center, garden center, hands-on math center, and woodworking center. Each center included a variety of materials and manipulatives as well as an opportunity for children to interact through independent cooperative groups.

Through interaction, children develop and use conversation in different forms (Tabors 1998). Children working in cooperative groups get a chance to exercise leadership, communication, and social skills (Grant, Johnson, & Richardson 1995).

According to Heath (1990), Mexican American children lack school-valued language experiences. I believe that giving such children a chance to work in cooperative groups offers them the language experience that they lack. Children learn to verbalize what they have learned by helping and teaching others, taking turns talking, listening to other points of view, and resolving conflicts.

We used an integrated literature-based curriculum

Our program was an integrated literature-based curriculum. We taught literacy skills in the context of a whole (Weaver 1900). Good children's literature, not textbooks, formed the foundation of instruction. The literature was integrated across the entire curriculum: math, science, social studies, and other grade-level skills were all drawn from the literature. Children learned through experiences, not fragmented drills, workbooks, or dittos.

Perez and Torres-Guzman (1992) acknowledge that there are discrep-

From *Young Children,* May 1999, pp. 74-79. © 1999 by the National Association for the Education of Young Children (NAEYC). Reprinted by permission.

ancies between the Hispanic culture and that of the traditional skill-based schools. They believe that these discrepancies can be minimized by offering Spanish-speaking children an integrated literature-based curriculum. Spanish-speaking children can thrive academically given an appropriate learning environment, effective teaching strategies, and integrated literature-based instruction (Kuball 1993).

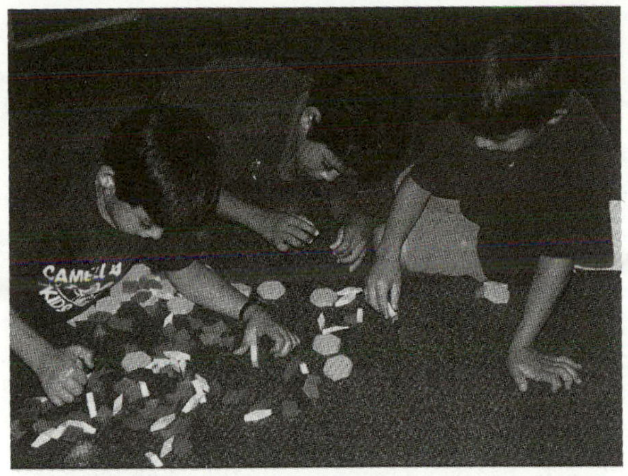

Three different grade levels use the same manipulatives but work on different learning tasks. Here, one child sorts, one tries to produce a pattern, and a third, who has already mastered patterning, shows how it's done.

The children took charge of their learning

Decorating the classroom. Throughout the year the children decorated the room using their creative work for each unit we studied. They helped us label the entire room in Spanish and English. They even made the calendar every month. Commercial bulletin board decorations were never used. Planning and making everything for the classroom taught the children to work cooperatively, manage time and space, plan, and take responsibility. This helped give them a sense of ownership: This was *their* room.

Working in activity centers. While the teachers taught skills to children in small groups, the other children chose activity centers to work in. They were free to rotate from center to center. Kagan (1990) points out that children of minority groups showed significant gains in academic achievement through cooperative learning.

Freedom to rotate among centers builds a sense of responsibility in the children for their own learning. Our children knew it was their responsibility to make a "purposeful choice" (Grant & Johnson 1995, 7). Choice empowered them by giving them control of their learning. Choice also reduced behavior problems because the children were engaged in tasks that were meaningful to them.

Freedom to rotate among centers also allows physical movement. Young children find it hard to sit down for an extended period of time. They also have different attention spans and complete assignments at different speeds. Free rotation among learning centers meets the needs of each child. The children choose whether to stand, sit, or lie down when working at a center. As Bredekamp and Copple (1997) state, physical activity is an integral part of children's cognitive growth.

Learning through talking. Kindergartners worked in cooperative groups as teachers facilitated. We selected children to work in small groups depending on the lesson and the children's needs; there were no set groupings (for example, by ability). The makeup of groups changed daily.

According to Young (1990), Hispanic children identify themselves as being part of a group. They feel comfortable in noncompetitive situations. Cooperative group projects offer them the comfort of learning in a noncompetitive group situation.

Children develop socially and emotionally through cooperative projects (Grant & Johnson 1995). Our children talked all day. Talking was valuable because they were teaching, coaching, helping, encouraging, and learning from each other. This was *meaningful conversation* (Grant & Johnson 1995). Our kindergarten room was seldom quiet. If it was, we knew something was wrong. Quiet meant that no learning was taking place.

Creative writing. By attending educational conferences and reading, my room partner and I became great believers in the developmental writing stages young children progress through (Calkins 1986). Therefore, a lot of child-initiated creative writing took place in our classroom. This ranged from scribbles through pre-phonetic stages, and toward the end of the year, it included the phonetic stages (Clay 1987).

In a year-long case study, Kuball (1993) demonstrated that the overall writing skills of Spanish-speaking children were not as advanced as those of the English-speaking children at the beginning of the school year. However, by offering the Spanish-speaking children a whole language learning environment, their writing skills developed as well as those of English-speaking children. Both groups' performances were very similar in the post-tests given at the end of the year.

Assessing children's progress

We developed different techniques—through observation, checklists, and work samples—to assess each child's progress (Weaver 1990). For this type of assessment to be beneficial, one needs to be aware of all the developmental stages through which children progress (Grant & Johnson 1995).

We lacked continuity between grade levels

By the end of each year, our kindergartens had flowered into children who took learning into their own hands. They planned together, helped each other, discovered ways to settle conflicts together. They became critical thinkers, decisionmakers, and problem solvers. They became "a family."

Why was it then that all I heard from first-grade teachers were complaints?

Many kindergarten teachers have heard such complaints before: Children coming from kindergarten can't sit still! Their letter formation is not neat and perfect! They can't recite the entire alphabet in order! They don't know how to use workbooks! They never stop talking! These are only a few of the complaints heard annually.

I realized that we lacked continuity between grade levels. There was no continuity in room environment, educational philosophy, teachers, or even acquisition of skills.

Children should not have to adjust to major changes; they should be able to start a new school year feeling comfortable enough to go straight into learning and experiencing (Barbour & Seefeldt 1993). So much time is lost each fall as teachers retrain children according to their new rules and different philosophies. Teachers need time to get to know the children's personalities, academic levels, strengths and weaknesses, and likes and dislikes, and the children need to get to know their teachers.

Children need time and opportunity to develop the skills involved in being self-directing, making plans, setting their own goals, and finding ways to achieve these goals (Barbour & Seefeldt 1993). Uprooting children every year does not allow them time to acquire these skills. The first few years of schooling are so critical. There is no time to waste.

Multiage, Ungraded, Multiyear, Looping: What Do These Words Mean?

The terms *multiage, ungraded, multiyear,* and *looping* are often used interchangeably, but in fact they represent different types of programs.

Multiage and ungraded programs are very similar. Two or three different grade levels are integrated to create one classroom. This facilitates teaching the wide developmental range that is usually found within one grade level (Grant 1991).

A traditional single-grade class is normally made up of children working below, at, or above grade level. Research has shown that most young children travel through the same stages of development; however, each child has his or her own rate of working through these stages (Ribowsky 1985). The multiage classroom offers children the chance to progress through developmental stages at their own rate without feeling frustrated or being left behind.

Children who are normally considered late bloomers have time to catch up to their peers without having to be referred to specialists or sent to a lower-grade classroom for certain subject areas. This also works for children working above grade level. They have the chance to move ahead and work at their more advanced developmental level. Children experience a "wider spectrum of learning as they work with other students ahead of them and behind them in the learning process" (Grant, Johnson, & Richardson 1995, 36).

Multiage is completely different from what most think of as splits or combinations (two different grades in one class). In a two-grade split or combination, the teacher focuses on two separate curriculums, one for each grade level. Each grade level is taught grade-specific skills. The children work within their grade level. Teachers find it difficult because of the double planning and double teaching. In a multiage classroom one integrated curriculum is planned.

Multiyear and looping are similar. In both programs the children stay with the same teacher for two or three years. Looping involves a team of teachers working together. For example, a kindergarten teacher and a first-grade teacher might work together. At the end of the year, the kindergarten teacher carries her own class with her to first grade and the first-grade teacher moves back into kindergarten. The process repeats itself at the end of each year.

We turned to the multiage setting

I first heard about multiage and multiyear classrooms at the NAEYC Annual Conference. They sounded like the answer to my problem. Children in multiage continuous-progress programs seem to achieve not only in academic and cognitive areas but also in social, emotional, attitudinal, and physical areas (Grant & Johnson 1995). I did a lot of reading research and realized that I could make a difference by following my class through another year.

A multiage continuous-progress program is a combination of multiage and multiyear programs. The teacher stays with her class of multiage children for more than one year. For example, in a K–1–2 group the kindergarten children would stay with the same teacher through second grade. (For further discussion of multiage and multiyear, see "Multiage, Ungraded, Multiyear, Looping: What Do These Words Mean?" (above) and "The Role of Learning Centers in Multiage Classrooms" next page.)

Grant, Johnson, and Richardson (1995) provide the following list of benefits that one can attribute to multiage continuous progress:

- fewer student/teacher transitions
- a cohesive family atmosphere
- a higher level of discipline
- improved student attendance
- an increased sense of stability for children as a result of continued classroom routines and consistency
- only six to nine new children for the teacher to get to know each year
- an increase in mental health benefits for the children

- a tendency for a decrease in special needs referrals
- fewer grade-level retentions
- postponement of teachers' high-stakes decisions about retention and special education retentions
- an increased cooperative spirit between children and teacher
- an increase in parental involvement
- more time-efficient instruction
- a semiseamless curriculum
- increased child observation time for the teacher

The Role of Learning Centers in Multiage Classrooms

Learning centers are extremely important in multiage settings. In them children engage in meaningful, hands-on activities. They allow the individualizing of education to meet all the different developmental levels within the class. Learning centers promote experiential learning and cooperative activities among children of all levels. The use of manipulatives and open-ended activities help in meeting the needs of children with different abilities.

Learning centers also allow small-group teaching, which is very important in the multiage setting (Grant, Johnson, & Richardson 1995). Small-group teaching assists teachers in providing individualized instruction and checking on the progress of each child. Everyone in a multiage program is considered a teacher/learner (Grant, Johnson, & Richardson 1995).

My experience creating a multiage classroom

So, after five years as a bilingual kindergarten teacher, I decided to carry my class with me into first grade.

Things did not go completely as planned. I was not given my entire kindergarten class to carry over; I was randomly given only half (15) of my kindergartners. The other half of my new class was second-graders. I was given a first/second-grade split. However, because most of the second-graders had been with me in kindergarten two years earlier, I decided to run the class as a multiage rather than a split grade.

Children, teachers, and parents adjusted easily

The beginning of the year was the easiest I had ever experienced. My first-graders came into the room and began working as if there had been no changes. They retrained the second-graders on the computers and the use of the room environment. The second-graders were able to exercise real leadership qualities. All were comfortable and happy.

I picked up where I had left off. I knew at exactly what level the children were. I knew their families. Their parents had had a whole year to get to know me and felt very comfortable talking with me. This gave me the parental support I needed from the home.

The parents knew my style of assignments and my expectations. I did not have to spend time familiarizing them with my philosophy. Knowing from the start what was expected of them made the parents feel comfortable and eager to help. The parent-teacher relationship evolved into a friendly, trusting, personal one. Parents felt comfortable about dropping in to help; they felt at home. I found that parental involvement increased dramatically in the second year.

The class became much like a family

It was a wonderful experience. We became a very family-like classroom community—something that does not happen in one year. I had never experienced this closeness in my 10 years of teaching. I became almost like an additional parent to most of the children.

The parents were pleased to see their children enjoying class and really wanting to come to school. I had the best attendance ever. Grant, Johnson, and Richardson (1995) state that research shows that children in a multiage setting seem to have a more positive attitude and are happier about school. This may be attributed to the success they experience in the classroom, the feeling of belonging to a caring community of learners, and the security of knowing what to expect from year to year.

The children treated each other with respect and cared for each other very much the way siblings might. Because they'd had the experience of working in cooperative groups two years in a row, they were able to relate very well to one another. I experienced very few discipline problems during the year.

The children thrived intellectually

The class also flourished intellectually. Vygotsky (1986) believed that giving children the chance to work together helps them generate thoughts and build individual consciousness by making it necessary to compromise, offer explanations, teach each other, learn from each other, and respect others' ideas.

My job was easier. I was able to build on children's previous experiences and go into great depth. All of my class, first- and second-graders, ended the year performing at grade level or above. All were reading at grade level three-quarters of the way through the school year.

I was so proud of the children and so were their parents. The children were proud of themselves. We did it together. All in all, I experienced every benefit that Grant, Johnson, and Richardson (1995) attribute to the multiage classroom.

Designing a continuity program

The continuity we experienced was wonderful and relaxing for all of us. I was so excited by the children's social and intellectual gains in these two years that I, with the help of a few coworkers, worked to design a K–2 developmental continuity program wherein a team of teachers would follow the students through for three years.

The best-laid plans . . .

Unfortunately, the program became a political issue among the rest of the staff. We ran into difficulty because in our district teachers pick grade levels by seniority. Senior teachers would not allow the team to hold their positions or children for the three years needed. Therefore, the team of teachers could not be secure in the knowledge that they would follow the children through for three years. They might be bumped out of the position by a teacher with more seniority.

Looping would not work either in this situation because there was no guaranteed space in the next grade level the following year. It was sad that we were not able to continue giving children the benefits and wonderful experiences of the developmental continuity program.

Children in kindergarten, first grade, and second grade enjoy reading together, often stopping to share with each other or to ask for assistance.

Grant and Johnson (1995) explain that to have a multiage program within a graded school, administrators and peers must be advocates for the program. Administrators who believe in the program are in a critical position to inform the staff and foster an understanding of multiage in a positive way in order not to divide the staff. An administrator needs to pave the way by creating a cooperative and supportive environment for the teachers. Grant and Johnson (1995) declare that without administrators' undivided support, the school atmosphere can be too stressful for multiage teachers.

They are right. Although we had our principals' support, she placed upon the shoulders of the multiage teachers the responsibility for informing and persuading the other staff members about the program. She never took an official stand, and the rest of the staff misconstrued the program as a form of favoritism. This created conflict and divisiveness among the staff. We were not able to get a majority vote approving the multiage program within the graded school.

Individual children add their own expertise to a cooperative project. Here, kindergartners, first-graders, and second-graders create a city together.

Working around the problems

We believed in the program, however, and found a way around this problem. We developed a semimultiage program.

Each of the three multiage team teachers chose a different grade level or split grade. Because most teachers do not like them, split grades are usually left for the less senior teachers to pick from. I chose a 1–2 split, the second teacher chose a K–1 split, and the third teacher got a 5–6 split. We mixed the five grade levels among us for writers' workshop and other activities. Therefore, at times in each of our classrooms, we had kindergartners, first-, second-, fifth-, and sixth-graders.

Satisfying results

The children loved working with their classroom family. Although this was not a true multiyear or multiage continuous-progress program, it did work. We saw many benefits and growth in all the children. I personally observed among the children the positive effects in Grant, Johnson, and Richardson's list of multiage benefits.

My experience with multiage/multiyear was very satisfying. I am convinced that such programs would be beneficial to all children including those who speak limited English. I only hope that more teachers and administrators are willing to learn about them and give them a try.

References

Barbour, N., & C. Seefeldt. 1993. *Developmental continuity across preschool and primary grades.* Wheaton, MD: Association for Childhood Education International.

Bredekamp, S., ed. 1987. *Developmentally appropriate practice in early childhood programs serving children from birth through age 8.* Exp. ed. Washington, DC: NAEYC.

Bredekamp, S., & C. Copple, eds. 1997. *Developmentally appropriate practice in early childhood programs.* Rev. ed. Washington, DC: NAEYC.

Calkins, L. 1986. *The art of teaching writing.* Portsmouth, NH: Heinemann.

Clay, M. 1987. *Writing begins at home.* Portsmouth, NH: Heinemann.

Grant, J. 1991. *Developmental education in the 1990s.* Rosemont, NJ: Modern Learning.

Grant, J., & B. Johnson, 1995. *A common sense guide to multiage practices.* Columbus, OH: Teachers' Publishing Group.

Grant, J., B. Johnson, & I. Richardson. 1995. *Multiage Q&A 101: Practical answers to your most pressing questions.* Peterborough, NH: Crystal Springs.

Heath, S. B. 1990. Sociocultural context of language development. In *Beyond language: Social and cultural factors in schooling language minority students,* 143–86. Los Angeles: Evaluation, Dissemination and Assessment Center.

Kagan, S. 1990. Cooperative learning and sociocultural factors in schooling. In *Beyond language: Social and cultural factors in schooling language minority students,* 231–98. Los Angeles: Evaluation, Dissemination and Assessment Center.

Kuball, Y. 1993. A comparison of the writing development between Spanish-speaking children and English-speaking children. California State University, Northridge. Typescript.

Perez, B., & M. E. Torres-Guzman. 1992. *Learning in two worlds: An integrated Spanish/English biliteracy approach.* White Plains, NY: Longman.

Ribowsky, H. 1985. *The effect of a code emphasis approach and a whole-language approach upon emergent literacy of kindergarten children.* ERIC, ED 269720.

Tabors, P. O. 1998. What early childhood educators need to know: Developing effective programs for linguistically and culturally diverse families. *Young Children* 53 (6): 20–26.

Vygotsky, L. 1986. *Thought and language.* Cambridge, MA: MIT Press.

Weaver, C. 1990. *Understanding whole language from principles to practice.* Portsmouth, NH: Heinemann.

Young, P. 1990. *Cultural foundations of education.* Columbus, OH: Merrill.

For further reading

Banks, J. C. 1995. *Creating the multiage classroom.* Edmonds, WA: CATS Publications.

Goodlad, J. I., & R. H. Anderson. 1987. *The nongraded elementary school.* New York; Teachers College Press.

Goodman, K. S. 1986. *What's whole in whole language?* Portsmouth, NH: Heinemann.

Harding, E. A. 1997. Kindergarten teachers—Move up to first grade! *Young Children* 52 (3): 80–81.

Kasten, W., & B. Clark. 1993. *The multiage classroom.* Katonah, NY: Richard Owen.

Katz, L., D. Evangelou, & J. A. Hartman. 1990. *The case for mixed-age grouping in early education.* Washington, DC: NAEYC.

Maeda, B. 1994. *The multi-age classroom.* Cypress, CA: Creative Teaching.

Miller, B. 1994. *Children at the center: Implementing the multiage classroom.* Portland, OR: Northwest Regional Educational Laboratory.

Homework Doesn't Help

Every night, millions of parents and kids shed blood, sweat and tears over the kitchen table. Now some researchers say these dreaded lessons are generally pointless until middle school.

BY SHARON BEGLEY

THERE ARE AS MANY THEORIES ABOUT why so many of America's children need remedial tutoring as there are failing students. But more and more education researchers are drawing lessons from kids like Adam, whose long, sad battle with homework began in the first grade. His school, outside Chicago, assigned just a little in the beginning—maybe 15 minutes a night, plus reading. Now, in fourth grade, his load has rocketed to three hours a night, and Adam, identified as a gifted student, "is completely frustrated," says his mother. "Last night he was up until 10:15 finishing a project, and he is crying more and more. He asks me, 'I work hard six hours a day in school—how much do I have to do?' He is having trouble focusing in school, and I suspect it's because he is exhausted."

There was blood, sweat and a puddle of tears on kitchen tables across America this morning, the detritus of a long afternoon, stretching into evening, of yesterday's homework. Sure, some students probably whipped out their perfectly organized assignment pad, did each task cheerfully and finished with time to spare for reading, television or play. We just don't know any. Something that infuriates parents, sabotages family time and crowds out so much else in a child's life might be tolerable if it also helped kids learn and if it imbued them with good study habits and a lifelong love of learning. Unfortunately, "for elementary-school students the effect of homework on achievement is trivial, if it exists at all," concludes psychologist Harris Cooper of the University of Missouri, whose analysis of more than 100 studies has stood up for 10 years.

The drive to discover why homework is not more useful in the early years, and to explain how to make it so, has generated more scientific interest in the subject "than ever before," says Cooper. Next month, at the annual meeting of the American Educational Research Association in San Diego, a symposium will examine the value of homework and ask what constitutes good assignments. For the new study he will present there, Cooper collected data on 709 students in grades two through four and six through 12. In lower grades, "there was a significant *negative* relationship between the amount of homework assigned and student attitudes," Cooper says, reflecting the not-surprising fact that kids resent the stuff. But in grades six and up, the more homework students completed, the higher their achievement. It is not clear, however, what is cause and what is effect: are already good students finishing more assignments because they are motivated and good at academics, or is completing assignments causing students to do better? "You can't identify anything as causal," says Cooper. "But we do think that how much homework helps is a function of grade level. There is a tipping point where homework has negative consequences."

That suggests that the trend among schools to pile on more homework, starting in kindergarten, could backfire. In the lower grades, since homework does not improve student performance, it should fulfill different goals: fostering a love of learning, honing study skills. Instead, there is ample anecdotal evidence that it breeds poor attitudes, as Cooper finds, and resentment. Too many teachers are still assigning useless, even counterproductive, homework—work that duplicates without reinforcing material covered in class. Homework that frustrates or angers a child or otherwise makes learning unpleasant "is a quick route to academic dread," says Lyn Corno of Columbia University's Teachers College, convincing a child early on that school stinks and he's a rotten student. "Homework becomes a grind to get through, rather than a learning experience," Corno says. The prevalence of bad homework might explain the lack of a connection between homework and student achievement in elementary school.

What is good homework? Especially for younger children, short assignments quickly completed should be the goal; long assignments uncompleted or completed with tears and tantrums are deadly. Also, homework should be different from classwork. It "is most beneficial when it moves out of the drone mode and into the creative mode," says Gary Griffin of Teachers College. "Homework should be an opportunity to engage in creative, exploratory activity—doing an oral history of your family or determining the ecological effects of a neighborhood business." Rather than memorizing names, dates and battles of the Civil War, students might write fictional letters from a Northerner to a Southerner, expressing their feelings about the issues dividing the nation. The assignment should also be crucial to the next day's classwork to emphasize to students that homework matters and isn't just a plot to make them miserable. It should be focused: for example, don't ask the students to write about an open-ended theme from a novel the class is reading, ask them to pick one character and explain why he or she behaved in a particular way.

Even good assignments can be overdone, however. "If homework gets piled on, and if it's boring, kids will go through satiation and frustration, and parents will express negative attitudes that kids will pick up," warns Lyn Corno. David, a third grader in Oak Park, Ill, regularly spends from 7 to 9 p.m. on homework, "but sometimes we're up until 10:30 trying to finish," says his mother, a lawyer. "David is a very bright and inquisitive kid who has come to dislike school because of the homework."

More than 100 studies find that it is not until middle school that homework begins to pay off. Julian Betts of the University of California, San Diego, for instance, followed 3,000 seventh and 10th graders. "The amount of math homework assigned had a huge effect on math test scores," he finds. A seventh grader given 15 minutes of math homework every school night through 11th grade would wind up one full grade ahead in achievement compared with one who did no math homework for those years.

How can homework have little to no effect on learning in the elementary grades, but a noticeable effect beginning in sixth grade? It is easier in higher grades to assign imaginative, focused, substantive homework that requires students to integrate and apply knowledge—the kind of homework that promotes learning. "The theory," says Corno, "is that assignments given in high school relate more directly to the school curriculum and become more challenging. Also by high school, students usually have resigned themselves to the routine. Working hard after school, and having good study skills, is less of an issue." But teaching the high schooler to work independently and to value academics requires that a good foundation of attitudes and aptitude be laid in the early years. Because homework is too often turning kids off to school, says Corno, "homework is more a part of the problem than a part of the solution." If young students fail to acquire the basic foundation of learning, thanks to dumb homework or staggering amounts of it, tutors can look forward to more paying customers.

Make or Break

By Debra Viadero

Springfield, Mass.

'Transition years'—when students move to a new school or new kinds of learning—are too often the points where children stumble.

First grade is a big year for KeAusha Scott-Cummins, a tallish 7-year-old with plastic beads on her pigtails and eyes the color of Hershey's Kisses. This year in Room 12 at Arthur T. Talmadge Elementary School, she will learn how to tell time by the hour, to identify vowels and their sounds, and to master sums up to 12. Even so, KeAusha would rather be in kindergarten. Like many children her age, Keausha had a hard time moving up from kindergarten. The transition is one of several crucial bridges she must cross before earning her high school diploma years from now.

In 3rd grade, she'll have to move from "learning to read" to "reading to learn," and she'll tackle more-complex mathematics concepts.

In 5th grade, KeAusha will have to gear up for the big move the following year to middle school, a daunting place that may be three times as large as her small, 350-student elementary school.

And after 8th grade, there is high school.

Research has identified these as some of the most pivotal points in a child's educational career, places where grades and test scores falter and a few more children fall—or get pushed—between the cracks.

"Children's long-term success can be made more certain or placed in jeopardy by how they negotiate school transitions," Johns Hopkins University researchers Karl Alexander and Doris Entwistle say in their book *Children, Schools, and Inequality.*

Though researchers and educators know where these rough passages lie on the long educational journey, they still don't know enough about how to make all of them easier. And while transitions are hard for all children, they may be especially hard for those from less affluent families such as KeAusha's.

To think about transition as a set of onetime activities that take place at the end of one school year to prepare children for the next is to put too narrow a lens on the issue, experts say.

Children are constantly undergoing transitions. Babies and toddlers move from home care to day-care settings and preschools. Immigrant children move from speaking their native languages to speaking English. Inner-city

Reprinted with permission from *Education Week,* Vol. 18, No. 34, May 5, 1999, pp. 24-29. © 1999 by Editorial Projects in Education. Reprinted by permission.

> "Going from kindergarten to 1st grade is like going from high school to college. There's a shock the first couple of weeks of school."
>
> **John M. "Jack" Fitzgerald,** Principal, Talmadge Elementary School

children may make a daily journey from chaotic neighborhoods to the more orderly world of schools and classrooms.

And getting children ready for kindergarten is a process that should begin early in their young lives—not just a few days before the start of school.

"We now understand that [such preparation has] got to be much deeper and more systematic," says Sharon Lynn Kagan, a senior research scientist at Yale University's Bush Center for Child Development. "There's got to be pedagogical continuity, continuity in how people approach discipline. It's more than 'let's plan a visit.' "

KeAusha entered day care at age 1, years before she stepped off the bus for her first day at Talmadge Elementary, a tidy, one-story school just a few minutes from her apartment complex.

In 1997, a few days before KeAusha started kindergarten, her mother, Denise Scott, attended an orientation session for parents of incoming kindergartners. Scott, a single mother, learned everything from the school's discipline policies to what to pack in KeAusha's book bag.

And KeAusha herself visited the classroom beforehand so that her teachers could screen her individually, as they did for every child entering school that year. Brief as it was, KeAusha's introduction to schooling was more than many schools offer.

A study released last year suggests that few teachers do anything to help children and their families adjust to school before that critical first day—mostly because they don't get their class lists early enough. (Talmadge teachers know by June who will be in their classes the following year.) And far fewer teachers forge any kind of relationship with the preschool programs that feed their classrooms.

For KeAusha, the introduction must have helped. Scott remembers how eager her daughter was to board the bus her first day. "She was excited because it was going to be a new school," the 38-year-old mother says. Within a few weeks, though, KeAusha ran into some problems. Teachers called Scott in once or twice when her daughter's tantrums disrupted the class. The outbursts subsided as the year went on.

Like most kindergartners, KeAusha got comparatively little orientation to 1st grade—a transition that may well be the biggest she will make in her entire school career. "Going from kindergarten to 1st grade is like going from high school to college," says John M. "Jack" Fitzgerald, Talmadge's principal. "There's a shock the first couple of weeks of school to many of the students' systems. We're still feeling our way with the transition from K to 1."

KeAusha had to get used to a full day of school. (The 25,500-student Springfield school system is shifting from half-day to full-day kindergarten programs now.) She was placed in a reading group and began to take spelling tests for the first time. There were more rules to follow, no naps, and less freedom to wander about. Hardest of all, she had to learn to sit quietly at rectangular tables of four.

"In kindergarten, you get to play more," says KeAusha, who is dressed this day in a magenta-pink sweatsuit speckled with milk and crumbs from her lunch. "You get to go outside longer. I had friends that I like."

Then, intrigued by her memories of kindergarten, she takes a pencil between fingers dotted with chipped nail polish and painstakingly writes down her reasons for preferring it.

At some point there's sort of a collision in the way we approach kids educationally," says Robert Pianta, a University of Virginia education professor who is studying the transitions children make in the early years. "They move from a less directive to a more directive environment, from where there are fewer expectations in terms of discrete academic skills to more," he explains. "Sometimes that happens in kindergarten, but more times it happens in 1st grade."

Earlier this year, KeAusha's tantrums reappeared, and Scott found herself summoned to the school once again. But the calls stopped coming after two months. KeAusha doesn't talk about school much at home, preferring instead to play on the patio with her dolls or to watch television.

"I think she's doing very well now," says Scott, noting that her daughter earned a B in reading.

"Doing well" is critical right now for KeAusha, experts say, because a child's performance in 1st grade sets the stage for the years to come.

The time is so critical, in fact, that Entwistle and Alexander compare the kindergarten and 1st grade years to the "imprinting" period that occurs in the first 24 hours of a duckling's life. During those critical hours, the tiny birds form a lifetime attachment to the nearest large animal they can find, regardless of whether it's a mother duck.

Yet, for too many children, 1st grade means a first encounter with failure. Studies show that more pupils are

Transition programs in the early grades try to address "the incredible variability that kids come to school with," says University of Virginia professor Robert Pianta.

Ingredients for Successful Transitions

Good preparation of children, families, and schools for elementary school.

+

Comprehensive support for children, families, and schools in early elementary school.

+

Positive expectations for the future

↓

Successful transitions throughout schooling

- Children have good feelings about schools, teachers, parents, and peers.
- Children show good progress in physical, social, emotional, and intellectual development
- Parents and key adults express positive attitudes toward school and promote children's learning.
- Teachers and school personnel provide programs adapted to children's individual development and cultural/linguistic diversity.
- Mutually supportive relationships occur among families, school personnel, service providers, communities

Positive school adjustment and successful transitions to adolescence and adulthood

SOURCE: Craig Ramey, University of Alabama at Birmingham

retained in 1st grade than in any other year of schooling. Talmadge Elementary, in that regard, is no different from other schools. Of the 29 children in KeAusha's class, three or four will have to repeat the year, says teacher Colleen Whitman.

The numbers may yet rise as Talmadge and other schools in Massachusetts work to meet rigorous, new state standards for academic achievement—a change that is already infusing more academics into kindergarten and 1st grade.

"It's very important to stop and make sure that children are learning basic-level reading skills because that becomes more important as they move up the grades," Principal Fitzgerald says.

The decision to hold pupils back a year is not one that Fitzgerald or Whitman takes lightly. Talmadge educators have an extensive before- and after-school reading-intervention system in place in 1st grade that is designed to head off potential retentions.

And they, too, have seen the studies suggesting that being held back increases a child's chance of dropping out later on. But if a student is going to have to repeat a year of schooling, they reason, better to do it sooner rather than later.

To avoid having children start out in school on an unhappy note, educators have experimented for years with different configurations in the early grades. There are "developmental" kindergartens for students not ready for regular kindergarten, "transitional" 1st grades for children not up to the rigors of more formal classrooms, and multiage classes that allow children to progress at their own rates without being labeled failures. Yet so far, studies show, most of those attempts have either mixed or poor track records.

"What these are attempts by schools to address the incredible variability that kids come to school with," says Pianta. "But, in a sense, what they're also trying to do is create a more continuous system for the whole population."

Talmadge Elementary, for example, sits in a community of modest, single-family homes and commercial strips close to Springfield's border with its eastern suburbs. But the school draws a high proportion of children from the apartment complexes and housing projects closer to downtown, which has shared in the economic downturns that have afflicted many of New England's manufacturing centers.

With 65 percent of the school's children coming from families poor enough to qualify them for free or reduced-price lunches, mobility is high. As many as a quarter of Talmadge students move in and out during the course of the year, bringing with them a wide range of abilities and experiences.

While some students such as KeAusha Scott-Cummins come to kindergarten with years of preschool, others have spent their first five years at home. A few can identify colors and read a word or two; others cannot yet utter a complete sentence.

When KeAusha gets to 3rd grade and 4th grade, she will encounter a less visible transition—the "3rd grade slump."

The term comes in part from studies of Head Start, Follow Through, and other federally funded preschool programs for disadvantaged children. Those studies show that the academic gains that students make in such programs early on tend to fade by 3rd grade.

But experts disagree over whether the phenomenon is real, with some researchers pointing to other intervention studies showing that children—even those born poor and with low birthweights—can indeed make steady progress throughout the middle childhood years.

What is undoubtedly true, however, is that academic tasks become different for children at those grade levels. Learning mathematics, for example, becomes more complex as students move from addition to multiplication and tackle other, more abstract concepts.

And, rather than primarily learning to read, as they did in earlier years, children spend more time reading to learn other things. They may use textbooks for the first time to read about social studies and science.

"Some kids do well in the beginning with decoding, but they don't seem to get much meaning out of words," says Joanna P. Williams, a professor of psychology and education at Teachers College, Columbia University. "It's not too much of a problem early on, but at the 4th grade level, people expect that kids will begin to get something out of the material."

Vocabulary grows in importance, giving an edge to children who have amassed a bigger storehouse of words.

"Much is known about getting children started in reading," a national panel of prominent researchers recently concluded. "But less is known about what competencies and programs help children to succeed beyond 3rd grade."

Playtime Is CANCELLED

BY KELLY KING ALEXANDER

In the push to improve test scores and pack more subjects into the curriculum, schools across the country are sacrificing one of the most important elements of learning—the need to take a recess every now and then.

At first, Julie Moorhead, of Algiers, Louisiana, was unfazed when her four children came home from elementary school complaining that they weren't having recess. "Give it a couple of days," she reassured her kids. "Things may be disorganized because it's the first week."

But Moorhead soon received a bulletin from the principal of Alice M. Harte Elementary School explaining that recess had, in fact, been cut to comply with a state mandate increasing the amount of time students must spend on academics. "No time for recess?" asked Moorhead, a former teacher. "How could this happen?"

Parents across the country have been similarly shocked by the elimination of what many fondly remember as the best part of the school day. In the scramble to improve standardized test scores, as many as 40 percent of the country's school districts are considering doing away with recess or modifying it in some way, according to an informal poll conducted by the American Association for the Child's Right to Play.

In the 1990s, American students' poor showings on standardized tests have spawned a back-to-basics movement that regards recess as frivolous.

And the no-recess movement may be more than just a passing educational fad. In Atlanta, which scrapped recess in all of its 69 elementary schools more than a decade ago, at least two elementary schools have been constructed without playgrounds, and a third is on the drawing board. This makes it unlikely, if not impossible, for these schools to one day reverse their policies. "It's sad," says Rhonda Clements, Ed.D., author of *The Case for Elementary School Recess* (American Press, 1999). "An entire generation may never experience games like jump rope, hopscotch, or freeze tag."

Until recently, recess was almost the fourth "R" in American education. In colonial times, educators had a "religious duty" to give students breaks from their studies, and healthy play in fresh air was considered an essential counterbalance to the confinement of one-room schoolhouses. Recess periods were much longer—a typical lunch break might last 90 minutes—as children played in nearby woods or meadows.

By the turn of the 20th century, most American schools held 15- to 20-minute morning and afternoon recesses in addition to hour-long lunch breaks. Until the 1950s, three daily recesses were still the norm; then, as fine arts, physical education, and other specialty areas were added to the curriculum, the afternoon break began to disappear. Since the 1970s, the lunch hour has been cut in half, and the

From *Parents,* November 1999, pp. 114-118.

length of the periods devoted to traditional academics has increased.

All work and no play

In the 1990s, American students' poor showings on standardized tests have spawned a back-to-basics movement that regards recess as frivolous. Although concerns such as school-yard safety, liability for injuries, and teachers' unwillingness to supervise are sometimes cited, the overwhelming reason for the decline of recess is the intense pressure on schools to improve test scores.

"We're here to educate children," says Mike Jordan, principal of Magellan Charter School, a middle school with no formal recess, in Raleigh, North Carolina. "To take thirty minutes out of our instructional day just to let kids play doesn't sound good—to parents, to legislators, or to taxpayers."

Child-development experts, who are unanimous in their belief that play is an essential part of a child's day, don't have much say in the matter. Nor do kids themselves. Certainly no one asked Julie Moorhead's son, David, 7, an active first-grader who began returning home from first grade every afternoon with a headache, or Nicholas Maxwell, 10, a straight-A fourth-grader at Asliwortli Elementary, in Arlington, Texas, who often complains of being exhausted after a seven-hour recessless school day followed by two hours of homework.

But such a rigid emphasis on work, not play, along with the force-feeding of academics, could backfire, experts say, creating kids who despise school and misbehave more often. After all, if adults need coffee breaks and lunch hours, don't kids as well? "It really isn't normal for children to sit quietly in chairs all day," says Jane McGrath, M.D., school health officer for the state of New Mexico.

There is also growing evidence that the dramatic increase over the past two decades of children with attention disorders may be related to the decline in physical activity. "We have an epidemic of attention-deficit disorder in this country," says educational psychologist Jane M. Healy, Ph.D., author of *Failure to Connect* (Simon and Schuster, 1999). "This is partly because children lack the physical and emotional outlets found in active play"

Keli Strain, of Arlington, doesn't believe that lack of recess caused her 10-year-old son Benjamin's ADD, but she's convinced that his sitting for seven hours a day without a play break has made it worse. In fact, Benjamin's ADD was not diagnosed until he was in the fourth grade, when his class suspended recess in order to buckle down for state standardized tests.

Even children who do not have attention disorders will struggle to stay focused when they go for long periods without a break, says Olga Jarrett, Ph.D., an assistant professor of early-childhood education at Georgia State University, in Atlanta. Dr. Jarrett and her colleagues found that kids who have regular recesses were less fidgety and spent more time "on task"—teacher-speak for being engaged in schoolwork—than kids who did not. "There's this misguided idea that you can just pump information into kids all day," says Dr. Jarrett. "Learning doesn't happen that way."

Even the highly rigorous Japanese system offers more outdoor recess time than the average American elementary school.

Let's get physical

In many ways, however, child burnout is the least of it. In an era when childhood obesity is at an all-time high, and many kids are enrolled in before- and after-school day-care programs (which are usually indoors and highly structured), or return home from school only to spend several latchkey hours in front of the TV or computer, Dr. McGrath believes that outdoor free play at school is more essential than ever.

Indeed, last year, the National Association for Sport and Physical Education (NASPE) released its first-ever guidelines for elementary-school children, recommending that young kids be physically active for at least one hour a day. No-recess proponents often argue that kids move around in the classroom during group work or as they change classes. But a brief episode of controlled movement, such as "walking quietly to the library, finger on your lips, does not constitute physical activity," says Judy Young, NASPE's executive director.

Similarly, some school administrators maintain that their students don't need recess because they run around in physical-education class. But even Young, whose Virginia-based group represents over 25,000 PE teachers, coaches, and sports professionals, rejects that argument. PE is to recess, she says, what phonics drills are to reading comic books at home: The former teaches a structured curriculum, while the latter gives kids a chance to practice what they've learned in ways of their own choosing.

The views of children themselves highlight another critical difference between recess and PE. In another study by Dr. Jarrett and Darlene Maxwell, of Mercer University, in Atlanta, fourth-graders said they needed a time in the day when they had choices about what to play and whom to play

AMERICAN KIDS too busy to play?

If children aren't getting the unstructured playtime they need at school, there's little reason to believe they're making up for it at home. According to a 1998 University of Michigan study, kids today have far less free time than they did in 1981, and there are big differences in the way they spend the little they have.

In 1981, for example, they spent 16 hours a week playing; by 1997, playtime had dropped to 12 hours a week. Meanwhile, time spent on structured activities—school, homework, organized sports—increased dramatically.

Sociologist Sandra Hofferth, senior research scientist at the University of Michigan's Institute for Social Research, attributes the changes to a cultural shift toward dual-career couples. When one parent is at home, Hofferth says, children tend to have more after-school play. But since other neighborhood kids are rarely available at this time, even at-home parents have moved away from spontaneous outdoor play in favor of scheduled playdates and structured activities.

with. Or as Elisabeth Bayer, a freckle-faced 8-year-old, puts it, "In PE, you have to do certain things. At recess, you do whatever you want."

New research suggests that 10- to 15-minute bursts of varied activity throughout the day aren't just good for the body, they actually stimulate brain development, especially in children. Other studies suggest that aerobic exercise pumps oxygen into the brain, thereby improving alertness and memory. "We are about to see an upsurge in research about the connection between motor development and brain development that will make recess critics look even more foolish," says Dr. Healy, who also notes that in countries where students academically outperform those in the United States, recess has not been sacrificed. Even the highly rigorous Japanese system offers more outdoor recess time than the average American elementary school.

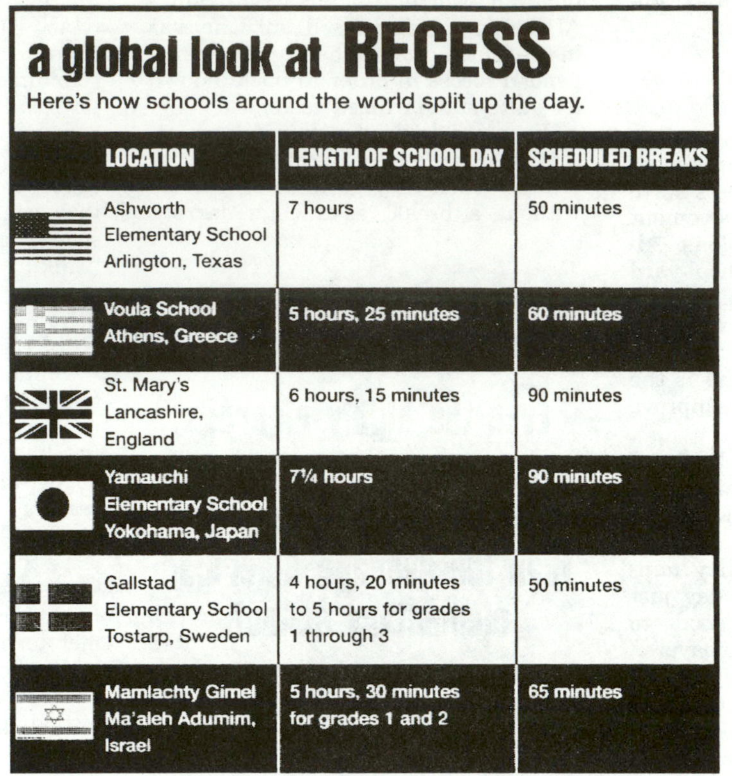

a global look at RECESS

Here's how schools around the world split up the day.

LOCATION	LENGTH OF SCHOOL DAY	SCHEDULED BREAKS
Ashworth Elementary School Arlington, Texas	7 hours	50 minutes
Voula School Athens, Greece	5 hours, 25 minutes	60 minutes
St. Mary's Lancashire, England	6 hours, 15 minutes	90 minutes
Yamauchi Elementary School Yokohama, Japan	7¼ hours	90 minutes
Gallstad Elementary School Tostarp, Sweden	4 hours, 20 minutes to 5 hours for grades 1 through 3	50 minutes
Mamlachty Gimel Ma'aleh Adumim, Israel	5 hours, 30 minutes for grades 1 and 2	65 minutes

Playing to learn

Anyone harboring doubts that play spurs learning need only listen in on a group of kindergartners engrossed in sculpting a hamlet out of pea gravel during morning recess at St. George School, in Baton Rouge. "We're reptiles, and this is our reptile village," says Bradley, 6, who will not formally study cold-blooded vertebrates for at least another two years. "This is our bridge, this is our lake, and these are our houses. We're snakes and alligators and Tasmanian devils."

"Sometimes we build a volcano and turn it into a castle," adds Paige, 5, "or pretend we're unicorns."

As important as the flights of imagination gleaned from this quarter hour of play is the socialization taking place. During the freedom of recess, children figure out how to get along. Bradley and the other kids settle a dispute over who will be the reptilian king. Paige and two other girls agree on a game without interference from their teacher, who observes from a distance.

"Recess is sort of like the sandlot of life before kids go to the major leagues," says June Lange Prewitt, state developer for the Parkway School District, in Missouri. "It allows them to develop emotional and social skills. To learn to say, 'Can I play?' is an important skill. And so is being able to handle the answer when it's no."

The National Education Association and the National Association of Elementary School Principals have adopted resolutions encouraging members to preserve recess at their schools.

Ironically, kids' difficulty in getting along has been the reason for some principals' decisions to revoke recess. As many of us remember, recess is often the time when bullies hold sway. Annette Maiden, principal of Ames Elementary School, in Marrero, Louisiana, declined to talk to *Parents* but told *The Times-Picayune,* a New Orleans newspaper, that the number of fights and disciplinary infractions at her school has dropped by 80 to 90 percent since recess was cut. Many of Philadelphia's 176 public elementary schools have implemented "socialized recess" periods—a kind of cross between free play and PE class—to reduce bullying and other playground violence.

Yet most experts believe that such statistics only point to a greater, rather than lesser, need for recess. Children who have little free play lose not only a positive outlet for excess energy but also, gradually, the ability to entertain themselves. "In my neighborhood, kids don't know how to go out and organize a game,' says NASPE's Young. "A fight breaks out in five minutes. We referee every minute of our children's lives, and then we wonder why they're bored and out of control when they reach adolescence."

Of course, few educators disagree with the myriad benefits of recess. But, they ask defensively, how can they fulfill all their responsibilities to the children in a six- or seven-hour day? Although the length of the American school day has changed very little in 30 years, much has been squeezed into the curriculum, including mandated courses in everything from self-esteem and sex education to character building and conflict resolution.

"Because so much has been heaped on the curriculum, teachers struggle to fit everything in," says Judy Underman, principal of Ashworth Elementary, in Arlington. "We're constantly forced to choose what's more or less important." Linderman has left the recess decision up to the discretion of individual teachers, but recent complaints from parents whose kids miss recess have prompted her to reexamine the policy.

There has been no research to determine whether kids without recess perform better academically, but past studies have shown a link between higher scores and more time spent on schoolwork. One solution might be to lengthen the school day or year to allow time for play and rest as well as for the teaching of core courses and enrichment programs. Proponents cite the success of some European schools with extended days and add that the change would relieve many working parents of the burden of securing child care during latchkey hours, as well as cut down on crime by unsupervised minors. Opponents include teachers' groups, which worry that longer hours will mean additional responsibilities without commensurate pay.

In the meantime, a counterrevolution is afoot. The National Education Association and the National Association of Elementary School Principals have adopted resolutions encouraging members to preserve recess at their schools. Private and parochial schools, which have traditionally put a high premium on recess, have strengthened that commitment by extending free-play periods, according to Rhonda Clements.

And some districts and individual schools have actually retracted their no-recess policies. Last year; the superintendent of elementary schools in the Evanston and Skokie, Illinois, district reinstated recess within months of its elimination because of parental outrage. Recess has also returned to Alice M. Harte Elementary—thanks to Julie Moorhead and other parents who believe so strongly in its value that they have volunteered to supervise kids during lunch and for one 15-minute recess per day. Student conduct has since improved in the cafeteria and on the playground, says principal Stacy Rockwood, because kids don't want to waste valuable free time misbehaving.

Moorhead fondly recalls the day students first got their freedom back. "One little boy was standing in line as we were preparing to leave the cafeteria," she says. " 'I know what we have to do now,' he said in a monotone. 'Walk in a straight line back to class.' I looked at him and said 'No, we don't. It's recess now. Go play.'

"I wish I'd had a video camera, Moorhead says, laughing. "The kids were whooping and running around the playground. You'd have thought I'd given them a million bucks. In fact, I gave them something better."

"But What's Wrong With Letter Grades?"

Responding to Parents' Questions About Alternative Assessment

Linda Doutt Culbertson and Mary Renck Jalongo

Linda Doutt Culbertson is Teacher, Edinboro Elementary School, Edinboro, Pennsylvania. Mary Renck Jalongo is Professor, Indiana University of Pennsylvania, Indiana, Pennsylvania, and Editor, Early Childhood Education Journal

Imagine attending a parent/teacher conference, this time as a parent without any professional training in the field of education. You have just been presented with a folder of information that documents your child's progress. This portfolio includes notes about daily achievement, checklists showing areas of strength, child-selected work samples, and even artwork and interest inventories that show that the school recognizes talents beyond academics. Your child enjoys coming to school and you have seen steady improvement in his or her reading and math capabilities; in fact, your child is blossoming not only in schoolwork, but also in everyday situations.

While you understand that the portfolio folder shows your child's academic growth for this term, nagging questions about the process of student evaluation remain. You wonder, "What is wrong with a simple letter grade? I had them in school and so did my parents. Why make a sudden change in the way my child is evaluated? Can you convince me that portfolios are superior to report cards?"

From *Childhood Education,* Spring 1999, pp. 130-135. Reprinted by permission of Linda Doutt Culbertson and Mary Renck Jalongo, and the Association for Childhood Education International, 17904 Georgia Avenue, Suite 215, Olney, MD.

"What is wrong with a simple letter grade? I had them in school and so did my parents. Why make a sudden change in the way my child is evaluated? Can you convince me that portfolios are superior to report cards?"

Parents are the most significant influence in a child's life (Gelfer, 1991), and they expect and deserve answers to questions about alternative assessment. This article attempts to answer some of parents' most common questions, including:

- Why is there a need for change?
- Just what is alternative assessment?
- How can parents recognize an alternative assessment?
- What contributions can alternative assessment make to a comprehensive evaluation plan?

Why Is There a Need for Change?

We all have experienced the pounding hearts and churning stomachs when we realize that the exam in front of us does not cover the material we studied. A feeling of powerlessness overcomes us, and we wish we were anywhere else but sitting in that chair taking that test. Thoughts such as "Why didn't I study something else?" and "Will I fail?" triumph over the more important questions of "What do I know?" and "How can I improve?" The feeling of panic that results can last for a day or for a lifetime, as when people say, "I always 'freeze up' on tests."

Unfortunately, the practice of testing specific material at one particular point in time is a common practice in many American classrooms. Our children are now experiencing the same feelings of powerlessness that we experienced as students when confronted by the pressures of testing. Schools' testing procedures often serve to both label and demoralize children by separating them into groups. Those who obtain high test scores are likely to be placed into the "academic" group and will receive the best teachers and the best learning opportunities; those who do not score as well often are left with drill-and-practice exercises, presumably to compensate for their deficiencies (Goodwin, 1997).

Because technology has expanded the amount of information available, we can no longer base education on a factory model of learning in which knowledge is poured into children, who memorize it for tests and forget it shortly thereafter. Fairness to children demands that we teach them the skills necessary to think and to make decisions about the knowledge that is available to them. Traditional testing offers no opportunity for a child to stop and say, "But wait! This test doesn't show what I can do! I didn't understand the question you were asking, but when you word it differently, I know the answer. Give me a chance to

Name ____________ Score ______

CHAPTER TEST — Chapter 9

Read each sentence.
Circle the picture answer.

1. Which shows a summer day?
2. Which day is cold and rainy?
3. Which is a sign of spring?
4. What do people do in cold winter weather?
5. Which shows the tree in fall?

Traditional test used to assess seasonal changes © Silver, Burdett & Ginn.
Figure 1

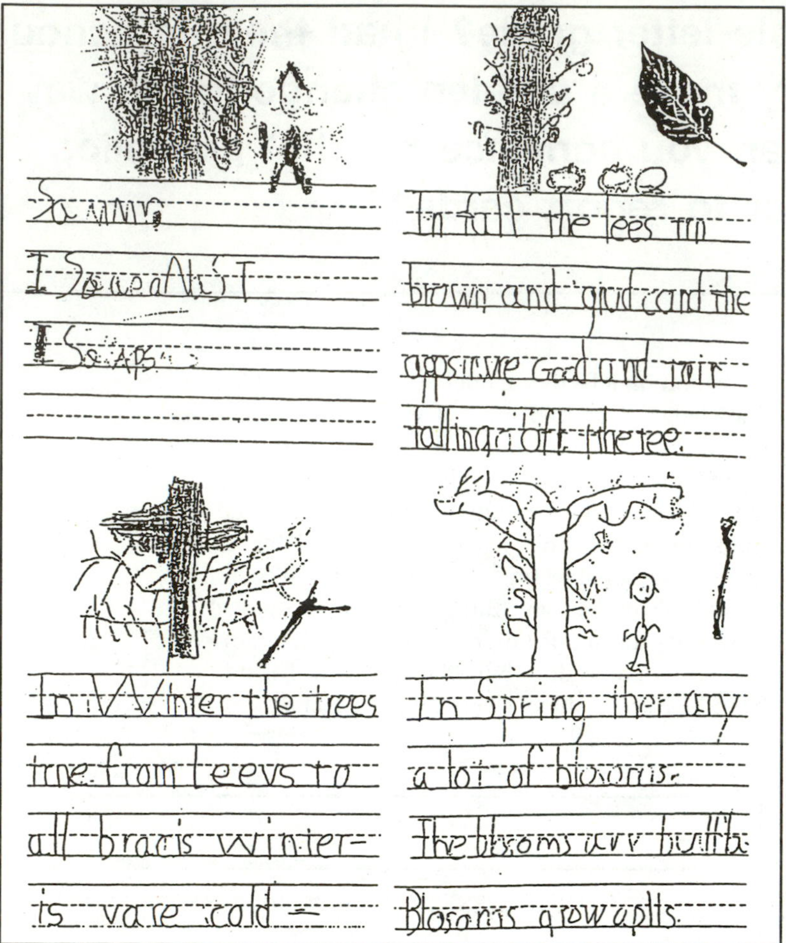

Alternative assessment used to evaluate knowledge of seasonal changes. "Summer. I saw a nest. I saw apples. In Fall the leaves turn brown and gold and the apples are very good and they're falling off the tree. In Winter the trees turn from leaves to all branches. Winter is very cold. In Spring there are a lot of blossoms. The blossoms are very beautiful. Blossoms grow apples."

Figure 2

explain . . . then you'll see!" It is no longer reasonable to provide advantages only to those who are good test takers; we must base students' evaluations on the quality of their work and not merely on their ability to recall information for a test.

Just What Is Alternative Assessment?

What if you were asked to rate a loved one on a scale of 1 to 10? Perhaps you would use all kinds of information (e.g., emotional strength, physical appearance, social skills) to arrive at the final number. Now imagine that only the number itself is reported to your loved one. Would you feel comfortable sharing the number without any explanation?

In the same manner, it makes more sense for teachers to determine what children know and can do based upon experiences that can be explained and expanded upon, rather than on multiple-choice, true/false, or other traditional forms of testing that offer no opportunities for explanation. Alternative assessment is based upon the performance of a task that the child is likely to encounter outside the classroom (Hamayan, 1995); therefore, it provides for a more natural and less stressful way of evaluating students than traditional testing does. It makes more sense, for example, to evaluate students on their ability to make correct change by setting up a classroom store than by having them complete a worksheet of addition and subtraction problems. Too often, the abilities demanded on a simple task like basic computation do not "translate" well to a practical situation. If you go to a fast food restaurant, for example, you will see that the cash register is set up with icons of the food items and that the cash register distributes the correct change. This way of making change came about mainly because while employees could pass a simple math test, they still did not know how to handle money. Clearly, it is possible to master "the basics," yet still be unable to function well on the job.

Informal methods of assessment are an integral part of daily life. We evaluate waiters and waitresses on performance—their efficiency in taking our order and delivering our food. It would mean very little to us that they might get a good grade on a multiple-choice "Server's Examination." In the same manner, we evaluate our accountants based upon the amount of money they save us at tax time, and our children's teachers based upon how well our children respond to their instruction. In fact, a national survey (conducted by the Carnegie Foundation for the Advancement of Teaching) found that parents' number one criterion for evaluating teachers was the teacher's ability to motivate their child to learn (Boyer, 1995), an ability that would be extremely difficult to measure on a test. Thus, basing evaluation on real-world evidence and actual job performance makes learning more relevant.

Figure 1 shows a traditional science examination given to assess 1st-graders' knowledge of seasonal changes. Figure 2 provides an alternative assessment in which children made seasonal visits to an apple tree and then recorded their observations. Although the alternative assessment measures the same information as the traditional test does, it provides a much more meaningful, easily remembered way to learn about seasonal changes. Traditional and alternative methods of assessment are not necessarily in opposition to one another; rather, the alternative methods are ways of providing a more complete picture of children's knowledge, understanding, and ability to apply what has been learned.

How Can I Recognize an Alternative Assessment?

Alternative assessment operates on the assumption that students should be evaluated according to criteria that are important for the performance of a given task (Wiggins, 1989). The measures used should give teachers and parents a clear picture of what the child can or cannot do in order to help the child in a given area. Many parents are accustomed to seeing their children arrive home from school each day with a backpack full of worksheets and papers. They assume by the amount of paperwork that their child is learning certain skills. The notion of equating a large amount of paperwork with learning, however, is a false one; children are learning all of the time even without direct instruction. In fact, they learn best if they are actively involved in the process (Newmann & Wehlage, 1995). Ironically, the same adults who speak despairingly of becoming "paper pushers" at work are often the first to demand that children begin doing this as soon as possible in school. Outside the classroom, the opposite assumption is made. When teaching children to use inline skates, play a musical instrument, or build a model airplane, we expect learning to occur when children are actively involved in firsthand experiences.

The specific form of alternative assessment will depend upon the subject area, the students being instructed, and an individual teacher's preference. The following examples provide insight into the most common types of alternative assessment (Darling-Hammond, Ancess, & Falk, 1995). They can be used to help parents recognize the many different ways that a child's effort, growth, and academic achievement are being recognized and documented.

Teacher Observation. Imagine calling your mechanic after your car has broken down on the freeway. After explaining how the car performed, you ask the mechanic to diagnose the problem over the telephone; your mechanic, however, insists upon actually *seeing* the car before making any kind of assessment. Although observing the car is not the only way to determine what is wrong, it certainly helps the mechanic make a more accurate assessment of the problem.

Teachers likewise use observation to become more informed about children. It allows teachers to get to know students as individuals, with talents and abilities uniquely their own (Wortham, 1995). Observation is a way for teachers to familiarize themselves not only with the academic aspects of a child's development, but also with social, emotional, physical, and cultural influences on learning. Many circumstances—both in and out of school—influence learners, and observation paints a clearer picture than testing ever can.

FIRST QUARTER SKILL CHECKLIST
FIRST GRADE

Language Arts:			
Identifies capital letters			
Identifies lower case letters			
Identifies initial consonant sounds			
Identifies final consonant sounds			
Recognizes vowels (a, e, i, o, u)			
Recognizes basic sight words (to current level)			
Uses temporary spelling to express ideas			
Uses spaces between words in writing			
Math:			
Forms sets using objects and numerals			
Writes numerals correctly from 1-10			
Can count aloud to . . .			
Recognizes numbers to . . .			
Can complete and identify basic patterns			
Can combine sets to form a new number			

A check in the box indicates mastery to grade level expectancy.

Parent Signature: ____________________ Date __________
Teacher Signature: ____________________ Date __________

A checklist used for first grade.
Figure 3

Checklists. Think about your last visit to a physician's office. Did the receptionist ask you to fill out a checklist so that the doctor would know about your family history and prior illnesses? If you checked "yes" for an illness, you were probably asked to provide further information. The doctor could then refer to the checklist during your visit to make sure that all pertinent questions had been asked and that no possible factor had been overlooked. The checklist provided an easily accessible and consistent manner in which to record your medical history, and it gave the doctor concrete information with which to work.

For the classroom teacher, checklists provide a way to make sure that all areas of a child's education have been evaluated. Checklists are designed and based upon a particular grade level's curriculum, and they provide a framework for as-

Dear Mom or Dad,

This is my portfolio. It is a collection of my best work in different subjects in school. My portfolio is so special because my teacher did not choose the pieces of work for it . . . I DID! Sometimes with your help, I picked out the pieces that I felt good about.

I have included some of my journal wirting from September of this year so that you can see my improvement. You will see that I have learned how to express my ideas much better and use lots more periods, capital letters, and other punctuation marks in the right places.

You will also see some of my best work in math, reading, art, and other subjects. There is even a book I've written! Please be sure to notice my improvement throughout the year. I've been working so hard. What a change you'll see!

I have met with my teacher to talk about why I chose what I did for my portfolio. I know you will see how I have grown this year by looking at it. I am very proud of my work and hope that you are too!

Love from your child,

____

A letter sent to parents describing their child's portfolio.
Figure 4

sessment that can be used to communicate a child's progress to parents (Wortham, 1995). By providing specific details concerning a child's performance, the checklist in Figure 3 provides parents with more information than a letter grade does. Brief comments also can be recorded on the checklist for elaboration.

Projects and Exhibitions. Think about the displays and exhibits that are used to advertise new products at a home show, grocery store, or shopping mall. Posters, videos, and photographs—along with actual samples—invite passersby to take a closer look. The displays provide succinct information about each product.

In the school setting, projects and exhibitions are types of alternative assessment that can furnish concrete evidence of a child's most significant accomplishments. Book reports, creative writing, computations, photographs, videotapes, audiotapes, and other media are highly motivating, because these methods allow students to demonstrate and document understanding. They also enable children to share their successes as learners in a tangible way with peers and family members. Because projects and exhibitions provide a tangible measurement of learning, children can learn to take pride in their accomplishments and strive for excellence.

Portfolios. Did your parents proudly keep a folder stuffed with your papers, photographs, drawings, and so forth from kindergarten through 12th grade? Perhaps you still own some of these items or have since reviewed them with your child. Collections of documents like these are worth a second look because they chronicle a child's developmental changes and new skills.

Unlike the folders kept by parents, classroom portfolios are organized, purposeful collections of student work that help to tell the story of a student's efforts, progress, or achievement in a given area. Portfolios provide an alternative to drill worksheets, standardized tests, and other measures that reflect skills development rather than developmental progress (Graves & Sunstein, 1992). Portfolios can represent all areas of the curriculum and may include papers, checklists, summaries, or other items that adequately demonstrate a student's performance. Portfolios offer a wonderful opportunity for students, parents, and teachers to not only see test scores, but also actually experience a child's growth. Figure 4 shows a sample letter sent home to parents to explain a child's portfolio.

When Does Alternative Assessment Occur?

In the workplace, you may have had a supervisor observe and assess your performance over a long period of time, perhaps for an entire year. Even if (or because) we know such evaluations are coming, our nervousness may impair our ability to perform. As adults, we appreciate it when the quality of our work is judged fairly, and in the right context. Most of us also prefer to have continuous feedback from supervisors rather than have everything depend upon one brief sample of behavior that may not be representative of our overall performance.

One of the greatest strengths of alternative assessment is its ability to allow the teacher to see the child as a whole person and not purely as a learner of basic skills. Instead of assessing children at one time on a given measure, alternative assessment allows the teacher to evaluate children's work on various projects as they proceed. The teacher is able to gain a comprehensive view of student progress from many sources and can collect varied work samples to gain an understanding of how students think about and learn new skills (Campbell, 1997).

Many children, just like adults, grow apprehensive, become demoralized, or give up entirely when given only one "high stakes" chance to prove themselves. Alternative assessment is based upon the premise that students grow and change continuously, and that measurement of their knowledge, abilities, and skills is seriously limited by a one-shot approach to testing (Isenberg & Jalongo, 1997).

How Does Alternative Assessment Contribute to Children's Learning?

1. *Alternative assessment makes sense to students.*
Would you be happy if you were given one test to determine your salary, benefits, and promotion opportunities for the upcoming year? Furthermore, would such a procedure make sense to you? Being judged by our performance is much more meaningful than being judged by a contrived measure that is unrelated to our daily lives. This concept makes sense to children as well.

Alternative assessment invites students to think about what they have learned, and it gives children the opportunity to make connections from classroom experiences to the outside world (Gardner, 1993). When learning is personally relevant, children can continuously monitor their progress and assess their own learning (Glazer, 1992). Because alternative assessment makes sense to students, they have a much better understanding of what is expected of them and, therefore, have a much better chance of meeting those expectations (Earl & LeMahieu, 1996).

2. *Alternative assessment fosters responsibility in students.*
Students can develop responsibility for their own learning by having opportunities to choose work for portfolios, discuss their observations, and determine where they need help. Whereas multiple-choice tests promote competition among students, alternative assessment promotes skill in self- and peer evaluation. Students develop responsibility and independence by learning to help, share, cooperate, and care about others (Osin & Lesgold, 1996).

Alternative assessment allows children to make choices, and it gives them responsibility for living with those choices within a classroom setting where the teacher is a guide and facilitator. Before students are placed in real-life decision-making situations, alternative assessment provides them with plenty of practice in making decisions within classroom walls. Students become problem-solvers in a non-threatening atmosphere that encourages them to learn from their mistakes.

3. *Alternative assessment emphasizes the process, rather than the product, of learning.*
By focusing on the entire learning process, rather than on one small product (e.g., a test at the "end" of learning), alternative assessment helps children to realize that what they do each day in school is part of an important and ongoing process. By focusing on intense, concentrated involvement in an activity (Osin & Lesgold, 1996), students gain more information than they would from a single evaluation product or test. Rather than memorizing facts for a test that will soon be forgotten, children build upon their knowledge and are encouraged to evaluate their own growth. This meaningful process helps to create an environment in which learning is remembered. Alternative assessment provides opportunities for the process of work to be challenging, pleasurable, and rewarding (Osin & Lesgold, 1996).

4. *Alternative assessment motivates children to continue learning.*
If each of us were assigned the task of constructing a birdhouse, we would probably approach it in very different ways. Some would prefer to work with a group; others would work better alone. Some would be able to create an original from materials found at home, while others would buy a kit and follow the directions to the letter. Most of us would want to find out which structures attract which birds and study examples of birdhouses before beginning our task. Having choices motivates us much more than being told, "Your birdhouse must look exactly like the other 25 in your neighborhood, and you must complete it at exactly the same time and in the same sequence as everyone else." By the same token, students either can be motivated by having choices in reaching high standards, or they can be defeated by being forced to do things exactly as others in their class are doing. Alternative assessment allows for student selection of learning opportuni-

ties, based upon the assumption that having an interest in something will be motivation to learn more about it. Teachers and parents can work together with the child to choose projects that are "natural challenges," and that lead to real accomplishments (Osin & Lesgold, 1996). Alternative assessment motivates children by giving them a voice in their own education (Schneider, 1996).

Conclusion

No parent wants his or her child to fail in the school system. Although looking at a letter grade on a report card or a percentage score from a traditional test is familiar, based on our own experiences as children, it does little to help us form accurate, detailed perceptions about a child's strengths or academic needs (Newman & Smolen, 1993). Alternative assessment can provide us with information about daily progress and insight into the process of learning. It also encourages children to become lifelong learners, rather than memorizers and forgetters" of information. The major purposes of any assessment practices in schools should be to help children really understand what they are learning, enable them to concentrate and investigate ideas in depth, and encourage them to produce high-quality work that will be useful to them, not just in school but also throughout their lives (Newmann & Wehlage, 1995). Although changes in assessment practices may be disconcerting at first, adults who really care about children and their learning will need to concentrate more on children's futures than on their distant pasts, if they are to improve education for all students.

References

Boyer, E. L. (1995). *The basic school: A community for learning.* Princeton, NJ: The Carnegie Foundation for the Advancement of Teaching.

Campbell, L. (1997). Variations on a theme: How teachers interpret MI theory. *Educational Leadership, 55*(1), 14–19.

Darling-Hammond, L., Ancess, J., & Falk, B. (1995). *Authentic assessment in action: Studies of schools and students at work.* New York: Teachers College Press.

Earl, L. M., & LeMahieu, P. C. (1996). Rethinking assessment and accountability. In A. Hargreaves (Ed.), 1997 ASCD Yearbook: *Rethinking educational change with heart and mind* (pp. 149–168). Alexandria, VA: Association for Supervision and Curriculum Development.

Gardner, H. (1993). *Frames of mind: The theory of multiple intelligences.* New York: Basic Books.

Gelfer, J. I. (1991). Teacher-parent partnerships: Enhancing communications. *Childhood Education, 67,* 164–167.

Glazer, S. J. (1992). Assessment in classrooms: Reality and fantasy. *Teaching K-8, 22*(8), 62–64.

Goodwin, A. L. (1997). *Assessment for equity and inclusion: Embracing all our children.* New York: Routledge.

Graves, D. H., & Sunstein, B. S. (1992). *Portfolio portraits.* Portsmouth, NH: Heinemann.

Hamayan, E. V. (1995). Approaches to alternative assessment. *Annual Review of Applied Linguistics, 15,* 212–226.

Isenberg, J. P., & Jalongo, M. R. (1997). *Creative expression and play in early childhood* (2nd ed.). Upper Saddle River, NJ: Merrill/Prentice Hall.

Newman, C., & Smolen, L. (1993). Portfolio assessment in our schools: Implementation, advantages, and concerns. *MidWestern Educational Researcher,* 6(1), 28–32.

Newmann, F. M., & Wehlage, G. G. (1995). *Successful school restructuring: A report to the public and educators.* Madison, WI: University of Wisconsin-Madison, Wisconsin Center for Educational Research, Center on Organization and Restructuring of Schools.

Osin, L., & Lesgold, A. (1996). A proposal for the re-engineering of the educational system. In F. B. Murray & J. Raths (Eds.), *Review of education research: Winter 1996* (pp. 621–656). Washington, DC: American Educational Research Association.

Schneider, E. (1996). Giving students a voice in the classroom. *Educational Leadership,* 54(1), 22–26.

Science test masters grade 1. (1987). Morristown, NJ: Silver, Burdett & Ginn.

Wiggins, G. (1989). A true test: Toward more authentic assessment. *Phi Delta Kappan,* 703–713.

Wortham, S. C. (1995). *Measurement and evaluation in. early childhood education.* Englewood Cliffs, NJ: Prentice Hall.

From Philosophy to Practice in Inclusive Early Childhood Programs

Tom Udell
Joyce Peters
Torry Piazza Templeman

Two 4-year-olds are playing at the water table. Their teacher observes that Michelle splashes her hand on the surface repeatedly, chortling with delight. Carlos is busy pouring water from a large container into several smaller ones and then arranging them in a pattern to his liking.

These children of the same age are at different developmental points in their lives. How can a teacher or a child care provider allow Michelle to do all the splashing she needs to do, teach her social skills in water play, and also encourage Carlos to continue his absorption in measuring and artistic design—as well as learn the social skills of playing with Michelle? A simple water table activity is more complicated than it seems. Why is this play activity important? How can an inclusive program meet the needs of both children?

The Individuals with Disabilities Education Act has challenged all providers of service to young children with disabilities to provide services in natural community settings where young children without disabilities participate. Educators are looking for ways to merge developmentally appropriate practices with practices found effective in the field of early childhood special education. Although these two sets of practices converge at certain points, professionals agree that differences remain (Bredekamp & Rosegrant, 1992).

The Teaching Research Early Childhood Program has developed a conceptual framework to meet the challenge of blending developmentally appropriate practices with early childhood special education recommended practices. This blended approach has resulted in the delivery of quality services within an inclusive preschool/child care setting.

Elements of an Inclusive Program

In the context of early childhood education, what are the differences among practices known as *mainstreaming, reverse mainstreaming, integration,* and *inclusion?* All these terms denote the introduction of children with disabilities into a "typical" environment for some portion of the day, or in the case of reverse mainstreaming, the introduction of some typically developing peers into what is essentially a special education program.

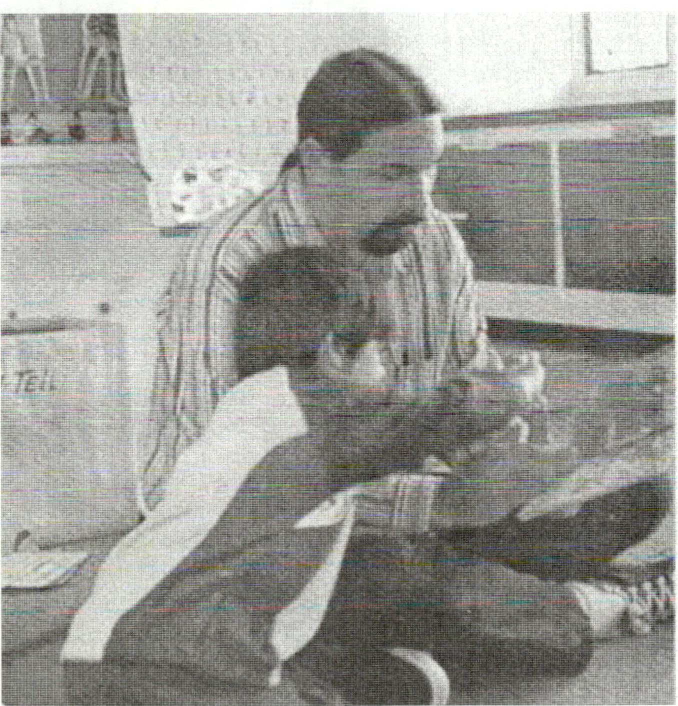

Inclusion goes further in that no one is introduced into anyone else's program. All children attend the same program, all of the time. Each child is given the support he or she needs to be successful in the setting. For children age 3 to school age, these settings are most often public and private community preschool and child care programs.

The most comprehensive and widely disseminated guidelines defining quality services in these settings are *developmentally appropriate practices,* as defined by the National Association for the Education of Young Children (NAEYC).

Research in early childhood special education indicates that those using these developmental guidelines as the *sole* principles for providing services to young children with disabilities would fall short of providing the full range of services these children need. Carta, Schwartz, Atwater, and McConnell (1991) warned against the adoption of these guidelines to the potential exclusion of principles and practices that we know are effective for children with disabilities, but also suggest that educators not overlook developmentally appropriate practices in providing inclusive services for these children. Indeed, Bredekamp and Rosegrant stated in a 1992 NAEYC publication:

> Experiences with mainstreaming over the past two decades suggest a conclusion that probably will be made concerning the guidelines . . . and children with special needs 20 years from now: The guidelines are the context in which appropriate early education of children with spe-

From *Teaching Exceptional Children,* January/February 1998, pp. 44-49.

Principles of Early Childhood Special Education

- **Intervention focused on functional goals**
- **Family-centered services**
- **Regular monitoring and adjustment of intervention**
- **Transition planning**
- **Multidisciplinary services**

cial needs should occur; however, a program based on the guidelines alone is not likely to be sufficient for many children with special needs. (p. 106)

Let's look at both recommended practices—developmentally appropriate practices and early childhood special education practices—and find points where educators, children, families, and communities can work together to make inclusive programs successful.

Developmentally Appropriate Practice

NAEYC published a widely used position statement about developmentally appropriate practices for serving young children from birth to age 8 in early childhood programs (Bredekamp, 1987). The association compiled and published this statement in reaction to the concern of early childhood educators with the increasing academic demands made of young children in early childhood programs and general misconceptions about how teachers should provide instruction to young children.

This position statement became the most widely recognized guideline in the field of early childhood education. In 1997 NAEYC published the revised *Developmentally Appropriate Practice in Early Childhood Programs* (Bredekamp & Copple, 1997), clarifying the misunderstandings and misinterpretations that arose from a decade of extensive dissemination of the original position statement.

Based on the developmental theories of Piaget and Vygotsky, the NAEYC guidelines convey the primary message that *learning occurs through exploratory play activities* and that formal instruction beyond the child's current developmental level will result in nonfunctional, rote learning at best. Developmentally appropriate practice suggests that teachers should not attempt to direct or tightly structure learning experiences and that formal academic instruction at the preschool level should not occur.

These guidelines have three dimensions, as follows:

1. *Age appropriateness.* According to child development knowledge and research, all children grow and change in a universal, predictable sequence during the first 9 years of life. This knowledge about typical child development allows teachers to plan appropriate environments and experiences.
2. *Individual appropriateness.* Each child has his or her own unique pattern of growth, strengths, interests, experiences, and backgrounds. Both the curriculum and adults' interactions with children should be responsive to these individual differences.
3. *Cultural appropriateness.* To truly understand each child, teachers and child care providers must recognize and respect the social and cultural context in which the child lives. When teachers understand the cultural context in which children live, they can better plan meaningful experiences that are relevant for each child (Bredekamp & Copple, 1997).

Teachers should use knowledge of child development to identify the range of appropriate behaviors, activities, and materials for a specific age group. As well, they should use this knowledge in conjunction with an understanding of each child in the classroom and his or her unique personalities, backgrounds, and abilities to design the most appropriate learning environment.

NAEYC recommends that instructional practices emphasize child-initiated, child-directed play activities, based on the assumption that young children are intrinsically motivated to learn by their desire to understand their environment. Teaching strategies include hands-on exploratory activities with emphases on the use of concrete, real, and relevant activities.

Rationale of Early Childhood Special Education

Early childhood special education is based on the premise that early and comprehensive intervention maximizes the developmental potential of infants and children with disabilities. Such intervention produces child outcomes that would likely not occur in the absence of such intervention (McDonnell & Hardman, 1988).

Since the initiation of publicly supported services for preschool children with disabilities in the mid-1970s, professionals in early childhood special education have developed a body of practices. This body of practice has evolved from research, model demonstration, and evaluation efforts and is currently referred to as *early childhood special education recommended practices.* Researchers have documented syntheses of desired characteristics, or recommended practices, of exemplary, early childhood special education models (DEC, 1993; McDonnell & Hardman, 1988; Wolery, Strain & Bailey, 1992; Wolery & Wilbers, 1994). We have selected components of these models and practices that researchers have shown to be essential, effective, and compatible with the NAEYC guidelines (see Carta et al., 1991, for evaluation criteria). These components include setting functional goals and monitoring children's progress toward these goals, planning for transitions, and working closely with families.

Intervention Focused on Functional Goals

Intervention for children with disabilities should focus on producing specific and measurable child goals. To make meaningful changes in children's behavior, these goals need to be functional for each child and for the environments in which the child participates. A *functional* skill is one that is essential to participation within a variety of integrated environments. In early childhood settings, functional skills are those that assist children to interact more independently and positively with their physical and social environments.

For example, it is probably more functional for a child to be able to carry out his or her own toileting functions independently than to be able to name 10 farm animals. Shouldn't we give preference to skills that will enable the child to participate more fully in an integrated setting, as

---

Effective early childhood instructional practices emphasize child-initiated, child-directed play activities, based on the assumption that young children are intrinsically motivated to learn by their desire to understand their environment.

---

opposed to those skills that would be indicated in the developmental hierarchy or sequence? If our answer is yes, these goals then become the focus for providing individualized intervention. Teachers or care providers design services and instruction to produce a specific outcome—like independent toileting—and this outcome becomes the standard against which the success of an intervention is measured.

Family-Centered Services

The family is the heart of all early childhood programs. Families participate in planning and decision making in all aspects of their children's program.

A good school-family partnership includes a system for a child's family to have regular communication with the classroom staff and have frequent opportunities to participate in their child's program. Quality programs also include procedures for helping families link into existing community resources.

Regular Monitoring and Adjustment of Intervention

Educators and care providers should systematically monitor the effects of specific interventions. Researchers have shown the effectiveness of using *formative* assessment data to monitor children's progress toward their individual goals and objectives. (McDonnell & Hardman, 1988).

We know that such data must be gathered frequently enough to monitor the subtleties of progress or failure. Data-collection systems must measure child progress toward the acquisition of predetermined goals, including the application of skills in a variety of settings.

Transition Planning

Educators and care providers of all children—and particularly children with disabilities—must plan for transition from one school or child care setting to the next one. Early childhood special educators are particularly concerned with transition from preschool to kindergarten because this move signals a major change for the child and the family from familiar and secure surroundings to a new, unknown setting.

This is a time of considerable stress, and teachers and child care providers must engage in careful, timely planning to smooth the process. Many people are involved in the transition planning process: the child's family, the sending teacher, the early intervention specialist, support personnel, and the future receiving teacher. An effective transition plan often begins 1–2 years before the actual move. This preliminary planning enables the sending teachers to identify skills needed in the future environment. These skills are included in the child's curriculum during the last preschool years.

Key Aspects of Developmentally Appropriate Practices

- **Developmental evaluation of children for program planning and implementation**
- **High staff qualifications**
- **High ratio of adults to children**
- **Strong relationship between home and program**

Multidisciplinary Services

Professionals from many disciplines need to participate in the planning of comprehensive services for children with disabilities and their families. Because many of these children and their families have complex needs, no single professional and no one discipline can provide a full range of services.

The specific needs of each child and family determine what disciplines should be involved in assessing, planning, implementing, and monitoring services. The following disciplines are commonly involved in early childhood special education:

- Speech and language therapy.
- Occupational and physical therapy.
- Health and medical services.
- Audiology.
- Disability-specific specialists, such as a vision specialist or autism specialist.

Professionals in these disciplines provide services in an integrated manner: They share knowledge and methods across disciplines, and the entire team develops and implements one comprehensive plan. Following this plan, team members provide consultation services within the early childhood environment.

Merging Programs Through Developmentally Appropriate Practices

The first step to merging these approaches is to recognize the advantages a program adhering to developmentally appropriate practices offers for the successful inclusion of children with disabilities. Such a program will have high-quality components, many of which facilitate the inclusion process.

Facilitating Inclusion

The nature of developmentally appropriate practices allows for the inclusion of children with great variation in development within the same setting. Even in a group of young children without disabilities, of the same age, children can be as much as 2 years apart developmentally.

Thus, planning developmentally appropriate activities and providing equipment and materials for the preschool setting already accommodates children in a wide development range. This allowance in planning and material selection makes it possible to include children with mild and moderate disabilities without additional adaptation.

This developmental approach to planning creates an ideal environment for embedding instruction on individually targeted skills. The developmental emphasis on learning as a process rather than a product also facilitates targeting a variety of individualized objectives. To illustrate the process-versus-product approach, let's look at ways teachers might provide art experiences—and individualized instruction—for children.

The *process* approach to art allows children to explore available materials, experiment, and create individual designs with little regard for the end product. This approach also allows for intervention on a variety of instructional objectives for children with disabilities while all children are involved in the same activity. For example, all children are involved in a finger-painting activity; one child may be working on requesting objects, another on identifying colors, and yet another on staying with the group.

Providing Quality Indicators

Developmentally appropriate practices are not a curriculum, nor do they dictate a rigid set of standards. Developmental programs will not all look the same, but they will have a similar framework that pays careful attention to child development knowledge and will assist educators in providing quality services for children. The use of developmentally appropriate practices ensures quality in programs in many ways, such as developmental evaluation of children for program planning and implementation, high staff qualifications, a high ratio of adults to children, and strong relationship between home and program.

- *Developmental evaluation.* Decisions about enrollment and placement have a major effect on children. Educators and care providers base these decisions on multiple assessment data emphasizing observations by teachers and parents. Teachers use developmental assessment of child progress and achievement to adapt curriculum, communicate with families, and evaluate program effectiveness. Developmental evaluations of children use valid instruments developed for use with young children; these assessment tools are gender, culture, and socioeconomically appropriate (Bredekamp, 1987).

Children of the same age can be as much as 2 years apart developmentally.

- *Staff qualifications.* The NAEYC guidelines for developmentally appropriate practice emphasize the need for staff with preparation and supervised experiences specific to working with young children. Early childhood teachers should have college-level preparation in early childhood education and child development.
- *High adult/student ratios.* A key to implementing developmentally appropriate practices is to have a small number of children per classroom and a high ratio of adults to children. Ratios suggested in the NAEYC position statement are higher than those required for licensing in most states. NAEYC recommended standards describe a ratio of 2 adults to 20 children ages 4–5, with younger children requiring smaller groups with higher adult-to-child ratios.
- *Home-to-program relationship.* NAEYC guidelines recommend parent involvement in all decision making, regular communication between parents and teacher, and encouragement of parent involvement in the day-to-day happenings of the program. These practices help in building a strong relationship between home and the child's community program.

Developing a Conceptual Base

We have developed a conceptual base, recognizing the two sets of practice, that will allow both developmentally appropriate practices and special education principles to exist within the same setting. The Teaching Research Early Childhood Program has developed a philosophy that views developmentally appropriate practices as the foundation on which individualized programs are built, adding special education instruction when needed for individual children. We believe that the two approaches to early childhood are not mutually exclusive.

Figure 1 illustrates this dilemma. The builder has two sets of clearly different materials and cannot decide which to use. The key to moving beyond this dilemma is to recognize that these practices serve distinctively different purposes—and we can view them as different types of resources.

- *Developmentally appropriate practices* are used to design an age-appropriate, stimulating environment supportive of all children's needs. These practices, however, were not developed to reflect or address specific individual needs of children with disabilities and offer little information about specific intervention strategies needed to serve these children.
- *Early childhood special education practices* are used to complement the basic program for children with exceptional developmental needs and to emphasize individualized strategies to maximize children's learning opportunities. These practices, however, do not provide guidelines for designing a quality early childhood learning environment.

When educators recognize these practices as being different, but compatible, they can then plan a single comprehensive program, as shown in Figure 2. The completed school uses developmentally appropriate practices as the material from which the foundation is built and special education practices as the material that completes the structure.

Implementing Both Practices Within the Same Setting

Let's look more closely at how this merger might work. A well-designed early childhood education program, following developmentally appropriate practices, uses a planned, well-organized environment where children interact with materials, other children, and adults. Here the NAEYC guidelines are apparent: Young children are intrinsically motivated to learn by their desire to understand their environment; the program is set up to allow children to self-select activities from a variety of interest centers.

When children show they need further support, educators use special education strategies that are made available in the program. These strategies include the following:

- *Directly prompting practice* on individually targeted skills, based on functional behavioral outcomes.
- *Reinforcing* children's responses.
- *Collecting data* to monitor children's progress and make intervention changes.

Some educators view these strategies as conflicting with developmentally appropriate practices. Some people liken this direct prompting to the formal instruction that NAEYC deplored for use with young children. We believe that this view is a misinterpretation of NAEYC's position statement and the guidelines for developmentally appropriate practices.

As we mentioned earlier, however, NAEYC guidelines do not exclude intervention strategies for children with identified special needs (Bredekamp & Rosegrant 1993). We hope that by clarifying this misinterpretation, we might encourage teach-

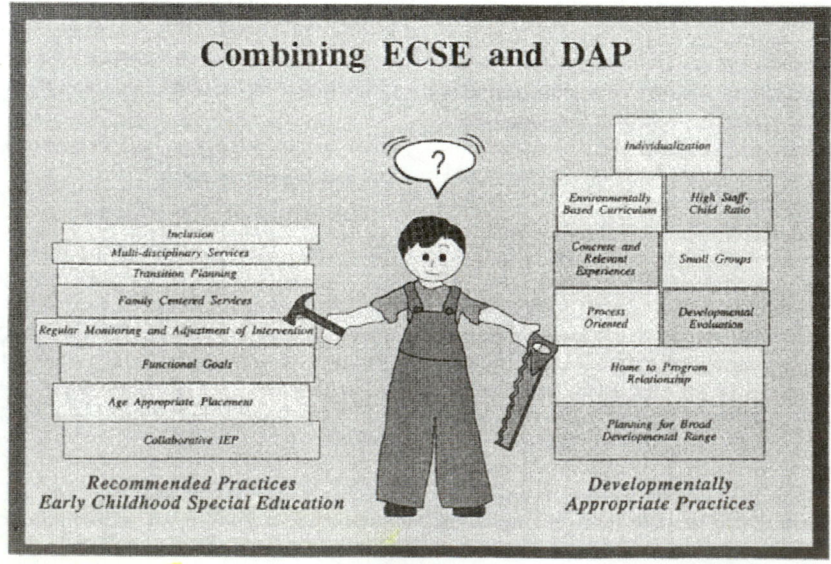

Figure 1

ers to view these intervention strategies as individually appropriate for some children.

As educators begin to merge these two approaches to early childhood education, we will find all children participating in the same well-organized, systematically planned environment—with direct instruction being provided to children who need this type of intervention. This direct instruction is blended into naturally occurring opportunities throughout the ongoing daily routine, such as play at the water table or learning independent toileting. An early childhood program adhering to developmentally appropriate practices provides a strong foundation for the provision of consultation services from professionals across different disciplines.

Consider transition services—an area of special education services that some educators believe conflicts with a child-centered developmental program. The transition planning process has an apparent conflict with developmentally appropriate practice because it presumes that the needs of some future environment should drive the child's curriculum at present. Guidelines for developmentally appropriate practices reject the idea of current curriculums being driven by the needs of a future environment.

To resolve this conflict we can look to the *foundation* concept. In developmentally appropriate practice, we find children participating in an environment planned to fit their current developmental demands and individual backgrounds and interests. Within this environment, children with special needs receive instruction on specific skills that will assist them to be successful in their next setting. Teachers have selected these specific skills or objectives with direct regard to the child's current needs and level of functioning, with some, but not predominant, focus on transition skills needs as dictated by future environments. Skills selected because of the demands of a future environment are ones that can be facilitated without disruption in the current environment. These skills are also within the boundaries of being developmentally appropriate in the future environment.

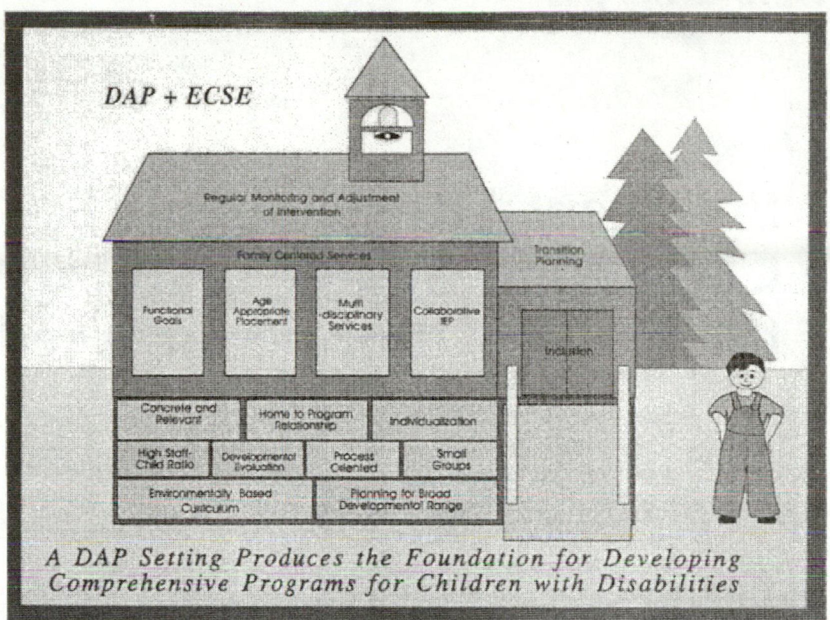

Figure 2

Mutually Beneficial, Not Mutually Exclusive

In inclusive early childhood education programs, we must caution against adopting developmentally appropriate practices to the exclusion of research-supported special education practices. Similarly, we must not fail to recognize the benefits offered by placing children with disabilities in developmentally appropriate programs. We need to develop an understanding of both sets of practices and to develop a program, from philosophy to practice, that merges practices.

References

Bredekamp, S. (Ed.). (1987). *Developmentally Appropriate Practices in Early Childhood Programs Serving Children from Birth Through Age 8* (Exp. ed.). Washington, DC: National Association for the Education of Young Children.

Bredekamp, S., & Copple, C. (Eds.). (1997). *Developmentally Appropriate Practices in Early Childhood Programs* (Rev. ed.) Washington, DC: National Association for the Education of Young Children.*

Bredekamp, S., & Rosegrant, T. (Eds.). (1992). *Reaching potentials: Appropriate curriculum and assessment for young children* (Vol. 1, pp. 92–112). Washington, DC: National Association for the Education of Young Children.

Carta, J. J., Schwartz, I. S., Atwater, J. B., & McConnell, S. R. (1991). Developmentally appropriate practice: Appraising its usefulness for young children with disabilities. *Topics In Early Childhood Special Education 11*(1), 1–20.

DEC Task Force on Recommended Practices. (1993). *DEC recommended practices: Indicators of quality in programs for infants and young children with special needs and their families.* Reston, VA: The Council for Exceptional Children, Division of Early Childhood Education. (ERIC Document Reproduction Service No. ED 370 253)

McDonnell, A., & Hardman, M. (1988). A synthesis of "best practice" guidelines for early childhood services. *Journal of the Division of Early Childhood, 12,* 328–337.

Wolery, M., Strain, P. S., & Bailey, D. B. (1992). Reaching potentials of children with special needs. In S. Bredekamp & T. Rosegrant (Eds.), *Reaching potentials: Appropriate curriculum and assessment for young children* (Vol. 1, pp. 92–112). Washington, DC: National Association for the Education of Young Children.*

Wolery, M., & Wilbers, J. S. (Eds.). (1994). *Including children with special needs in early childhood programs.* Washington, DC: National Association for the Education of Young Children.*

Tom Udell, *Assistant Research Professor;* **Joyce Peters,** *(CEC Oregon Federation), Associate Research Professor;* **Torry Piazza Templeman,** *(CEC Oregon Federation), Associate Director, Teaching Research Division, Western Oregon University, Monmouth.*

Address correspondence to Tom Udell, Teaching Research Division, Western Oregon University, 345 N. Monmouth Ave., Monmouth, OR 97361 (e-mail:udellt@wou.edu).

We would like to thank Kathy Haydon for her illustrations.

Emergent Literacy in an Early Childhood Classroom: Center Learning to Support the Child with Special Needs

Margaret Genisio[1,2] and Mary Drecktrah[1]

A child with special needs will flourish and benefit from an early childhood environment that empowers learning. Center learning empowers a child to to be actively engaged in self-directed learning based on strength, ability, and interest. Center learning can enhance interactive language, story response, art, reading and writing-like behavior, collaboration, buddy activity, and independence. All of these empowering areas of development are strongly related to the child's emergent literacy development. The variety of center learning experiences is limited only by the imagination; this article provides a selection of start-up ideas for the early childhood educator.

KEY WORDS: emergent literacy; early childhood; special needs.

INTRODUCTION

Choice, engagement, experimentation, risk taking, opportunity to see and use print, and hear and use language, are all closely linked early childhood education components related to emergent literacy development in the young child (Allen & Mason, 1989; Teale, 1986). The child with special needs requires scaffolding crafted to empower the child to progress towards personal literacy fulfillment (Salinger, 1996).

Center learning is one way to offer a personally nurturing and stimulating environment that scaffolds learning, sometimes taking it beyond the classroom walls and into the home.

The *child with special needs* is one who learns in different ways and at different rates. Children ages 3 to 5 years with disabilities must be educated in the least restrictive environment according to Public Law 99-457, which means that today's classrooms will enhance learning opportunity for all children (Wood, 1993).

Although many educators use the broad term of developmental delays to categorize young children with disabilities, we use particular categories with specific characteristics to help define the type of child for which our suggestions would be suited. The following are areas of special need (Tompkins, 1995, pp. 59–61), with a range of suggestions for early childhood educators (Ysseldyke & Algozzine, 1995). Center learning is one positive, empowering option that can effectively address the suggestions that follow:

Students with Specific Learning Disabilities (Tompkins, 1995). These children are capable of learning, but demonstrating significant problems in one or more of the following areas: listening, speaking, reading (reading-like activity), writing (writing-like activity).

[1] College of Education and Human Services, The University of Wisconsin-Oshkosh, Oshkosh, Wisconsin 54901.
[2] Correspondence should be directed to Margaret Genisio, Department of Reading, University of Wisconsin-Oshkosh, 800 Algoma Boulevard, Oshkosh, Wisconsin 54901.

From *Early Childhood Education Journal,* Vol. 26, No. 4, 1999, pp. 225-231.

Suggestions for Teachers of Students with Learning Disabilities

- Help youngsters focus on important activities
- Use concrete examples when demonstrating new ideas
- Provide more experiences for practice than necessary for classmates
- Allow youngsters to progress at their own speed
- Modify activities to compensate for learning problems

Students with Mental Retardation (Tompkins, 1995). These children have below average intellectual functioning, coupled with limitations in two or more of the following areas: communicating, self-care, home living, social skills, self-direction, health, safety, and play.

Suggestions for Teachers Working with Mental Retardation

- Use varied and concrete examples when demonstrating new ideas
- Break activities into smaller parts
- Provide more experiences for practice than necessary for classmates
- Give corrective and supportive feedback more often than for others
- Repeat teaching and experiences more often than necessary than for peers

Student with behavior disorders (Tompkins, 1995): these children exhibit frequent frustration and find it difficult to communicate frustrations to another either verbally, in art or in drama. The limited ability to communicate may make this child feel uncomfortable at school.

Suggestions for Teachers of Students with Emotional Disturbance

- Establish rules and consequences for behavior with the youngster
- Teach appropriate behaviors, modeling and practicing often
- Praise and reward youngsters for appropriate behaviors
- Be consistent with all youngsters
- Help youngsters monitor their own behavior

Students with language disorders (Tompkins, 1995): This area includes children with needs in listening and speaking; the child finds difficulty in using language to express ideas, interest, feelings or to engage in conversation, descriptions, retelling or made up stories.

Suggestions for Teachers of Students with Speech/Language Disabilities

- Encourage youngsters to talk to each other and adults
- Provide good speech models
- Integrate language activities into all centers
- Value speech and language diversity
- Be aware of developmental language levels, use areas of strength

Students who are gifted (Tompkins, 1995): These children demonstrate the need for more challenge, are able to engage in more advanced reading and writing activities, can communicate ideas and stories and can activate conversation at an advanced level.

Suggestions for Teachers of Students Who Are Gifted and Talented

- Model higher-level thinking skills and creative problem-solving
- Offer challenging activities in centers that generate different types of thinking and solutions
- Encourage independent learning activities
- Provide advanced content through enrichment activities
- Provide challenging instructional activities using youngster's interest and preferences

Students who are visually impaired

Suggestions for Teachers of Students with Visual Impairments

- Organize classroom so student knows where things are
- Verbalize information along with pictures, videos
- Give students freedom to move close to areas of interest and discussion
- Reduce distance between youngster and speaker
- Check that the youngster's glasses or other visual aids are working correctly

A center in the classroom that focuses on the alphabet not only reinforces activity that is engaged in at home between parent and child, but also extends this learning into the classroom and perhaps back home once again.

SCAFFOLDING THE EXPERIENCE: CRAFTING AN EMPOWERING LEARNING ENVIRONMENT

Darlene Nugent, an early childhood educator, described one parent's reaction to center learning:

> Charlene frequently used baby talk and rarely conveyed ideas or messages from school to home. She has been enthusiastic about bringing home the class traveling alphabet book in the special "ABC" tote bag. This is the first time she has been able to tell us about her school activity. In fact, she wants me to help her find print to slip into each letter bag page in the binder. Last night she completed two pages in the book. She placed a box top from vanilla wafers in the "v" section, and an empty package from hot chocolate in the "h" section. Later, when I asked her to tell a story about the pages, she said she has hot chocolate and vanilla cookies when she comes home from school.

A center in the classroom that focuses on the alphabet not only reinforces activity that is engaged in at home between parent and child, but also extends this learning into the classroom and perhaps back home once again. An ABC Center, such as the one described below, enhances this learning:

ABC Center

Goal: To provide children with an opportunity to interact with a variety of materials that depict letters of the alphabet.

Number of Children: Four at one time.

Activity: In the alphabet center are magnetic alphabet letters, both upper and lower case. These can be used with individual magnetic trays, cookie sheets, or burner covers purchased at variety store in sets of four. Children experiment with letter combinations, copying words from books. The center also contains letter picture cards, alphabet stamps, jigsaw letter puzzles, and a traveling alphabet book. A traveling alphabet book is a loose-leaf binder, containing 26 clear plastic pockets, one for each letter of the alphabet. Use an inexpensive supermarket variety of an alphabet book that has been cut up, placing each letter of the alphabet at the top of each page as a guide. The book is sent home with a different child each night. The child then inserts environmental print that contains the featured letter of the alphabet within each pocket. **"Environmental print"** is print that features very familiar logos, such as "McDonalds." When the book is brought back to class each child reads the logo selection to the class, page by page.

Adaptation: A grabber that has a pincher on the end of a stick that a child can operate offers a motorically impaired child the opportunity to manipulate the letters in this center. Another way to participate is to use a flashlight to indicate which letters she/he wants a peer to move to form a sequence. This provides an opportunity for collaborative activity for all children. Wikki Stix are colorful 6-inch lengths of bendable, wax-like strips similar to pipe cleaners, that can be manipulated into letters by all children, providing a different tactile experience. Multisensory opportunities can encourage all students to experiment with letter writing. Sugar or corn meal, instead of sand for writing with their fingers, are environmentally friendly to children with allergies or breathing problems. Sandpaper letters and foam form letters are other three-dimensional materials that may intrigue children.

Nugent explained that Charlene's parent had been provided with supporting directions to use as needed. A main point of emphasis was to encourage Charlene's efforts to tell what she planned to do with the alphabet book she brought home. When Charlene was prompted with key phrases and given time to remember what had happened at school, she was able to tell her mother what she planned to do. Phrases such as the following were used to prompt Charlene: "This looks very interesting! What will we do with this book? What could these pock-

Some children with special needs or disabilities may not have had a literature-rich home environment.

ets be used for?" This language scaffolding was especially prepared by the teacher for Charlene because she had delayed language development.

"I give the children enrolled in my program time to decide what they would like to do, and time to try it. Center activity provides the backdrop for so much individual learning," said Nugent. Nugent has 16 children and 2 assistants in her Oshkosh, Wisconsin classroom.

> When the children decide to spend time at a center they are making a choice based on their interest at the time. I encourage this. I want the children to enjoy themselves as they activate personal learning. To help children's experimentation and risk taking I suggest that they rotate among my changing centers and explore each one during free visit time. There is lots of opportunity for experimentation and small group activity. Some of my children have special needs or are developmentally delayed. I closely observe to make sure they benefit from the center time and can actively enjoy participating with their peers. Enhancing the emerging literacy of each child is the major goal of the center activity. I keep each child's strengths and needs in mind as I use center learning to promote literacy development.

What Nugent is stressing is based on sound educational principles. She creates a nurturing and safe environment by leading children through enjoyable activities in language-based centers, and then encourages movement, choice-making, and experimentation. This activity, coupled with language interaction and negotiation, cooperative learning, socialization, book handling, and reading- and writing-like activity, form core basics in the development of sound emergent literacy (Butler & Clay, 1979; Salinger, 1996; Teale, 1982).

EMERGENT LITERACY

Early childhood classroom environments that provide the child with authentic opportunity to become engaged in learning by listening, talking, reading, writing, and playing, nurture emerging literacy. The term *emergent literacy* (Clay, 1966) acknowledges children's natural growth and awareness of print in the environment. Literacy development is an ongoing, cumulative activity. This means that the child becomes acquainted with literacy in personally satisfying ways, building on what is learned as time passes. We know that the early childhood child in a literacy-rich home environment acquires a lot of personally satisfying and useful information about literacy through natural learning (Butler & Clay, 1979).

Pretending to write a letter to a friend, telling a story that is similar to one heard while holding the book and turning pages, talking to stuffed animals, and engaging in dramatic play are all literacy-related activities that begin first as home-based endeavors for most children. Observing parents and caregivers as they perform everyday literacy-related activities, such as reading the newspapers, or writing out a grocery list, contributes to the child's natural learning about literacy.

Some children with special needs or disabilities may not have had a literature-rich home environment. The early childhood classroom may be their first encounter with rhyming chants, dramatic play, telling stories, or being read to in a nurturing environment. This background presents a particular challenge to the early childhood professional. Scaffolding and modeling techniques used with center learning strengthen the opportunity for learning success.

SCAFFOLDING AND MODELING FOR THE YOUNG CHILD

Verbal interaction between teacher and child that helps the child to solve a problem, carry out a task or achieve a goal beyond efforts that are unassisted is referred to as *scaffolding* (Applebee & Langer, 1983). Talking about the way the Reading Center is used, and then providing the child with an opportunity to use the Center, is strong verbal scaffolding.

Modeling an activity at the same time scaffolding is provided further enhances the learning opportunity. Modeling involves physical demonstration, showing the child what needs to occur, while demonstrating the activity for the child. For example, if the activity involves using a pointer to "Read the Room," the teacher demonstrates holding the pointer, drawing it under words and pictures in the room (modeling), while telling the child

> I am going to start reading the room at the door. Even though I may not be able to read like mom, dad or the teacher, I can do kid reading, and I can say what I think words are. The first thing I see is Susan's picture with her name, "Susan" on it. When I use the pointer I hold it at this end, and I can put the other end under the word "Susan," and read it. When I come to words I cannot read, I can say what I remember about them, until I have read the room from here where I am standing at the door.

A verbal framework and a physical demonstration have been modeled and scaffolded, providing the child with positive motivation to continue exploring literacy-related activity. For some children, the teacher may have to lead them through the activity. The teacher may have to help guide the pointer so words are not skipped, verbally prompting the child with words.

Providing the child with information about how to enter a center, and about center scheduling, is part of the learning associated with participating in this learning experience.

CENTER LEARNING: ADAPTATIONS TO ENHANCE EMERGENT LITERACY

Learning environments, such as the Center, enhance opportunities to grow in emerging literacy and to interactively use the communicative arts of speaking, listening, reading, and writing. Centers are exciting learning environments for the child. At once small groups of friends gather to meet to share in an activity that has become familiar through modeling and scaffolding. Yet, there are some unresolved mysteries, choices, and a little risk available for the child to consider. Here, the child can anticipate success. Perhaps there are artifacts at the center that are so intriguing that she/he wants to carry learning beyond the classroom, sharing it with a parent or sibling, as was the case with Charlene and the ABC tote bag containing the traveling alphabet book.

In order to be an ordered environment out of which learning can occur, the center should have a designated location accessible to all, focused on a particular topic, using a prescribed routine to enter and exit, as well as to use the artifacts contained within it. Center goals and outcomes are predetermined by the teacher, with the strengths and needs of each child in mind. Several centers can be in operation at the same time in a classroom, depending on the arrangement of the room. A center may be a spot in the room, or it may be a collection of items the child carries to a particular spot to use. A Dress-up/Costuming Center, for example, may be a carton containing costuming items which can be carried from the closet to a location in the classroom for use. A Reading Center is usually a permanent classroom location outfitted with cushions, rugs, a rocking chair, and baskets of books, along with stuffed animals that can be read to.

Providing the child with information about how to enter a center, and about center scheduling, is part of the learning associated with participating in this learning experience. At the early childhood level, a 10- to 15-minute time frame is a maximum length of time to be within a center. The child can rotate from one center to another center during specific periods using charts with names and time frames to enhance movement, which is also supervised by the teacher.

Centers are most effective when there is high anticipation by the children about choices and participation. Activity in each center can be for small groups or for one child alone.

"Jason and Lor spent ten minutes at the Sequencing Center reordering loose, duplicated pictures from *Mrs. Wishy-washy* (Cowley, 1980), a story read with a small group of children in the morning. They paged through *Mrs. Wishy-washy* deciding what happened first, next, and so on. The children organized the pages and put them into plastic page savers, placing the pages in a three-ring binder to make their own book. Lor's first language is Hmong and he requires extensive language immersion activity. This activity provided Lor with an opportunity to orally plan with his partner about the organization and order of the story they were working with. The project was visual, linguistic, cooperative and was based on the auditory comprehension of a story. After the children created their picture book they sat together, turned the pages and talked about the story. They had the option of taking their book to the Shared Reading (or Library) Center, a station in close proximity to the Sequencing Center, to 'read' it to a stuffed rabbit, or to the Overhead Projector Corner, to make an overhead drawing to share," continued Nugent. This scenario took 20 minutes, and included two center activities chosen by the 4½ year-old boys.

Centers that reinforce this learning and scaffold new adventures, such as the Sequencing Center, Shared Reading Center, Library Center, Read the Room Center, and Overhead Projector Corner, extend learning through choice, movement, language interaction, art, reading and dexterity.

Sequencing Center

Goal: To provide an opportunity to understand the order of a story by looking at the pictures and placing them in sequence, and to provide children with an opportunity to work together in a small group.

Number of Children: Four children at one time.

Activity: Purchase several identical copies of inexpensive and very familiar supermarket variety books. Videos with accompanying books work well with this project when viewing is followed by reading the story. Share the story in small groups. Disassemble one copy of the book, placing each page in a plastic page saver pocket. Provide a small three-ring binder and the pages of the story at a table. The children work together to reassemble the story, telling about their decisions, placing their pages inside the binder. They can retell the story by reading it, or by retelling using the pictures as a guide. Another version of the story can be made by reordering the pages in a different way. Pages that are cut to fit inside the remaining cardboard cover can be clipped together so that another version of the story can be drawn.

Adaptation: Children who have difficulty putting items in order can be paired with children who can sequence. They can complement and enhance one another as they work together. For example, children who respond to the story though listening and viewing the video can work with children who enjoy oral interaction and planning. Together they can sequentially organize the story.

Shared Reading Center

Goal: To provide the child with an opportunity to reread, or re-experience, a familiar, class shared big book in personal ways.

Number of Children: Two children at one time.

Activity: In this center an easel displays the recently read big book. Children can decide to "reread" the book, taking turns reading it, or retelling while turning the pages, to one another. Or, they can buddy read, with one child reading a page to a partner. They can chorally read, which focuses on reading the story together.

Library Center

Goal: To engage the children in reading activity within a comfortable area of the classroom dedicated to encouraging self selection of a wide variety of children's books, enhancing reading and reading-like activity, comfort and relaxation.

Number of Children: Four at one time.

Activity: The books should represent a variety of early childhood education literature, such as picture books, big books, predictable books, fairy tales, poetry, nursery rhymes, and short stories. Books within the library center should be rotated about every 2 weeks, and the quantity should be approximately four books per child within the center. Books can be categorized by the children in plastic, color-coded cartons for ease of selection (e.g., green cartons contain books about animals; blue cartons contain books about friends and family; red cartons contain Big Books; orange cartons contain books that you can read along with, that are predictable). Books made by the children should also be included in the library center. Children should be aware of how to check out books, and they should know how long they may be inside the center. Books read to the class by the teacher should be available at the library center.

Adaptation: For the child with visual problems, or special needs in screening out external stimuli, earphones with recorded books on tape can enhance the enjoyment here. Pairing children with special needs who have beginning print awareness with children who are more aware of the conventions of print, in the sharing of a book can benefit both. The child who knows how books are read (front to back, top to bottom, left to right) can demonstrate her/his knowledge in relaxed activity as they both hold the book.

Goal: To engage the child in reading and reading-like activity involving familiar, prominently posted classroom material.

Number of Children: Four at one time.

Activity: This center comprises a container housing three pointers and three sets of lenses-out sunglasses. Children pick up the container, obtain a pointer and pair of sunglasses without lenses (optional). They walk around their classroom, pointing the pointer at posted material, "reading" it. If they are unable to read they name what they see. This causes the child to read in a continuous manner, and is a satisfying experience. Reading occurs in a soft whisper to one's self, or to an accompanying child. For example, holding a pointer, John read the calendar and said: "This is the November month, and today is Thursday." He pointed to the words as he read. He also said, "This is Calley's picture," when he pointed to his classmate's art. Prior to reading the room the teacher should provide modeling and scaffolding so that what is displayed around the room is familiar. Naming what is pointed to is as important as is actual reading. Children can walk around the room alone, or in pairs of two.

Adaptation: For children with motor impairments, a flashlight can substitute for the pointer so they can more easily participate in this activity. It should be pointed out here that the classroom must be barrier free, and the flashlight serves only to enhance bridging distance at the option of the child.

Overhead Projector Corner

Goal: To facilitate manual dexterity in the handling of materials that are used with the overhead projector, and to aid in story comprehension. This center fosters planning together and conveying ideas to others in the class.

Number of Children: Four children at one time.

Activity: Following careful modeling and scaffolding four children move to the location of the overhead projector. The projector is located in a confined space, such between two file cabinets, or in a corner. Four tickets are near the projector. When four tickets are taken no others will enter the space for the projector. Children know how to turn the machine on and off and they know that the machine casts shadows on the wall. In fact, they probably have already had a chance to experiment in this capacity! The children also know how to draw on acetate sheets. A maximum of 4–6 acetate sheets are provided to the group accompanied by washable markers in a variety of colors. The children select a familiar book to work with, and before retelling the story on the acetate sheets, they sit together to talk about the story and about who will draw what. They then plan to retell the story by illustrating major ideas on the acetate sheets. After they complete the art, they retell it using the art. During retelling the acetate sheets are displayed on the overhead. Acetates can be washed and reused by other youngsters in the class.

Adaptation: Some children require additional guidance through spatial learning activity. To enhance learning Styrofoam trays can serve as a frame for the acetate sheets and help contain the pictures.

CONCLUSION: BENEFITING THE CHILD WITH SPECIAL NEEDS

Engaging children in activities that enhance the natural progression of emergent literacy includes opportunity for active learning and participation in decision making. We know that language interaction, handling of literacy-related materials, and social communication is part of emergent literacy that can be enhanced during the scaffolding and modeling of experiences at center play. The centers presented in this article provide strong opportunity to strengthen emergent literacy through literacy-related play.

Emergent literacy early childhood classrooms with center activity support the child with special needs by providing a variety of literacy-related opportunities that build on strength (Morrow, 1993). Participation and choice are crucial elements of center activity.

Nugent's contact with 4-year-old Charlene and her family continues. Her parents, familiar with Child Find, a process that identifies children with disabilities and provides parents with information about typical childhood development, want more information about her development in the crucial area of language. Following a series of oral exchanges between Charlene and her mother observed by a trained practitioner, her family learned that she was experiencing some developmental delay in language. The observation led to the crafting of a plan (Individual Family Service Plan) intended to address her strengths and needs [to] benefit Charlene, her teachers, as well as her family.

Nugent talks about responding to Charlene's personal plan within her emergent literacy program: Charlene continues baby talk at school, even though she is 4½ years old. She sometimes does not respond to her name, and finds it hard to listen to a story in small groups during shared book reading time. After we were given information about Charlene's language differences, we focused on providing Charlene with more opportunity to listen to familiar stories followed by time for one-on-one interaction, such as we make available for her at the Sequencing Center. A variety of scaffolded and modeled experiences, designed to be brief, such as drawing on acetate with markers in response to reading and sharing this with a small group at Overhead Corner, scaffold Charlene's active language opportunities. Charlene wears a name tag, as do other children. We notice that she is calling others by their name, and responding as well to hers. As Charlene progresses at her personal rate, she will have a buddy to work with on special projects to encourage additional language interaction.

Center learning has provided Charlene, and others with special needs, with a sense of empowerment, choice, and excitement in daily learning adventures. Ideas for center learning grow throughout the school year and become part of the learning environment as needs of the children are understood and met.

REFERENCES

Allen, J., & Mason, J. (Eds.). (1989). *Risk makers, risk takers, risk breakers.* Portsmouth, NH: Heinemann.

Applebee, A. N., & Langer, J. (1983). *Instructional scaffolding: Reading and writing as natural language activities. Language Arts,* 60, 168–175.

Butler, D., & Clay, M. (1979). *Reading begins at home.* Portsmouth, NH: Heinemann.

Breen, M. J., & Fiedler, C. R. (1996). *Behavioral approach to assessment of youth with emotional/behavioral disorders.* Austin, TX: Pro-Ed.

Cowley, J. (1980). *Mrs. Wishy-washy.* Bothell, WA: Wright Group.

Clay, M. M. (1966). *Emergent reading behavior.* Doctoral dissertation, University of Auckland, New Zealand.

Morrow, L. (1993). *Literacy development in the early years: Helping children read and write.* Boston: Allyn & Bacon.

Salinger, T. (1996). *Literacy for young children.* Columbus, OH: Merrill.

Teale, W. (1982). Toward a theory of how children learn to read and write naturally. *Language Arts,* 58, 555–570.

Teale, W. (1986). The beginnings of reading and writing: Written language development during the preschool and kindergarten and preschool years. In M. Sampson (Ed.), *The pursuit of literacy: Early reading and writing.* Dubuque, IA: Kendall Hunt.

Tompkins, G. E. (1995). *Language arts: Content and teaching strategies.* Englewood Cliffs, NJ: Merrill/Prentice-Hall.

Wood, J. W. (1993). *Mainstreaming: A practical approach for teachers.* (2nd ed.). New York: Merrill/MacMillian.

Ysseldyke, J. E., & Algozzine, B. (1995). *Special education: A practical approach for teachers.* Boston: Houghton Mifflin.

Inclusion of Young Children with Special Needs In Early Childhood Education: The Research Base

Samuel L. Odom
University of North Carolina at Chapel Hill

Karen E. Diamond
Purdue University

Increasingly, early childhood programs include children with disabilities and typically developing children. The purpose of this paper is to review the recent empirical literature that underlies the practice of inclusion at the early childhood level in order to provide a context for the research articles appearing in this issue of ECRQ. We first describe the definitions of inclusion, rationales for inclusive classes, and demographics of inclusive programs and staff. Using Bronfenbrenner's ecological systems theory as a conceptual framework, we review research related to variables proximal to the program (i.e., microsystem and mesosystem levels) such as classroom practices, children's social interactions, teacher beliefs, and professional

Direct all correspondence to: Samuel L. Odom, School Education, CB-3500. University of North Carolina at Chapel Hill, Chapel Hill, NC 27599-3500.

From *Early Childhood Research Quarterly,* Vol. 13, No. 1, 1998, pp. 3-25. © 1998 by Ablex Publishing Corporation. Reprinted by permission.

collaboration. Next, we examine research associated with variables occurring more distally from the classroom program (i.e., ecosystem and macrosystem levels): families' perspectives, social policy, community and culture. We conclude this review with an examination of research that illustrates the influence of variables a[t] one level of the ecological system on those occurring at a different levels and recommend directions for future research.

When a mother brings her child to the preschool program in her community, when a child steps off the bus to go into his Head Start classroom, and when the Montessori teacher looks around the class before beginning the day's activities, they all are likely to see children with different abilities and different family backgrounds. Developmental and cultural diversity characterizes early childhood education in the late 1990s, and these themes are likely to become more prominent in the next century. Including young children with disabilities in early childhood programs is one trend that exemplifies this diversity.

Although specific references to inclusive practices were missing from the original NAEYC publication of Developmentally Appropriate Practice (Bredekamp, 1987), the most recent revision contains some strategies for including children with special needs (Bredekamp & Copple, 1997). Leaders from the fields of early childhood education and early childhood special education have collaborated to identify ways in which programs might be modified to accommodate the individual needs of children with disabilities (Allen & Schwartz, 1996; Chandler, 1994; Wolery, Strain, & Bailey, 1992; Wolery & Wilbers, 1994). Researchers have noted the similarities between accepted practices in early childhood education and early childhood special education (Fox, Hanline, Vail, & Galant, 1994; McLean & Odom, 1993), and a call for collaboration among professionals providing services for both groups of children has been clear and persistent (Bredekamp, 1993; Burton, Hains, Hanline, McLean, & McCormick, 1992; Stayton & Miller, 1993; Wolery & Bredekamp, 1994).

Given the momentum generated by this movement toward inclusion, an examination of the research that underlies practice is timely and important. The current special issue of *ECRQ* provides a venue for the most recent research on inclusion. The purpose of this introductory article is to provide an "empirical" context for the articles in this issue through a review of the recent literature that has appeared in other journals and publications. Comprehensive reviews of the literature on inclusion, integration, and mainstreaming have appeared in the past (Karnes & Lee, 1979, Odom & McEvoy, 1988; Peck & Cooke, 1983), with Buysse and Bailey (1993) and Lamorey and Bricker (1993) having conducted the most recent reviews. Our review takes up where these earlier reviews left off—with research published in the early 1990s to the present. The review focused specifically on research with young children, primarily from the toddler years through kindergarten. Also, unless authors reported conducting research with children having a single type of disability or diagnosis, the general descriptor, "children with disabilities" is used. A common practice in early childhood special education has been to identify children as having developmental delays, so often specific disability information is not available beyond a general identification of the magnitude of delay. In most cases, we report empirical research that has appeared or will appear in refereed journals, although in extending this discussion to issues of social policy, we expand our review to scholarly publications in which policy analyses appear.

CONCEPTUAL FRAMEWORK FOR REVIEW

An ecological systems framework, based on the work of Bronfenbrenner (1979), serves as the conceptual organizer for this review. Bronfenbrenner proposed that events occurring within specific settings affect children's behavior and development, and he identified these specific settings as *microsystems.* For our purposes, the microsystem is conceptualized as the inclusive classroom. Variables operating outside the immediate classroom setting influence the implementation of inclusion inside and outside the microsystem. A second level of the ecological system, identified as the *mesosystem*, consists of factors occurring in other settings in which the child or other key participants in the microsystem might participate. For example, mesosystem variables may include an event occurring in the home or family or interactions occurring among professionals outside of the immediate classroom setting (e.g., collaborative interactions among professionals).

The *exosystem,* the third ecological system level, consists of events or individual's actions occurring in settings in which microsystem participants do not participate, but which have an influence on events or actions in the microsystem. For example, social policies established by individuals not directly participating in the inclusive setting represent exosystem variables. *Macrosys-*

tem variables are cultural or societal values and beliefs that affect participants or events in the microsystem. For example, cultural values related to disability or cultural roles related to authority represent macrosystem variables. Last, influences between variables at different levels could exist and Bronfenbrenner assumed that such influences could be reciprocal (e.g., influences could go from exosystem to microsystem or visa versa). For a more in-depth discussion of the ecological systems models and inclusion research, see Peck (1993) and Odom et al. (1996). In this paper, we will follow Bronfenbrenner's lead by first examining research on microsystem variables like classroom practices and teacher beliefs, and follow this initial section with reviews of research related to meso-, exo-, and macrosystem variables (e.g., family, social policy, and cultural influences on inclusive programs). We begin with a discussion of the definition of and rationales for inclusion.

DEFINITION OF INCLUSION

A commonly agreed upon definition of inclusion does not exist, and in fact the terminology associated with inclusion has changed over the years. Programs that first placed young children with and without disabilities in early childhood classroom settings were called *integrated* (Allen, Benning, & Drummond, 1972; Bricker & Bricker 1971; Guralnick, 1976). *Mainstreaming,* a term originating in public school settings for older children, was later applied to such programs. However, Bricker (1995) has noted that the mainstreaming term has never fit exactly, because often public school programs have not provided programs for typically developing preschool-aged children (although this trend is changing). The term *inclusion* began appearing in the early 1990s (Stainback & Stainback, 1990) in part as a reaction to the way in which mainstreaming was being poorly implemented in some public school settings for elementary school-aged children, and the term was rapidly applied to early childhood programs. The definition implied a more embedded (in regular education) and comprehensive (e.g., community as well as school settings) form of involvement of children with and without disabilities than occurred in mainstreamed programs. However, when authors currently write about inclusion at the early childhood level, they tend to define inclusion in different ways (compare Bricker, 1995; Filler, 1996; Odom et al., 1996; Salisbury, 1991; Siegel, 1996).

The single commonality across definitions of inclusion is that children with and without disabilities are placed in the same setting, which is most often a classroom. The specific contexts vary across organizations (e.g., private community-based child care programs, Head Start programs, pre-kindergarten programs in public schools) and service delivery models (e.g., itinerant-direct service, itinerant-collaborative, team teaching, etc.) (Odom et al., 1997; Wolery, Holcombe et al., 1993a). The ratio of children with disabilities to typically developing children also varies; however, researchers and practitioners appear to apply the term *inclusion* most frequently to programs in which the majority of the children are typically developing. Other descriptors such as *reverse mainstreaming, inclusive early childhood special education, or integrated special education* are often applied to programs in which the majority of children have disabilities and some typically developing children are also enrolled (Odom & Speltz, 1983). In this review, we will use the terminology that authors use in their respective papers (when describing their papers) or the generic term "inclusion" when multiple papers are cited.

RATIONALES FOR INCLUSION

Educational, legal, and philosophical rationales for inclusive programs are noted by Bricker (1978) and Bailey, McWilliam, Buysse, and Wesley (1998). In practice, these rationales appear to be implemented in ways that differentially affect the nature of inclusive programs. One philosophical rationale for placing children with disabilities in inclusive settings has been that all children have the right to a life that is as *normal* as possible. This philosophical/ethical rationale emphasizes that children with disabilities should experience the same quality preschool classroom program (presumably high quality) as typically developing children (Bailey et al., 1998); that they become members of the classroom community through participation in class activities (Schwartz, 1996); and that they develop positive social relationships with class members and teachers (Guralnick, in press; Storey, 1993).

Legal and legislative issues also provide a rationale for inclusive programs for preschool children. The Individuals with Disabilities Education Act (IDEA), passed in 1986 and recently re-authorized with similar language, extended its support for special education to preschool children and maintained the provision in the earlier law that children be placed in classes with typically developing peers to the extent appropriate. In addition, the Americans with Disabilities Act has stipulated that enrollment in regular child care settings cannot be denied to children with disabilities because of their disability. In combination, these laws provided impetus for the placement of children with disabilities in settings with typically developing children. However, as will be discussed in a later section on social policy, these laws are implemented through state and local policies, which sometime create barriers to inclusion.

An educational rationale is sometimes used to support inclusion. Following this rationale, children with disabilities are placed in inclusive settings because professionals and family members believe that the developmental benefits in inclusive settings are superior to nonintegrated settings. For some of these children, however, these settings may need to be adapted (Carta, Schwartz, Atwater, & McConnell, 1991; Wolery et al, 1993b) so that learning experiences become embedded in the ongoing developmentally appropriate curriculum (Cavallaro, Haney, & Cabello, 1993). In fact, Bailey et al. (1998, this issue) propose that the question of whether or not to place a child with a disability in an inclusive program would not be an issue if professionals and parents were confident that the program was [a] high quality program and staff planned individual learning experiences to meet the children's needs.

DEMOGRAPHICS OF INCLUSION

Inclusion appears to occur frequently in this country. In a series of studies, Wolery and his colleagues have examined the frequency of inclusion and personnel involved in such programs. Employing national random sampling strategies, they have found that children with disabilities have been included in Head Start (i.e., reported by 94% of the respondents), public school prekindergarten (73% of respondents), public school kindergarten (81.5% of respondents), and community-based programs (59.2% of respondents) (Wolery et al., 1993a). Across a four year period from 1986–1990, the percentage of programs enrolling at least one child with disabilities increased from 37% to 74.2% (Wolery et al., 1993b). In a recent study of AEYC accredited preschools, McDonnell, Brownell, and Wolery (1997) found a smaller percentage (56%) of programs, than in previous survey research, enrolling children with disabilities.

Other researchers have confirmed the finding by Wolery and colleagues that inclusion occurs in different organizational settings. Buscemi, Bennet, Thomas, and Deluca (1995) and Sinclair (1993) have noted that Head Start has become a frequent setting for inclusion, which corresponds to the mandate to enroll children with disabilities given to Head Start over a quarter century ago. In some states, inclusive preschool programs are beginning to be implemented in public schools. Barnett and Frede (1993) found that in Massachusetts, 67% of the 3 and 4 year old children with disabilities were in some form of inclusive placement within the public schools. In other states (TN and CT), Brown, Horn, Heiser and Odom (1996) and Bruder, Staff, and McMurrer-Kaminer (1997) have noted that community-based child care programs serve as inclusive placements. . . .

THE MICROSYSTEM: CLASSROOM AND TEACHER VARIABLES

Inclusive early childhood classes may be seen as a microsystem within a child's social ecology. Aspects of this microsystem, such as classroom characteristics, affect children's development. These characteristics include overall quality, the make-up of the class (e.g., same-age, mixed-age), the ways that teachers arrange the classroom environment, and their teaching strategies. In the next sections, we will discuss research that has examined the influence of classroom variables on children's experiences in inclusive preschool classes.

Curriculum

In inclusive early childhood programs, the curriculum followed will affect children's participation and outcomes. As noted earlier, NAEYC (Bredekamp & Copple, 1997) has proposed developmentally appropriate curriculum guidelines for all early childhood programs, including those that include children with disabilities. In their study of the quality of developmentally appropriate practice inclusive and segregated special education early childhood classrooms, Laparo, Sexton, and Synder (1998) found the quality of developmentally appropriate practice to be moderately high in both types of programs. They found no significant differences in quality across the two groups of programs.

Providing children the freedom to select their own play activities is an aspect of developmentally appropriate practices that may have an important influence on children's development. Hauser-Cram, Bronson and Upshur (1993) conducted naturalist study of 153 children with disabilities enrolled in community-based preschool programs. In classrooms where teachers offered more choice of activities, children with disabilities engaged in "more and higher levels of peer interaction . . . and appeared to be less distracted and more persistent when involved in mastering tasks" (p. 494). Similarly, Antia, Kreimeyer, and Eldredge (1994) found more positive interactions between children with and without hearing impairments when teachers provided consistent opportunities for children to work together in the same small groups.

Mixed-age Grouping

The age-grouping of children in inclusive programs also affects children's participation and development. Roberts, Burchinal, and Bailey (1994) found that children (2-, 3-, and 4-year-olds) in mixed-age groups took more turns in conversations with partners with disabilities and received more turns from partners with disabilities than did children in same-age groups. Other research in inclusive mixed-age group, has revealed that developmental trajectories for communication, motor, and cognitive development were enhanced for younger children (Bailey, Burchinal, & McWilliam, 1993) and interactions with peers were higher for younger children (Bailey, McWilliam, Ware, & Burchinal, 1993) when compared with children in same-age groups. Furthermore, children with disabilities in mixed-aged inclusive settings engaged in higher levels of play mastery (Blasco, Bailey, & Burchinal, 1993) when compared with peers with disabilities in same-age classes. McWilliam and Bailey (1995) reported, however, that attentional engagement (i.e., attending to another child or adult or playing nearby with similar materials) was affected only modestly by age grouping, and there was no effect of age grouping on other measures of engagement.

Social Competence in Classroom Settings

In the 1970s and 1980s, most research focused on the effectiveness of different interventions in promoting cognitive, communicative, and motor outcomes for children with disabilities. When these variables were used to define outcomes for children, research demonstrated that children with disabilities benefited from early intervention, and that having a well-defined curriculum was associated with more positive outcomes for children regardless of the curriculum that was chosen (Shonkoff & Hauser-Cram, 1987). With the emergence, in the early 1980's, of social competence as an important developmental construct (Hartup, 1983), research that focused on social competence as an important outcome for children with disabilities soon followed.

Guralnick and Neville (1997) describe social competence as the way "individuals define and solve the most fundamental problems in human relationships" (p. 579). To develop social competence requires that children integrate cognitive, communication, affective and motor skills to meet their own interpersonal goals. A young child's social competence has important implications for later development, since young children's difficulties in peer interaction are predictive of social adjustment problems during later childhood and adolescence (Parker & Asher, 1987). While social competence includes cognitive (information-processing) and emotional components (Dodge, Pettit, McClaskey, & Brown, 1986), interactions with peers provide an avenue for children to put into practice their social skills.

Recent research examining social interaction among peers with and without disabilities supports earlier findings that peer interaction for children with disabilities occurs more frequently in inclusive settings than in noninclusive setting containing only children with disabilities. Using play groups of boys with mild developmental delays and boys without disabilities, Guralnick, Connor, Hammond, Gottman, and Kinnish (1996) found that all children were more interactive when in an inclusive setting than when they were in segregated settings including only children with disabilities (similar to special education preschools) or only typically developing children (similar to regular preschools). The difference was evident in the first week and was most consistently apparent for children with developmental disabilities. . . .

As noted earlier, social competence includes cognitive and emotional components, as well as peer-related behaviors. In a recent study, Diamond, Hestenes, Carpenter, & Innes (in press) examined the influence of children's participation in an inclusive preschool program on acceptance of classmates with disabilities. They found that typically developing children in inclusive classes gave higher social acceptance ratings in response to scenarios about imaginary classmates with physical and sensory disabilities than did children in noninclusive early childhood programs. Children without disabilities in both types of classes gave the highest social acceptance ratings to imaginary classmates without disabilities. To examine the relationship of acceptance ratings and children's behavior in the classroom, Okagaki,

Diamond, Kontos, & Hestenes (1988, this issue) observed children in university-based and community-based classrooms. Typically developing children with more positive attitudes toward children with disabilities (i.e., as measured through a hypothetical assessment) also played more often with children with disabilities in their class than did children with less positive attitudes. These authors also found a positive relationship between parental attitudes toward their children's play with children with disabilities and their children's interaction with children with disabilities. The studies just reported, along with recent work by Stoneman and her colleagues (Stoneman, Rugg, & Rivers, 1996) suggest that teachers and parents may play important roles in promoting children's acceptance of peers with disabilities.

Understanding the ways in which adults influence children's ideas about, and interactions with, other children is an area for future research. Bailey (1997) suggests that a primary factor that differentiates approaches to adult-child interaction, including teaching, is whether the adult (teacher or parent) assumes a directive or responsive role in relationship to the child. A question that has been of particular interest in recent years has been the ways in which such directive or responsive classroom teaching practices may promote interactions among children in inclusive classrooms . . .

Collaboration and Consultation. Cooperation, collaboration and mutual respect between "regular" and "special" early childhood teachers and therapists are important components of successful inclusive programs (Kontos & File, 1993). When receiving services and supports by consultants, early childhood teachers report preferring a consultative model rather than a medical or expert model approach (Buysse, Schulte, Pierce, & Terry, 1994). This finding is consistent with the work of Peck et al. (1993) who found that collaborative relationships among early childhood teachers and specialists were a hallmark of successful inclusive programs.

Barriers to successful collaboration also exist. In this issue, research by Stoiber, Gettinger, and Goetz (1998, this issue) suggests that limited time and opportunities for collaboration among teachers and therapists are viewed by practitioners as major barriers to inclusion. Similarly, Buysse, Wesley and Keyes (1998, this issue) found that the complexities of coordinating services for children with disabilities and their families often serves as a barrier to inclusion, at least from the perspective of practitioners and administrators. In their examination of the relationships among professionals working in inclusive programs, Lieber et al. (1997) identified a range of factors that functioned as barriers to or—alternatively—as facilitators of collaboration. These included having a shared philosophy, perceived "ownership" of the child with disabilities, staff communication, role release, and administrative support.

MESOSYSTEM VARIABLES: FAMILY PERSPECTIVES

For inclusive programs, most research related to families may be viewed as mesosystem level variables in that families represent a second microsystem context in which the child participates and which may affect the inclusive program. A rich history of research on family members' perspectives on early childhood inclusion exists (Bailey & Winton, 1987; Turnbull & Winton, 1983; Winton & Turnbull, 1981) and has been summarized well in an earlier review (Winton, 1993). The general findings across studies have been that family members: (a) have positive feelings about inclusive settings; (b) have identified some benefits for their children, and (c) share some fears or concerns about inclusive placements. . . .

EXOSYSTEM VARIABLES: SOCIAL POLICY

Social policies that affect inclusive programs often are formulated outside of the microsystem and, as such, can be considered exosystem variables. Gallagher, Harbin, Eckland, & Clifford (1994) have defined policy as: "the rules and standards that are established in order to allocate scarce public resources to meet a particular social need (p. 235)." Policies that affect preschool inclusion occur at the national (Federal regulations of Education or Head Start), state (State Departments of Education or Human Resources), and local levels (individual programs, see Smith & Rose, 1993). Kochanek and Buka (1997) noted that, along with families' desires for their child's placement, the increasing incidence of inclusion at the preschool level has been given impetus by the congressional action and statutes related to the Individual with Disabilities Education Act (PL 99-457) and Civil Rights legislation (i.e., Americans with Disabilities Act). However, the translation of national policy at the state level may also affect early childhood inclusion. Smith and Rose (1993) surveyed administrators, state policy makers, family members, and other constituents from 10 states. These respondents felt that state policies influenced most the provision of inclusive services at the local level. In their study of implementation of policy in Colorado, North Carolina, and Pennsylvania, Harbin, McWilliam, and Gallagher (in press) identified three policy factors that affected the number of children served in inclusive settings: (a) policymakers' interpretations of the federal law; (b) the emphasis (on inclusion) they choose to follow in policy development; and (c) the specificity of the policy created. . . .

Across this range of studies, key issues consistently appear as barriers. The first set of issues relates to *program standards or policies* regulating programs; such policies often require that children with disabilities be served in categorical (i.e., Special Education) classes in public school buildings. These policies have been identified as barriers that prevent placement of children in community-based or Head Start settings (Janko & Porter, 1997; Smith & Rose, 1993). *Financial or fiscal policies* represent a second set of issues; these refer to policies that prevent the use of special education funds for services involving typically developing children, the blending of funds across agencies, and the availability of funds (ACF, 1997; Bailey et al., 1998 this volume; Harvey et al., 1997; Janko & Porter, 1997; Smith & Rose, 1993). *Personnel issues and staffing* represent another policy issue that can be a barrier. For example, regulations sometimes specify that young children with disabilities be placed only in classes with a licensed special education teacher, which precludes services in many community-based or Head Start programs (ACF 1997; Harvey et al., 1997; Smith & Rose, 1993). Another personnel issue relates to *preservice and inservice training*. In several states a barrier was identified because personnel were not trained to work in inclusive early childhood programs (Harvey et al., 1997; Janko & Porter, 1997; Smith & Rose, 1993). Although not a formal policy issue, the *attitudes of policy makers and implementers* (e.g., special education administrators, program directors) toward preschool inclusion exert a major influence on the provision of services (Rose & Smith, 1993). Likewise, Kochanek and Buka (1997) found attitudes and beliefs of adults in decision making roles to be a more powerful influence on placement decisions than either the availability of community placements or the families' attitudes toward inclusion.

MACROSYSTEM VARIABLES: CULTURE AND COMMUNITY

Issues related to community and culture fall within Bronfenbrenner's conceptualization of macrosystem variables. Attention to cultural values is a key and distinctive feature of accepted practice in early childhood education (Bredekamp & Copple, 1997) and early childhood special education (McLean & Odom, 1996). However, research on the relationship between cultural values and inclusive practices is just beginning to appear. In their examination of cultural variables, Hanson et al. (1996, this issue) found that cultural beliefs influenced family members' explanations for and understanding of their child's disability; the concerns and desires by families from different cultures for their children were sometime in conflict with classroom goals; cultural differences sometimes affected the social relationships children with disabilities and families formed with others; and programs varied in how they responded to cultural diversity and difference. . . .

Separating culture, community, and family is somewhat artificial. Characteristics of the community certainly affect the availability and nature of inclusive classroom programs for young children with disabilities (Beckman et al., this issue; Hanson et al., this issue: Kochanek & Buka, 1997). However, "inclusion" as a concept extends beyond classroom settings to the broader participation of individuals with disabilities in communities (Allen & Schwartz, 1996). Research describing community participation of young children with disabilities and their families is just emerging. Ehrman, Aeschleman, and Svanum (1995) surveyed parents of children with and without disabilities about the community activities in which their children participated. Although noting similarities for the two groups, the authors found that children with disabilities participated in fewer community activities than typically developing children, with the primary difference occurring for activities related to family enrichment (e.g., eating in a restaurant, going to a movie, activity with a sibling). To examine factors in the community that may serve as barriers to or facilitators of community inclusion for young children, Beckman et al. (1998, this issue) drew upon a cross-site qualitative data base. Facilitators included the family's sense of community, school-community connections, families' social contacts, deliberate strategies to foster participation, and environmental adaptations. Factors that limited community participation included neighborhood safety and stability, limited resources, family schedules, and unavailability of peers.

CONCLUSION

The research base on early childhood inclusion in the mid- to late-1990s is extensive. While much research continues to address questions related to classroom practices and families' perspectives, the topics have expanded greatly. Studies have generated information on practical issues such as the frequency of inclusive placements, the characteristics of personnel in inclusive settings, and the barriers to and facilitators of inclusion. Important new directions in research on cultural values, community, and social policy are emerging and may well influence practice in the future.

Using Bronfenbrenner's ecological systems theory as our conceptual organizer, it seems appropriate to note that research is rich and active within system levels, and researchers are beginning to examine linkages of variables across systems. For example, Janko, Schwartz, Sandall, Anderson, and Cottam (1997) examined the organizational features (i.e., policies, rules and regulations) of inclusive programs (an exosystem variable) and their linkages to the way inclusion occurred at the classroom level (microsystem). Kochanek, Harbin, and their colleagues have examined how social policy characteristics (exosystem) affect program provision (microsystem) (Harbin, McWilliams & Gallagher in press; Kochanek & Buka, 1997). In a study that illustrates the reciprocal influences across system variables, Harvey et al. (1997) described a process by which factors operating at the local program level (microsystem) influenced the development of policy at the state level (exosystem level), which in turn influenced local program practice. Hanson and colleagues (1998, this issue) have begun to examine cultural values (macrosystem) and issues within classrooms (microsystem). This systems analysis of factors related to inclusion may well contribute to our understanding of how inclusive programs work well for children and families and the range of factors related to such operation.

The emerging themes for future research come from each level of the ecological system model Bronfenbrenner proposed. At the microsystem level, specific practices for promoting developmental outcomes for children and for influencing the quality of inclusive settings are fertile areas for future research. At the mesosystem level, research on strategies for collaboration among professionals and between professionals and families will contribute strongly to the implementation of inclusive programs. At the exosystem level, research on the development and implementation of social policy, the reciprocal influences between policy and practice, the analysis of costs and flexible models for funding may well serve as the foundation for future inclusive programs. At the macrosystem level, our understanding of how cultural and linguistic diversity affect inclusive preschool programs is just beginning to become apparent. The significant and far reaching challenge for investigators in the future will be to step beyond the research *within* levels to examine how linkages *across* levels affect the everyday experiences of children in inclusive early childhood programs and their families.

Acknowledgment: Support for preparation of this paper was provided by Grant No. HO24K60001-97 from the U.S. Department of Education. The authors wish to thank Ruth Wolery and Sylvia Mewborn for assistance in final preparation of this manuscript.

REFERENCES

Administration for Children and Families. (1995). *Passages to inclusion.* Washington, DC: Administration for Children and Families Child Care Bureau (Available on WWW through http://ericps.crc.uiuc.edu/ncci/nccicome.html).

Allen, K. E., Benning, P. M., & Drummond, W. T. (1972). Integration of normal and handicapped children in a behavior modification preschool: A case study. In G. Semb (Ed.), *Behavior analysis and education* (pp. 127–141). Lawrence, KS: University of Kansas.

Allen, K. E., & Schwartz, I. S. (1996). *The exceptional child: Inclusion in early childhood education,* 3rd Ed. Boston: Del Mar Publishers.

Antia, S. D., Kreimeyer, K. H.,& Eldredge, N. (1994). Promoting social interaction between young children with hearing impairments and their peers. *Exceptional Children, 60,* 262–275.

Arnold, D., & Tremblay, A. (1979). Interaction of deaf and hearing preschool children. *Journal of Communication Disorders, 12,* 245–251.

Bailey, D. B., & Winton, P. (1987). Stability and change in parents' expectations about mainstreaming. *Topics in Early Childhood Special Education, 7,* 73–88.

Bailey, D. B. (1996). An overview of interdisciplinary training. In D. Bricker & A. Widerstrom (Eds.), *Preparing personnel to work with infants and young children and their families: A team approach,* (pp. 3–22). Baltimore, MD: Paul Brookes.

Bailey, D. B. (1997). Evaluating the effectiveness of curriculum alternatives for infants and preschoolers at risk. In M. J. Guralnick (Ed.), *The effectiveness of early intervention* (pp. 227–248). Baltimore, MD: Paul H. Brookes.

Bailey, D. B., Burchinal, M. R., & McWilliam, R. A. (1993). Age of peers and early childhood development. *Child Development, 64,* 848–862.

Bailey, D. B., McWilliam, R. A., Buysse, V., & Wesley, P. W. (1988). Inclusion in the context of competing values in early childhood education. *Early Childhood Research Quarterly, 15*(1).

Bailey, D. B., McWilliam, R. A., Ware, W. B., & Burchinal, M. A. (1993). The social interactions of toddlers and preschoolers in same-age and mixed-age play groups. *Journal of Applied Developmental Psychology, 14,* 261–276.

Barnett, W. S., & Frede, E. C. (1993). Early childhood programs in the public schools: Insights from a state survey. *Journal of Early Intervention, 17,* 396–413.

Beckman, P., Barnwell, D., Horn, E., Hanson, M., Gutierrez, S., & Lieber, J. (1998). Communities, families, and inclusion. *Early Childhood Research Quarterly, 15*(1).

Bennett, T., Delucca, D., & Bruns, D. (1997). Putting inclusion into practice: Perspectives of teachers and parents. *Exceptional Children, 64,* 115–131.

Bennett, T., Lee, H. & Lueke, B. (in press). Expectations and concerns: What mothers and fathers say. *Education and Training in Mental Retardation and Other Developmental Disabilities.*

Blasco, P. M., Bailey, D. B., & Burchinal, M. R. (1993). Dimensions of mastery in same-age and mixed-age integrated classrooms. *Early Childhood Research Quarterly, 8,* 193–206.

Bredekamp, S. (1987). *Developmentally appropriate practice in early childhood programs serving children from birth through age 8.* Washington, D.C. NAEYC.

Bredekamp, S. (1993). The relationship between early childhood education and early childhood special education: Healthy marriage or family feud? *Topics in Early Childhood Special Education, 13*(3), 258–273.

Bredekamp, S., & Copple, C. (1997). *Developmentally appropriate practice in early childhood programs,* Revised ed. Washington, D.C.: National Association for the Education of Young Children.

Bricker, D. D. (1978). A rationale for the integration of handicapped and nonhandicapped preschool children, in M. Guralnick (Ed.), *Early intervention and the integration of handicapped and nonhandicapped children* (pp. 3–26). Baltimore, MD: University Park Press.

Bricker, D. (1995). The challenge of inclusion. *Journal of Early Intervention, 19,* 179–194.

Bricker, D., & Bricker, W. (1971). Toddler Research and Intervention Project Report—Year 1. *IMRID Behavioral Science Monograph No. 20,* Nashville, TN: Institute on Mental Retardation and Intellectual Development, 1971.

Bronfenbrenner, U. (1979). *The ecology of human development: Experiments by nature and design.* Cambridge, MA: Harvard University Press.

Brown, W. H., Horn, E. M., Heiser, J. G., & Odom, S. L. (1996). Project BLEND: An inclusive model of early intervention services. *Journal of Early Intervention, 20,* 364–375.

Bruder, M. B., Staff, I., & McMurrer-Kammer, E. (1997). Toddlers receiving early intervention in child care centers: A description of a service delivery system. *Topics in Early Childhood Special Education, 17,* 185–208.

Burton, C. B., Hains, A. H., Hanline, M. F., McLean, M., & McCormick, K. (1992). Early childhood intervention and education: The urgency of professional unification. *Topics in Early Childhood Special Education, 11*(4), 53–69.

Buscemi, L.,Bennett, T., Thomas, D., & Deluca, D. A. (1995). Head Start: Challenges and training needs. *Journal of Early Intervention, 20,* 1–13.

Buysee, V., & Bailey, D. B. (1993). Behavioral and developmental outcomes in young children with disabilities in integrated and segregated settings: A review of comparative studies. *Journal of Special Education, 26,* 434–461.

Buysse, V. (1993). Friendships of preschoolers with disabilities in community-based child care settings. *Journal of Early Intervention, 17,* 380–395.

Buysse, V., Bailey, D. B., Smith, T. M., & Simeonsson, R. J. (1994). The relationship between child characteristics and placement in specialized versus inclusive early childhood programs. *Topics in Early Childhood Special Education, 14,* 419–435.

Buysse,V., Schulte, A. C., Pierce, P. P., & Terry, D. (1994). Models and styles of consultation: Preferences of professionals in early intervention. *Journal of Early Intervention, 18,* 302–310.

Buysse, V., Wesley, P., Keyes, L., & Bailey, D. B. (1996). Assessing the comfort zone of child care teachers in serving young children with disabilities. *Journal of Early Intervention, 20,* 189–203.

Buysse, V., Wesley, P. W., & Keyes, L. (1998). Implementing early childhood inclusion: Barrier and support factors. *Early Childhood Research Quarterly, 13*(1), 169–184.

Carta, J. J., Schwartz, I. S., Atwater, J. B., & McConnell, S. R. (1991). Developmentally appropriate practice: Appraising its usefulness for young children with disabilities. *Topics in Early Childhood Special Education, 11*(1), 1–20.

Cavallaro, C. C., Haney, M., & Cabello, B. (1993). Developmentally appropriate strategies for promoting full participation in early childhood settings. *Topics in Early Childhood Special Education, 13,*293–307.

Chandler, P.A. (1994). *A place for me: Including children with special needs in early care and education settings.* Washington, D.C.: National Association for the Education of Young Children.

Cole, K. N., Mills, P. E., Dale, P. S., & Jenkins, J. R. (1991). Effects of preschool integration for children with disabilities. *Exceptional Children, 58,* 36–45.

Derman-Sparks, L. And the A.B.C. Task Force (1989). *Anti-Bias Curriculum: Tools for empowering young children.* Washington, D.C.: NAEYC.

Diamond, K., Hestenes, L., Carpenter, E., & Innes, F. (in press). Relationships between enrollment in an inclusive class and preschool children's ideas about people with disabilities. *Topics in Early Childhood Special Education.*

Dodge, K. A., Petit, G. S., McClaskey, C. L., & Brown, M. M. (1986). Social competence in children. *Monographs of the Society for Research in Child Development, 51,* (2, Serial No. 213).

Ehrmann, L., Aeschleman, S., & Svanum, S. (1995). Parental reports of community activity patterns: A comparison between young children with disabilities and their nondisabled peers. *Research in Developmental Disabilities, 16,* 331–343.

English, K., Goldstein, H., Schafer, K., & Kaczmarek, L. (1997). Promoting interactions among preschoolers with and without disabilities: Effects of a buddy skills-training program. *Exceptional Children, 63,* 229–243.

Erwin, E. J. (1993). Social participation of young children with visual impairment in specialized and integrated environments. *Journal of Visual Impairments and Blindness, 87,* 138–142.

Favazza, P. C., & Odom, S. L. (1997). Promoting positive attitudes of kindergarten-age children toward people with disabilities. *Exceptional Children, 63,* 405–418.

Filler, J. (1996). A comment on inclusion: Research and social policy. *Social Policy Report: Society for Research in Child Development, 10(2 & 3),* 31–33.

File, N. (1994). Children's play, teacher-child interactions, and teacher beliefs in integrated early childhood programs. *Early Childhood Research Quarterly, 9,* 223–240.

File, N., & Kontos, S. (1993). The relationship of program quality to children's play in integrated early intervention settings. *Topics in Early Childhood Special Education, 13,* 1–18.

Fishbein, H. D., & Imai, S. (1993). Preschoolers select playmates on the basis of gender and race. *Journal of Applied Developmental Psychology, 14,* 303–316.

Fox, L., Hanline, M. F., Vail, C. O., & Galant, K. R. (1994). Developmentally appropriate practice: Applications for young children with disabilities. *Journal of Early Intervention, 18,* 243–257.

Gallagher, J. J., Harbin, G., Eckland, J., & Clifford, R. (1994). State diversity and policy implementation: Infants and toddlers. In L. Johnson, et al. (Eds.), *Meeting early intervention challenges: Issues from birth to three,* (pp. 235–250). Baltimore: Paul H. Brookes.

Gemmel-Crosby, S., & Handik, J. R. (1994). Preschool teachers' perceptions of including children with disabilities. *Education and Training in Mental Retardation, 19,* 279–290.

Goldstein, H., Kaczmarek, L. A., & Hepting, N. H. (1996). Indicators of quality in communication interventions. In S. Odom & M. McLean (Eds.), *Early intervention and early childhood special education: Recommended practices* (pp. 197–221). Austin, TX: PRO-ED.

Graham, M. A., & Bryant, D. M. (1993). Characteristics of quality, effective service delivery systems for children with special needs. In D. M. Bryant & M. A. Graham (Eds.), *Implementing early intervention: From research to effective practice* (pp. 233–252). NY: Guilford Press.

Guralnick, M. J. (in press). The nature and meaning of social integration for young children with mild developmental delays in inclusive settings. *Journal of Early Intervention.*

Guralnick, M. J. (1976). The value of integrating handicapped and nonhandicapped preschool children. *American Journal of Orthopsychiatry, 46,* 236–245.

Guralnick, M. J. (1994). Mothers' perceptions of the benefits and drawbacks of early childhood mainstreaming. *Journal of Early Intervention, 18,* 168–183.

Guralnick, M. J. (1997). Second generation research in the field of early intervention. In M. Guralnick (Id.), *The effectiveness of early intervention* (pp. 3–23), Baltimore: Paul H. Brookes.

Guralnick, M. J., Connor, R., & Hammond, M. (1995). Parents' perspectives of peer relations and friendships in integrated and specialized programs. *American Journal on Mental Retardation, 99,* 457–476.

Guralnick, M. J., Connor, R. T., Hammond, M. A., Gottman, J. M., & Kinnish, K. (1996a). Immediate effects of mainstreamed settings on the social interactions and social integration of preschool children. *American Journal on Mental Retardation, 100,* 359–377.

Guralnick, M. J., Gottman, J. M., & Hammond, M. A. (1996b). Effects of social setting on the friendship formation of young children differing in developmental status. *Journal of Applied Developmental Psychology, 17,* 625–651.

Guralnick, M. J. & Neville, B. (1997). Designing early intervention programs to support children's social competence. In M. Guralnick (Ed.), *The effectiveness of early intervention* (pp. 579–610). Baltimore, MD: Paul H. Brookes.

Hanline, M. F. (1993). Inclusion of preschoolers with profound disabilities. An analysis of children's interactions. *Journal of the Association for Persons with Severe Handicaps, 18,* 28–35.

Hanson, M. J., Guitierrez, S., Morgan, M., Brennan, E. L., & Zercher, C. (1997). Language, culture, and disability: Interacting influences on preschool inclusion. *Topics in Early Childhood Special Education, 17,* 307–336.

Hanson, M. J., Wolfberg, P., Zercher, C., Morgan, M., Gutierrez, S., Barnwell, D., & Beckman, P. (1998). The culture of inclusion: Recognizing diversity at multiple levels. *Early Childhood Research Quarterly, 13* (1), 185–210.

Hartup, W. (1983). Peer relations. In E. M. Hetherington (Ed.), P. H. Mussen (Series Ed.), *Handbook of child psychology,* Vol 4: *Socialization, personality, and social development* (pp. 103–196). New York: John Wiley.

Harbin, G. L., McWilliam, R. A., & Gallagher, J. (in press). Services to young children with disabilities: A descriptive analysis. In S. Meisels & J. Shonkoff (Eds.), *Handbook of early childhood intervention,* 2nd ed. New York: Cambridge University Press.

Harvey, J., Voorhees, M. D., & Landon, T. (1997). The role of the State Department of Education in promoting integrated placement options for preschoolers: Views from the field. *Topics in Early Childhood Special Education, 17,* 387–409.

Hauser-Cram, P., Bronson, M. B., & Upshur, C. C. (1993). The effects of the classroom environment on the social and mastery behavior of preschool children with disabilities. *Early Childhood Research Quarterly, 8,* 479–498.

Hundert, J., Mahoney, B., Mundy, F., & Vernon, M. L. (1998). A descriptive analysis of developmentally appropriate and social gains of children with severe disabilities in segregated and inclusive preschools in southern Ontario. *Early Childhood Research Quarterly,* 13 (1).

Hundert, J., Mahoney, W. J., & Hopkins, B. (1993). The relationship between the peer interaction of children with disabilities in integrated preschools and research and classroom teacher behaviors. *Topics in Early Childhood Special Education, 13,* 328–343.

Janko, S., & Porter, A. (Eds.). (1997). *Portraits of inclusion through the eyes of children, families, and educators.* Seattle, WA: Early Childhood Research Institute on Inclusion.

Janko, S., Schwartz, I., Sandall, S., Anderson, K., & Cottam, C. (1997). Beyond microsystems: Unanticipated lessons about the meaning of inclusion. *Topics in Early Childhood Special Education, 17,* 286–306.

Johnson, R., & Johnson, D. W. (1986). Building friendships between handicapped and nonhandicapped students: Effects of cooperative and individualistic instruction. *American Educational Research Journal, 18,* 415–424.

Karnes, M. D, & Lee, R. C. (1979). Mainstreaming in the preschool. In L. Katz (Ed.), *Current topics in early childhood education, Vol. 2* (pp. 13–42). Norwood, NJ: Ablex.

Kochanek, T. T., & Buka, S. L. (1997). *Influential factors in inclusive versus noninclusive placements for preschool children with disabilities.* Manuscript submitted for publication.

Kontos, S., & File, N. (1993). Staff development in support of integration. In C. Peck, S. Odom, & D. Bricker (Eds.), *Integration of young children with disabilities into community programs* (pp. 169–186). Baltimore: Paul H. Brookes.

Lamorey, S., & Bricker, D. D. (1993). Integrated programs: Effects on young children and their parents. In C. Peck, S. Odom, & D. Bricker, (Eds.), *Integrating young children with disabilities into community-based programs: From research to implementation* (pp. 249–269). Baltimore: Paul H. Brookes.

LaParo, K. M., Sexton, D., & Snyder, P. (1998). Program quality characteristics in segregated and inclusive early childhood settings. *Early Childhood Research Quarterly, 13* (1), 151–168.

Lieber, J., Beckman, P. J., Hanson, M. J., Janko, S., Marquart, J. M., Horn, E., & Odom, S. L. (1997) The impact of changing roles on relationship between professionals in inclusive programs for young children. *Early Education and Development, 8,* 67–82.

Lieber, J., Capell, K., Sandall, S. R., Wolfberg, P., Horn, E., & Beckman, P. (1998). Inclusive preschool programs: Teachers' beliefs and practices. *Early Childhood Research Quarterly.*

Maccoby, E. E. (1988). Gender as a social category. *Developmental Psychology, 55,* 755–765.

McConnell, S. R., Sisson, L. A., Cort, C. A., & Strain, P. S. (1991). Effects of social skills training and contingency management on reciprocal interaction of preschool children with handicaps. *Journal of Special Education, 24,* 473–495.

McDonnell, A. P., Brownell, K., & Wolery, M. (1997). Teaching experience and specialist support: A survey of preschool teachers employed in programs accredited by NAEYC. *Topics in Early Childhood Special Education, 17,* 263–285.

McLean, M. E., & Odom, S. L. (1996). Establishing recommended practices in early intervention/early childhood special education. In S. Odom & M. McLean (Eds.), *Early intervention and early childhood special education: Recommended practices* (pp. 1–22). Austin, TX: PRO-ED.

McLean, M. E., & Odom, S. L. (1993). Practices for young children with and without disabilities; A comparison of DEC and NAEYC identified practices. *Topics in Early Childhood Special Education, 13,* 274–293.

McWilliam, R. A., & Bailey, D. B. (1995). Effects of classroom structure and disability on engagement. *Topics in Early Childhood Special Education, 15,* 123–147.

McWilliam, R. A., Lang, L., Vandeviere, P., Angell, R., Collins, L., & Underdown, G. (1995). Satisfaction and struggles: Family perceptions of early intervention services. *Journal of Early Intervention, 19,* 43–60.

Miller, L. J., Strain, P. S., Boyd, K., Hunsicker, S., McKinley, J., & Wu, A. (1992). Parental attitudes toward integration. *Topics in Early Childhood Special Education, 12,* 230–246.

Odom, S. L., & McEvoy, M. A. (1988). Integration of young children with handicaps and normally developing children. In S. Odom & M. Karnes (Eds.), *Early intervention for infants and children with handicaps: An empirical base* (pp. 241–268). Baltimore: Paul H. Brookes.

Odom, S. L., & Speltz, M. L. (1983). program variations in preschools for handicapped and nonhandicapped children: Mainstreaming vs. integrated special education. *Analysis and Intervention in Developmental Disabilities, 3,* 89–104.

Odom, S. L., Horn, E. M., Marquart, J., Hanson, M. J., Wolfberg, P., Beckman, P., Lieber, J., Li, S., Schwartz, I., Janko, S., & Sandall, S. (1997). *On the definition(s) of inclusion: Organizational context and service delivery models.* Manuscript submitted for publication.

Odom, S. L., Peck, C. A., Hanson, M., Beckman, P. J., Kaiser, A. P., Lieber, J., Brown, W. H., Horn, E. M., & Schwartz, I. S. (1996). Inclusion at the preschool level: An ecological systems analysis. *Social Policy: Society for Research on Child Development, 10 (2 & 3),* 18–30.

Okagaki, L, Diamond, K. E., Kontos, S. J., & Hestenes, L. L. (1988). Correlates of young children's interactions with classmates with disabilities. *Early Childhood Research Quarterly, 13* (1), 67–86.

Parker, J. G., & Asher, S. R. (1987). Peer relations and later personal adjustment: Are low-accepted children at risk? *Psychological Bulletin, 102,* 357–389.

Peck, C. A. (1993). Ecological perspectives on the implementation of integrated early childhood programs. In C. Peck, S. Odom, & D. Bricker, (Eds.), *Integrating young children with disabilities into community-based programs: From research to implementation* (pp. 3–15). Baltimore: Paul H. Brookes.

Peck, C. A., & Cooke, T. P. (1983). Benefits of mainstreaming at the early childhood level: How much can we expect? *Analysis and Intervention in Development Disabilities, 3,* 1–22.

Peck, C. A., Carlson, P., & Helmstetter, E. (1992). Parent and teacher perceptions of outcomes for typically developing children enrolled in early childhood programs: A statewide survey. *Journal of Early Intervention, 16,* 53–63.

Peck, C. A., Furman, G. C., & Helmstetter, E. (1993). Integrated early childhood programs: Research on the implementation of change in organizational contexts. In C. Peck, S. Odom, & D. Bricker (Eds.), *Integration of young children with disabilities into community programs* (pp. 187–206). Baltimore: Paul H. Brookes.

Ramsey, P. G., & Myers, L. C. (1990). Salience of race in young children's cognitive, affective, and behavioral responses to social environments. *Journal of Applied Developmental Psychology, 11,*49–67.

Roberts, J. E., Burchinal, M. R., Bailey, D. B. (1994). Communication among preschoolers with and without disabilities in same-age and mixed-aged classes. *American Journal on Mental Retardation, 99,* 231–249.

Rose, D. F., & Smith, B. J. (1993). Preschool mainstreaming: Attitude barriers and strategies for addressing them. *Young Children, 48* (4), 59–62.

Salisbury, C. L. (1991). Mainstreaming during the early childhood years. *Exceptional Children, 58,* 146–155.

Schwartz, I. S. (1996). Expanding the zone: Thoughts about social validity and training. *Journal of Early Intervention, 20,* 204–205.

Siegel, B. (1996). Is the emperor wearing clothes? Social policy and the empirical support of full inclusion of children with disabilities in the preschool and early elementary grades. *Social Policy Report: Society for Research in Child Development, 10 (1 & 2),* 2–17.

Shonkoff, J. P., & Hauser-Cram, P. (1987). Early intervention for disabled infants and their families: A quantitative analysis. *Pediatrics, 80,* 650–658.

Sinclair, E. (1993). Early identification of preschoolers with special needs in Head Start. *Topics in Early Childhood Special Education, 13,* 184–201.

Smith, B. J., & Rose, D. F. (1993). *Administrator's policy handbook for preschool mainstreaming.* Cambridge, MA: Brookline Books.

Stainback, W., & Stainback, S. (Eds), (1990). *Support networks for inclusive schooling: Interdependent integrated education.* Baltimore, MD: Paul H. Brookes.

Stayton, V. D., & Miller, P. S. (1993). Combining general and special early childhood education standards in personnel preparation programs: Experience of two states. *Topics in Early Childhood Special Education, 13,* 372–387.

Stoiber, K. C., Gettinger, M., & Goetz, D. (1998). Exploring factors influencing parents' and early childhood practitioners' beliefs about inclusion. *Early Childhood Research Quarterly.*

Stoneman, Z., Rugg, M. E., & Rivers, J. (1996, December). *How do young children learn about peers with disabilities? Examining the role of parents as teachers of values, attitudes and prosocial behavior.* Paper presented at the International Early Childhood Conference on Children with Special Needs.

Storey, K. (993). A proposal for assessing integration. *Education and Training in Mental Retardation, 28,* 279–287.

Task Force on Recommended Practices (1993). *DEC Recommended Practices: Indicators of quality in programs for infants and young children with special needs and their families.* Reston, VA: Council for Exceptional Children.

Turnbull, A. P., & Winston, P. (1983). A comparison of specialized and mainstreamed preschools from perspectives of parents of handicapped children. *Journal of Pediatric Psychology, 8,* 57–71.

Winton, P. J. (1993). Providing family support in integrated settings: Research and recommendations. In C. A. Peck, S. L. Odom, & D. D. Bricker, (Eds.), *Integrating young children with disabilities into community programs: Ecological perspectives on research and implementation* (pp. 65–80). Baltimore: Brookes.

Winton, P. J., & Turnball, A. (1981). Parent involvement as viewed by parents of handicapped children. *Topics in Early Childhood Special Education, 1* (2), 11–20.

Wolery, M., & Bredekamp, S. (1994). Developmentally appropriate practice and young children with disabilities: Contextual issues in the discussion. *Journal of Early Intervention, 18,* 331–341.

Wolery, M., Holcombe, A., Brookfield, S., Huffman, K., Schroeder, C., Martin, C. G., Venn, M. L., Weits, M. G., & Fleming, L. A. (1993). The extent and nature of preschool mainstreaming: A survey of general early educators. *Journal of Special Education,* 27, 222–234.

Wolery, M. R., Martin, C. G., Schroeder, C., Huffman, K., Venn, M. L., Holcombe, A., Brookfield, J., & Fleming, L. A. (1994a). Employment of educators in preschool mainstreaming: A survey of general early educators. *Journal of Early Intervention, 18,* 64–77.

Wolery, M., Holcombe, A., Venn, M. L., Brookfield, J., Huffman, K., Schroeder, C., Martin, C. G., & Fleming, L. A. (1993). Mainstreaming in early childhood programs. Current status and relevant issues. *Young Children, 49,* 78–84.

Wolery, M., Strain, P. S., & Bailey, D. B. (1992). Reaching potentials of children with special needs. In S. Bredekamp & T. Rosegrant (Eds.), *Reaching potentials: Appropriate curriculum and assessment for young children,* Vol. 1 (pp. 92–113). Washington, D.C.: National Association for the Education of Young Children.

Wolery, M., Venn, M. L., Schroeder, C., Holcombe, A., Huffman, K., Martin, C. G., Brookfield, J., & Fleming, L. A. (1994b). A survey of the extent to which speech-language pathologists are employed in preschool programs. *Language, Speech, and Hearing Services in Schools, 25,* 2–8.

Wolery, M., & Wilbers, J. S. (1994). *Including children with special needs in early childhood programs.* Washington, D.C.: National Association for the Education of Young Children.

Unit 4

Unit Selections

Key Points to Consider

❖ When is the best time to try to change a child's challenging behaviors?
v What are the reasons for young children's diminishing motivation as they reach school age?

❖ What television programs did you watch as a young child? How violent were they? What television programs do young children watch today? How violent are they?

❖ In order to work effectively with a child who has been traumatized by violence, what characteristics does a teacher need to display?

Links **www.dushkin.com/online/**

21. **Child Welfare League of America (CWLA)**
http://www.cwla.org
22. **Early Intervention Solutions (EIS)**
http://www.earlyintervention.com
23. **National Network for Family Resiliency**
http://www.nnfr.org

These sites are annotated on pages 4 and 5.

Guiding and Supporting Young Children

Early childhood teaching is all about problem-solving. Just as children work to solve problems, so do teachers. Every day, teachers make decisions about how to guide children socially and emotionally. In attempting to determine what could be causing a child's emotional distress, teachers must take into account a myriad of factors. They consider physical, social, environmental, and emotional factors in addition to the surface behavior of a child. Whether it's an individual child's behavior or interpersonal relationships, the pressing problems involve complex issues that require careful reflection and analysis. Even the most mature teachers spend many hours thinking and talking about the best ways to guide young children's behavior: What should I do about the child who is out of bounds? What do I say to parents who want their child punished? Should intrinsic motivation be taught to every child? How do I guide a child who has experienced violence and now acts out violently?

Teachers who work with children whose behavior is challenging can serve as a protective presence and increase children's resilience. This is the premise of the lead article, "The Why and Wherefore." Information from a national study supports the strategies given in this article for dealing with challenging behaviors of young children. Regardless of the risk factors leading to challenging behavior, it is never helpful to blame the child. High expectations and support are much more productive in helping children to develop coping skills.

Conflict resolution and social responsibility are important skills for all of us, whether adult or child. Teaching children to live at peace starts in the preschool classroom by helping children to be generous to each other and teaching through community projects. Teachers can learn techniques for conflict resolution to incorporate into the routines of everyday classroom life. They can also integrate peace into the curriculum in a variety of ways, according to author Anarella Cellitti in her article, "Teaching Peace Concepts to Children."

Viewing violence, whether in real life or on television, makes children more aggressive. They may believe they are unable to control their own behavior and blame themselves for the violent events they have witnessed. Two articles in this unit deal with the latest research on the effects of violence on young children. "Television Violence and Its Effects on Young Children" is a thorough discussion of the links between children's behavior and programming for young children. We now know that television violence can lead to imitating violent acts in real life, for it is the actions, not the plot, that children remember. In "Adverse Effects of Witnessing Violence," Victor LaCerva defines the brain's response to trauma. Many children become fearful and less sensitive as a result of violence, while others become angry and emotional. Unfortunately, what we know about violence is not being effectively translated into action against it. These articles outline important recommendations for guiding individual children and for banding together to decrease the amount of violence in children's lives.

The theory article for this unit is "Fostering Intrinsic Motivation in Early Childhood Classrooms." It is an in-depth review of the patterns of motivation established during the early childhood years. Martha Carlton and Adam Winsler's premise is that young children are born with an innate need to interact with the environment, yet this need diminishes as children reach school age. The authors include a comprehensive definition of mastery motivation at four age ranges and conclude with principles for fostering the development of intrinsic motivation in early childhood programs.

The Why and Wherefore

from

Meeting the Challenge

EFFECTIVE STRATEGIES FOR CHALLENGING BEHAVIORS IN EARLY CHILDHOOD ENVIRONMENTS

Project Manager: Anne Maxwell, Director of Information Services, Canadian Child Care Federation
Authors: Barbara Kaiser and Judy Sklar Rasminsky

What is challenging behaviour?

Challenging behaviour is any behaviour that:

- interferes with children's learning, development and success at play;
- is harmful to the child, other children or adults;
- puts a child at high risk for later social problems or school failure.[1]

Estimates of the prevalence rate of aggressive and antisocial behaviour among preschool-age children range from 3 to 15 percent.[2]

We have limited our focus to aggressive behaviours, but many of the ideas here work equally well with children who have timid and withdrawn behaviours, which certainly also qualify as challenging.

But isn't this behaviour sometimes appropriate for the child's age?

Human beings are not born with social skills; they learn them. Very small children don't have words to express their feelings and needs. They don't yet connect actions to consequences, they are impulsive and self-centered, and even though they may notice others' feelings, they don't begin to develop the ability to empathize until they are about two years old.[3] They use any means at their disposal to get what they want and to make themselves understood. The National Longitudinal Survey of Children and Youth, a random sample of 22,831 children living in Canada, found that physical aggression starts at

A Rose by Any Other Name

Challenging behaviour can be direct (like hitting, pushing, biting, pinching, kicking, spitting or hair-pulling) or indirect (like bullying, teasing, ignoring rules or instructions, spreading rumours, excluding others,[6] name-calling, destroying objects, refusing to share, not paying attention or having temper tantrums). Now we call these behaviours "challenging," but we've also labeled them—or the children who use them—as:

difficult	*aggressive*
unsociable	*violent*
antisocial	*assaultive*
a handful	*low threshold*
high needs	*high impulsive*
bad	*oppositional*
out of control	*non-compliant*
acting out	*mean*
hard to manage	*problem*
at risk	*attention-seeking*
disruptive	*willful*

Excerpted from *Meeting the Challenge: Effective Strategies for Challenging Behaviors in Early Childhood Environments*, 1999, pp. 7-14.

about nine months and peaks between 27 and 29 months, when 53.3 percent of boys and 41.1 percent of girls try it out.[4] By about the age of three, most children learn to use alternative, prosocial strategies rather than physical aggression.[5]

What causes challenging behaviour?

Theories about the origin and development of aggressive behaviour abound. Some emphasize social learning, others cognition, problem-solving or attachment. The only certainty is that the causes of challenging behaviour are extremely complex and intricately interconnected.

However, research does show that certain factors increase a child's risk for developing challenging behaviour. The factors fall into two broad categories, biological and environmental.

Biological risk factors

- *Pregnancy complications, perinatal stress, prematurity, birth trauma and congenital defects* may put children at risk by causing neurological damage.[7]
- *When mothers use drugs, drink alcohol or smoke during pregnancy,* their children are at increased risk for behavioural, cognitive, learning and developmental problems. Babies exposed to cocaine and babies with Fetal Alcohol Syndrome (FAS) or Fetal Alcohol Effects (FAE) may exhibit severe and long-lasting effects."[8]
- *Developmental delays, especially language delays,* are often associated with challenging behaviours. Studies report a 50 percent overlap between language delays and behaviour problems.[9] Sensory integration problems—which include poor motor coordination, hypersensitivity to sensation, distractibility, hyperactivity and slow speech—may also be linked to challenging behaviours.[10]
- *Attention deficit disorder (ADD) and attention-deficit hyperactivity disorder (ADHD)* can also contribute to antisocial and violent behaviour.[11] ADD/ADHD is a neurological syndrome whose major symptoms include inattention, impulsivity and sometimes hyperactivity. Now thought to be largely genetic,[12] it isn't usually diagnosed until a child is at least five, although the hyperactive symptoms appear earlier.[13]
- *Temperament* is a significant factor. In 1956 New York University psychiatrists Alexander Thomas and Stella Chess began the first longitudinal study of personality traits and discovered that children are born with distinct temperaments. Thomas and Chess identified three types: easy, difficult and slow to warm up.

  In trying to figure out why only half of the children with difficult temperaments developed emotional or behavioural disturbances, Thomas and Chess evolved the concept of "goodness of fit": serious problems are more likely to arise, they said, when the temperament of the child and the expectations of the parent or caregiver are out of sync. A child's temperament has a major impact on her environment—caregivers included.[14]
- *Gender* plays a part in challenging behaviour, but it's not clear whether this is a matter of biology or environment. In the National Longitudinal Survey, boys rated higher than girls on physical aggression in every age group,[15] but aggressive behaviour in girls is becoming more common.[16]

Environmental risk factors

- *Poverty and the social conditions surrounding it*—poor housing, poor nutrition, parental unemployment, victimization, discrimination—provide fertile ground for challenging behaviours.[17] According to the National Longitudinal Survey, "Boys and girls from the lowest socioeconomic levels clearly had the highest physical aggression scores." They also ranked higher on indirect aggression.[18]
- *Exposure to violence* brings a high risk of challenging behaviour. Children who witness violence at home or who have been physically, emotionally or sexually abused are especially vulnerable.[19]
- *Parenting style and family factors* also figure in the development of challenging behaviours. When one or both parents use arbitrary, harsh, inconsistent, coercive discipline, when they respond negatively and are uninvolved with their children, when they model antisocial ways to resolve disagreements and when they don't supervise their children, the children may respond with defiant, aggressive, impulsive behaviours.[20]
- *Viewing violent television* makes children more aggressive and seduces them into watching

even more violent television to justify their increasingly aggressive behaviours.[21]

- *Low quality child* care can put a child at risk. Groups that are too large, spaces that are too small or too big, untrained or too few educators, lack of structure, not enough or too many toys, can all contribute to challenging behaviour. So do too many transitions, too much noise and too many demands on children who aren't developmentally ready to handle them.[22]

Is there any way to protect a child against risk?

Challenging behaviour is not inevitable, even when a child is at high risk. On the contrary, some factors protect children. Researchers refer to this ability to stave off risk as "resilience." Here are some of the factors that enable children to cope well despite adversity:

- an easy temperament;
- problem-solving skills, including the ability to plan;
- sociability;
- skill-based competence;
- self-esteem;
- involvement in hobbies;
- having responsibility.

Families and other people in their lives can increase children's resilience by:

- having high expectations and supporting the child as she tries to extend her reach;
- encouraging the child to participate in activities and to take responsibility;

Stress Test

Stressful life events leave parents short of the time and energy that good parenting demands. These factors may put children at risk:

- a mother who had her first child when she was very young;
- parents who completed fewer than 10 years of school;
- parents who don't live together;
- parents who fight;
- a parent with mental illness, especially depression;
- a parent who is abusing alcohol or drugs;
- a parent with criminal behaviour.[24]

Batteries Included

Two books—*The Difficult Child* by Stanley Turecki and Leslie Tonner and *Raising Your Spirited Child* by Mary Sheedy Kurcinka—expanded and popularized Thomas and Chess's work. A difficult—or spirited—child comes endowed with several of the following character traits, which can seem either positive or negative, depending on your point of view:

Activity level: always on the move; active, restless.
Perceptiveness or distractibility: notices everything; difficulty concentrating.
Intensity: powerful reactions; loud whether happy or angry.
Regularity: unpredictable about sleeping, eating, etc.; changeable moods.
Persistence: committed to tasks; stubborn, can't be reasoned with.
Physical sensitivity: responds to the slightest touch, smell, sound, sight, etc.
Adaptability: uncomfortable with transitions and changes in routine.
Approach/withdrawal: withdraws from new situations, people, places, foods, etc.
Mood: serious and analytical; seldom shows pleasure, cranky.

Roughly 20 percent of children have difficult or spirited temperaments. There is no correlation between temperament and intelligence, gender, birth order or social and economic status.[23]

- being a caring, supportive adult presence (in addition to the parents).

As the National Crime Prevention Council puts it, "An interested, caring adult [like a grandmother, older sibling, teacher, child care provider or coach] can serve as a protective factor for the child by role modeling social competence and by providing support."[26]

The bottom line

No matter which risk factors are present, it is not productive to blame—especially to blame the child, the parents or ourselves. It makes more sense to focus on elements in the child's immediate environment that we can influence directly and to try to boost his capacity to overcome risk. When we work with a child over a period of time, we can help him to develop the skills he needs to function successfully with other people. What we teach him stays with him and protects him in a variety of settings.

Do children outgrow their challenging behaviour?

Sometimes yes, sometimes no. Studies show that preschool-age children with behavioural problems often turn into difficult school-age children, delinquent teens and violent adults.[27] Richard Tremblay and his colleagues at the University of Montreal found that eight percent of the boys in a low income neighborhood were highly physically aggressive every year from kindergarten to grade 6. On the other hand, another 16 percent who had been aggressive in kindergarten were no longer aggressive in grade 6. The boys with good social skills were less likely to remain aggressive.[28]

What happens to these children if their challenging behaviours continue?

They have poor self-esteem, and they remain at high risk for a prodigious number of problems. Their aggressive behaviour, along with their disregard for others and their tendency to think everyone is against them,[29] leads their peers to reject them; and without friends they have no chance to learn the social skills they need. Because their teachers often don't like them either, and because they find it hard to solve problems, they don't do well at school, and they're likely to be held back or placed in a special class.[30] All of this raises their risk for delinquency, gang membership, substance abuse and psychiatric illness. As adults they are more likely to commit violent crimes.[31] The boys may become batterers, and new research is finding that the girls, who are at risk for early pregnancy and single parenthood,

Words Hurt

According to Toronto psychologist Tom Hay, emotional punishment can cause even more developmental problems than minor physical punishment.

Emotional punishment damages the relationship between the punisher and the punished, creates a climate for confrontation, hurts a child's sense of safety and interferes with learning. Children who've been controlled with punishment may learn to use aggression to control others. Punishment can destroy self-esteem by sending the message, "You're bad and you deserve to be punished."

People who work with children agree that physical punishment is never appropriate. But did you know that the following practices are also punitive and unacceptable:

- threatening
- scaring
- humiliating
- yelling
- embarrassing
- annoying
- insulting or putting someone down
- teasing
- intimidating.[25]

lack parenting skills and may be mothering the next generation of children with challenging behaviours.[32] . . .

Notes

1. L. K. Chandler and C. M. Dahiquist, "Confronting the challenge: Using team-based functional assessment and effective intervention strategies to reduce and prevent challenging behaviour in young children," workshop presented at SpeciaLink Institute on Children's Challenging Behaviours in Child Care, Sydney, N.S., April 26–27, 1997; J. Ritchie and C. Pohl, "Rules of thumb workshop, "*The Early Childhood Educator* 10 (Nov.-Dec. 1995): II; C. S. Klass, K. A. Guskin and M. Thomas, 'The early childhood program: Promoting children's development through and within relationships," *Zero to Three* (Oct-Nov. 1995): 9.
2. F. Vitaro, M. Dr Civita and L. Pagani, "The impact of research-based prevention programs on children's disruptive behaviour," *Exceptionality Education Canada,* 5 (1995): 106.
3. S. Landy and R. De V. Peters, "Understanding and treating hyperaggressive toddlers," *Zero to Three* (Feb. 1991): 24.
4. R. E. Tremblay et al., "Do children in Canada become more aggressive as they approach adolescence?" in *Growing Up in Canada: National Longitudinal Survey of Children and Youth* (Ottawa: Human Resources Development Canada and Statistics Canada, 1996) 129–130.
5. Landy and Peters 24; R. E. Tremblay et al., "From childhood physical aggression to adolescent maladjustment: the Montreal prevention experiment," in R. De V. Peters and R. J. McMahon, eds., *Preventing Childhood Disorders, Substance Abuse, and Delinquency* (Thousand Oaks, CA: Sage Publications, 1996) 271.
6. N. R. Crick, J. R. Cases and M. Mosher, "Relational and overt aggression in preschoolers," *Developmental Psychology,* 33 (1997): 579–588.
7. P. Brennan, S. Mednick and E. Kandal, "Congenital determinants of violent and property offending," in D. J. Pepler and K. H. Rubin, eds., *The Development and Treatment of Childhood Aggression* (Hillsdale, NJ: Lawrence Erlbaurn Associates, 1991) 87–90; A. J. Reiss, Jr. and J. A. Roth, eds., *Understanding and Preventing Violence* (Washington D.C.: National Academy Press, 1993) 364–365.
8. M. Leslie and G. DeMarchi, "Understanding the needs of substance-involved families and children in a child care setting," *Ideas, 3* (Dec. 1996): 12–16; K. Shore, *Rethinking the Brain: New Insights into Early Development* (New York: Families and Work Institute, 1997) 43–46; M. R. Burch, "Behavioral treatment of drug-exposed infants," *Children Today,* 21 (1992): 12–14.
9. S. B. Campbell, *Behavior Problems in Preschool Children* (New York: Guilford Press, 1990) 50.
10. A. J. Ayres, *Sensory Integration and the Child* (Los Angeles: Western Psychological Services, 1979) 8, 56.
11. Shamsie 5–9.
12. Shamsie 8; D. K. Sherman, G. I. William and M. K. McGue, "Attention-deficit hyperactivity disorder dimensions: A twin study of inattention and inpulsivity-hyperactivity," *Journal of the American Academy of Child and Adolescent Psychiatry, 36* (1997): 745–753; F. Levy et al., "Attention-deficit hyperactivity disorder: A category or a continuum? Genetic analysis of a large-scale twin study," *Journal of the American Academy of Child and Adolescent Psychiatry,* 36 (1997): 737–744.
13. Shamsie 8; R. A. Barkley, *ADHD and the Nature of Self-Control* (New York: Guilford Press, 1997) 11.
14. S. Chess and A. Thomas, "Temperament and its functional significance," in S. I. Greenspan and G. H. Pollock, eds., *The Course of Life, Vol. 11, Early Childhood* (Madison, CT: International Universities Press, 1989) 163–227.
15. Tremblay et al., *Growing Up in Canada* 129–130.
16. D. J. Pepler and R. G. Slaby, "Theoretical and developmental perspectives on youth and violence," in Eron et al. 48,
17. National Crime Prevention Council Canada, *Preventing Crime by Investing in Families* (Ottawa, 1996) 9–10; Shore 47–49.
18. Tremblay et al., *Growing Up in Canada* 130–131.
19. Slaby et al. 8; National Crime Prevention Council 29.
20. J. D. Coie, "Prevention of violence and antisocial behavior," in Peters and MeMahon 6; L. D. Eron, L. K. Huesmaun and A. Zelli, "The role of parental variables in the learning of aggression," in Pepler and Robin 169–170; 3. Haapasalo and R. B. Tremblay, "Physically aggressive boys from ages 6 to 12: Family background, parenting behavior, and prediction of delinquency," *Journal of Consulting and Clinical Psychology, 62* (1994): 1044–1052.
21. E. Doonerstein, R. G. Slaby and L. D. Eron, "The mass media and youth aggression," in Eron et al. 219–250.
22. B. Kaiser and J. S. Rasminsky, *The Daycare Handbook: A Parents' Guide to Finding and Keeping Quality Daycare in Canada* (Toronto: Little, Brown & Co.,1991); Canadian Child Care Federation, *National Statement on Quality Child Care* (Ottawa: author, 1994).
23. S. Turecki and L. T. Tonner, *The Difficult Child* (New York: Bantam Books, 1989); M. S. Kurcinka, *Raising Your Spirited Child* (New York: Harper Perennial, 1992).
24. R. E. Tremblay, "Early identification and intervention," presented at Dealing with Violence in Children and Youth Conference, Hamilton, ON, May 8, 1997; Coie in Peters and McMahon 6; A. K. Kazdin, "Interventions for aggressive and antisocial children," in Eron et al. 346; Haapasalo and Tremblay 1044–1052.
25. T. Hay, "The case against punishment," *IMPrint* (Winter 1994–95): 10–11.
26. National Crime Prevention Council 10; E. E. Werner and R. S. Smith, *Overcoming the Odds: High Risk Children from Birth to Adulthood* (Ithaca: Cornell University Press, 1992).
27. Tremblay et al., "Predicting early onset" 733; Reiss and Roth 358; Coie in Peters and McMahon 6.
28. Tremblay, "Early identification and intervention."
29. K. A. Dodge, "Social cognition and children's aggressive behaviour," *Child Development, 51* (1980): 162–170; K. A. Dodge and C. L. Frame, "Social cognitive biases and deficits in aggressive boys," *Child Development, 53* (1982): 620–635.
30. A. B. Kazdin, "Treatment of antisocial behavior in children: Current slams and future directions," *Psychological Bulletin, 102* (1987): 189; D. J. Pepler and K. H. Rubin, "Current challenges in the development and treatment of childhood aggression," in Pepler and Rubin xv.
31. National Crime Prevention Council 30–31.
32. National Crime Prevention Council 29; L. A. Serbin et al., "Aggressive, withdrawn, and aggressive/withdrawn children in adolescence: Into the next generation," in Pepler and Rubin 64–66; R. E. 'Tremblay, "Aggression, prosocial behavior, and gender," in Pepler and Rubin 75–76.

Resources

Behavior - Development - Individuality: A Newsletter about Caring for the High Maintenance Child. Available only online; www.temperament.com

Canadian Centre on Substance Abuse, FAS/FAE Information Service, 75 Albert St., Suite 300, Ottawa, ON K1P 5E7; 1-800-559-4514 or 613-235-4048; fax 613-235-8101; www.ccsa.ca/fasgen.htm

Carey, W. B. and S. C. McDevitt, *Coping with Children's Temperament: A Guide for Professionals* (New York: Harper Collins, 1995).

Essa, E., *A Practical Guide to Solving Preschool Behavior Problems* (New York, Delmar, 1998).

Fields, M. V. and C. Boesser, *Constructive Guidance and Discipline: Preschool and Primary Education* (Upper Saddle River, NJ: Prentice-Hall, 1998).

Flick, G. L., *ADD/ADHD Behavior-Change Resource Kit: Ready-to-Use Strategies and Activities for Helping Children with ADD* (West Nyack, NUY: Center for Applied Research in Education, 1998).

Grene, R. W., *The Explosive Child: A New Approach for Understanding and Parenting Easily Frustrated "Chronically Inflexible" Children* (New York: Harper Collins, 1998).

Greenspan, S. I. and J. Salmon, *The Challenging Child: Understanding, Raising and Enjoying the Five "Difficult" Types of Children* (Reading, PA: Addison Wesley, 1995).

Hallowell, E. M. and J. J. Ratey, *Driven to Distraction: Recognizing and Coping with Attention Deficit Disorder from Childhood through Adulthood* (New York: Simon and Schuster, 1994).

Irwin, S. H., ed., *Challenging the Challenging Behaviours: A Sourcebook Based on the SpeciaLink Institute on Challenging Behaviours in Child Care* (Wreck Cove, NS.: Breton Books, 1999).

Katz, L. G. and D. M. McClellan, *Fostering Children's Social Competence: The Teacher's Role* (Washington D.C.: National Association for the Education of Young Children, 1997).

Kleinfeld, J. and S. Wescott, eds., *Fantastic Antone Succeeds! Experiences in Educating Children with Fetal Alcohol Syndrome* (Fairbanks: University of Alaska, 1993). Available from BC FAS/E Support Network, 604-589-1854; fax 604-589-8438; E-mail fasnet@istar.ca

Kreidler, W. J. and S. T. Whittall, *Early Childhood Adventures in Peacemaking: A Conflict Resolution Activity Guide for Early Childhood Educators* (Cambridge, MA: Educators for Social Responsibility, 1999).

Kurcinka, M. S., *Raising Your Spirited Child* (New York: Harper Perennial, 1992).

LaForge, A. E., *Tantrums: Secrets to Calming the Storm* (New York: Pocket Books, 1996).

Levin, D. E., *Teaching Young Children in Violent Times: Building a Peaceable Classroom* (Cambridge, MA: Educators for Social Responsibility, 1994).

Making Friends. A series of four video programs. Image Media, #3-8755 Ash Street, Vancouver, BC V6P 6T3; 1-800-667-1500; fax 604-324-4855.

McCreight, B., *Recognizing and Managing Children with Fetal Alcohol Syndrome/Fetal Alcohol Effects: A Guide Book* (Washington, D.C.: CWLA press, 1977).

McGinnis, E. and A. P. Goldstein, *Skill-Streaming in Early Childhood: Teaching Prosocial Skills to the Preschool and Kindergarten Child* (Champiagn, IL: Research Press, 1990).

National Clearinghouse on Family Violence, Health Promotion and Programs Branch, Health Canada, Ottawa, ON K1A 1B4; 1-800-267-1291 or 613-957-2938; fax 613-941-8930; www.hc-sc.gc.ca/hppb/familyviolence

National Crime Prevention Council, *Preventing Crime by Investing in Families: An Integrated Approach to Promote Positive Outcomes in Children* (Ottawa: author, 1996).

National Crime Prevention Council, *Risks or Threats to Children* (Ottawa: author, 1995).

O'Neill, R. E. et al., *Functional Assessment and Program Development for Problem Behavior: A Practical Handbook* (Pacific Grove, CA: Brooks/Cole, 1997).

Parry, A. et al., *Choosing Non-Violence: The Rainbow House Handbook to a Violence-Free Future for Young Children* (Chicago: Rainbow House/Arco Iris, 1990).

Quinn, M. M. et al., *Addressing Student Problem Behavior: An IEP Team's Functional Behavior Assessment and Behavior Intervention Plans* (Washington D.C.: Center for Effective Collaboration and Practice, 1998); www.air-dc.org/cecp/resources/problembehavior

Reynolds, E., *Guiding Young Children: A Child-Centered Approach* (Mountain View, CA: Mayfield, 1996).

Rodd, J., *Understanding Young Children's Behavior: A Guide for Early Childhood Professionals* (New York: Teachers College, 1996).

Second Step: A Violence Prevention Curriculum (Preschool-Kindergarten), Committee for Children, 2203 Airport Way South, Suite 500, Seattle, WA 98134-2027; 1-800-634-4449 or 206-343-1223.

Shore, R., *Rethinking the Brain: New Insights into Early Development* (New York: Families and Work Institute, 1997).

Slaby, R. G. et al., *Early Violence Prevention: Tools for Teachers of Young Children* (Washington D.C.: National Association for the Education of Young Children, 1995).

Turecki, S. and L. T. Tonner, *The Difficult Child* (New York: Bantam Books, 1989).

WEVAS (Working Effectively with Violent and Aggressive Students). Workshop information: 204-888-4759; E-mail spencler@mts.net

Wichert, S., *Keeping the Peace: Practicing Cooperation and Conflict Resolution with Preschoolers* (Philadelphia and Gabriola Island, BC: New Society, 1989).

Zirpoli, T. J. and K. J. Melloy, *Behavior Management: Applications for Teachers and Parents* (New York: Macmillan, 1993).

Teaching Peace Concepts to Children

ANARELLA CELLITTI

Children's everyday group experiences contain important opportunities for adults to model and teach skills and understandings that can lead to a more peaceful world.

Subjects & Predicates

Look for active, contemporary, positive pictures of people of various ages, from many cultures, with a range of capacities.

> **Components of teaching peace**
> - create a peaceful classroom
> - teach conflict resolution and social responsibility

Many children today are exposed to acts of violence on television, in their communities, and sometimes within their families. Although the violence is frightening and puts children in danger, some children become accustomed to high levels of violence in their surroundings. As a result of their observations and experiences, many children are learning that violence is an apparently viable way to resolve conflicts between people (Eisenberg & Mussen, 1989).

In other homes, early childhood programs, and schools, young children learn that violence is not the only option, nor is it even an effective one, to resolve problems. Children in these peaceful environments routinely experience and use nonviolent ways to relate to peers and adults.

As early educators, it is our responsibility to expand children's thinking, to help them learn positive social skills if they are not familiar with them, and to assure that children know how to engage in peaceful interactions with others.

Teaching peace to young children involves two major components: creating a peaceful classroom environment, and teaching children conflict resolution and social re-

From *Dimensions of Early Childhood,* Spring 1998, pp. 38-42. © 1998 by the Southern Early Childhood Association (SECA), Little Rock, AR. Reprinted by permission.

sponsibility for themselves, others, and the world. The environment and curriculum can be shaped in ways that enable children to learn positive concepts about how people can live in harmony.

Create a Peaceful Atmosphere

In order to create a peaceful learning environment, teachers first establish an atmosphere in which adults model and facilitate peaceful interactions. Teachers maintain a climate of caring tolerance and mutual respect at all times, among children, staff, families, and visitors. Adults and children model communication skills, conflict resolution, tolerance, and honesty. Children in the group are expected to be generous to each other, to exhibit empathy, and to be increasingly aware of how their behaviors affect others.

Learning materials and activities are free from gender, racial, age, and other stereotypes. Caring adults build on typical everyday incidents (disagreements about turns on equipment, for example) to promote appropriate peacemaking skills such as communication, accepting no for an answer, standing up for what is fair, and taking turns. Children develop a sense of understanding about and empathy for others when they engage in meaningful community projects. Collect items for a toy or food drive, make cards or sing for nursing home residents or children in the hospital.

Families are an important ally in the peace-learning process. Talk with parents or guardians about how their children use their positive social skills and are learning to respect people. Encourage families to observe children at play, or videotape representative classroom interactions to show during conferences or meetings. Include information about conflict resolution, anti-bias activities, and other topics when you exchange information about children's progress.

Consider a peace center

In addition to incorporating peace into the daily routine, some teachers may want to set up a Peace Center in which children can read, listen to music, and practice their conflict resolution strategies. These are a few suggestions about how to set up such an area.

1. Designate a comfortable space. Decorate it with children's words and artwork depicting their ideas about peace. Post pictures of children engaged in activities at the Peace Center. Choose soothing music from a variety of cultures. "Peace Is the World Smiling" (Music for Little People, 1989) is one such recording. Select children's books in which the characters model peaceful behaviors.

2. Display pictures and posters that depict human diversity. Hang them at children's eye level. Look for active, contemporary, positive pictures of people of various ages, from many cultures, with a range of capacities. Catalogs, travel brochures, and magazines are excellent sources. Local newspapers often publish pictures of community members who are volunteers.

3. Set a few positive rules about expectations for children's behavior in the group, such as "We use our words to solve problems."

4. Teach children how to resolve conflicts with others. Explain all four steps (Table 1) as children resolve their disagreements. At first, and nearly always with toddlers, an adult is there to assure that children follow each step. Preschoolers soon learn to use these strategies independently. This democratic conflict resolution process also can be used by adults.

5. Post the program's rules and conflict resolution steps, so that adults are aware of what is expected. Explain their purpose. Encourage families to implement similar positive childrearing strategies.

Table 1

Steps to teach children conflict resolution

Step	Action
1. "Tell us what happened."	Allow each child to explain the problem.
2. Summarize.	Summarize what they say. Include each child's point of view.
3. "What could you do about this problem?"	Ask children for possible solutions. Consider all possibilities. You may say, "I wonder if there is another way to handle this problem," but don't suggest any solution.
4. Help the children choose a solution.	Do not give any hint of what you think they should do—it is their decision.

Note. From *Helping Children Love Themselves and Others: A Professional Handbook for Family Day Care* (p. 26), by J. McCracken (ed.), 1990, Washington, DC: The Children's Foundation. Copyright © 1990 by The Children's Foundation.

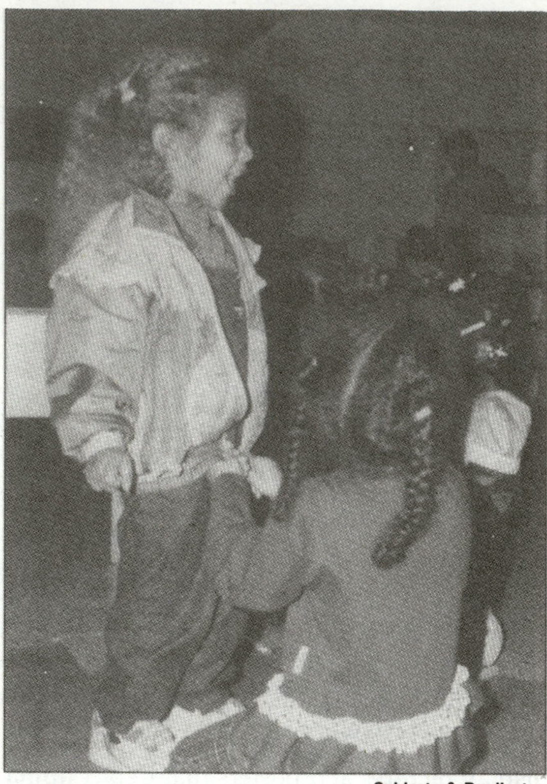

Subjects & Predicates

Teaching peace to children is a daily process.

6. Have a log that children fill in each time they use the center. Activities to be logged could include being at the center to resolve problems, read, write, or chat. For children who are still learning to read, use symbols to denote each activity.

7. Create a "Getting Along" word bank for your readers.

Suggest words that children can use to express their feelings and or describe actions so they can communicate more effectively. Offer substitute words for hurtful language (hate, stupid), such as angry or confused.

Integrate Peace in The Curriculum

Peace concepts are effectively taught only when they make sense to children and are embedded within the curriculum and classroom routines. Teaching peace to children is a daily process, rather than a special week or a project. These ideas describe how peace concepts can be incorporated into traditional academic areas, all of which are integrated in a developmental early childhood curriculum.

1. Social studies. Broaden children's true understanding about the uniqueness and similarities among individuals, families, communities, states, and countries around the world. Make sure information is accurate and about real people. Ask community volunteers to share aspects of their heritage, such as artifacts or family photos. Ensure that children realize all people, including themselves, are unique individuals within a particular culture. Regularly incorporate authentic ethnic foods and real clothing into the pretend play area. Engage children in appropriate ways to solve current social problems in the community, such as writing letters about trash on their playground. Children learn about the democratic process when they vote on meaningful issues (Gunnels, 1997), build consensus in small groups, and use negotiation skills.

2. History/news. Read children's stories that recognize and celebrate people who work to establish human rights and a better life for others. Select such books often, rather than reading about Martin Luther King, Jr. only on his birthday holiday, for example. Talk with children about people they know who are working for peace and justice—neighbors, educators, decision makers in their community. Invite these people to describe their work to children. The president of the library board, for example, might explain how he talks with people and writes letters to ask for donations to buy new books.

3. Music and oral traditions. Music from any time periods and cultures can be integrated into discussions about geography and social studies. Find out what children know about a topic, and then build on that information. In what states or countries do children's friends and relatives live? What areas have they heard about in the news? To what kinds of music do they listen? Choose authentic music—familiar and new—from many different styles. Select songs, games, and finger plays that promote the values of understanding and helping others. Learn the words to songs in several languages, including signing.

4. Authentic literature. Books can greatly enhance children's knowledge of others. Look for accurate, balanced portrayals of diverse peoples. Limit the number of books that deal only with holidays or offer a "tourist" approach—make sure children gain a more realistic perspective of daily life. Choose children's books that portray children and adults engaging in friendly, peaceful behaviors. Extend children's literature experiences by providing hands-on activities that enable them to gain a fuller understanding of the situation portrayed.

5. Visual arts. Art experiences that relate to taking care of the earth or that come from different cultures can promote children's social responsibility and their understanding of other perspectives. Show children paintings or weavings, for example and talk with them about these pieces. Provide children with the necessary materials and tools, and demonstrate new techniques. Then encourage them to represent their own ideas and concepts.

6. Natural sciences. Science activities concerning recycling, reforestation, and taking care of sea animals and the ocean could be included as children discover the process of erosion, decomposition of waste, and animal life. Or follow up on children's understanding about human similarities and differences in skin color, hair texture, and teeth.

7. Number concepts. Math could incorporate studies of the classroom population such as helping children create graphs of classmates' eye color, food preferences, or other characteristics. Prepare ethnic foods using favorite recipes provided by families in the program. Children make a shopping list for, measure, and mix ingredients, and when it is done, divide the food in portions. Nutrition, money, and many other concepts could be explored.

Teachers have daily opportunities to increase children's abilities to communicate, respect each other, resolve conflicts, and accept social responsibility—skills they will carry into adulthood. Inclusion of peace-making skills in the curriculum is as important as learning to read and write.

References

Damon, W. (1988). *The moral child: Nurturing children's natural moral growth.* New York, NY: Free Press.

Eisenberg, N., & Mussen, P. (1989). *The roots of prosocial behaviors in children.* Cambridge, MA; Cambridge University Press.

Gunnels, J. A. (1997, Fall). A class pet campaign: Experiencing the democratic process. *Dimensions of Early Childhood, 25* (4), 31–34.

Kostelnik, M., Stein, L., Whiren, A., & Soderman, A. (1993). *Guiding children's social development.* Albany, NY: Delmar.

Kreidler, W. (1984). *Creative conflict resolution.* Glenview, IL: Scott Foresman.

McCracken, J. (Ed). (1990). *Helping children love themselves and others: A professional handbook for family day care.* Washington, DC: The Children's Foundation.

Peace is the world smiling. (1989). A peace anthology for families (Cassette Recording No. MLP D-2104). Redway, CA: Music for Little People.

Wolfgang, C., & Glickman, C. D. (1986). *Solving discipline problems: Strategies for classroom teachers.* Boston, MA: Allyn & Bacon.

Anarella Cellitti, Ph.D., is Assistant Professor at Texas A&M University-Kingsville in Kingsville.

Television Violence and Its Effects on Young Children

Betty Jo Simmons,[1,2] Kelly Stalsworth,[1] and Heather Wentzel[1]

This article examines research on television violence and links violence to specific programs commonly watched by young children. Although there are some who try to disprove any connection between television and aggressive behavior, there is evidence to suggest that such linkages do exist.

KEY WORDS: television; violence; programs for young children.

INTRODUCTION

After the introduction of television in 1939, E. B. White said it was "going to be the test of the modern world. We shall stand or fall by the television—of that I am quite sure." (Asamen & Berry, 1993, p. 10) These prophetic words are proving to be more accurate on a daily basis. With its ability to inform, entertain, teach, and persuade, television unquestionably has tremendous effects upon its viewers. Indeed, television has become the central activity in most homes today. Currently, in the United States, 98% of all households have at least one set. Even more astounding is the fact that it is watched an average of 7.5 hours per day (Asamen & Berry, 1993). Beckman (1997) concurs, saying that children watch more than 28 hours of television each week and in the process the average child, before the age of 12, has viewed over 8,000 murders.

RESEARCH ON TELEVISION VIOLENCE

In order to clean up the airways for young audiences, the Federal Communications Commissions (FCC) enacted The Children's Television Act in 1990. Many television stations show strictly positive programs, but the negative ones are also still being aired. This point is important because preschool children are curious and easily influenced. They tend to mimic and repeat what they hear and see on television without knowledge of right and wrong.

One of the main concerns with television programming is the violence viewed by children. Berk (1993) says that because young folks cannot fully understand what they see

[1]Longwood College, Farmville, Virginia.
[2]Correspondence should be directed to Betty Jo Simmons, Professor of Education, Longwood College, 201 High Street, Farmville, Virginia 23909: e-mail; bjsimmon@longwood.lwc.edu

From *Early Childhood Education Journal*, Vol. 26, No. 3, 1999, pp. 149-153. © 1999 by Human Sciences Press, Inc. Reprinted by permission.

on television, they are very much under its influence. Davidson (1996) agrees that children are extremely vulnerable to television between the ages of 2 to 8 years because of their maturational inability to separate what they view from reality. Attention to violence on television became a matter of serious consideration in the 1950s, with the first congressional hearing taking place in 1952. From 1952 to 1967, many analyses were done of the content of television programs. In the late 1960s and early 1970s, the scrutiny shifted from content alone to specifically discerning the effects of violence on viewers. The resulting findings supported the idea that a casual relationship existed between television violence and aggressive behavior (National Institutes of Mental Health, 1983).

IMITATING VIOLENCE

Levin and Carlsson-Paige (1996) lament the 1984 deregulation of broadcasting, noting that subsequently teachers began to observe an escalation of violence in their classrooms. They state that "Today, U.S. crime rates are increasing most rapidly among youth who were in their formative early years when children's TV was deregulated and violent programs and toys successfully deluged childhood culture" (p. 17). Governmental investigation led to several studies about the effects of violence. Two of the most well known were done by Bandura and Berkowitz. Bandura (1973), a social learning theorist, purported that children learn primarily through social modeling. From his studies, he concluded that children went through three stages—exposure, acquisition, and acceptance (Moody, 1980). He maintained that increased exposure to aggressive models led to reduced inhibitions toward violence. For example, when a television character acts violently and the consequences are positive, then the viewer is more likely to assume this behavior. Today, unfortunately even the "good" guys feel obligated to blow away their opponents (Munson, 1996).

Berkowitz (1962) examined the effects of television on aggressive drives. He concluded that exposure to televised violence does arouse aggressive behaviors, especially if viewers believe that aggression is justified. Noble (1975) maintains that aggressive behavior is harder to inhibit if viewers have a target which is associated with a television victim. Similarly, a study involving five different countries in which children were subjected to violence through television found evidence that even brief exposures caused them to be more accepting of other aggressive behavior. This research also concluded that the more children watched television, the more accepting they became of aggressive actions (Huesmann & Eron, 1986). Davidson (1996) reports that research done by Leonard Eron of the University of Michigan shows that violence children watched as eight-year-olds became a better predictor of adult aggression than socioeconomic and childrearing factors.

Cullingford (1984) reports on a study done by Shaw and Newell in which they interviewed families about their concerns over television. One of the major findings was that violence went almost unnoticed. Even when people were shown killings and then heavily prompted, most did not think of it as violent. The frightening truth was that "objectionable content" had become so acceptable that it was invisible. Later investigations by Drabman and Thomas (Geen, 1981) used observation to determine the effects of violent films on the way children resolved conflict. They, like Geen, who used blood pressure as the indicator concluded that violence leads to desensitization (Molitor, 1994; Voojis & Voort, 1993). Thus, it is not hard to understand what Minnow, former chair of the Federal Communications Commission, meant when he said that in the 1960s, he worried that his children would not greatly benefit from television, but in the 1990s, he worries that his grandchildren may be harmed by it (Minnow, 1995).

VIOLENCE AND FEAR

In addition to theories that television can cause children to be more aggressive and less sensitive to the results of violence, there is also the theory that televised violence causes viewers to be afraid. According to this theory, the misconstrued world presented on television is seen as a mirror of reality and viewers become convinced they will fall victim to violence. It is reasoned that viewers absorb information without analyzing it and subsequently develop false beliefs about law enforcement and crime. Chen (1994), who found that crime during prime time is depicted 10 times greater than in reality, gives credence to the notion that television is distorted in its portrayal and resolution of crime and violence.

Levine (1996) says 3-to 5-year-old children live in a magical world that often leaves them terrified of things which completely surprise adults. On the other hand, there are those who disagree that television makes them afraid. According to Hamilton (1993), today's children are much more preoccupied with violence. Therefore, according to Dr. Daniel Koenigsberg, chief of child psychiatry at Saint Raphael Hospital, it is not so much that children are scared by it, as it is that they accept it and are intrigued by it. Thus, it is easy to see that not everyone agrees about the effects that violence has; however, it is generally agreed that it does play a significant role in the children's construction of social reality (Voojis & Voort, 1993).

CHILDREN'S PROGRAMS FEATURING VIOLENCE

According to Kaplan (1998), the National Coalition on Television Violence has classified the Mighty Morphin Power Rangers as the most violent program "ever studied, averaging more than 200 violent acts per hour" (p. 16). Furthermore, in an experimental study involving 5-to 11-year-olds (26 boys and 26 girls with ethnically diverse backgrounds), Kaplan (1998) reports that children who watched Power Rangers committed 7 times more aggressive acts than those who did not. Recognizing that children imitate what they see, several day care centers, nursery schools, and elementary schools have outlawed Power Rangers in play.

According to Evra and Kline (1990), "One of the dangers for preschoolers or early school-age children is their lack of ability to relate actions, motives, and consequences, and they may simply imitate the action they see" (p. 83). Levin and Carlsson-Paige (1996) purport that children cannot assimilate the Power Rangers into their own naturally limited experiences. Thus, unable to devise meaningful play from what they have seen, they act out "what they are unable to understand, primarily the kicking, fighting, and shooting" (p. 18). Teachers, according to Levin and Carlsson-Paige (1996), have observed that children become so fascinated by the Power Rangers that they excuse their own aggressiveness by saying they must do as the Power Rangers do.

Another show, similar in content, is the Teenage Mutant Ninja Turtles. Violence is also the main attraction in this program. The four heroes are pumped-up turtles named after four famous artists: Michaelangelo, Donatello, Leonardo, and Raphael. Their mentor is a skilled ninja rat. Each has a distinctive personality and each fights best with specific weapons. The main "bad guy," Shredder, is so named because he has blades protruding from his clothes, which he does not hesitate to use when fighting. In one episode on the Cartoon Network, Shredder tried to use a robot to take over the world and the Turtles stopped him by fighting. At the end of the show, the characters discuss what is supposed to have been learned by the viewers. However, young children watching these shows would not necessarily learn from these messages because they can take in only so much information at a time. According to Evra and Kline (1990), the lack of understanding and well-developed behavioral control causes the main attraction to be primarily the action.

In what may be called the "Dynamic Duos" are found Bugs Bunny and Elmer Fudd, Tweetie and Sylvester, the Roadrunner and Wyle E. Coyote, and Tom and Jerry. Each pair takes turns trying to outsmart and pummel one another. The goofy and colorful characters attract children and the only message that might be sent to children is how to solve problems through fighting.

Similarly, a new wave of cartoons, such as Beavis and Butthead, The Simpsons, King of the Hill, and Daria, are aimed at an adult audience; yet many children are intrigued by these animated cartoons. Most of the themes in these shows focus on adult life, things that young children would not understand. For example, those that focus on teenage life, such as Beavis and Butthead and Daria, show lazy characters concerned only with materialistic and selfish things. These programs also use adult language that is not appropriate for small children to hear. However, since children do watch these shows, they tend to repeat certain things that they see and hear.

For example, at the beginning to Beavis and Butthead, words come across the screen saying that the cartoon is not realistic and the acts in the show should not be repeated. However, such disclaimers do not register in the minds of children who are more intrigued by action than consequences. For example, in the early 1960s, Schramm, Lyle, and Parker (1961) were pointing out the inherent danger involved in televised violence. They noted that a 6-year-old told his father he wanted real bullets because toy ones did not kill like Hopalong Cassidy's bullets. It appears that when children watch shows, they often do not remember the plot, but they do remember the actions of their favorite characters. Evra and Kline (1990) found that even 14-month-old children have a tendency toward some type of imitation of television.

PUBLIC REACTION

Even though there are shows on television that are designed for preschoolers, many American adults feel that there are still not enough programs for young children. In a press release on October 5, 1995, the Center for Media Education (CME) published the results of a national poll which showed strong public support of more educational programs. To quote from the poll:

> More than four in five American adults (82%) believe there is not enough educational children's programming on commercial broadcast television. Three in five adults surveyed (60%) support specific requirements that broadcasters air an hour of educational programming—or more—for children each day. More than a third of all parents (35%) would require two hours daily. 80% of Americans believe there are good reasons to regulate children's TV more strictly than programming intended for general or adult audiences. The two most frequently cited reasons for the lack of quality in children's broadcast programming are violent (43%) and insufficient educational programming (25%). (Poll on Children's Television, 1995, Center for Media Education)

These complaints are slowly being attended to with new educational programs and the revival of old ones, such as Schoolhouse Rock and Sesame Street. A rating system has recently been enacted. At the beginning of each show, letters and numbers, ranging from "G" to "Adult" appear at the top left-hand corner of the television screen, stating the appropriateness of the television show.

In 1997, in response to the public's demand for improvement in the quality of children's television, the Federal Communications Commission (FCC) issued stronger rules to regulate the Children's Television Act of 1990. According to the new expectations, broadcasters must produce 3 hours weekly of educational programming. These programs must make education the major focus with clearly articulated objectives, and a designated target age group. Fortunately, more stations are appearing and many of them do show programs that are, for the most part, appropriate for all audiences. Channels such as PBS, Animal Planet, The Family Channel, and the Disney channel are examples. However, there is still the question of violence on television. Especially so, since the Children's Television Act is not definitive about the meaning of educational programming. The act simply says that programs must contribute to the well-being of children "in any respect." The "in any respect" seems to be a loophole that dilute the original intent (*U.S. News and World Report*, 1997).

Even when educational programs are produced, problems remain. One of them lies with the competition. With the availability of cable, violence continues to be prevalent. Children can and do quickly switch the channel to the Cartoon Network (*New York Times*, 1997). Furthermore, since educational programs are not big moneymakers, producers tend to schedule many of them early in the morning or in spots which are not the most normal viewing times. Another major consideration is what Zoglin contended in 1993, namely, that children are not much attracted to educational shows. He says, "The very notion of educational TV often seems to reflect narrow, school-marish notions" (p. 64). Five years later, Mifflin (1997) pointed out that broadcasters agree because they have a hard time finding educational programs that children will watch (*New York Times*, 1997).

RECOMMENDATIONS

Naturally, children are easily confused when they watch the superhero beat up other characters. Therefore, recognizing and taking a proactive position against televised violence becomes a prime responsibility for all those involved in the care and nurturance of young children. With this premise in mind, the following recommendations are offered:

1. Parents, teachers, and communities must work together to combat the violence that is permeating society. They must work to build community programs to prevent violence and diffuse aggressive behavior. They must work on an individual level to teach acceptable and unacceptable standards.

2. Children must have their television viewing supervised and regulated which means that adults have to show responsible behavior themselves by refusing to watch programs that are violent in nature. If they are unwilling

to abolish violent programs in their homes, they must take the time to ask questions of their children, explain the seriousness of violence to them, and help them to evaluate what they witness.

3. Parents must not let television become the dominant part of their family's life. It is imperative that drastic steps be taken to curtail the kind of socially unacceptable behavior, which is routinely and daily invited into the average home.

4. Parents and teachers must help young children develop appropriate behavior for social interactions. Children need guidance in learning to settle disagreements with verbal rather than physical skill.

5. Schools need to take television violence seriously, especially so, since it transfers to inappropriate behavior in the classroom. Thus, school personnel should take immediate steps to involve parents and the community in open dialog through newspaper articles, PTA meetings, and public forums.

6. The curriculum must be based upon the developmental needs of young children. Consideration must be given to fantasy, animism, and the inability of children to separate real from the pretend. Young children should be taught how to make decisions and how to work through problems by finding acceptable alternatives to violent acts.

REFERENCES

Asamen, J., & Berry, G. (1993). *Children and television: Images in a changing sociocultural world.* London: Sage Publications.

Bandura, A. (1973). *Aggression: A social learning analysis.* Englewood Cliffs, NJ: Prentice Hall.

Beckman, J. (1997). *Television violence: What the research says about its effect on young children.* Winnetka, IL: Winnetka Alliance for Early Childhood.

Berk, L. (1993). *Infants, children, and adolescents.* Boston: Allyn and Bacon.

Berkowitz, L. (1962). *Aggression: A social psychological analysis.* New York: McGraw-Hill.

Center for Media Education (1995). Poll on children's television. Press release, October 1995 (also available online).

Chen, M. (1994). *The smart parent's guide to kid's TV.* San Francisco, CA: KQED Books.

Cullingford, C. (1984). *Children and television.* New York: St. Martin's Press.

Davidson, J. (February 2, 1996). *Menace to society.* Rolling Stone, pp. 38–39.

Defining the "educational" in educational TV for children (September 12, 1994) *U.S. News and World Report,* p. 90.

Evra, J., & Kline, W. (1990). *Television and child development.* Hillsdale, NJ: Lawrence Erlbaum Associates.

Geen, R. (1981). Behavioral and physiological reactions to observed violence: Effects of prior exposure to aggressive stimuli. *Journal of Personality and Social Psychology, 40,* 868–875.

Hamilton, R. (May/June, 1993). TV violence—What influence on young minds? *St. Raphael's Better Health,* pp. 7–11.

Huesmann, R., & Eron, L. (1986). *Television and the aggressive child: A cross national comparison.* Hillsdale, NJ: Lawrence Erlbaum Associates.

Kaplan, P. (1998). *The human odyssey.* Pacific Grove, CA: Brooks and Cole.

Levin, D., & Carlsson-Paige, N. (1996). Disempowering the "Power Rangers." *The Education Digest, 61,* 17–21.

Levine, M. (1996). Handling the "boob tube." *Parents Magazine, 71,* 55–57.

Mifflin, L. (September 11, 1997). Can you spell "compliance," boys and girls? *New York Times,* p. C13.

Minnow, N. and LaMay, C. (August 6, 1995). Abandoned in the wasteland. *Detroit Free Press,* Magazine Section, pp. 12–16.

Molitor, F., & Hirsch, K. (1994). Children's toleration of real life aggression after exposure to media violence: A replication of the Drabman and Thomas studies. *Child Study Journal, 24,* 191–203.

Moody, K. (1980). *Growing up on television.* New York: Times Books.

Munson, M. (1995). Media mayhem. *Prevention, 47,* 86–89.

Noble, G. (1975). *Children in front of the small screen.* Thousand Oaks, CA: Sage Publications.

Schramn, W., Lyle, J., & Parker, E. (1961). *Television in the lives of our children.* Stanford, CA: Stanford University Press.

Television and behavior: Ten years of scientific progress and implications for the eighties (1983). Washington, DC: National Institutes of Mental Health.

Voojis, M., & Voort, T. (1993). Learning about television violence: The impact of critical viewing curriculum on children's attitudinal judgment of crime series. *Journal of Research and Development in Education, 26,* 133–141.

Zoglin, R. (1993). If not the Jetsons, what? *Time,* March 22, p. 64.

Fostering Intrinsic Motivation in Early Childhood Classrooms

Martha P. Carlton[1,3] and Adam Winsler[2]

Young children are born with an innate curiosity to learn about their world. This intrinsically instigated learning is often called mastery motivation. Patterns of motivation are established at an early age. The early childhood years are crucial for establishing robust intrinsic motivational orientations which will last a lifetime. By the time many children reach school, much of their motivation has been lost or replaced with extrinsically motivated learning strategies. Preschools and elementary schools have been criticized for contributing to such negative motivational patterns in children. This can be changed. Early child care situations and preschools can instead be instrumental in the strengthening of children's motivation. The goal of this paper is to show that through an understanding of the beginnings of motivation, we can begin to find ways to build strong motivational patterns in children that can carry on to later years of learning.

KEY WORDS: Motivation; classroom, preschool; infant.

INTRODUCTION

When a child is born, there is within that child an innate need to interact with the environment. These interactions lead to learning and the acquisition of knowledge. The motivation that drives this learning is based solely within the child and requires no outside rewards for its continuation. This motivation has been seen as humans' inherent intrinsic motivation to learn (Deci, 1975). As children reach school age, however, many do not seem to possess this interest in learning (Stipek, 1988). What happens to this motivation? What can we do to foster its development? By looking at the origins and development of intrinsic motivation, it is possible to identify some of the factors that can result in the strengthening or weakening of motivational patterns in young children. The purpose of this article is to explore the development differences in children from birth to 5 years with respect to motivation, and to provide several ideas, activities, and principles that early childhood educators can use to foster intrinsic motivation in all young children. Children's development will be divided into four age ranges: birth to 9 months, 9–24 months, 24–36

[1] College of Education, University of Alabama, Tuscaloosa, Alabama.
[2] Department of Psychology, George Mason University, Fairfax, Virginia.
[3] Correspondence should be directed to Martha Carlton, Educational Psychology, College of Education, University of Alabama, Box 870231, Tuscaloosa, Alabama 35487; email: mcarlton@bamaed.ua.edu.

From *Early Childhood Education Journal,* Vol. 25, No. 3, Spring 1998, pp. 159-166. © 1998 by Plenum Publishing Corporation. Reprinted by permission.

months, and 3–5 years. During each of these age ranges, specific activities will be discussed that can foster the development of intrinsic motivation in early childhood settings and at the close, a table will be given summarizing ten major motivational principles for early childhood professionals.

A DEFINITION OF MOTIVATION

Motivation can be defined as the process by which children's goal-directed activity is instigated and sustained (Pintrich & Schunk, 1996). Goal-directed behavior may be intrinsically motivated, extrinsically motivated, or motivated by a combination of the two. Intrinsic motivation refers to the desire to participate in an activity merely for the pleasure derived from that activity (Pintrich & Schunk, 1996). Conversely, an extrinsically motivated activity would be one that is engaged in for the sake of a desirable outcome, such as praise or reward. Intrinsic motivation is associated with greater learning and achievement in children (Gottfried, 1985; Pintrich & Schunk, 1996). This enhancement of learning occurs presumably because intrinsically motivated students are more involved in their learning, and they use strategies to promote deeper understanding and future application of that learning. Intrinsically motivated children experience more enjoyment from their learning, gain greater knowledge and insight, feel better about themselves, and are more likely to persist in goal-directed activities (Barrett & Morgan, 1995; Deci, Vallerand, Pelletier, & Ryan, 1991; Ford & Thompson, 1985; Harter, 1978; Pintrich & Schunk, 1996). If intrinsically motivated learning is better than extrinsically motivated learning, then it would appear to be to the benefit of all educators to understand the functioning and development of this type of motivation.

INTRINSIC MOTIVATION IN THE EARLY CHILDHOOD YEARS

Intrinsic motivation is made up of three basic psychological needs that are thought to be innate in human beings: the needs for competence, relatedness, and autonomy or self-determination (Deci *et al.*, 1991). Competence is understanding how to achieve various outcomes and having the belief that you are capable of obtaining those outcomes. Relatedness involves the ability to develop secure and stable relationships with others in a social context. Autonomy is the self-regulating and self-initiating quality of one's own actions. The development of these three areas can be seen in the context of the young child.

The newborn is filled with the desire to respond to the many stimuli presented by her environment. As the child interacts with the environment, certain events occur. If the child can relate her action with the reaction of the environment, a sense of control over the environment is gained. This sense of control strengthens feelings of competence within the child and leads to further exploration and experimentation. With each successful interaction, the sense of competence grows (Ford & Thompson, 1985).

This growing sense of competence is closely linked with the child's attachment to significant caregivers. As children develop secure relationships with caregivers, they become freer to exhibit more exploration within the environment. They are also able to use the caregiver as a secure base for explorations as they attempt to master the environment (Ford & Thompson, 1985). The security of initial warm attachment relationships facilitates the ability to develop other meaningful relationships in later childhood. Feelings of relatedness to early childhood teachers motivate and free children to explore the learning environment (Ryan & Powelson, 1991).

As the child becomes older, autonomy becomes more important. Autonomy is the need to regulate one's own behavior and to govern the initiation and direction of one's actions (Ryan & Powelson, 1991). Children from homes where autonomy is supported tend to transfer their feelings of autonomy to school situations. Learning environments can also be seen as either autonomy-supportive or controlling. Autonomy denotes an inner sense that one's actions are coming from within one's self and that the individual has control of those actions. Controlling situations cause the individual to feel a lack of personal control over actions and little personal responsibility for those actions. Learning gained through autonomy-supportive events facilitates a feeling of self-determination and often results in greater understanding of the material being learned (Deci & Ryan, 1987).

As children become older, motivational patterns become differentiated by various subject and task areas. For example, each individual will have different motivational patterns for mathematics, reading, music, etc., depending on their history of experiences in those domains. All motivational levels do not have to be equal across demands for each individual (White, 1959). Infants and young children, conversely, are seen to have an undifferentiated need for competence; they have only a general need to master their environment. This is often referred to as "mastery motivation" (Barrett & Morgan, 1995). All mastery motivation is intrinsic in nature since children find the behavior rewarding in itself with no need for external rewards. Some aspects of mastery motivation include: (a) persistence at tasks that are somewhat difficult, (b) a preference for one's own control over environmental events (as opposed to passive observation), and (c) preference for some degree of challenge (Barrett & Morgan, 1995). All children start out with an optimal degree of motivation at birth, with the exception of some children whose special needs may compromise their motivation. The differences in older children's motivation is determined by what happens to them in their early years.

How does motivation manifest itself within the early childhood classroom? Here are two different children in the same preschool classroom. Sarah is 3 years old. She enjoys coming to school and is seldom ready to go home at the end of the day. She chooses activities that present a challenge to her and she persists until completing the activity to her own satisfaction. She decides what she would like to do during the day, and is pleased with her own abilities. Although she occasionally seeks the teacher's help with more difficult activities, she is content to work on her own, and she persists on activities for extended periods of time. Sally, on the other hand, needs constant help from the teacher. She seldom is able to select her own activity or plan what she would like to do during the day. When she does make a decision, she selects only those activities that are easy enough to complete rapidly, and demands the teacher's approval when she is finished. Sally quits an activity at the slightest obstacle, and rarely completes anything. One essential difference between these two children is their motivational orientation. While Sarah is very intrinsically motivated, Sally's activities are mostly extrinsically motivated.

As can be seen from this illustration, motivation is an important topic for early childhood educators. It determines a child's total functioning in learning environments. There is little published material dealing with these issues that caretakers can turn to for information. While much is known about different motivational patterns seen in children and their relation to academic performance and achievement in the later school years (Pintrich & Schunk, 1996), less information is available about the development of early motivation in the preschool years.

A DEVELOPMENTAL SEQUENCE FOR MOTIVATION

Infants (Birth to 9 Months)

Description of Infant Motivation. At birth, infants are capable of limited voluntary motor movements. They can turn their heads, kick their legs, and fling their arms about. They are also capable of controlling their sucking responses. From this state, infants rapidly gain control of more motor functions as muscle coordination develops. Within 9 months, the average infant has progressed from a state of random movements to a child who can crawl across the room and pull himself to a standing position, possibly even move a few steps. During these great changes, what can help maintain the child's motivation?

Research on Infant Motivation. Infants are predisposed to try to control their environments from birth. When infants can see the actual consequences of their actions, they are motivated to continue the actions. Young infants, of course, have a very limited behavioral repertoire for controlling their environment. Cries, vocalizations, facial expressions, and small limb actions are what most people can observe in the infant as attempts at control. Psychologists, however, in the laboratory have been able to capitalize on another important and natural infant behavior—sucking. By using pressure-sensitive pacifiers wired to computers which control the presentation of different stimuli, researchers have learned that infants within the first few weeks of life will control the rate of their sucking (i.e., increase or decrease sucking speed) in order to view or repeatedly view pleasant visual stimuli. That is, infants will systematically suck on the pacifier at the rate that presents desired (i.e., face-like) stimuli rather than the rate that presents either other, less attractive stimuli or no stimuli, and infants early on prefer to use the pacifier which controls the presentation of stimuli rather than one that does not (Rovee-Collier, 1987). Also, infants remember (in terms of repeating/increasing their sucking rates later) which stimuli were previously under their control and which stimuli were not (DeCasper & Carstens, 1981). Such research suggests that infants are much more sophisticated than had been previously thought and that infants' motivation and goals can be assessed if one carefully interprets infant behavior from the perspective of their own behavioral repertoire.

Slightly older infants begin to gain additional control over muscle movements and use more involved means to interact with their environment. Several studies have illustrated this point. Infants who are given a mobile that is activated by their own movements, become more active and escalate the frequency of their movements when viewing the mobile again later (Shields & Rovee-Collier, 1992). Continued exposure will also result in social reactions to the movements, such as smiling and cooing (Watson & Ramey, 1972). Children react similarly to a string tied around their wrists which activates pictures and pleasant music. If the pulled string no longer results in music and pleasant pictures, the child will become angry and unhappy (Lewis, Alessandri, & Sullivan, 1990). Although infant care centers are not likely to have computerized pacifiers which present stimuli, nor might they wish to attach strings between infants' arms and their mobiles, infant caregivers can learn to recognize infants' cues and attempts at mastering the environment and arrange the environment such that infants have multiple opportunities to do so.

Recommendations for Caregivers. Caregiver actions are also critical in the development of the infant's motivation. The beginnings of mastery feelings develop as a child sees that his actions upon the environment have an effect. If the child's actions are consistently responded to and reinforced by caregivers, the infant develops an expectancy that his/her actions have an effect on the environment (Lewis & Goldberg, 1969). By providing toys that would reinforce this feeling of environmental control (i.e., toys that actually manifest a change when manipulated), the caregiver can insure that the child will continue to experience feelings of control over the environment.

Both the inanimate environment (including the physical surroundings and the toys presented to the child) and the social environment (including the individuals that the child comes in contact with) function independently to foster mastery motivation within the child (Yarrow, Rubenstein, Pedersen, & Jankowski, 1972). Social stimulation extends the development of social responsiveness and language, and occurs when caregivers respond to the child's social actions. This might include responding to the child's verbalizations, playing peek-a-boo, or responding to smiles by smiling back. Social stimulation also leads to stronger attachment to caregivers and feelings of relatedness to others. Stimulation from the inanimate environment furthers exploratory behaviors. This can be facilitated by providing toys that are interesting and responsive to the child. The infant's orientation to both objects and people become part of a feedback system with the environment which influences the infant's functioning over a long time period. A wider variety of inanimate objects leads to a greater amount of exploratory behavior exhibited by the child. The responsiveness of both the social and the inanimate environments facilitates motivational and skill development (Yarrow *et al.*, 1972).

Specific activities that are appropriate for this age group and that would enhance exploratory behavior are: mobiles that are activated by the child's movements; brightly colored objects that can easily be grasped, and that make sounds when moved; objects with interesting taste, texture, and smell; small, soft dolls or animals with emphasis on the face, especially the eyes.

Infants/Toddlers (9–24 Months)

Description of Infant/Toddler Motivation. During the period from 9 to 24 months, infants continue to try to control events and are better able to decide what to do to accomplish particular ends (Barrett & Morgan, 1995). Success is still not based on externally imposed standards because caregivers tend to reward all attempts, but is based on the infant's ability to accomplish desired ends. Infants begin to evaluate themselves and are motivated to do things for themselves. (Barrett & Morgan, 1995)

Research on Infant/Toddler Motivation. Although most research has been done with mothers and their children, it is likely the same for all caregivers. It has been found that the mother's responsive behavior to the child is the most important factor of determining future competence across all types of exploratory behavior (Hendrickson & Hansen, 1977). Mothers who were responsive, but who did not instantly answer every request from the children were more likely to rear motivated and competent children. These children are able to independently explore with little mother–child interaction, knowing that mother is there when needed. This enhanced freedom of exploration leads to greater development of competence. On the other hand, infants whose mothers are constantly choosing and directing the child's activities tend to initiate fewer of their own explorations, resulting in infants who show less competence and mastery motivation. Mothers who interact less often but facilitate discovery and exploration in their infants when they do play with them, tend to have children who persist longer on difficult tasks (Jennings, Harmon, Morgan, Gaiter, & Yarrow, 1979).

There appears to be a negative relation between the level of a child's mastery with objects and the amount of parental interference in the child's interactions with those objects (Wachs, 1987). The more a parent interferes with the child's independent exploration of objects, the less the child will progress toward mastery of that object. It is the independent exploration that leads to mastery. Providing responsive toys in one setting also helps the child learn strategies to deal with new toys in other settings. The child has learned the necessary strategies to deal with responsive toys at home, and these strategies can be applied to unfamiliar situations away from home. If a child has not learned how to deal with these toys at home, he faces difficult circumstances when in an unfamiliar situation. He not only has to deal with the new situation, but also with new toys, which may cause unmanageable stress (Wachs, 1987).

Infants of mothers who support their child's autonomy by allowing them to freely explore the environment tend to exhibit more overall persistence plus more competence and positive affect at 20 months of age (Frodi, Bridges, & Grolnick, 1985). Maternal sensitivity, defined as effectively reading infant cues and being responsive to the child's communications, relates highly with persistence and competence. Finally, these authors found that mothers who control their children's behaviors through the use of supportive rather than punitive corrections tend to have children who score higher on ratings of persistence, competence, and positive affect.

Adult attention-focusing skills become an important factor in caregiver interactions with the older infants (Yarrow *et al.*, 1984). Maternal stimulation teaches a child how to focus his or her own attention, enhancing the child's exploratory competence (Belsky, Goode, & Most, 1980). Infants who display the greatest amount of competence while exploring have mothers who frequently focus their attention on objects and events within the environment, in a responsive, respectful, and nonintrusive manner.

Recommendations for Caregivers. Caregivers can be effective in many ways when focusing the child's attention. The caregiver can arouse a child's interest when it is waning, redirect attention to a new area, or inhibit actions in an overstimulated child. While demonstrations can increase a child's interest in a particular toy, extended demonstrations can decrease that same interest. A single demonstration of a new object may be enough to interest the child, with the adult then allowing the child to explore on its own (Ruff & Rothbart, 1996). An important principle for adults to follow when trying to foster joint attentional states with infants while simultaneously trying to avoid being intrusive, is for adults to present various toys and stimuli but for them to follow the gazes, cues, and interests of the infant.

Language development is also influenced by joint attention with the caregiver. When the adult focuses verbally on an object that the child is interested in, the child can more easily establish the joint attentional focus with the adult. This facilitates greater opportunities for verbal development and other nonlinguistic scaffolding of the child's language development (Tomasello & Farrar, 1986).

A mother's emotional response to particular aspects of the environment can also have consequences for the child's responses in ambiguous situations (Gunnar & Stone, 1984). If mother is happy and positive, the infant is reassured and can respond positively to an uncertain situation. Infants look to adults for ways of reacting and positive caregiver responses can elicit the same responses in children.

Appropriate activities for children in this age range that would support autonomy and help focus attention are: play songs that are repetitive and simple enough for the child to repeat; flutter/action balls; bristle-type blocks; grasping toys that require complex manipulations (dials, switches, doors that open); push toys with sturdy handles for walking; puzzles with large knobbed pieces; round nesting materials.

Toddlers/Preschoolers 24–36 Months)

Description of Toddler/Preschooler Motivation. By the age of 24–36 months, children are developing an appreciation for standards, self-awareness, and self-evaluation. They are also developing the ability to execute a sequence of behavior to achieve a goal. By 3 years of age, children become interested in doing well rather than just accomplishing socially valued tasks (Barrett & Morgan, 1995).

Research on Toddler/Preschooler Motivation. Children in this age group are able to evaluate their own behavior and to respond appropriately to successes and failures. Children are able to sense which activities are harder for them, and experience greater pride when accomplishing these difficult tasks, with less shame when failing to accomplish them. When tasks are determined to be easy, shame is apparent if the task is failed, but only minimal pride is exhibited for successes (Lewis, Alessandri, & Sullivan, 1992).

Adult teaching styles remain of importance during the toddler years. Parents and teachers can help their children work through tasks by giving less support after success and more support after failures (Pratt, Kerig, Cowan, & Cowan, 1988). Successful parents respond to improvements of their children by systematically reducing their own involvement and allowing children to participate and accomplish as much of the task on their own as possible, using a strategy that is known as "scaffolding."

The basis of scaffolding is the establishment of a joint problem solving situation where two individuals interact while trying to reach a common goal. The adult is warm and responsive to the child's needs, but provides only enough support to keep the child engaged in the task and interacting. The adult carefully structures the task to maintain the child's interest by providing an obtainable challenge at all times. The amount of adult involvement lessens as the child gains competency in the task and is more able to function on his own. By allowing the child more freedom and by providing questions that allow the child to discover his own solutions to the problem, self-regulation skills, motivation, and learning are increased (Berk & Winsler, 1995).

Children early in the toddler years are becoming increasingly aware of the multistep nature of tasks (Barrett & Morgan, 1995). While simple cause-and-effect toys such as a pop-up toaster, were appropriate at earlier ages, more complex combination toys are now needed. A ring stacking toy that requires a sequence of actions for solution would be a more appropriate example for the toddler. Early in their second year, children become able to select appropriate tasks on their own due to a rapidly developing self-awareness (Busch-Rossnagel, Knauf-Jenson, & DesRosiers, 1995). Since the provision of appropriately challenging toys is positively related to persistence, the caregiver still has a very necessary role in selecting the range of activities that will be at the child's disposal and in providing the guidance and scaffolding necessary for children's effective learning of these more complex, sequential skills.

Recommendations for Caregivers. Appropriate activities for this age range that allow for self-evaluation, encourage multistep solutions, and provide situations for scaffolding would include: all sizes of balls to throw and catch; simple pop-up books; dress-me dolls; simple matching games; rhythm instruments to play with accompanying music; tunnels to crawl through; boards with magnetic shapes; 5–10 piece wooden puzzles; rocking horses; house-cleaning sets; matching and sorting materials.

Preschoolers (3–5 Years)

Description of Preschooler Motivation. By three years of age, children are becoming more involved with the use of verbal problem solving skills, and the internalization of speech. Children are beginning to direct their own learning, with private speech, or children's self-talk, being a critical component in this development. Private speech begins as social conversation, but develops into a means of self-regulation of activity (Berk & Winsler, 1995). The child uses overt verbal communication to direct her own behavior in problem solving situations. When the young child is challenged by an activity, she will talk herself through the solution to the problem. Just as the adult scaffolded the child's behavior in joint problem solving situations earlier, the child can now scaffold her own behavior through the use of private speech (Winsler, Diaz, & Montero, in press). The child is now able to accept the role of self-regulator which was once fulfilled by the adults in his environment.

Research on Preschooler Motivation. When children have reached a level of self-regulation, they are able to feel that they have gained some level of control over their own environment which leads to feelings of self-competence. This ties back to two of the three innate needs that are required for the development of intrinsic motivation: competence and autonomy. The ability to be self-regulated is the basis for autonomy, while the establishment of that autonomy leads to feelings of competence, all of which lead to strengthened intrinsic motivation. Private speech is an indicator that the child is involved in motivated, engaged activity. Rather than urging children to work quietly, caregivers should encourage children to verbalize about their activities, carefully scaffolding their interactions to provide the child with the appropriate level of help (Berk & Winsler, 1995).

The appropriate use of rewards is also of extreme importance at this age. As caregivers of young children, our intuition may tell us that if we reward children for completing a task, we will strengthen their motivation for engaging in that task. This notion is linked to the idea that children are devoid of their own motivation and that it is the job of caregivers to motivate children from the outside. However, we now know from a large body of research that this is simply not true. Giving rewards to children for an activity that is already interesting to them actually reduces their motivation for the activity and makes them less likely to repeat the activity later (Cameron & Pierce, 1994). Lepper, Greene, and Nisbett (1973), for example, compared two groups of preschool children who initially liked to draw. One group was given rewards (an award) for drawing and another group did not receive rewards for drawing. The two groups were then measured as to how much time children voluntarily spent drawing a week or so later. Children who received the rewards spontaneously chose to draw significantly less often than those who were not rewarded for drawing earlier. The reason is that young children are filled with their own internal, intrinsic motivation for various activities. When children are rewarded for doing a task for which they were already intrinsically interested, they tend to reinterpret that the reason for doing the activity is to get rewards rather than to do the activity for fun. The child can become focused on the extrinsic reward and lose sight of the intrinsic nature of learning. Another problem is that children often feel like they are under external rather than internal control when they receive excessive rewards, praise, and punishments. What results is that children are less likely in the future to want to repeat the task simply for fun (Lepper, 1983).

When rewards are used, they should be infrequent and given only as feedback that focuses on the effort of the child rather than the quality of the final accomplishment (Ames, 1992). By focusing on the accomplishment, rewards can lead to feelings of inadequacy and focus the child on his work in relation to others rather than on his own abilities and efforts (Solomon, 1996). Praise of the child's effort, on the other hand, will help instill feelings of self-worth that strengthen motivation (Deci *et al.*, 1991).

Recommendations for Caregivers. The role of the teacher is significant at this age level. The teacher provides the framework of goals and multiple activities for obtaining those goals. If the goals are appropriate for the children and the activities are well organized, then the teacher should be able to step back and allow the children to pursue their own learning with guidance from the teacher as needed. However, it is important that early childhood teachers not conclude from the above that the role of the teacher is to stand back and not intervene or get involved with the children's activities. Teachers need to provide structure and assistance, without completely controlling every learning activity. Neither extreme of the totally teacher-directed or the completely child-centered classroom seen in many early childhood programs is optimal for promoting motivation and self-regulation (Berk & Winsler, 1995). Rather, preschool programs which fall in the middle of the continuum, in which children are given independence within intermediate amounts of structure and adults sensitively direct children's activities, are perhaps the best models for developing children's intrinsic motivation and competence (Berk & Winsler, 1995). Children's persistence, motivation, and participation in learning-directed activities is greatest during early childhood curricular activities which are pursued in a semistructured environment (Winsler & Diaz, 1995).

When applied to older children who are moving on to preschool classes and pre-kindergarten situations, the same suggestions for activities should apply. Children need structure that allows for free exploration. They should be challenged and allowed to set their own goals and to evaluate their own successes. Setting the environment up for this type of learning is of utmost importance. Activities need to be carefully selected to provide the correct amount of challenge and to engage curiosity. Guidance and scaffolding techniques properly utilized will help children develop to their highest potential.

Appropriate activities for this age range which will provide the atmosphere for learning may include: large and small trucks, cars, animals of all types; simple machines; mea-

Table 1. Ten Key Principles For Strengthening Children's Intrinsic Motivation in Early Childhood Classrooms

1. *Provide a Responsive Environment.* Present toys and activities that allow the child to actually see the effect that s/he has on the environment.
2. *Give Consistent and Responsive Caregiving.* Respond to the child in consistent ways. This allows the child to develop a sense of expectancy for reactions to his/her behavior. Responding to the child's cries and vocalizations builds the child's sense of agency in the world.
3. *Support Children's Autonomy.* Allow for children's free exploration and choice within the parameters you have set up in your classroom.
4. *Establish Close Relationships.* Young children are more comfortable exploring and challenging themselves when they are in the presence of caregivers with whom they have close, warm, and caring relationships.
5. *Establish Joint Attention.* Provide many opportunities for joint attention and joint collaboration with children on specific objects and/or tasks and talk about the object/task. Such episodes increase feelings of relatedness and agency and advance language, a tool children will use later to regulate their own motivation.
6. *Provide a Good Motivational Role Model.* By showing confidence in your abilities as a teacher, keeping a positive emotional tone and attitude, modeling persistence and a preference for challenge, and showing enthusiasm in learning for learning's sake, early childhood professionals can maximize the chances that young children will exhibit these same motivational qualities.
7. *Provide Challenge.* Children's self-efficacy is increased as they succeed at more and more challenging tasks. Provide developmentally-appropriate, yet challenging, activities for the children and gradually increase the difficulty level as children become more competent.
8. *Scaffold Children's Problem Solving.* In order to insure that children remain engaged in goal-directed pursuits and succeed on challenging tasks, teacher guidance may be needed in the form of sensitive scaffolding. Scaffolding refers to an adult–child interaction style during joint collaboration in which the adult carefully and dynamically modifies task difficulty and adult verbal assistance (i.e., asking leading questions) to allow the child to become increasingly more responsible for completing the task on his or her own.
9. *Foster Self-Evaluation.* Give children opportunities to evaluate their own activities and performances. Explicit questions to children may be needed to get the children to do this (i.e., "How do you feel about your (product)?" "Are you happy with that or do you want to do more?"), or to get the children to realize that they are already self-evaluating (i.e., "I like the way you looked at your (product), decided it wasn't the way you wanted it, and changed it.")
10. *Use Rewards Sparingly and Cautiously.* External rewards can reduce children's intrinsic motivation. Rewards should be used sparingly in the classroom. When rewards are used, they should emphasize the child's effort, persistence, and process, rather than performance, and they should be given in an informational, rather than controlling, manner.

suring materials; beginning computer software; props for dress-up and pretend play; more complex puzzles including jigsaw as well as fit-in pieces; realistic ride-on toys; puppets and elaborate puppet theater; mosaic blocks; climbing structures; picture bingo, and matching games.

SUMMARY

From birth, children are instilled with an innate desire to learn about their world. What happens during the early years may determine the strength and type of motivation the child will have in later years. Caregivers play an extremely important role in the motivational life of the developing child. Table 1 provides a summary of what we feel are the ten most important principles for fostering intrinsic motivational patterns in early childhood classrooms. If the caregiver can remain flexible and respond to the changing needs of the child, then mastery motivation can be enhanced throughout the child's early development. Scaffolding techniques can be employed to further enhance the development of motivation, self-regulation, and learning skills. The careful and selective use of appropriate rewards focusing on the process of learning rather than the product will also enhance motivational skills. Allowing children to develop to their fullest potential can help them maintain their motivation and excitement in learning throughout the school years.

REFERENCES

Ames, C. (1992). Classrooms: Goals, structures, and student motivation. *Journal of Educational Psychology, 84,* 261–271.

Barrett, K. C., & Morgan, G. A. (1995). Continuities and discontinuities in mastery motivation during infancy and toddlerhood. A conceptualization and review. In R. H. MacTurk & G. A. Morgan (Eds.) *Mastery moti-*

vation: Origins, conceptualizations and applications (pp. 57–94). Norwood, NJ: Ablex.

Belsky, J., Goode, M. K., & Most, R. K. (1980). Material stimulation and infant exploratory competence: Cross-sectional, correlational, and experimental analysis. *Child Development, 51,* 1163–1178.

Berk, L. E., & Winsler, A. (1995). *Scaffolding children's learning: Vygotsky and early childhood education.* Washington, DC: National Association for the Education of Young Children.

Busch-Rossnagel, N. A., Knauf-Jensen, D. E., & DesRosiers, F. S. (1995). Mothers and others: The role of the socializing environment in the development of mastery motivation. In R. H. MacTurk & G. A. Morgan (Eds.), *Mastery motivation: Origins, conceptualizations and applications* (pp. 117–145), Norwood, NJ: Ablex.

Cameron, J., & Pierce, W. D. (1994). Reinforcement, reward, and intrinsic motivation: A meta-analysis. *Review of Educational Research, 39,* 363–423.

DeCasper, A. J., & Carstens, A. A. (1981). Contingencies of stimulation: Effects on learning and emotion in neonates. *Infant Behavior and Development, 4,* 19–35.

Deci, E. L. (1975). *Intrinsic motivation.* New York: Plenum Press.

Deci, E. L., & Ryan, R. M. (1987). The support of autonomy and the control of behavior. *Journal of Personality and Social Psychology, 53,* 1024–1037.

Deci, E. L., Vallerand, R. J., Pelletier, L. G., & Ryan, R. M. (1991). Motivation and education: The self-determination perspective. *Educational Psychologist, 26,* 325–346.

Ford, M. E., & Thompson, R. A. (1985). Perceptions of personal agency and infant attachment: Toward a life-span perspective on competence development. *International Journal of Behavioral Development, 8,* 377–406.

Frodi, A., Bridges, L., & Grolnick, W. (1985). Correlates of mastery-related behavior: A short-term longitudinal study of infants in their second year. *Child Development, 56,* 1291–1298.

Gottfried, A. E. (1985). Academic intrinsic motivation in elementary and junior high school students. *Journal of Educational Psychology, 77,* 631–645.

Gunnar, M. R., & Stone, C. (1984). The effects of positive maternal affect on infant responses to pleasant, ambiguous, and fear-provoking toys. *Child Development, 55,* 1231–1236.

Harter, S. (1978). Effectance motivation reconsidered: Toward a developmental model. *Human Development, 21,* 34–64.

Hendrickson, N. J., & Hansen, S. L. (1977). Toddlers: Competence and behavior patterns. *Child Study Journal, 7,* 79–97.

Jennings, K. D., Harmon, R. J., Morgan, G. A., Gaiter, J. L., & Yarrow, L. J. (1979). Exploratory play as an index of mastery motivation: Relationships to persistence, cognitive functioning, and environmental measures. *Developmental Psychology, 15,* 386–394.

Lepper, M. R. (1983). Extrinsic reward and intrinsic motivation: Implications for the classroom. In J. M. Levine & M. C. Wang (Eds.) *Teacher and student perceptions: Implications for learning* (pp. 281–317). Hillsdale, NJ: Erlbaum.

Lepper, M. R., Greene, D., & Nisbett, R. E. (1973). Undermining children's intrinsic interest with extrinsic rewards: A test of the overjustification hypothesis. *Journal of Personality and Social Psychology, 28,* 129–137.

Lewis, M., Alessandri, S. M., & Sullivan, M. W. (1990). Violation of expectancy, loss of control, and anger expressions in young infants. *Developmental Psychology, 26,* 745–751.

Lewis, M., Alesssandri, S. M., & Sullivan, M. W. (1992). Differences in shame and pride as a function of children's gender and task difficulty. *Child Development, 63,* 630–638.

Lewis, M., & Goldberg, S. (1969). Perceptual-cognitive development in infancy: A generalized expectancy model as a function of the mother-infant interaction. *Merrill-Palmer Quarterly, 15,* 81–100.

Pintrich, P. R., & Schunk, D. H., (1996). *Motivation in education: Theory, research, and applications.* Englewood Cliffs, New Jersey: Prentice-Hall.

Pratt, M. W., Kerig, P., Cowan, P. A., & Cowan, C. P. (1988). Mothers and fathers teaching 3-year-olds: Authoritative parenting and adult scaffolding of young children's learning. *Developmental Psychology, 24,* 832–839.

Rovee-Collier, C. K. (1987). Learning and memory. In J. D. Osofsky (Ed.), *Handbook of infant development* (2nd ed., pp. 98–148). New York: Wiley.

Ruff, H. A., & Rothbart, M. K. (1996). *Attention in early development: Themes and variations.* New York: Oxford University Press.

Ryan, R. M., & Powelson, C. L. (1991). Autonomy and relatedness as fundamental to motivation and education. *Journal of Experimental Education, 60,* 49–66.

Shields, P. J., & Rovee-Collier, C. K. (1992). Long-term memory for context-specific category information at six months. *Child Development, 63,* 245–259.

Solomon, M. A. (1996). Impact of motivational climate on students' behaviors and perceptions in a physical education setting. *Journal of Educational Psychology, 88,* 731–738.

Stipek, D. J. (1988). *Motivation to learn: From theory to practice.* Englewood Cliffs, New Jersey: Prentice-Hall.

Tomasello, M., & Farrar, M. J. (1986). Joint attention and early language. *Child Development, 57,* 1454–1463.

Wachs, T. D. (1987). Specificity of environmental action as manifest in environmental correlates of infants' mastery motivation. *Development Psychology, 23,* 782–790.

Watson, J. S., & Ramey, C. T. (1972). Reactions to response-contingent stimulation in early infancy. *Merrill-Palmer Quarterly, 18,* 219–227.

White, R. W. (1959). Motivation reconsidered: The concept of competence. *Psychological Review, 66,* 297–333.

Winsler, A., & Diaz, R. M. (1995). Private speech in the classroom: The effects of activity type, presence of others, classroom context, and mixed-age grouping. *International Journal of Behavioral Development, 18,* 463–487.

Winsler, A., Diaz, R. M., & Montero, I. (in press). The role of private speech in the transition from collaboration to independent task performance in young children. *Early Childhood Research Quarterly.*

Yarrow, L. J., MacTurk, R. H., Vietze, P. M., McCarthy, M. E., Klein, R. P., & McQuiston, S. (1984). Developmental course of parental stimulation and its relationship to mastery motivation during infancy. *Developmental Psychology, 20,* 492–503.

Yarrow, L. J., Rubenstein, J. L., Pedersen, F. A., & Jankowski, J. J. (1972). Dimensions of early stimulation and their differential effects on infant behavior. *Merrill-Palmer Quarterly, 18,* 205–218.

Adverse Effects of Witnessing Violence

by Victor LaCerva

Brain Basics

Mounting evidence reveals that the adverse neurological effects of experiencing or witnessing violence are considerable. The brain is designed to sense, process, store, and then act on information related to survival. The more activated a particular area of the brain becomes, the more stimulated it will be to organize and develop—often at the expense of other areas of the brain. This process is known as *use dependent learning.*

Essentially we have three brain structures, composed of a midbrain (which we share with the reptiles), a limbic system emotional brain (which we share with the other mammals), and a cortex thinking brain (which is distinctly human). We store memories and information at each of these sites. The stored material is later activated in several ways. We use cognitive memory to recall a phone number or a person's name. Emotional memory brings on sadness when we hear an oldies song reminiscent of a long lost love. Relying on spatial memory, we are able to find our way home without a map. Kinesthetic memory helps us ride a bike even when we haven't been on one for years.

A type of memory we don't often think about also exists. It is called *state* memory or reflexive memory, and it is associated with the midbrain. Research has shown that a Vietnam vet, after hearing a helicopter overhead, may exhibit an elevated pulse rate and increased blood pressure as well as general body tension and irritability for a period of time. This constellation of symptoms occurs because his internal alarm system designed to set off a fight-or-flight response has been activated by the state memory he experienced in combat. His body, informed by his midbrain, *remembers* the trauma of combat, although he may not consciously associate the helicopter with his battleground experience.

The same phenomenon occurs in children who have been traumatized. The younger a child is, the more likely she is to internalize a state memory of a traumatic event. The more often her brain's fight-or-flight response is stimulated with repeated exposures to trauma, the more enhanced and *turned on* her midbrain functions will be. A toddler who has been harshly punished or who has watched mom being beaten by dad, for example, will, in a moment reminiscent of the trauma, very quickly pass from a state of relative calm to one of either vigilance, alarm, fear, or terror. Correspondingly, her body will prepare to either run or do battle, and her pulse rate will increase significantly, indicating precisely where she is on the response-to-threat continuum. The traumatized toddler has, like the Vietnam vet, internalized a state memory. Her physiology has been altered as a result of her exposure to violence. With repeated exposure, her

Victor LaCerva, MD, has been actively working in violence prevention for more than 12 years. He currently is medical director of the Family Health Bureau, New Mexico Department of Health, and holds a clinical faculty appointment with the Department of Pediatrics at the University of New Mexico Medical School. He has two daughters who constantly teach him what he most needs to know about raising children in a violent world. Victor cares deeply about preventing violence and believes that solutions are found by strengthening what is already good within ourselves, our families, our communities, and our culture.

From *Child Care Information Exchange,* November 1999, pp. 44-47.

baseline pulse rate will be reset at increasingly higher levels, and her brain development will be adversely affected.

Post Traumatic Stress Disorder (PTSD)

Infants and young children who repeatedly experience fear-provoking situations eventually begin showing signs of post-traumatic stress disorder. PTSD is, in essence, a persistent triggering of the alarm system by an exaggerated state memory. What was originally a protective bodily response has become detrimental. PTSD is typically accompanied by three patterns of behavior:

■ **Recurrent and intrusive recollections, also called flashbacks, in which a threatening event is relived with all one's senses.** These recollections often manifest as nightmares or a repetitive reenactment of the traumatic events during play. Children whose play becomes focused on trauma have fewer opportunities to engage in forms of play that stimulate brain development in areas other than the midbrain.

■ **Avoidance of stimuli or numbing of general responsiveness to the environment.** In the first instance, children will become extremely withdrawn and cautious in their play. In the second, they may *space out* when asked about a behavior related to the original trauma. Having observed that adults are unable to restrain themselves, the children may believe they cannot learn to control their own behavior. They may also blame themselves for post-traumatic events, and out of fear and inadequacy, shut down completely. In addition, they will most likely avoid triggers—key reminders of the trauma that elicit intense distress. An infant may pull away from someone with a beard, for example, or a young child may refuse to go to a park with rope swings.

■ **Persistent symptoms of increased arousal.** Children may experience night terrors, hypervigilance, frequent startle responses, or sudden angry outbursts. Unable to concentrate, due to sleep deprivation and the constant search for clues to a threatening situation, children often have difficulty in school.

In summary, infants, toddlers, or other children who experience or witness violence at home or on the street are apt to feel fear, anger, powerlessness, guilt, confusion, despair, sadness, or shame. These feelings are most often expressed through bodily pains and acting-out or withdrawn behaviors. Changes in the brain result in behavioral characteristics that are detrimental to learning and development (see *Post Traumatic Stress Disorder in Children Exposed to Violence*).

Post Traumatic Stress Disorder in Children Exposed to Violence

PTSD is a continuation and an exaggeration of the normal protective fight or flight response. In the body's attempt to protect itself, symptoms appear which can be destructive, especially in children.

Symptoms of PTSD include recurring intrusive recollection of the traumatic event, persistent avoidance of stimuli associated with the trauma or numbing of general responsiveness, and persistent symptoms of increased arousal and physiological hyperarousal.

A child with PTSD may appear anxious, behaviorally impulsive, hypervigilant, motorically hyperactive, withdrawn or depressed, have sleep difficulties, have increased heart rate or blood pressure.

Diagnostic labels given to a child with PTSD include attention deficit hyperactivity disorder, conduct disorders, anxiety disorders, mood disorders.

Factors important in the development of PTSD following trauma include the nature of the trauma, degree of threat, available support system, availability of early intervention, and sense of control.

Children exposed to violence thus may have differences in baseline state of arousal, differences in cognitive processing, over-reading of nonverbal cues and under-reading of verbal information.

What we need to do to help children resolve PTSD:

1. Realize it is a normal reaction to crazy circumstances, and deal with the anxiety and fear as it arises.
2. Mobilize support and educate family and teachers on what to expect.
3. Cognitive focus on how we explain to ourselves and others what happened.
4. Consistent, predictable nurturance and safety.

Effects on Caregivers

Parents living in violent settings experience stress, which further affects their children's development. Many parents, unable to protect their children from the violence, develop a debilitating sense of helplessness during these episodes and become increasingly overprotective in other aspects of child care. Some become so immersed in their own grief that they are unable to meet their children's needs for comfort. Others, wrestling with their own traumatic responses, become demanding, irritable, and angry because their children are unable to help them. Violence in the household can take an even heavier toll on the caretaker-child relationship. Recurrent out-

Working with a Traumatized Child

Stability, Predictability, and Information!

A person that is calm, deliberate, and *in control* will significantly calm the fearful child. Use familiar adults to help calm the child.

Tell the child who you are, what you are doing, and what you will be doing. Be a *play-by-play* announcer.

Tell the child what happened in simple age-appropriate words. Let him know someone is taking care of the other people. Repeat often.

The way in which you talk is as important as the actual words. Children read nonverbal cues more than hear words in traumatic situations.

breaks of rage and abuse may bring back painful memories for parents who prefer not to deal with the past, causing them to withdraw further from their children. Living with violence can also produce depression, in which case a parent's TLC turns to *Talk less, Look sad, and Can't control mood swings*. Depressive states have devastating consequences, particularly for young infants, who are programmed to interact with lively, talkative, and consistently caring adults. Infants who experience the *unholy triad* of early exposure to family violence, substance abuse, and depression in effect have a triple negative impact on their developing brain.

When the sociological incubators in which children are evolving become so damaged, service providers must organize effective responses. Current responses, as we know, are pitifully inadequate. Due to the failure of early identification, fragmented intervention, and a dearth of mental health resources, we are left with a large pool of untreated victims of violence, each of whom invariably experiences more neglect, unpredictability, chaos, and violence.

The Action Agenda

The challenge before us is to begin viewing victims of violence through the lens of social ecology, and to build solid inroads into this previously impenetrable landscape. Resiliency research tells us that the ongoing presence of a caring adult in the life of a child can make all the difference. If we examine the various domains of a child's life, we can build on this concept and support children through the trauma of witnessing violence.

■ **Crisis support.** All families exposed to violence must be given on-the-spot assistance. Front-line law enforcement and emergency services personnel must understand how to minimize the adverse effects of witnessing (see *Working with a Traumatized Child).*

■ **Recognition and immediate referral.** Instances of suspected child abuse and sexual assault need to be acknowledged, and children living in violent households need to be placed in the hands of knowledgeable case-management teams.

■ **Improved management of the violent scene.** Children should be removed from the scene as quickly as possible. If they must be interviewed, it should take place once, in a session conducted collaboratively by law enforcement and health professionals; this is especially important in cases of sexual trauma. Follow-up services must be provided to assist children in processing the event and to minimize the onset of PTSD (see *Important Messages for Children).*

■ **Stress debriefing for all service providers.** On-the-scene teams as well as follow-up teams require assistance in processing the complexity of emotions and high stress levels that accrue from intervening in trauma. The growth of Critical Incident Stress Debriefing (CISD) ca-

Important Messages for Children (EASY)

E Address child at her **eye** level.

A Talk with simple, direct **age appropriate** language.

S Use a **soft** voice and calm, neutral tone; nonthreatening, comforting body language.

Y **Yield**, for a moment, to seeing the situation through the child's eyes.

Helpful phrases:

This must be scary for you.
Who can you talk to about this?
It's not your fault.
It is not your responsibility to solve the problem.
We'll do everything we can to keep you safe.

Be the fair witness: What happened to you isn't right, or fair, or your fault, and things will get better.

pability for service providers in various communities has been encouraging. Debriefing will help these individuals deepen their understanding and enhance their readiness to help other victims in the future.

■ **Security and consistency.** For improved chances of recovery, children exposed to violence require close relationships with caring adults; consistent and reliable child care routines; and safe, familiar environments (see *Principles of Support*).

■ **A fundamental shift in how we handle the response to domestic violence cases, where children are witnessing but are not physically abused.** Many of the programs around the country set up to specifically assist children witnessing violence find that this population represents their greatest caseload. Yet, in most areas of the country, there is no adequate response to these children, and social services is most often not involved unless there is physical abuse. A few model programs are paving the way by coordinating a combined domestic violence and social service intervention.

PTSD and compromised brain development can be prevented through early support and intervention—both of which are best provided by a strong community response to violent events. With well-integrated teamwork, we can also reduce the suffering of these untreated victims of violence.

Principles of Support

(Adapted from Boston Medical Center)

Healing begins with relationships. The adult nurturing relationship is the most powerful tool we have to help children heal from traumatic events.

Help children know what to expect at home and at school. Provide a highly structured, predictable environment for children. Establish and reinforce routines.

Give children permission to tell their stories. It helps children to talk about the violence in their lives with trusted adults.

Give parents help and support. Help parents understand that young children think differently than adults and need careful explanations about scary events.

Foster children's self-esteem. Children who live with violence need reminders that they are lovable, competent, and important.

Don't try it alone. Identify and collaborate with other caregivers in the child's life.

Teach alternatives to violence. Help children learn conflict resolution skills and nonviolent ways of playing.

Model nurturing in our interactions with children. Serve as role models for children by resolving issues in respectful, nonviolent ways.

Unit 5

Unit Selections

28. **Play As Curriculum,** Francis Wardle
29. **Why Curriculum Matters in Early Childhood Education,** Lawrence J. Schweinhart and David P. Weikart
30. **Isn't That Cute? Transforming the Cute Curriculum into Authentic Learning,** Lynn Kirkland
31. **Productive Questions: Tools for Supporting Constructivist Learning,** Mary Lee Martens
32. **Beginning to Implement the Reggio Philosophy,** Lynn Staley
33. **Documenting Children's Learning,** Judy Harris Helm
34. **Challenging Movement Experiences for Young Children,** Stephen W. Sanders and Bill Yongue
35. **What Role Should Technology Play in Young Children's Learning?** Susan W. Haugland

Key Points to Consider

- What should be the role of play in an early childhood classroom?
- How does a teacher begin to implement the Reggio philosophy?
- Why should teachers move beyond providing cute activities to learning experiences that provide for authentic learning?
- How does a teacher document the learning taking place in his or her classroom? What are important considerations for teachers and parents when planning for initial experiences with technology?

Links

www.dushkin.com/online/

24. **California Reading Initiative**
    http://www.sdcoe.k12.ca.us/score/promising/prreading/prreadin.html
25. **Early Childhood Education Online**
    http://www.ume.maine.edu/cofed/eceol/welcome.shtml
26. **Kathy Schrock's Guide for Educators**
    http://www.discoveryschool.com/schrockguide/
27. **Phi Delta Kappa**
    http://www.pdkintl.org
28. **Reggio Emilia**
    http://ericps.ed.uiuc.edu/eece/reggio.html
29. **Teachers Helping Teachers**
    http://www.pacificnet.net/~mandel/
30. **Tech Learning**
    http://www.techlearning.com

These sites are annotated on pages 4 and 5.

Curricular Issues

At a time when communities and individuals are spending millions of dollars to provide additional opportunities for adult play time in the form of golf courses and recreational facilities, educators are continuing to defend the offering of free choice play time for young children in school settings. Teachers are also encouraging parents to provide fewer structured activities for their children and to allow for more free time. Children are increasingly being denied the chance to participate in what many adults remember as their fondest childhood memories. Leisurely passing away the hours while attempting to dam up a little stream and float leaves and sticks, finding secret hiding places for games of hide and go seek, or using every available cushion, pillow, and blanket to make a fort are memories many adults have of childhood. What will be your children's memories of their play experiences? For years teachers have been justifying the inclusion of play in the curriculum. With new schools being built without playgrounds (see "Playtime Is Cancelled" in unit 3) and teachers being criticized for taking too much time away from learning by allowing children to play, the battle will not end soon. In "Play As Curriculum" Francis Wardle brings the importance of play in the curriculum to light once again in an article that presents play as a positive learning experience. We can only hope that all children will experience play early and often throughout their childhood.

Lawrence Schweinhart and David Weikart discuss the ongoing debate about early childhood curriculum in "Why Curriculum Matters in Early Childhood Education." They provide information on curriculum and the role of the teacher in early childhood settings. With many still teaching in a teacher-directed format we now have clear evidence of the importance of children participating in child-initiated, active, hands-on learning experiences. Just as we now know not to put butter on a burn because medical research has proved that to be harmful, we must use educational research to change those ingrained educational practices that do not provide for optimal learning.

Young children are eager to delve into curriculum that is compelling. Activities that will allow them to investigate, dig deep, and roll up their sleeves and get involved are the types of learning experiences that send the message, "learning is fun, and I can be successful." What children often are presented with is watered-down, teacher-directed, and lacking in elements of true discovery. A number of the articles in unit 5 provide opportunities for the reader to reflect on the authentic learning experiences available to children. How can they investigate, explore, and create while studying a particular area of interest? One suggestion is to make children work for their learning, rather than presenting it to them all neatly cut into the appropriate shapes to be glued on a piece of paper. Classrooms where children spend day after day completing teacher-designed activities are robbing children of valuable learning experiences. Susan Haugland asks a further question: "What Role Should Technology Play in Young Children's Learning?" and provides some challenging answers to teachers and parents.

Play as Curriculum

BY FRANCIS WARDLE, PH.D.

Play! There are two radically different views on the value of play. Early childhood educators, child development specialists, and some parents believe play is the best way for young children to learn the concepts, skills, and tasks needed to set a solid foundation for later school and life success. School administrators, many parents, and most politicians believe play is a waste of time, off task behavior, needless coddling of young children, messy and noisy, unstructured and uneducational—an unaffordable luxury in an ever-more competitive world. With the new emphasis on national and state standards and school accountability, many early childhood programs are eliminating play. Is play worth fighting for? If so, why?

Definition of Play

While most of us know play when we see it, academics have had trouble defining it (Johnson, Christie, & Yawkey, 1999). "Play involves a free choice activity that is non-literal, self-motivated, enjoyable and process oriented. Critical to this definition is the non-literal, non-realistic aspect. This means external aspects of time, use of materials, the environment, rules of the play activity, and roles of the participants are all made up by the children playing. They are based on the child's sense of reality" (Wardle, 1987, p. 27). "Children do not play for a reward—praise, money, or food. They play because they like it."(p. 28). Children who compete to make the best wooden ship are not playing. Children who are told they must use the block with an "A" on it to create a word are not playing, and children who are asked to label the colors of their paints, instead of using them to create a picture, are not playing.

This child-centered aspect of play creates the central dilemma. Increasingly, we expect education programs to meet prescribed adult objectives. Schools, funding sources, and curricular developers expect programs to teach specific outcomes and provide child-based results (Kagan & Cohen, 1997). And more and more parents expect their young children to be learning specific academic skills. If adults develop these standards and outcomes, there is no room left for child-centered learning—play. Ironically, at the same time we are eliminating play from the formal education of young children. Therefore, many of our children do not have access to the natural play experiences we experienced as children. They don't walk in the park collecting leaves, throw stones in the water to see the ever-expanding ripples, play racing-of-the-sticks under the bridge, build muddy castles on the banks of a cold stream, or create a frontier fort with their buddies. They don't scramble up gnarled trees, skip across meadows full of flowers, pick nuts from low branches, use a fallen tree as a natural balance beam, or sit on an old tractor imagining that they are leading a convoy of explorers across the Sahara Desert.

Why is Play Critical to Future Academic Success?

As we push more academics and computer instruction on young children; as we observe many of our children's home become dominated by passive TV watching and computer games; and as we see many of our publicly funded early childhood programs become downward extensions of public schools, we need to advocate for children's right to play. More and more parents question the value of young children climbing trees, playing in the sandbox, and splashing paint all over themselves. Below are some of the various kinds of play, and why they are important.

Types of Play

Motor/Physical Play

Motor play provides critical opportunities for children to develop both individual gross and fine muscle strength and an overall integration of muscles, nerves, and brain functions. Recent research has confirmed the critical link between stimulating activity and brain development (Shore, 1997). Young children must have ample opportunities to develop physically, and motor play instills this disposition toward physical activity. With so many American adults experiencing health problems from being overweight, we have a responsibility to encourage physical activity in young children.

Social Play

A variety of opportunities for children to engage in social play are the best mechanisms for progressing through the different social stages. By interacting with others in play settings, children learn social rules such as, give and take, reciprocity, cooperation, and sharing. Through a range of interactions with children at different social stages, children also learn to use moral reasoning to develop a mature sense of values. To be prepared to function effectively in the adult world, children need to participate in lots of social play.

Constructive Play

Constructive play is when children manipulate their environment to create things. This type of play occurs when children build towers and cities with blocks, play in the sand, construct contraptions on the woodworking bench, and draw murals with chalk on the sidewalk. Constructive play allows children to experiment with objects; find out combi-

From *Early Childhood News,* March/April 1999, pp. 6-9. © 1999 by *Early Childhood News.* Reprinted by permission.

nations that work and don't work; and learn basic knowledge about stacking, building, drawing, damming, and constructing. It also gives children a sense of accomplishment and empowers them with control of their environment. Children who are comfortable manipulating objects and materials also become good at manipulating words, ideas, and concepts.

Fantasy Play

Children learn to abstract, to try out new roles and possible situations, and to experiment with language and emotions with fantasy play. In addition, children develop flexible thinking; learn to create beyond the here and now; stretch their imaginations; use new words and word combinations in a risk-free environment; and use numbers and words to express ideas, concepts, dreams, and histories. In an ever-more technological society, lots of practice with all forms of abstraction—time, place, amount, symbols, words, and ideas—is essential.

Games With Rules

Developmentally, most children progress from an egocentric view of the world to an understanding of the importance of social contracts and rules. Part of this development occurs as they learn that games like Follow the Leader, Red Rover, Simon Says, baseball, and soccer cannot function without everyone adhering to the same set of rules. This "games with rules" concept teaches children a critically important concept—the game of life has rules (laws) that we all must follow to function productively (Wardle, 1987).

But Why Play?

Play opponents argue that the ever increasing amount of information and skills needed by young children require direct teacher instruction to specific goals and objectives. They believe we cannot afford to take valuable time away from important academic activities to allow children to hide in a fantasy world of play. But play is, in fact, the most efficient, powerful, and productive way to learn the information young children need.

First, children progress through stages of play, and through levels (complexity) of play. As children master new concepts and practice them through repetitive play, they progress to the next level. In essence, children create their own curriculum. Because children like to learn new information and want to master new tasks (ever watched a child persist in learning to ride a bike?) and because they hate to be bored, children self-diagnose what they know and what they can learn next. Play provides the ultimate curriculum for social, physical, and cognitive advancement. Secondly, by using materials, interactions with others, and mastery of tasks and skills to progress through levels of play, children develop a sense of control of their environment and a feeling of competence and enjoyment that they can learn. Finally, play provides a natural integration between all the critical brain functions and learning domains that are often missing with discrete teacher instruction. Recent brain research shows that this integration is very important to development (Shore, 1997).

Play is also a very effective way for children to accumulate a vast amount of basic knowledge about the world around them, knowledge needed for later learning in language, math, science, social studies, art, and medicine. When playing with sticks in the sand a child learns about the properties of sand, how posts are used for building, the way materials must be retained from rivers, roads, and mountainsides, the effect of moisture on materials, the impact of wind and the nature of gravity, and ways of creating patterns, shapes, and lines by drawing in the sand. A child playing with tadpoles in a pond learns about the cycle of life, the properties of water including sinking and floating, the effect of cold water on the body's thermal system, and concepts related to water safety and drowning. Children engaged in socio-dramatic play experiment with words, phrases, and idioms they have heard and learn new and more complex ways to express themselves.

Role of the Teacher

Somehow the phrase, "free play" has entered our vocabulary. "Free play" means play free of structure and adult involvement. This is unfortunate, because adults have a variety of critical roles in supporting children's play. These roles include providing materials that encourage high-quality play, structuring environments, modeling play (like when the teacher becomes a participant in a socio-dramatic activity), and introducing children to new play opportunities (girls on the workbench and boys in the dramatic play area). Vygotsky's idea of scaffolding (Berk & Winsler, 1995) is particularly useful in explaining the role of the teacher in extending play. Further, his concept of the use of private speech by children to structure, extend, and expand their own play, illustrates children's internalization of teacher scaffolding. The teacher does, in fact, have a central role in children's play.

Conclusion

To succeed in an ever-more complex and technological world, our children need a solid foundation based on play. We must be very careful about accelerating them too quickly into abstract skills and isolated concepts (Wardle, 1996). Lots of play at an early age enables children to develop the wide, integrated foundation required for future academic success. It also will develop in our children a love of learning, a love that is desperately needed by children who can look forward to a minimum of 13 years of formal education.

References

Berk, L.E., & Winsler, A. (1995). *Scaffolding children's learning: Vygotsky and early childhood education*. Washington, DC: NAEYC.

Johnson, J.E., Christie, J.F., & Yawkey, T.D. (1999). *Play and early childhood development.* (2nd ed.). New York: Longman.

Kagan, S.L., & Cohen. N.E. (1997) Not by chance. *Creating an early childhood and education system for America's children.* New Haven, CT: Yale University Press.

Shore, R., (1997). *Rethinking the brain. New insights into early development.* New York: Families and Work Institute.

Wardle, F. (1987). Getting back to the basics of children's play. *Child Care Information Exchange*, Sept., 27–30.

Wardle, F (1996). *Of labels, skills, and concepts.* Urbana, Ill. ERIC Clearinghouse.

Francis Wardle, Ph.D., teaches for the University of Phoenix (Colorado) and is the executive director for the Center for the Study of Biracial Children. He has just published the book, *Tomorrow's Children.*

Why Curriculum Matters in Early Childhood Education

A long-running study of the effects of preschool programs for children in poverty shows the benefits of a child-initiated, teacher-facilitated curriculum.

Lawrence J. Schweinhart and David P. Weikart

A widespread consensus has developed in favor of public support for preschool programs for young children living in poverty. Head Start and state prekindergarten programs today serve about two-thirds of U.S. 4-year-olds living in poverty. Federal Head Start spending has tripled in the past decade, and nearly two-thirds of the states provide similar programs for 4-year-olds (see box, "Children in Poverty").

Influential groups of citizens, such as the Committee for Economic Development, have lent their political clout to this development—partly because of the findings of the High/Scope Perry Preschool Study that a high-quality preschool program cuts participants' lifetime arrest rate in half, significantly improves their educational and subsequent economic success, and provides taxpayers a return equal to 716 percent of their original investment in the program, a return that outperformed the U.S. stock market during the same period of time (Schweinhart et al. 1993; Barnett 1996).

We have less consensus on the goals of preschool programs. The National Association for the Education of Young Children (Bredekamp and Copple 1997) strongly favors *developmentally appropriate practice,* but this position has found detractors. Academic critics, such as Mallory and New (1994), argue that developmentally appropriate practice is socially constructed, context-bound, and insensitive to cultural and individual differences in development. Conservative critics, such as Hirsch (1997), see it as progressive ideology without adequate research support.

Should early childhood curriculum be adult-directed or child-initiated? Or should there be a balance of these two approaches? Is there a well-defined, research-proven model we can follow? The High/Scope Preschool Curriculum Comparison Study (the study that followed the

From *Educational Leadership,* Vol. 55, No. 6, March 1998, pp. 57-60. Reprinted with permission of the Association for Supervision and Curriculum Development.

Because all three groups had biweekly home visits, home visits alone cannot explain the differences that were found.

High/Scope Perry Preschool Study), which was begun in 1969 and now includes data through age 23, sheds new light on these questions (Schweinhart and Weikart 1997 a and b).

This study assesses which of three theoretically distinct preschool curriculum models works best. The study has followed the lives of 68 young people born in poverty who were randomly assigned at ages 3 and 4 to one of three groups, each experiencing a different curriculum model.

Three Curriculum Models

The Curriculum Comparison Study included the following curriculum models:

- *Direct Instruction* was a scripted approach in which the teacher presented activities and the children responded to them. Classroom activities were sequences of academic lessons, emphasizing positive reinforcements of correct responses. Teachers clearly defined academic goals in reading, arithmetic, and language. The psychological tradition was behaviorist (Bereiter and Engelmann 1966).

- *The High/Scope Curriculum* was an open-framework approach in which teacher and child planned and initiated activities and worked together. Classroom activities were partly the result of the *plan-do-review* sequence, planned by the children themselves and supported by the teachers. These activities reflected experiences intended to promote intellectual, social, and physical development. The psychological tradition was constructivist and cognitive-developmental (Hohmann and Weikart 1995).

- *The traditional Nursery School* was a child-centered approach in which children initiated activities and the teachers responded to them. The teachers created classroom themes from everyday events and encouraged children to actively engage in free play. The goal was to create an environment in which children could develop naturally, and the psychological tradition was psychoanalytic (Sears and Dowley 1963).

Children in Poverty

Here are resources on the number of preschool children in poverty and the programs that serve them:

- The number of Head Start 4-year-olds living in poverty (http://www.acf.dhhs.gov/programs/hsb/statfact.htm).

- The number of children served by state prekindergarten programs (Adams and Sandfort 1994).

- The number of 4-year-olds living in poverty (one-sixth of the number of children under 6 living in poverty) (http://www.census.gov/hhes/poverty/poverty96/pv96est1.html).

Program staff implemented the curriculum models independently and to high standards, in two-and-a-half-hour classes five days a week and home visits every two weeks. Because all three groups had biweekly home visits, these visits alone cannot explain the differences that were found, although they may have intensified the curriculum models' effects. All other aspects of the program were virtually identical. So, having taken into account slight differences in the groups' gender makeup, we are confident that outcome differences represent the effects of the three curriculum models.

Advantages at Age 23

Based on reports by the young people, either the High/Scope group or the Nursery School group had a total of 10 significant advantages over the Direct Instruction group, but the Direct Instruction group had no significant advantages over these groups. The High/Scope and Nursery School groups did not differ significantly from one another on any outcome variable.

By age 23, the High/Scope and Nursery School groups had two significant advantages over the Direct Instruction group:

- *Only 6 percent of either the High/Scope or the Nursery School group needed treatment for emotional impairment or disturbance during their schooling, as compared to 47 percent of the Direct Instruction group.* Because 47 percent is well above the typical rate for this population (17 percent of the comparable no-program group in the High/Scope Perry Preschool Study required such treatment), the Direct Instruction program experience appears to have left some of its participants with serious negative emotional residue.

- *Forty-three percent of the High/Scope group and 44 percent of the Nursery School group at some time up to age 23 engaged in volunteer work, as compared to 11 percent of the Direct Instruction group.* The programs that encouraged children to initiate their own activities had more

Child-initiated learning activities help children develop social responsibility and interpersonal skills.

graduates engaging in volunteer work in the community as young adults, suggesting greater awareness of the needs of others and their responsibility to take action to help.

The High/Scope group had six additional significant advantages over the Direct Instruction group:

• *Only 10 percent of the High/Scope group had ever been arrested for a felony, as compared to 39 percent of the Direct Instruction group.* Given the intractability of crime, this fourfold reduction in felony arrests is of great importance. It parallels the finding of the High/Scope Perry Preschool Study through age 27 that only 7 percent of the program group (which used child-initiated activities) but 35 percent of the no-program group had been arrested five or more times (Schweinhart et al. 1993). These data indicate the clearly different levels of personal and social responsibility that the High/Scope and Direct Instruction groups developed.

• *None of the High/Scope group had ever been arrested for a property crime, as compared to 38 percent of the Direct Instruction group.* Property crime may be distinguished from violent and drug-related crimes by its emphasis on assaulting authority. The High/Scope model places authority (teachers) in the role of resource and support. Direct Instruction gives teachers power and control and requires children to submit. As young adults, more of the former Direct Instruction preschoolers strike out at authority.

• *Twenty-three percent of the High/Scope group reported at age 15 that they had engaged in 10 or more acts of misconduct, as compared to 56 percent of the Direct Instruction group.* Although this finding did not reappear in self-reports at age 23, it presaged the age-23 arrest findings.

• *Thirty-six percent of the High/Scope group said that various kinds of people gave them a hard time, as compared to 69 percent of the Direct Instruction group.* Apparently, the High/Scope group more willingly accepted responsibility for their own actions than did the Direct Instruction group and had developed ways to relate positively to authorities and others, rather than to blame or attack them for their actions.

• *Thirty-one percent of the High/Scope group had married and were living with their spouses, as compared to none of the Direct Instruction group.* Marriage may be seen as a step that takes personal responsibility and a willingness to adapt to others.

• *Seventy percent of the High/Scope group planned to graduate from college, as compared to 36 percent of the Direct Instruction group.* While no differences were found in actual high school graduation rates or in the highest year of schooling, such planning by the High/Scope group reflects greater optimism, self-confidence, and aspirations for the future.

The Nursery School group had two additional significant advantages over the Direct Instruction group, both of which resemble the felony arrest difference between the High/Scope group and the Direct Instruction group.

• *Only 9 percent of the Nursery School group had been arrested for a felony at ages 22–23, as compared to 34 percent of the Direct Instruction group.*

• *None of the Nursery School group had ever been suspended from work, as compared to 27 percent of the Direct Instruction group.*

Goals of Early Childhood Education

This study through age 23 found that young people born in poverty experienced fewer emotional problems and felony arrests if they had attended a preschool program based on child-initiated learning activities focused broadly on children's development, rather than scripted direct instruction focused specifically on academics.

These findings suggest that the goals of early childhood education should not be limited to academic preparation for school, but should also include helping children learn to make decisions, solve problems, and get along with others. Scripted teacher-directed instruction, touted by some as the surest path to school readiness, may purchase a temporary improvement in academic performance at the cost of a missed opportunity for long-term improvement in personal and social behavior. On the other hand, child-initiated learning activities seem to help children develop their social responsibility and interpersonal skills so that they become more personally and socially competent, fewer of them need treatment for emotional impairment or disturbance. Fewer are arrested for felonies as young adults.

Although the High/Scope and Nursery School groups did not differ significantly on any outcome variable at age 23, the High/Scope curriculum model is easier to replicate than the Nursery School approach because of High/Scope's extensive documentation, training program, and assessment system. Well-documented, research-proven curriculum models based on child-initiated learning appear to have the best potential for supporting successful child development.

References

Adams, G., and J. Sandfort. (1994). *First Steps, Promising Futures: State Prekindergarten Initiatives in the Early 1990s.* Washington, D.C.: Children's Defense Fund.

Barnett, W.S. (1996). *Lives in the Balance: Age 27 Benefit-Cost Analysis of the High/Scope Perry Preschool Program* (Monographs of the High/Scope Educational Research Foundation, 11). Ypsilanti, Mich.: High/Scope Press.

Bereiter, C., and S. Engelmann. (1966). *Teaching the Disadvantaged Child in the Preschool.* Englewood Cliffs, N.J.: Prentice-Hall.

Bredekamp, S., and C. Copple, eds. (1997). *Developmentally Appropriate Practice in Early Childhood Programs,* rev. ed. Washington, D.C.: National Association for the Education of Young Children.

Hirsch, E.D. (June 18, 1997). "On Faddism, Guruism and Junk Research." *Los Angeles Times.* (Available online for $1.50; use search terms E.D. Hirsch and 1997 at http://www/latimes.com/home/archives).

Hohmann, M., and D.P. Weikart. (1995). *Educating Young Children: Active Learning Practices for Preschool and Child Care Programs.* Ypsilanti, Mich.: High/Scope Press.

Mallory, B.L, and R.S. New. (1994). *Diversity and Developmentally Appropriate Practices: Challenges for Early Childhood Education.* New York: Teachers College Press.

Schweinhart, L.J., H.V. Barnes, and D.P. Weikart. (1993). *Significant Benefits: The High/Scope Perry Preschool Study Through Age 27* (Monographs of the High/Scope Educational Research Foundation, 10). Ypsilanti, Mich.: High/Scope Press.

Schweinhart, L.J., and D.P. Weikart. (1997a). "The High/Scope Preschool Curriculum Comparison Study Through Age 23." *Early Childhood Research Quarterly* 12: 117–143.

Schweinhart, L.J., and D.P. Weikart. (1997b). *Lasting Differences: The High/Scope Preschool Curriculum Comparison Study Through Age 23.* (Monographs of the High/Scope Educational Research Foundation, 12). Ypsilanti, Mich.: High/Scope Press.

Sears, P.S., and E.M. Dowley. (1963). "Research on Teaching in the Nursery School." In *Handbook of Research on Teaching,* edited by N. L. Gage. Chicago: Rand McNally.

Lawrence J. Schweinhart is Research Division Chair and **David P. Weikart** is President of High/Scope Educational Research Foundation, 600 North River St., Ypsilanti, MI 48198-2898 (e-mail: LarryS@highscope.org).

Isn't That Cute?

Transforming the Cute Curriculum Into Authentic Learning

Lynn Kirkland, University of Alabama at Birmingham
Jerry Aldridge, University of Alabama at Birmingham
Patricia Kuby, Athens State University

Twenty-five years ago James Hymes, Jr. (1974), told early childhood educators that "cute" was a four-letter word. Unfortunately, the "cute curriculum" still exists in many programs. In the everyday world of many preschool and kindergarten classrooms, "many of the noneducative and miseducative activities . . . can be categorized in a single word—cute" (Jalongo, 1996, p. 67). This article will address three questions related to the cute curriculum: 1) What is the cute curriculum? 2) What is an example of the cute curriculum?, and 3) How can we transform the cute curriculum into authentic learning experiences?

What Is the Cute Curriculum?

For the purpose of this article, the cute curriculum is defined as pedagogical activities that teachers implement because of their mistaken notions of what children find appealing. Cute activities are used as a candy coating for the bits of knowledge teachers believe they need to transmit. These activities have no intrinsic connection to the topic being studied. The cute curriculum is most noted for its lack of content and process. Little consideration is paid to children's backgrounds, prior knowledge, the real world, or the purpose of the study unit. While some units are more worthy than others, it is most often not the topic that makes a cute curriculum, but rather what the students are asked to do. Teachers who use the cute curriculum often believe that children do not want to learn something unless it is "dressed up" as a fun activity. Some teachers do not consider the fact that children's questions can help guide the study of the topic; instead, they create cute activities to entice children's interest.

What Is an Example of the Cute Curriculum?

Finding out more about the community is a worthy topic of investigation in most preschool and kindergarten classrooms. Young children are interested in their families, the school, and their community, and are curious to know more about their immediate surroundings. Still, a unit on the community can easily become cute.

When children are asked to participate in predetermined packaged activities on community helpers, without consideration for their questions and interests, the result is the cute curriculum. Bulletin boards and pictures depicting figures of stereotypical careers (such as male doctors and female nurses), inflatable community helpers, and color books and worksheets of helpers, for example, all represent the cute curriculum. A cute activity might be one in which children manipulate cut-out figures or stickers meant to represent people's jobs. Unfortunately, they often resort to stereotypes, and often have no connection to the children's natural questions about their own communities. Another example would be making hats or badges of community helpers. While these activities are cute, real-world community helpers rarely parade around in paper hats and law enforcement personnel may or may not wear uniforms or badges. Many teachers do not see a problem with this practice, and so much of the time that could be spent more wisely on authentic experiences is wasted participating in these noneducative practices.

How Can We Transform the Cute Curriculum Into Authentic Learning?

The most important and crucial feature of authentic learning is that it always deals with the real world of children. Thus, an inquiry framework is necessary to move beyond the cute curriculum to more authentic learning. This section describes how Lynn, one of the authors of this article, used five questions to prepare more authentic learning activities for her kindergar-

From *Focus on Pre-K & K*, Fall 1999, pp. 1-3. Reprinted by permission of Lynn Kirkland, Jerry Aldridge, Patricia Kuby, and the Association for Childhood Education International, 17904 Georgia Avenue, Suite 215, Olney, MD.

Young children are interested in their families, the school, and their community, and are curious to know more about their immediate surroundings.

ten class, and to reduce, or eliminate, time spent on cute projects:

1. Do children's questions guide the development of the project?
Lynn's unit on the community was first and foremost guided by her children's questions. At the beginning of the year the students began asking the following questions about the school, which led to an authentic study of the school and the neighboring community.

Why aren't all of our friends at this school?
Has the school always been here?
Who are the helpers for our schools?
Who is the boss here?
Who lives in the houses around the school?

2. Can I teach problem solving and collaboration in pursuit of this project?
The process of learning is just as important as the content. What strategies can children develop while investigating this topic? Lynn found that three salient features could be addressed while studying the community: developing a sense of classroom community and cooperation, practicing interviewing skills, and learning to compile data.

A sense of community and cooperation are developed through ownership. At the beginning of the year, Lynn decided that children would become more motivated if their ideas were a major part of the curriculum. By seriously considering the children's questions, an atmosphere of cooperation and community among the students thrived.

When children asked questions about who were the helpers at the school and who was the boss, Lynn realized that children could answer some of their questions through interviews with the principal, the secretary, the lunchroom workers, other teachers, and custodians.

The children worked together to compile the data, determining if, in fact, they had found answers to their questions. They also had to consider how to organize and share the data with others. Lynn carefully guided the children in developing a chart to represent their data visually. The chart listed the community workers' names, job titles, and how they did their work. The results were then shared with a 4th-grade class that was also studying the school and community.

3. Does the study encourage independence as well as collaboration?
In the real world, we sometimes work alone, while at other times we work with others. A good study unit will provide opportunities for children to work both independently and in concert with others. The interviews fostered children's independence, while the activities of compiling information developed cooperation.

4. Are children interacting with real objects and people?
Children learned about their immediate surroundings by answering the question, "Has the school always been here?," and by studying old photographs of the neighborhood and the school building. Daily walks in the neighborhood also provided many chances for the students to interact with real objects and people in the area. Guest speakers, including the school's first principal and the mayor, were invited to class.

5. Do experiences facilitate the construction of new relationships?
Does the study revisit (in more depth) previous topics? Is there some thought for continuity within and across the curriculum? Throughout the curriculum, do activities and strategies build on children's prior knowledge? To help build a classroom community, Lynn asked the children to share photographs or drawings of their families with the class. As the children discussed them, several wanted to know, "Why aren't all of our friends at this school?" This expanded the study of children's families to include the school and community. In attempting to answer this question, Lynn was able to move children from familiar to unfamiliar information, thus facilitating the construction of new relationships.

Conclusions

Young children naturally have inquiring minds. If we take their questions seriously, we can develop authentic experiences and avoid the cute curriculum. There is no need to sugarcoat a study unit if we allow children to actively seek answers to their own questions. Learn to reexamine what we do with children. When we hear ourselves saying, "Isn't that cute?," try to remember that "cute" is a four-letter word and that children deserve much more.

References

Hymes, J., Jr. (1974). *Teaching the child under six.* Upper Saddle River, NJ: Merrill/Prentice Hall.

Jalongo, M. R. (1996). Editorial: On behalf of children—Why cute is still a four-letter word. *Early Childhood Education Journal, 24* (2), 67–70.

Productive Questions:

Tools for Supporting Constructivist Learning

By Mary Lee Martens

PRODUCTIVE QUESTIONS, THOSE leading to either physical or mental activity, are not new. Jos Eltgeest (1985) proposed them more than 13 years ago, but their usefulness is still being discovered. Teachers struggling to embrace a constructivist approach to teaching often find themselves stuck when students fail to make connections necessary to arrive at a desired understanding. They are tempted to resort back to dispensing information in the form of hints and/or to reject constructivism outright. Productive questions provide an alternative that, with practice, gives teachers a way out of this dilemma.

Productive Questions

Many questions formulated by teachers have asked students to remember or revisit things that they supposedly learned. Students' ability to do this counted as success. Productive questions, however, have a different goal.

Productive questions purport to take a student *forward* in his or her thinking; they enable a teacher to provide scaffolding for students beginning to build their own understandings. The six types of questions—attention-focusing, measuring and counting, comparison, action, problem-posing, and reasoning (see sidebar, next page)—allow a teacher to meet students where they are and provide the kind of support needed at any given moment. These questions are not intended to be asked in any particular order, but rather to be responses to what the teacher hears and sees happening. The teacher's role becomes more of a monitor and facilitator as students become more actively involved and responsible for their own learning.

If strategically asked, productive questions keep students motivated and fruitful in their efforts. Interestingly, it is not only teachers who can contribute to this, students working successfully in groups can often be overheard asking their own productive questions.

Learning About Buoyancy

"Can you find a way to make this clay float?" This was my introduction to a unit on buoyancy that I was sharing with students in a college-level elementary methods class. In terms of understanding this concept, these preservice teachers were remarkably similar to elementary school children. My students did exactly what I have seen many elementary children do. They flattened the clay expecting their "rafts" to float. When this didn't work, they proceeded to make the clay thinner and/or smaller and quickly became discouraged at their lack of success. I noticed folded arms and general disengagement. Elementary school children having this same problem begin to misbehave, get off task, make comments that this activity is silly or stupid, and often show uncooperative behavior. The challenge for me as a teacher was to help students access stored information from their memories in order for them to move forward and successfully meet this challenge.

"What have you noticed that floats?" I asked. Some students began to brainstorm, "boats, tubes, balls. . . ." while others quietly picked up the clay and began reshaping it. I had just asked an attention-focusing question, and for many students, this was all that was needed. Students who still didn't see how to proceed needed an additional prompt in the form of a comparison question, "How are all these floating objects similar?"

By this time, all of my students had reshaped the clay into some kind of boat or cup-shaped structure and were feeling quite successful. I then challenged them to find a way to support the greatest amount of "cargo." (I used small ceramic tiles for this purpose but any small, uniform items would do.) The students had three trials, and the goal was to improve their design after each attempt.

I noticed that some groups shared observations (attention focusing) and exchanged ideas about what shape would hold the greatest mass (comparison and/or action questions),

MARY LEE MARTENS is an associate professor of science education at SUNY Cortland in New York.

From *Science and Children,* May 1999, pp. 24-27, 53.

Productive questions enable teachers to create a bridge between activities and students.

while others repeated the same solution taking time only to patch holes and repair minor damage to their sunken vessels. The former groups stayed engaged (in fact, it was hard to get them to stop), while the latter groups lost interest after their second trial and did not even seem interested in trying a third time. I found that when I interjected an attention-focusing question, "What are you noticing about the way you put the tiles in?" or an action question, "What happens if you build higher sides?", the lagging groups became interested and engaged again.

Thus far, I had used different kinds of questions in response to what students were saying and doing. I asked more challenging action questions to those students who seemed ready to go further in their thinking and posed attention-focusing questions to those students who needed help in activating pieces needed to solve the problem successfully.

I deliberately stayed away from reasoning questions. Asking "Why do you think?" prematurely would only cause my students to shut down. They weren't ready to think about *why* when they were still coming to understand that changing the shape of the clay changed its properties. However, they *were* gaining in understanding; their success in building boats and then improving the capacity of their creations was clear evidence that this was true.

At the elementary level, the fact that changing the shape of an object changes its properties is an age-appropriate understanding. Why this occurs is probably too abstract and beyond the ability of most students to grasp. I do, however, eventually ask the reasoning question, "Why do you think the clay can float when shaped like a boat but not when it is the shape of a ball?" It is important to note here that the question is *"Why do you think?"* and not just *"Why?"* The wording (if truly meant) encourages children to *do* science—that is, to use evidence to create an explanation.

If students overlook some piece of evidence in coming up with their theories, an attention-focusing question invites them to look again. Students often suggest that spreading the clay over a greater surface makes it float. Asking them to compare what happened when the clay was shaped like a ball and when it was made into a raft (comparison question) helps students to think about what else might contribute to the explanation.

A second- or third-grade student (the grade level at which this activity is normally taught) should not be expected to arrive at an adult understanding of buoyancy. Understanding the fact that changing the shape makes a difference lays an important foundation for understanding that will proceed easily when abstract thinking comes into play a few years down the road.

For brighter children who are ready for more of a challenge, there is no reason to hold them back. Productive questions that cause these children to notice the correspondence between changing the shape of the clay and the changing level of the water might enable them to begin to think about displacement and actually move close to an advanced understanding of buoyancy.

Students Understanding Levers

The following is an example of a teacher using productive questions with fifth-grade students. The teacher asked her students if they

Productive Questions

Attention-focusing questions help students fix their attention on significant details.
Have you seen . . . ? What have you noticed about . . .? What are they doing? How does it feel/smell/look?

Measuring and counting questions help students become more precise about their observations.
How many . . . ? How often . . . ? How long . . . ? How much . . . ?

Comparison questions help students analyze and classify.
How are these the same or different? How do they go together?

Action questions encourage students to explore the properties of unfamiliar materials, living or nonliving, and of small events taking place or to make predictions about phenomena.
What happens if . . . ? What would happen if . . . ? What if . . . ?

Problem-posing questions help students plan and implement solutions to problems.
Can you find a way to . . . ? Can you figure out how to . . . ?

Reasoning questions help students think about experiences and construct ideas that make sense to them.
Why do you think . . . ? What is your reason for . . . ? Can you invent a rule for . . . ?

A teacher's own style and knowledge of students' abilities should determine how much structure to set when using productive questions for learning science.

could find a way to balance two pennies on a ruler using just one penny as the counterweight. Some children, using a pencil for a fulcrum, began to experiment by moving the position of the pencil. Others solved the problem by moving either the load (two pennies) or the counterweight (one penny). As individual children experienced success, the teacher quietly whispered, "Now can you balance three pennies (then four, five, etc.) using just one? And what are you noticing?"

This teacher began the lesson with a problem-posing question and then shifted attention-focusing questions as she endeavored to help the children make sense of their experiences. Many children initially met the challenge through trial and error. It was critically important for the development of conceptual understanding that the students were led to the point of being able to articulate the pattern they were observing.

However, not all the children were able to meet the initial challenge. There were some who randomly moved the pencil and/or the pennies (or both) and looked around in frustration as the enthusiasm of classmates grew in proportion to their successes. The teacher responded to the less successful children with a more structured action question. "What happens if we place the load at one end and the counterweight at the other and move the fulcrum closer (from the center) to the two pennies?" At this point, the teacher was leading the children to be able to meet the challenge successfully. This was necessary in order for these children to begin to notice the pattern and then develop an understanding of the fact that levers enable us to do work with less effort by applying force over a distance.

The teacher's style was to begin the lesson in a very unstructured way. Students were free to adjust either the position of the fulcrum or the load and counterweight. The teacher was skilled enough in observing and listening to her students to make appropriate use of productive questions regardless of how students approached the problem. Many teachers would prefer to set tighter parameters, as did this teacher in response to students who were not successful at first. A teacher's own style and knowledge of students' abilities should determine how much structure to set. All students, however, can profit greatly from the strategic use of productive questions.

This was not the only activity the teacher used to develop an understanding of the benefit of this type of simple machine. Other activities involving teeter-totters enabled the teacher to use comparison questions to reinforce the relationship pattern between force and distance. These activities took a lot more time than merely telling students about levers. There is no doubt though that these students **understood** and **will remember** what they learned by doing and making sense of what they did as their teacher served as facilitator and guide through her use of productive questions.

A Bridge to Understanding

There are many teachers who engage students in hands-on activities and assume that since the children enjoy the activities, learning is occurring and understanding is developing. Few children, however, are able to construct understanding simply by engaging in an activity. Productive questions enable teachers to create a bridge between activities and students. They make it possible for *all* learners to arrive at understanding.

National Science Education Standards

The techniques discussed in this article relate to Teaching Standard B: Teachers of science guide and facilitate learning (National Research Council, 1996, p. 32). In doing this, teachers

- Focus and support inquires while interacting with students.
- Orchestrate discourse among students about scientific ideas.
- Challenge students to accept and share responsibility for their own learning.
- Recognize and respond to student diversity and encourage all students to participate fully in science learning.
- Encourage and model the skills of scientific inquiry, as well as the curiousness, openness to new ideas and data, and skepticism that characterize science.

Resources

Eltgeest, J. (1985). The right question at the right time. In W. Harlen (Ed.), *Primary Science: Taking the Plunge.* Portsmouth, NH: Heinemann.

National Research Council. (1996). *National Science Education Standards.* Washington, DC: National Academy Press.

Sink or Float Kit—Grades 2 and 3. Delta Science Module #38-738-3133, Delta Education, P.O. Box 915, Hudson, NH 03051-0915.

RETHINKING WHAT WE DO

Beginning to Implement the Reggio Philosophy

Lynn Staley

As an early childhood teacher educator and staff development professional, I find that the Reggio Approach, from Reggio Emilia, Italy, is by far the most requested topic for discussion. Following almost every workshop or inservice session I conduct on the subject, however, caregivers, preschool teachers, and kindergarten teachers all make the same plea for help: "I love what I hear about Reggio Emilia. It's everything I believe about young children, but it all seems so overwhelming. Where do I start? How do I begin?"

Hoping to encourage others, our university preschool teachers agreed to carefully and candidly document their own first steps toward implementation. In Reggio the teacher is not only a practitioner, but also a coleader, researcher, and risk-taker as adults and children experiment together. Our teachers too were taking risks as they stepped away from the traditional, very secure, teacher-directed curriculum and began asking serious questions about how young children learn best. Getting started was scary, but the results were well worth it!

Lynn Staley, Ed.D., is an assistant professor of early childhood education at Ball State University in Muncie, Indiana. She was a member of the 1995 Spring Study Tour to Reggio Emilia and is now serving as the director of the Indiana Reggio Network.

Our Story

While the Reggio Approach does not represent a new philosophy, it is the rare and remarkable synergy that exists in Reggio Emilia between theory and practice that inspired us to reflect upon our own philosophies, beliefs, and practices. As our teachers prepared to implement the Reggio Approach, they too were overwhelmed and asked, "Where do we start? How do we begin?"

The parent-teacher partnership

The first step was to develop a renewed partnership with parents. The staff wanted to elicit parental enthusiasm, involvement, and participation in this new adventure, so

From *Young Children,* September 1998, pp. 20-25.

The Reggio Approach

Who is the young child?

Children are seen as capable, competent, curious, and creative (Rinaldi 1993). They are natural researchers as they question what they see, hypothesize solutions, predict outcomes, experiment, and reflect on their discoveries. Children are not passive, empty vessels waiting to be filled; rather, they are self-motivated learners actively seeking to understand the complex world in which they live. They are intrinsically motivated to learn and can be trusted as partners in curriculum development.

How do young children learn best?

Loris Malaguzzi founded the Reggio schools within the context of educational theorists such as Montessori, Dewey, Piaget, and Vygotsky (Malaguzzi 1993). Reggio's eclectic philosophy is highlighted by the Italian tradition of Maria Montessori, who respected children as capable and competent learners in need of an environment carefully prepared to stimulate curiosity, exploration, inquiry, and self-learning (Montessori 1965). Dewey's emphasis on designing curriculum based on children's interests (Archambault 1964) is evident in Reggio as one observes children pursuing their own projects.

Piaget's appreciation for children's cognitive development as a process of ongoing adaptation to one's environment (Forman & Kuschner 1983) contributes to the Reggio school's emphasis on "active education" (Malaguzzi 1993, 52). Malaguzzi referred to the schools as "amiable" schools that allow "maximum movement, interdependence, and interaction" (p. 56). Consistent with Vygotsky's sociocultural philosophy is an emphasis on relationships in which adults and children come together in an active process of education.

> Value should be placed on contexts, communicative processes, and the construction of a wide network of reciprocal exchanges among children and between children and adults. (p. 62)

Thus, children acquire knowledge best by construction rather than instruction (DeVries & Kohlberg 1990). Children need many opportunities for hands-on, multisensory experiences and active exploration (Bredekamp 1987; Bredekamp & Copple 1997). It is only as children search for answers to their own questions via discussion, investigation, and experimentation that they begin to grasp and understand complex concepts that are foundational to later learning. Rather than use teacher-directed thematic units, teachers integrate curriculum goals carefully within open-ended projects of inquiry chosen by the children (Katz & Chard 1989). Learning is therefore an ongoing, flexible, open-ended process wherein children construct their own understanding. Teaching is not telling; teaching is guiding discovery.

In Reggio, learning often takes place within the structure of small-group projects. Opportunities for discussion with other children and adults is essential if children are to construct and reconstruct ideas for themselves (Rosa & Montero 1990; Berk & Winsler 1995). Only as children articulate to others that which they believe to be true do they come face-to-face with errors in their thinking. As children find it necessary to explain, support, or defend their position, they must define and redefine what they know. Children learn best by doing and talking.

Curriculum planning is understood in Reggio Emilia as a "sense of preparation and organization of space, materials, thoughts, situations, and occasions for learning" (Rinaldi 1993, 102). Vea Vecchi, *atelierista* (art specialist) from Reggio

they planned a meeting to introduce the Reggio Approach to parents.

In addition to sharing the key concepts, staff warned parents not to expect the familiar "refrigerator art"; rather, they encouraged parents to appreciate their children's first steps in contributing to an emerging curriculum and using authentic art materials to represent what they had learned.

The teacher-teacher partnership

A very important ingredient in the Reggio Approach is a sense of collegiality and support. The staff is open to comments, suggestions, questions, and criticisms as everyone seeks the best ways to ignite children's interests, provoke questions, and sustain learning.

Based on trust and mutual respect, teacher interaction is positive and supportive. To facilitate such collegiality, we scheduled a weekly staff meeting to reflect together on daily observations of the children as the basis for curriculum design.

The teacher-child partnership

The next step was to move away from preplanned, teacher-directed, thematic units and whole-group, structured activities. Preplanned lessons had fostered a sense of security and control for the staff; they knew what to expect.

Letting go of thematic units made them feel anxious, nervous, uneasy, and insecure. Even at the close of the year, one teacher recalled, "The hardest things to learn were to be flexible and to let go of themes. The 'negotiated curriculum' [Fyfe & Forman 1996] seemed so unpredictable at first." (For those teachers already familiar with project-based emergent curriculum, incorporating the Reggio Approach should prove to be much easier.)

Project #1—Dinosaurs

After listening to children's conversations and observing their play, the teachers pursued the topic of dinosaurs. Needing a little structure to

Emilia, tells a story about shadows that illustrates well how teachers thoughtfully prepare the environment to provoke interest and ignite inquiry:

> Once I noticed that the sun, shining behind one of the trees outside the window, cast a shadow of the leaves onto the glass. I taped a sheet of translucent white paper onto the glass. As children came in that morning, they exclaimed with surprise and pleasure at the sight of the shadow of leaves on the paper. Many things followed. The children even came to use the shadow as a clock. One said, "It's time to go to lunch. Look at the design on the paper." (Vecchi 1993, 126–27)

Something as simple as taping paper to the window provoked incredible learning of complex concepts. What a patient teacher and keen observer!

How do young children express what they know?

While young children socially construct knowledge as they communicate their understandings to others, spoken language is sometimes inadequate for such expression. Young children often have images and understandings of complex concepts in their minds, but they can't put them into words. Young children in particular need alternative languages to express themselves. Whether they use the language of paint, clay, wire, pen and ink, mosaic, collage, puppetry, music, or dance, the children of Reggio Emilia demonstrate an eagerness to create visual and symbolic representations of what they know and understand. How appropriate that the Italian educators speak of this expression as *The Hundred Languages of Children* (Department of Education 1987; Edwards, Gandini, & Forman 1993).

How do young children benefit from documentation?

Along the children's journey of cognitive development, the teacher must record or document the learning process. Much like recording a personal vacation, the teacher compiles photographs, videotapes, audio recordings, models, and notes of children's conversations and accomplishments. Documentation of children's learning abounds in the Reggio schools. Visitors view mobiles, photo stories, wind machines, mosaics, sculptures, and much more as a tribute to children's learning. When children's creations are displayed in the school, there is a clear message to those who visit that children do indeed pursue intelligent and important work.

In addition to serving as a historical record, documentation is a tool for assessing children's understanding in order to design effective curriculum. Upon observing, listening, and recording children's interests, questions, and hypotheses, the parents and teachers in Reggio can carefully structure learning environments that assist children in their quest for further understanding.

Who are the partners in learning?

Much attention is given in the Reggio Approach to facilitating an effective partnership with families. The parent is considered the child's first teacher and therefore worthy of respect, inclusion, involvement, consultation, and contribution to curriculum design.

Summary

The teachers in Reggio Emilia consider children to be active, competent, and capable of directing their own learning. Teaching strategies include (a) providing time and materials for children to explore their own topics, (b) supporting small group projects in which children coconstruct knowledge, (c) incorporating the use of authentic art materials, (d) documenting children's journeys of discovery, and (e) including parents as part of the education team.

guide their first steps, the teachers chose to adapt the KWL method (Ogle 1986; Carr & Ogle 1987). They hoped that by asking the children three questions,

K—What do you **know** about dinosaurs?

W—What do you **want** to know about dinosaurs?

L—What did you **learn** about dinosaurs?

this method would help build a framework of questions from which the project would develop.

The children loved sharing what they "knew" about dinosaurs; however, when the teachers asked them what they wanted to know, the children had no idea. We understood later that children need a substantial knowledge base for a topic before they can contemplate further questions. They didn't know enough about dinosaurs to ask questions!

Following a field trip, teachers and children incorporated dinosaurs into the computer center, block center, literacy center, and math center.

The children lost interest in the topic of dinosaurs after a few weeks. They had been very dependent upon the adults, who were always there and were familiar with previous conversations, discussions, and explorations related to the topic. Inconsistent staffing and peer-group attendance may have contributed to the lack of sustained interest.

Reflections on project #1

Asking good questions. The teachers were very frustrated with their perceived inability to ask effective, engaging, provoking questions that would ignite children's discoveries. They understood that good teachers ask questions that motivate children (Kramer 1994, 32), good questions help children find words for their thinking (Schifter 1996), and good questions help children solve problems (Berk & Winsler 1995).

A student teacher said, "It's hard to ask questions. . . . I sort of listen and don't know what to say next. I want to encourage [the children] to think, but I don't know how. How do I keep them going?"

Teachers work with each child to deepen and extend understanding and effort.

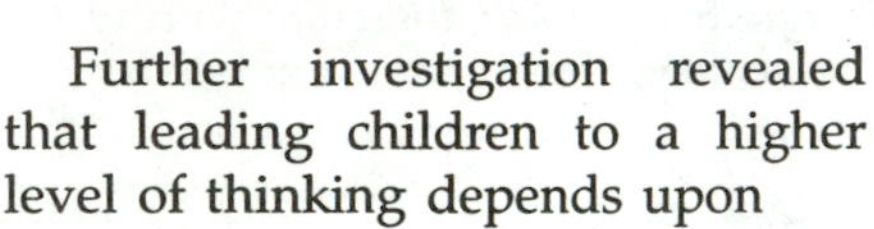

Drawing the costume on paper.

Making a pattern the right size.

Admiring a gown fit for a princess.

Further investigation revealed that leading children to a higher level of thinking depends upon

- asking questions that help children relate prior experiences to present learning;
- asking for literal details to assess understanding;
- helping children draw relationships;
- asking children for further clarification (Why? How? What if . . . ?), requiring children to rethink their beliefs and test their understanding;
- asking open-ended questions without any hint of appropriate or expected responses;
- asking open-ended questions that pose problems, contradictions, comparisons, alternatives; and
- waiting for responses (Sigel & Saunders 1977; Isbell 1979; Finkelstein & Ritter 1980; Berk & Winsler 1995).

Open-ended questions demand "active cognitive engagement" (Fowell & Lawton 1992, 419). Asking questions is like playing tennis. The "ball" (question) is served into the children's court, and they are expected to respond. By waiting, the teacher silently communicates a confidence in the children's ability to respond; the teacher validates the learner and gives the children time to organize their thoughts.

One teacher stated,

> I believe it is imperative that, as teachers, we listen to children intently and only interject ideas very occasionally that will assist each child in further construction of his or her knowledge. It is so tempting to lead a child to new understandings. It is difficult to wait for children to lead themselves. It is tempting to jump in with information that seems important and obvious to us. It is difficult to facilitate situations that allow the child to discover without directing the discovery.

Could it be that effective questioning depends first on our patient listening?

Project #2—Kites

After the dinosaur project a boy shared a book about kites. The class was so captivated with the topic that they decided to design, build, and test their own kite creations. Seeing design flaws, the teachers were silent and allowed some kites to fail. Surprisingly, this motivated the children to redesign and retest until they finally experienced success.

Reflections on project #2

This was the best project of the year. The staff noted that short-term projects might be the easiest way to begin using the Reggio Approach.

Project #3—Castles, princes, princesses

During the second half of the year, the children become interested in castles, princes, and princesses. The boys were primarily interested in how castles were built, and the girls were interested in the clothes the princesses wore. One little girl brought in several child-size princess gowns that generated great excitement in the dress-up corner.

The children wrote stories, researched books, and built catapults for complex block structures. A small group of girls decided to sew their own costumes. They drew designs on paper and prepared paper tube models from the designs. They then drew life-size patterns from the models, made adjustments, and cut out the patterns. They pinned the patterns to the fabric, cut them out, and sewed the pieces together. (The girls had difficulty pinning and cutting, so the teachers intervened to help the girls continue.)

Upon completion, a teacher reported, "One girl tried her outfit on, and she was really proud. She walked around and showed it to everybody. And one boy . . . said, 'Wow, that's really neat!' . . . She looked in the mirror. I wish you could have seen her face. . . . It got the other children excited too." One boy also became interested in sewing and made a long shirtlike costume.

Reflections on project #3

Who is our atelierista? An *atelierista* resides in each of the Reggio schools helping children and teachers continue the connection between art and learning. Our teachers longed for someone who could help the children use authentic art materials (for example, clay, wire, watercolors) to represent what they know. A university student with an art background volunteered to be our *atelierista*. As a result, the children began to incorporate clay into their thinking about castles.

Why do children revisit their work? The teachers observed that when children had repeated opportunities to revisit their ideas, they constructed more complex, detailed, and accurate representations than before. Commented one teacher, "For many of [the children], it's usually a one-time shot. A project is over in ten minutes, and then we go on to something else. This [project was] something special they revisited over and over and over."

What is the role of the teacher? Struggling to find the balance between child-directed and teacher-directed learning, the teachers were hesitant to instruct. If children learn best by discovery and exploration, then what is the role of the teacher?

Lella Gandini, Reggio Emilia liaison to the United States, visited our campus and explained that at times children depend on us to teach them a skill needed to pursue their goal. Without teacher intervention at points of frustration, children might be tempted to give up and never experience the joys of fruitful discovery. Teachers must still teach!

Closing reflections

What did the children learn?

"More than anything else, the children are learning to solve their own problems," concluded one teacher. "They are learning to negotiate with their friends. They are learning to work together. They are learning that they are competent learners."

Children are natural researchers as they question what they see, hypothesize, predict, experiment, and reflect.

The children used to come to school and say, "What are we learning today?" As the year progressed, they came prepared to direct their own course and make their own decisions about what they wanted to learn.

Adults valued their questions and suggestions for solutions; children were learning to be decisionmakers, thinkers, problem seekers, and problem solvers. Some parents noticed greater self-confidence in their child!

Topic selection

Reflecting further on the dinosaur and castles/princes/princesses projects, we teachers agreed that the topics were not the best choices. Topics should (a) be relevant to children's lives, (b) contribute to a balanced curriculum, (c) have the potential for artistic and expressive representation, and (d) prepare children for later life (Katz & Chard 1989; Chard 1996).

There are no universally successful project topics. Topics depend on careful observation and consideration of a particular group of children as well as the interests of the teacher. (In the second year of implementation, two topics, butterflies and mixtures, were very successful. The teachers attributed the success of these topics to the fact that they were real and, as they said, "the children could touch them.")

Documentation

The teachers took lots of pictures and the parents raved about the display panels, but the extensive time required to prepare scripted photos for formal display continued to frustrate the staff throughout the year.

"Following children and listening and interacting at the same time is frustrating," a teacher explained. "Even taping requires transcribing. We can't do everything . . . We want to stay involved, not with our heads in the paper all the time."

While taking quick notes was faster and more effective than taping and transcribing children's comments and conversations, the staff suggested that educators implementing the Reggio Approach for the first time might consider delaying the emphasis on formal documentation and instead focus on listening. Without undervaluing the importance of documentation to guide curriculum design and inform families, the teachers felt that learning to prepare documentation for formal display is a process that occurs over time and with much trial and error.

Learning what to document and how to document can easily distract a teacher from the most important component of the Reggio Approach—listening to the children.

Supportive collaboration

At the end of the year, successful implementation of the Reggio Approach appeared to be very dependent on the weekly staff meetings.

The group generated many more exciting and creative curriculum ideas than any one individual could have initiated. The meetings also contributed to a greater sense of collegiality and mutual respect among teachers than ever before. When teachers needed to talk through times of unknowing, insecurity, and confusion, the emotional support staff gave to one another fostered the confidence necessary to pursue new strategies.

Suggestions for future implementation

After a year of successes, failures, triumphs, and defeats, we offer the following advice to those interested in trying the Reggio Approach:

- study three key textbooks—*Engaging Children's Minds: The Project Approach* (Katz & Chard 1989), *First Steps Toward Teaching the Reggio Way* (Hendrick 1997), and *The Hundred Languages of Children* (Edwards, Gandini, & Forman 1993)—prior to implementation;
- include parents;
- find a teacher-partner willing to give professional support during curriculum experimentation and implementation;
- find an art specialist willing to serve as a resource person;
- begin with short-term small-group projects;
- choose topics that are real and relevant;
- experiment with effective questioning techniques;
- allow children time to revisit their work;
- delay emphasis on formal documentation, but continue to observe and record; and
- continue to teach, but perhaps teach differently.

With all that's been said, our best advice is to *listen* to your children, and there you will find the wonder and beauty of teaching the young child.

References

Archambault, R., ed. 1964. *John Dewey on education—Selected writings.* New York: Random House.

Berk, L. E., & A. Winsler. 1995. *Scaffolding children's learning: Vygotsky and early childhood education.* Washington, DC: NAEYC.

Bredekamp, S., ed. 1987. *Developmentally appropriate practice in early childhood programs serving children from birth through age 8.* Washington, DC: NAEYC.

Bredekamp, S., & C. Copple, eds. 1997. *Developmentally appropriate practice in early childhood programs.* Washington, DC: NAEYC.

Carr, E., & D. Ogle. 1987. K-W-L plus: A strategy for comprehension and summarization. *Journal of Reading* 30 (7): 626–31.

Chard. S. 1996. Highlights from the Reggio e-mail bulletin board. *Innovations* 4 (1): 4.

Department of Education. 1987. *The hundred languages of children.* Reggio Emilia, Italy: Author.

DeVries, R., & L. Kohlberg. 1990. *Constructivist early education: Overview and comparison with other programs.* Washington, DC: NAEYC.

Edwards, C., L. Gandini, & G. Forman, eds. 1993. *The hundred languages of children: The Reggio Emilia approach to early childhood education.* Norwood, NJ: Ablex.

Finkelstein, J., & V. Ritter. 1980. *Does anyone have any questions?* ERIC, ED 188768.

Forman, G., & D. Kuschner. 1983. *The child's construction of knowledge: Piaget for teaching children.* Washington, DC: NAEYC.

Fowell, N., & J. Lawton. 1992. Dependencies between questions and responses during small-group instruction in two preschool programs. *Early Childhood Research Quarterly* 7: 415–39.

Fyfe, B., & G. Forman. 1996. The negotiated curriculum. *Innovations* 3 (4): 4–7.

Hendrick, J. 1997. *First steps toward teaching the Reggio way.* Upper Saddle River, NJ: Prentice-Hall.

Isbell, C. 1979. Developing levels of thinking in young children. In *Collected papers: International Seminar in Childhood Education,* ed. R. Gardner. Ogden, UT: Weber State College. ERIC, ED 184690.

Katz, L. G., & S. C. Chard. 1989. *Engaging children's minds: The project approach.* Norwood, NJ: Ablex.

Kramer, J. F. 1994. Defining competence as readiness to learn. In *New perspectives in early childhood teacher education: Bringing practitioners into the debate,* eds. S. G. Goffin & D. E. Day, 29–36. New York: Teachers College Press.

Malaguzzi, L. 1993. History, ideas, and basic philosophy: An interview with Lella Gandini. In *The hundred languages of children: The Reggio Emilia approach to early childhood education,* eds. C. Edwards, L. Gandini, & G. Forman, 41–89. Norwood, NJ: Ablex.

Montessori, M. 1965. *Dr. Montessori's own handbook.* New York: Schocken.

Ogle, D. M. 1986. K-W-L: A teaching model that develops active reading of expository text. *The Reading Teacher* 39 (6): 564–70.

Rinaldi, C. 1993. The emergent curriculum and social constructivism. In *The hundred languages of children: The Reggio Emilia approach to early childhood education,* eds. C. Edwards, L. Gandini, & G. Forman, 101–12. Norwood, NJ: Ablex.

Rosa, A., & I. Montero. 1990. The historical context of Vygotsky's work: A sociohistorical approach. In *Vygotsky and education,* ed. L. C. Moll, 59–88. Cambridge, UK: Cambridge University Press.

Schifter, D. 1996. A constructivist perspective on teaching and learning mathematics. *Phi Delta Kappan* 77 (7): 492–99.

Sigel, I., & R. Saunders. 1977. *An inquiry into inquiry: Question-asking as an instructional model.* Urbana, IL: ERIC Clearinghouse on Early Childhood Education. ERIC. ED 158871.

Vecchi, V. 1993. The role of the *atelierista.* In *The hundred languages of children: The Reggio Emilia approach to early childhood education,* eds. C. Edwards, L. Gandini, & G. Forman, 119–27. Norwood, NJ: Ablex.

Documenting Children's Learning

Judy Harris Helm, Sallee Beneke and Kathy Steinheimer

Judy Harris Helm is an Early Childhood Specialist, Brimfield, Illinois.
Sallee Beneke is a Master Teacher, Oglesby, Illinois.
Kathy Steinheimer is a Preprimary Teacher, Peoria, Illinois.

doc·u·ment, -ment·ed, -ment·ing, -ments (dŏk'-ye-mènt')

2. To support (an assertion or a claim, for example) with evidence or decisive information.

The American Heritage Dictionary of the English Language, Third Edition

Documenting children's learning may be one of the most valuable skills a teacher can learn. When teachers carefully collect, analyze, interpret and display evidence of learning, they are better able to understand how children learn and to help others recognize that learning. Regular and consistent documentation of children's work can benefit teachers in five ways.

1. Teachers who can document children's learning in a variety of ways are able to respond to demands for accountability. An increased demand for accountability and program evaluation is a strong trend in education. Schools and other early childhood programs must prove their effectiveness to their constituencies. In an effort to meet these demands for accountability, some programs have turned to increased use of standardized tests. Such group administered tests, however, are especially inappropriate for assessing children younger than 3rd grade (Meisels, 1993). The Association for Childhood Education International's official position is that standardized testing should not occur earlier than Grade 3 (ACEI/Perrone, 1991). In contrast to achievement tests, comprehensive and quality documentation can:

- provide evidence of children's learning in all areas of their development: physical, emotional, social and cognitive
- provide insight into complex learning experiences when teachers use an integrated approach
- provide a framework for organizing teachers' observations and recording each child's special interests and developmental progress
- emphasize learning as an interactive process by documenting what children learn through active exploration and interaction with adults, other children and materials
- show the advantages of activities and materials that are concrete, real and relevant to young children, as opposed to abstract and artificial events such as group testing situations
- enable the teacher to assess children's knowledge and abilities in order to increase activities' difficulty, complexity and challenge as children develop understanding and skills.

From *Childhood Education,* Summer 1997, pp. 200-205.

2. Teachers who document are more often able to teach children through direct, firsthand, interactive experiences that enhance brain development.
Documentation enables the teacher to provide evidence that children are learning as a result of firsthand experiences. Recent research on brain development (Sylwester, 1995) suggests that children learn better when they are active, engaged and involved. Learning is related to children's feelings and emotions; therefore, their dispositions towards learning are important (Katz, 1995). How a child feels about reading, and whether or not the child wants to learn to read, will affect that child's reading achievement over the long term. Traditional methods for monitoring children's progress, such as standardized tests, do not reveal such attitudes.

Brain research also shows that learning is interconnected and cannot be isolated or compartmentalized into subject areas (Howard, 1994). Subject matter tests and standardized achievement tests do not provide information about how children integrate their learning and apply content knowledge to real life challenges. A systematic collection of children's work documents how children integrate and apply what they learn. Teachers can then assess that integration and provide more meaningful experiences.

Sylwester also showed that the brain adapts and develops by exposure to continuously changing and challenging environments. Children learn from hands-on, thought-provoking experiences that challenge them to think and stimulate their brain's growth and development. Such experiences cannot be assessed easily by conventional methods.

As teachers strive to develop curricula that is brain enhancing, they must also be mindful of assessing students' growth, development and intellectual and social learning. The two circles in Figure 1 represent these simultaneous challenges.

3. Teachers are more effective when they document.
Perhaps the greatest value of comprehensive documentation is its power to inform teaching. Teachers who. have good documentation skills will make more productive planning decisions, including how to set up the classroom, what to do next, what questions to ask, what resources to provide and how to stimulate each child's development. The more information a teacher can gather when making these decisions, the more effective a teacher is likely to be.

Lev Vygotsky's sociocultural theory explains the importance of teachers' decisions in maximizing learning. According to Vygotsky (1978), the teacher is most effective when teaching is directed towards a *zone of proximal development* for each child. Children learn best when learning experiences are within their zone of development. The teacher needs to assess a child's development, probe the child's thinking on the topic and provide learning experiences that will build a bridge, or "scaffold," to higher level thought processes (Berk & Winsler, 1995). Data that reveal what the child partially understands, what the child is beginning to be able to do, or what the child is trying to integrate are often the most helpful pieces of information for teachers. Standardized tests primarily provide a limited sample of what the student has already mastered. By focusing only on what children already know, teachers cannot be as effective in helping them reach the next learning steps.

Documentation can also help the teacher decide if and when a child needs additional support systems. If the teacher collects a child's work over a period of time, the teacher can see if the child is progressing as expected or if mastery of a skill is just around the corner. When the teacher does not see mastery or emerging skills, she can seek additional help, such as early special assistance.

4. Teachers who can document children's work are better able to meet special needs.
Because of changing demographics early childhood teachers need even more skills than ever. Children with special needs are now part of many prekindergarten and primary classrooms. Some of these special needs include giftedness, physical disabilities, learning problems requiring individualized education plans, and challenges resulting from growing up in poverty. Teachers who know how to gather information and assess children's development are better able to identify the appropriate

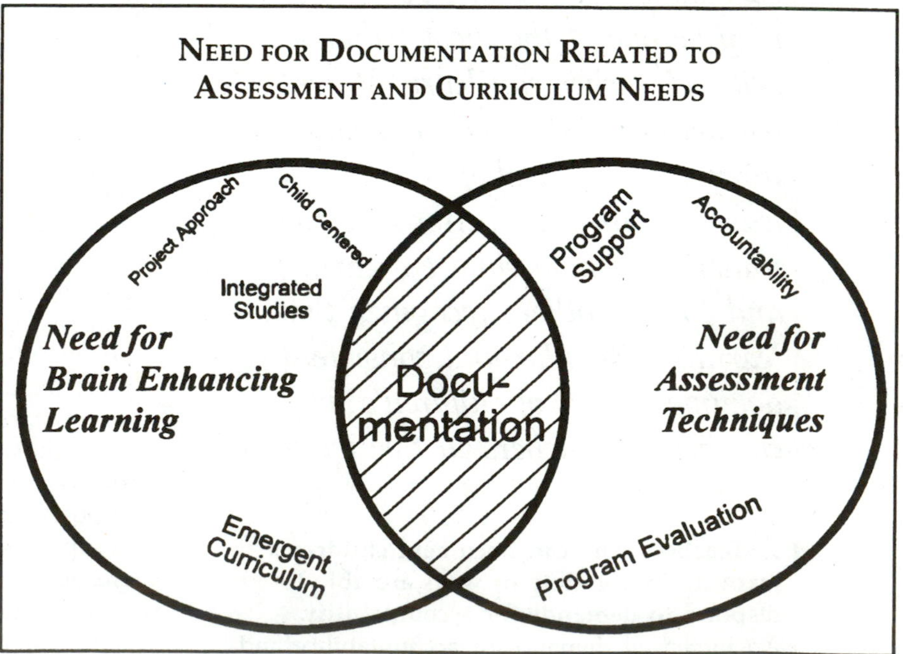

Figure 1

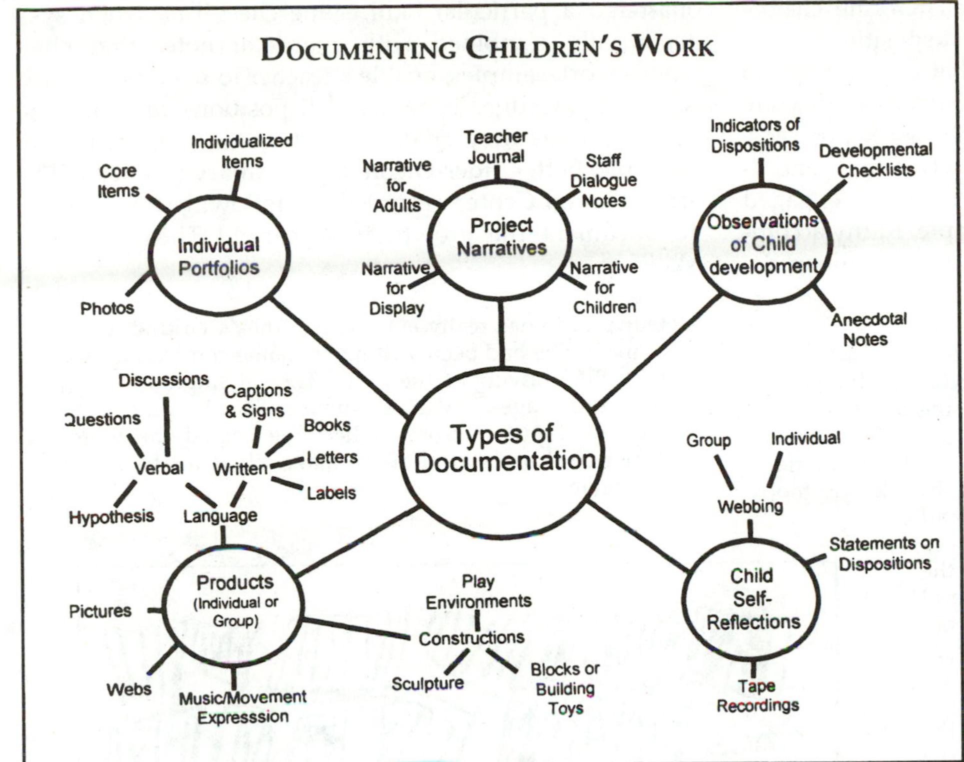

Figure 2

learning experiences for these children as well as for more typically developing children.

5. Children perceive learning to be important and worthwhile when teachers document their learning. Extensive documentation communicates to children that their efforts to learn are important and valued. As teachers pay more attention to documentation, they find their students become more careful about their work and more evaluative. By documenting children's first, second and even third attempts at a task, teachers encourage children to reflect upon their own skill development. Children also understand how tangible evidence of their learning, through documentation, affects their parents.

The Documentation Web and the Valeska Hinton Center

Most teachers have some familiarity with documenting children's learning. They may use a developmental checklist, take anecdotal notes or systematically collect some of children's work, such as self-portraits done at the beginning and the end of the year. Many teachers may not recognize, however, all the options for assessing and demonstrating children's learning. Greater familiarity with these methods helps teachers document meaningfully.

To be most effective, teachers should vary their documentation to match children's learning experiences and to meet the needs of the intended audience. A teacher who wants to discover what a child knows about a topic might collect the child's drawings and writings about that topic, but may not consider asking the child to help construct a beginning web about what he knows. The teacher may assemble a photographic display, but not think to have the child dictate an accompanying narrative. With a variety of ways to document at hand, the teacher will be able to obtain more accurate information about a particular child. A child who has not developed extensive language skills, for example, may not be able to dictate a narrative but may be able to draw a picture, or construct a block play environment, that shows his depth of understanding.

When teachers at the Valeska Hinton Early Childhood Education Center in Peoria, Illinois, introduced the project approach in their classrooms of children ages 3 through 6 they wanted to increase their documentation. The Professional Development Coordinator and Lead Teacher developed a web to illustrate the variety of ways that documentation could occur (see Figure 2). Teachers and other staff added to the web as they identified more ways to document. The resulting web classifies documentation methods into five clusters: Individual Portfolios, Project Narratives, Observations of Child Development, Products (both individual and group) and Self-reflections. Each of these types of documentation provides a way to view and understand children's work.

There are as many different ways to document learning as there are ways that active, engaged children try to make sense of their world. Therefore, the web is neither an exhaustive list nor an exclusive classification system. The documentation web informs and reminds teachers of the variety of ways they can document and provides a vocabulary and a structure for teachers to communicate with each other about documentation.

Project Narratives
Teacher Journal
Staff Dialogue Notes
Narrative for Adults
Narrative for Display
Narrative for Children

Project Narratives

A narrative statement, which tells the story or history of a learning experience or project, is the most traditional method of documentation. Stories are a powerful way of understanding other people's events and experiences. Such narratives can take the form of stories for and by children, records of conversations with other teachers, teacher journals, narratives for adults in the form of books and letters,or visual displays. They are usually created over a period of time, marking change and growth in knowledge, skills and dispositions.

To take advantage of the interest that comes from an evolving project, teachers can write narratives that are continuously updated as the children's work proceeds. Kathy Steinheimer's pre-kindergarten class of 3- and 4-year-olds at the Valeska Hinton Center became engaged in constructing a mail system, for example. Kathy accompanied a photo display that illustrated the mailbag design process with the following narrative:

> Karissa and Tim took on the job of creating a mailbag out of paper. This led to a lengthy interchange about the handle. Karissa drew a short handle using a picture on the cover of a book as her reference. Tim told her that it had to be bigger. Karissa drew a handle that was a little longer and wider. Tim told her that the handle was too fat. Karissa insisted that it would work and kept on cutting. Tim tried to convince Karissa that he needed the long strip on the edge of her paper. She did not agree and finished her cutting. Then, he showed her the picture on the book cover. Karissa kept on cutting. Next, she tried her handle on for size and discovered that it would not work. Therefore, she asked Tim to draw the handle. She cut out the long and narrow handle that he drew. It tore as she cut it out. However, they still thought that it would work after they cut it out. It did not. I gave them a yardstick and showed the pair how to draw a straight line with it. They made a long and wide handle for the bag, which they attached to the bag with tape. After a trial run without mail, they were satisfied with their accomplishment.

The problem-solving skills that the children developed through this experience would not be evident to others without the teacher's narrative.

mastered a particular skill, some checklists, when systematically combined with anecdotal notes and children's work samples, enable a teacher to reliably identify skills, knowledge, behaviors, dispositions and accomplishments as they emerge and become consistent. For example, Beth Crider-Olcott, a preprimary teacher at Valeska Hinton Center, recorded the following observation to document the growth in 4-year-old Thea's writing skills:

> Our project has really encouraged Thea's writing development. She had been writing her name consistently, but with the drawing of the cages, Thea attempted to copy the word "cages." With her success, Thea began to copy any word put in front of her! She copied the words "shampoo" and "alcohol" to make labels for bottles in the clinic.

Figure 3

Crider-Olcott was able to record on the developmental checklist that Thea was able to complete the skill, "Copies or writes words needed for work or play" (Jablon, Marsden, Meisels & Dichtelmiller, 1994). (See Figure 3.)

Observations of Child Development

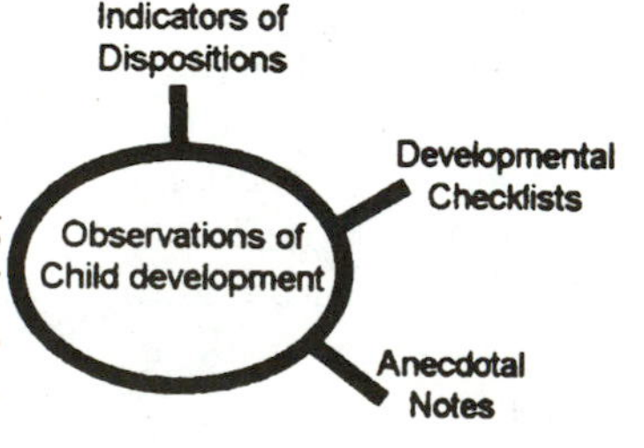

Observing and recording development is a familiar practice for many teachers of young children. In general, child development observations may be recorded as items on a developmental checklist, anecdotal notes or indicators of dispositions. These practices have been used primarily to report on mastery of discrete skills, to assess children's progress in school, or to indicate the frequency, duration and nature of a behavior at a particular point in time.

In recent years, observation systems such as the Work Sampling System have expanded the practical uses of checklists to document growth and skill development over time. Rather than focusing on whether a child has

Individual Portfolios

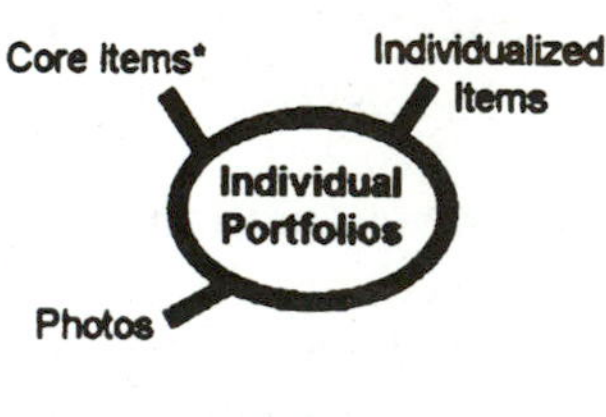

Collection of children's work is another familiar type of documentation. For years, teachers have saved children's work to share with parents and to use when evaluating a child's progress at the end of the year. Teachers often collect children's self-portraits or writing samples.

Teachers can observe and document growth by systematically collecting children's work over time. This documentation is more significant when it is linked to a "comprehensive and developmentally appropriate picture of what children can be expected to know and do across all domains of growth and learning" (Meisels et al., 1994, p. 8). Portfolio items are evidence of a child's progress, as measured on a checklist that is based on such a picture. Beth Crider-Olcott, for example, saved Thea's attempts to copy words, including a map that Thea labeled by copying names of vegetables (see Figure 4).

Child Self-reflections

Self-reflections provide the most accurate assessment of a child's emotional involvement with a project's content area. The teacher can assess whether an experience is developmentally appropriate and the extent to which it will contribute to the child's disposition to learn. Observations of child self-reflections provide the most direct evidence of appropriate classroom experiences.

As part of a water project, some children in Pam Scranton's multi-age pre-kindergarten class at Valeska Hinton made foil boats. Scranton recorded 4-year-old Antonio's self-reflections:

> Antonio has shown an increased disposition towards sticking with something. During the foil-boat activity, he struggled with his boat and how to connect the sides. He was beginning to become frustrated when he observed Rommel's boat and the way he pinched the sides closed. Antonio tried this and it worked. He exclaimed, "Look, Teacher, now my sides is gonna work good!" He manipulated both of his sides in this way and spent nearly 20 minutes perfecting the shape. Antonio's comments on his own progress and the length of his involvement with the boat indicate that Antonio was appropriately challenged and engaged.

Products

Products, the manifestations of children's learning, are the most obvious means of documenting learning. Adults probably consider writing samples to be the most visible signs of children's learning. Pictures, webs, musical expressions, constructions, and collections of data and oral language samples also produce significant documentation. These products can be produced either individually or by a group of children. Occasionally, the product speaks for itself; in general, however, this usefulness can be augmented by carefully selecting products for display and including an explanation of the product's significance. When displaying group work, a teacher may choose to select those products that are significant

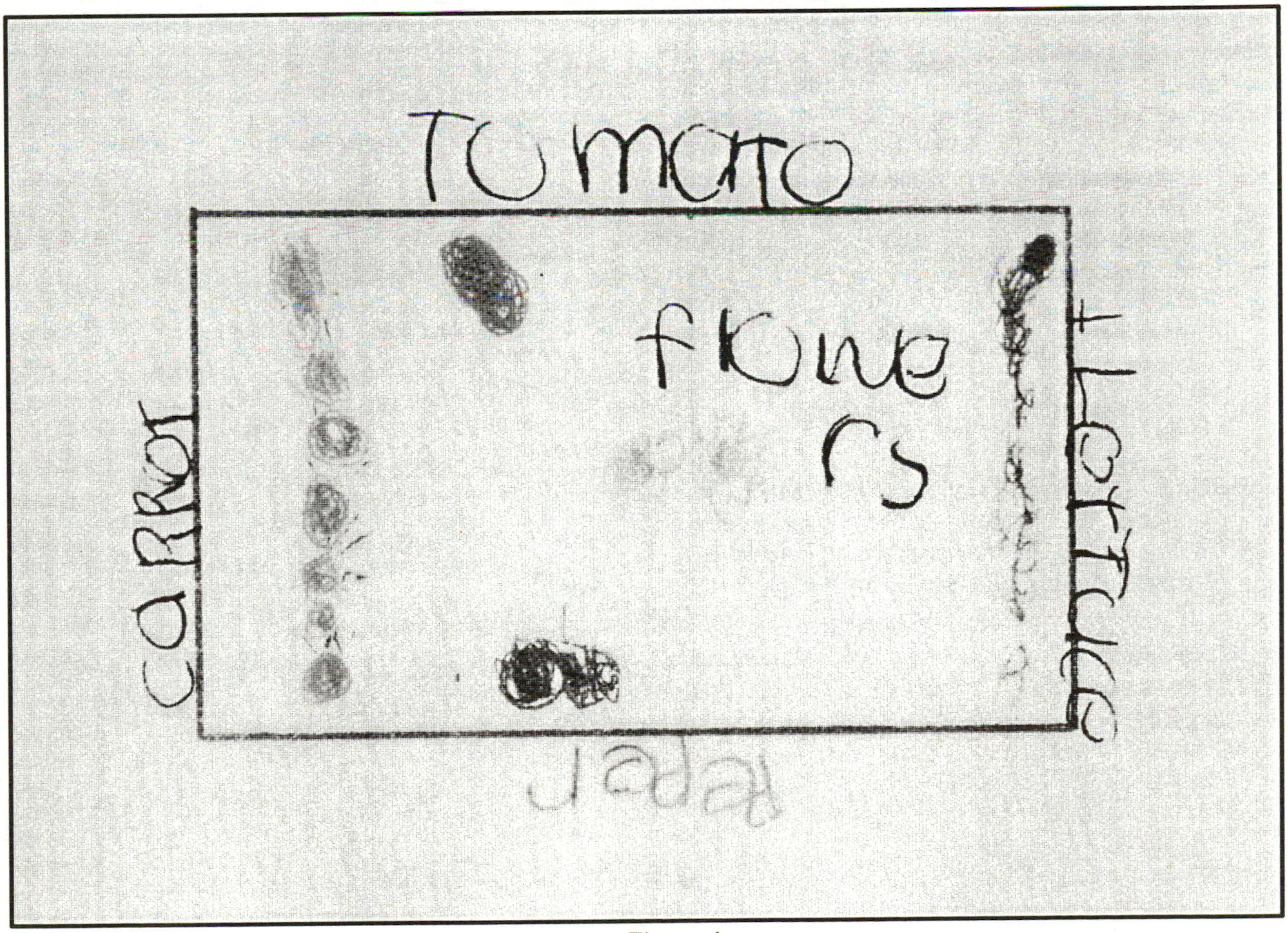

Figure 4

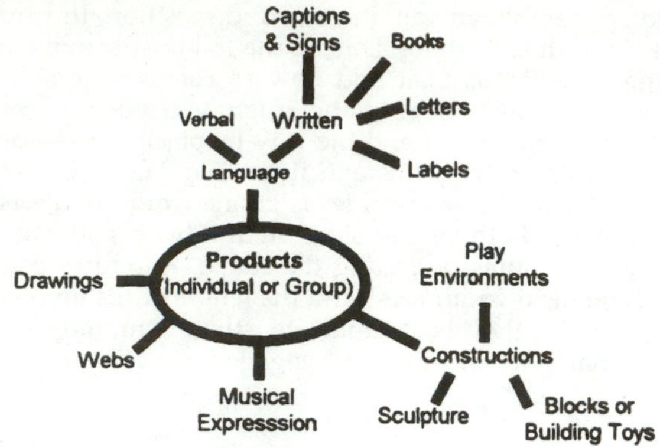

in telling the story of the project or in documenting an individual child's development through participation in the project. It is not usually necessary to display all of the children's pictures.

Group-constructed play environments are one of the most effective products to use when documenting children's knowledge and skills. What the children build reflects what they know, and the workmanship of the construction reflects their skills. Val Timmes' multi-age kindergarten/1st-grade class constructed a grocery store in their classroom, for example, as an outgrowth of their investigation of fruits and vegetables.

The children visited the grocery story, made sketches of what they saw, and then drew and refined floor plans for their store. They made lists and diagrams. They measured, cut and created, forming teams to construct the store's various departments. The resulting play environment was rich with examples of the children's knowledge of the grocery store and their ability to measure, read, write, problem-solve, work with number concepts and create. By documenting this play environment with written explanations of the various constructions, and by displaying photographs of the children in the process of constructing, Val Timmes was able to share the significance of these products with parents, children and other visitors.

Conclusion

Documentation is a powerful skill for the teacher. A letter from a parent at Valeska Hinton Center shows the effect that high quality documentation can have on parents' perceptions of a school. This parent was in the process of choosing a preschool program for her child and first encountered the project approach when she visited the center.

> My first actual encounter with projects occurred in late spring at an open house for prospective parents . . . I was skeptical—the so-called traditional approaches had worked for me, so why wouldn't it also provide success for our child? . . . Walking around the school that night, I began to be impressed. I studied [the documentation on] a project on reflections. I marveled at the insights shared by the children. The critical thinking skills [that] their work exhibited was phenomenal. Direct quotations included sentences of greater length and complexity than I would have expected. Their vocabulary was very specific. I went home and attempted to describe what I had seen to my husband . . . After our discussion, we became convinced that this was the place for our daughter to learn.
>
> —*Nancy Higgins, parent*

Ultimately, the teacher's skill and the time and effort spent in documentation benefited the children, the parents and the school.

References

Association for Childhood Education International/Perrone, V. (1991). On standardized testing. A position paper. *Childhood Education, 67,* 132–142.

Berk, L., & Winsler, A. (1995). *Scaffolding children's learning: Vygotsky and early childhood education.* Washington, DC: National Association for the Education of Young Children.

Howard, P. (1994). *The owner's manual for the brain.* Austin, TX: Leornian Press.

Jablon, J. R., Marsden, D., Meisels, S., & Dichtelmiller, M. (1994). *Omnibus guidelines: Preschool through third grade* (3rd ed.) Ann Arbor, MI: Rebus Planning Associates.

Katz, L. (1995). *Talks with teachers of young children: A collection.* Norwood, NJ: Albex Publishing.

Meisels, S. (1993). Remaking classroom assessment with the work sampling system. *Young Children, 48,* 34–40.

Meisels, S., Jablon, J., Marsden, D., Dichtelmiller, M., Dorfman, A., & Steele, D. (1994). *An overview* (3rd ed.) Ann Arbor, MI: Rebus Planning Associates.

Sylwester, R. (1995). *A celebration of neurons: An educator's guide to the human brain.* Alexandria, VA: Association for Supervision and Curriculum Development.

Vygotsky, L. S., edited and translated by M. Cole, V. John-Steiner, S. Scribner, & E. Souberman. (1978). *Mind in society: The development of higher mental processes.* Cambridge, MA: Harvard University Press.

Challenging Movement Experiences for Young Children

STEPHEN W. SANDERS
BILL YONGUE

Ten four-year-old children enter a large, carpeted room. A colorful parachute is on the floor in the middle. Against the wall are containers filled with a variety of balls and beanbags. The children move quickly in anticipation of what is about to happen. It is time for movement.

Every day, thousands of young children develop their physical skills by participating in a variety of movement experiences. Today we know more than ever about how to remain healthy. Regular participation in physical activity is one of the most important ways to live a longer, fuller life. Daily movement experiences are an integral part of high-quality early childhood programs. In the mid-1980s, the National Association for the Education of Young Children (NAEYC) published a position statement that described developmentally appropriate practice for children from birth through age eight (see Bredekamp & Copple, 1997).

The Council on Physical Education for Children (COPEC), a division of the National Association for Sport and Physical Education (NASPE), used NAEYC's model to develop *Developmentally Appropriate Practice in Movement Programs for Young Children Ages 3–5* (NASPE, 1992). The document consists of 25 integrated components, each suggesting guidelines for appropriate and inappropriate practice in movement programs for young children.

In a developmentally appropriate program for young children what kinds of movement experiences should children have? Four major areas from the NASPE guidelines are emphasized here: child development, teaching strategies, content, and assessment.

Developmentally Appropriate Practice in Movement Programs for Young Children Ages 3–5 (NASPE, 1992) can assist educators of young children to:

- make informed decisions about the curriculum and content of movement programs
- determine how to present content appropriately
- evaluate curriculum and teaching methods
- advocate for program improvement
- more fully integrate movement activities within the curriculum

Developmental Physical Education

Developmental physical education as defined by Gallahue (1995) is physical activity that emphasizes the acquisition of sequential movement skills and increased physical competency based on the unique developmental level of the individual. It recognizes and incorporates the many contributions that systemic, sensitive teaching can make to a child's cognitive and affective development. Developmental physical education encourages the uniqueness of individuals and is based on the fundamental proposition that although motor development is age related, it is not age dependent.

Three components that are critical in developmentally appropriate physical education are: age appropriateness, developmental appropriateness, and instruction (NASPE, 1992).

From *Dimensions of Early Childhood,* Winter 1998, pp. 9-17. © 1998 by the Southern Early Childhood Association (SECA), Little Rock, AR. Reprinted by permission.

Table 1.

Characteristics of 3- to 5-year-old children

Physical
1. Perceptual-motor abilities rapidly develop, but confusion often exists in body, directional, temporal, and spatial awareness.
2. Rapidly developing fundamental movement abilities in a variety of motor skills. Unilateral movements are easier than bilateral movements such as skipping.
3. Often active and energetic and would rather run than walk, but still need rest periods.
4. Body functions and processes become well regulated.
5. Body builds of boys and girls are very similar.
6. Fine-motor control is yet to be fully established, and gross-motor control is still developing.

Cognitive
1. Increasing ability to express thoughts and ideas verbally.
2. Learn through play.
3. Very imaginative and continue to investigate and discover.
4. This preoperational thought phase of development results in a period of transition from self-satisfying behavior to fundamental socialized behavior.
5. Attention span depends on whether activity keeps child's interest.

Affective
1. Some children may be somewhat egocentric and assume that everyone thinks the way they do. This may result in reluctance to share and cooperate with others.
2. May be fearful of new situations, shy, self-conscious.
3. Beginning to distinguish right from wrong.
4. Self-concept is rapidly developing. Success-oriented experiences and positive reinforcement are especially important.

Age appropriateness. High-quality programs are not based on chronological age or grade level but are influenced by both. The process of development proceeds from simple to complex and from general to specific as young children strive to increase their competence in all domains. As a result, patterns of behavior emerge that help guide the selection of movement experiences that are typically appropriate for specific age groups (Gallahue, 1995).

For example, most 5-year-old children do not yet have the skills to compete in a regulation soccer game, but they can participate in activities that involve kicking a ball. It would be developmentally inappropriate, then, to force all 5-year-old children to participate in a regulation soccer game.

Individual appropriateness. Each child has a unique timing and pattern of growth and development. Therefore, movement activities are based on children's individual stages of motor development and levels of movement skill learning. The inclusion of specific movement experiences is considerably influenced by children's fitness levels, as well as their cognitive and affective development (Gallahue, 1995).

Some children, for example, may not develop the necessary skills to play soccer until late elementary school; others may never achieve the skills or have interest necessary to participate in the game.

Instruction. In a developmentally appropriate program, it is also important to incorporate instructional strategies that maximize opportunities for learning and success for all children. Teacher decisions concerning what, when, and how to teach are based primarily on the appropriateness of the activity for the individual and secondarily on its suitability for a certain age group (NASPE, 1992, 1995).

It would be considered developmentally inappropriate to require children to participate in activities such as Duck-Duck-Goose or a relay race where activity time is limited because children spend most of their time waiting in lines for a turn.

Child Development

> Movement activities are designed with the physical, cognitive, and affective development of children in mind. (NASPE, 1992, p. 6)

Each child is a whole, integrated person (Gallahue, 1995). In order to plan an appropriate learning environment and develop suitable experiences for young children, adults first need to understand children's development, including the cognitive, affective, and psychomotor characteristics and needs of the age group.

The characteristics briefly reviewed in *Table 1* are among those that determine not only how teachers work with children but also the types of movement experiences provided (Gallahue & Ozmun, 1995). Based on these characteristics, the Council on Physical Education for Children (NASPE, 1992) developed five premises of a developmentally appropriate movement program for young children.

1. Three-, four-, and five-year-old children are different from elementary-age children. When teachers understand the continuum of development, their focus can be on teaching children rather than teaching activities.

Young children need a variety of experiences that will lead them to more mature movement patterns.

2. Young children learn through interaction with their environment. This well-established concept has been stated in many ways—children learn by doing; children learn through active involvement with people and objects. Developmentally appropriate movement programs for young children are designed so that all children are active participants, not passive listeners or observers except for brief demonstrations and explanations of the activity.

3. Teachers of young children act as guides or facilitators. Teachers construct the environment with specific objectives in mind, then guide children toward these goals. By carefully observing children's responses and interests, teachers can adapt learning experiences to best meet individual needs. In high-quality programs, children make choices and seek creative solutions. Teachers actively engage children in experiences to broaden and deepen their learning, a strategy which is called "child-centered" rather than "subject-centered" approach to curriculum.

4. Young children learn and develop in an integrated fashion. Children's physical, emotional, social, and cognitive development are interrelated, so learning through movement encompasses all areas of development. Regularly-scheduled movement experiences focus upon the development of physical skills which are incorporated in the child's total development and integrated into the entire curriculum.

5. Planned movement experiences enhance play. A combination of play and planned movement experiences, specifically designed to help children develop physical skills, are the most beneficial in assisting young children in their development. When frequent, regular, appropriate movement experiences are combined with daily indoor and outdoor play, children freely practice and develop their skills.

Teaching Strategies

> Movement exploration, guided discovery, and creative problem solving are the predominant teaching strategies employed. Children are provided the opportunity to make choices and actively explore their environment; while teachers serve as facilitators, preparing a stimulating environment and challenging activities. (NASPE, 1992, p. 6)

One of the most important tasks a teacher does is establish a safe, challenging environment in which all children can learn (Sanders, 1992). Make sure children know what is expected of them during movement activities. Children must be aware of any space restrictions, the movement patterns of other children, and their own potential for moving. A developmentally appropriate movement class for 4-year-old children might look something like the one described in *Figure 1.*

Table 2.

Skill themes in physical education for young children

Locomotor	**Nonmanipulative**	**Manipulative**
Walk	Push/pull	Throw
Run	Swing/sway	Catch
Leap	Bend/stretch	Strike
Hop	Twist/turn	Kick
Jump	Balance	Dribble
Gallop	Transfer weight	Bounce
Slide		Roll
Skip		

Curriculum Content

> The movement curriculum has an obvious scope and sequence based on goals and objectives that are appropriate for all children. It includes a balance of skills and concepts designed to enhance the cognitive, motor, affective, and physical development of every child. (NASPE, 1992, p. 6)

There are two parts to curriculum development in physical education for young children. First, the content of a movement program for young children is made up of movement skills and concepts. Skills themes, the actual physical movements or skills that children will learn and perform, can be divided into three categories: locomotor, nonmanipulative, and manipulative *(Table 2).*

Movement concepts modify skill themes and describe how skills are performed. For example, running is a skill. Fast, zigzag, and forward are concepts that describe running. During a lesson for older preschoolers, where the emphasis is on developing skill in running, the challenge might be, "Can you run very fast in a zigzag path while moving forward?" Movement concepts are expressed in categories of body awareness, (what the body can do), space awareness, (where the body moves), effort, (how the body moves), and relationships, (relationships of the body to its parts, objects, individuals, and groups).

The movement vocabulary in *Table 3* identifies appropriate concepts for young children to learn through movement (Graham, Holt/Hale, & Parker, 1993; Kruger & Kruger, 1989). This skill theme approach is developmentally appropriate with young children because it helps them become more capable movers. There is plenty of time to learn to play games such as soccer or basketball in later years after they have developed their skills.

The second part of a movement curriculum for young children includes providing children with information, or cues, on how to correctly perform the movement skills. *Cues* are key points children should learn about each skill (Graham et al., 1993). Some cues that are ap-

Figure 1.

Visit an appropriate movement class for four-year-olds

Ten four-year-old children walk quietly down a school hallway and enter a large, carpeted room. One of the first sights they see is the smiling face of Mrs. Phillips, their classroom teacher. "We are really going to have run learning today!" Mrs. Phillips tells the students.

Mrs. Phillips asks each child to pick a small carpet square from a pile and carry it to the center of the room. "Let's place our carpet squares in a circle and then sit on the carpets," she says. As the children sit, Mrs. Phillips observes that the shape is more a figure eight than a circle and that many children are sitting very close to each other. "Does this look like a circle?" she asks. Some children say no, others are not sure what a circle is supposed to look like. Mrs. Phillips helps arrange the carpets in a circle and then leads the children in a discussion about what a circle is, general and self-space, and not getting too close to friends while moving around the room. About two minutes have passed.

Mrs. Phillips explains the two rhythm sticks she holds. "These two sticks are my 'stop' signal. When I strike them together I would like you to stop, freeze your body, and not move." She demonstrates by striking the sticks together and freezing. "Can you stand up and start walking around the room and stay as far away from your friends as you can? If you see anyone getting close to you, it is your job to stay away from them." The children jump up and start moving. "This is fun!" David shouts.

Every 15 to 20 seconds, Mrs. Phillips strikes the sticks together and all children stop moving. Mrs. Phillips asks if they can move backward, and the children are off again. Each time Mrs. Phillips strikes the sticks, the children stop for about five seconds and she gives them the next challenge. "Show me you can hop on one foot." "Show me you can gallop around the room, but be careful not to get close to your friends." When the children have trouble with a challenge, Mrs. Phillips strikes the sticks together to stop the children so she can demonstrate how to do the challenge. The children move again, walking, hopping, galloping and running. Mrs. Phillips also guides the students in the directions, pathways, and speeds in which the movements can be performed.

After about four minutes, Mrs. Phillips can see the children are getting tired. She strikes the sticks together and points to three piles of beanbags. "Would you walk over, without touching any of your friends, pick up a beanbag, and then place it on your head? Can you balance the beanbag on your shoulder? Can you balance the beanbag on your elbow?" For the next four minutes the children practice balancing beanbags as suggested by the teacher. They also have ideas of their own, and Mrs. Phillips praises their creative efforts.

When the activity ends, the children place the beanbags in a box, and then Mrs. Phillips asks them to pick up large balloons [see note]. The balloons seem to spark an interest in the children, and they begin to bounce and strike them. After a short time, she gains their attention, talks about the balloons, and challenges the children to practice throwing, catching, and kicking. After about six minutes, Mrs. Phillips tells the children to put away their balloons and pick up hoops.

The hoops, spaced along a wall, are easy for children to pick up without collision. Children play with the hoops for a while without direction. Mrs. Phillips then asks them to line the hoops straight on the floor and challenges them to jump on two feet from hoop to hoop.

After practicing jumping for about five minutes or so, Mrs. Phillips wonders out loud, "How am I going to pick up all the equipment?" The children then eagerly volunteer to help.

The equipment stowed, Mrs. Phillips asks the children again to sit on their carpets. The children sing a song in which they touch parts of their bodies corresponding with the music. The children talk briefly about what they did during class and what they just learned, and Mrs. Phillips tells them they did an excellent job. The children then put their carpet squares away. The class period filled with movement activities, lasted about 30 minutes.

Note: **Balloons are an aspiration hazard and should only be offered to four- and five-year-old children if the balloons are properly inflated (American Public Health Association & American Academy of Pediatrics, 1992). Carefully supervise children whenever balloons are available, and remove all pieces of any popped balloons immediately. Infants and toddlers, who often explore items by chewing, should never be given balloons.**

Note: From Designing Preschool Movement Programs **pp. 11–12), by S.W. Sanders, 1992, Champaign, IL: Human Kinetics. Copyright © 1992 by Human Kinetics. Adapted with permission.**

propriate for assisting preschool children to develop movement skills are listed in *Table 4*.

Teachers who stress one cue at a time are less likely to confuse children (Graham et al., 1993). For example, the cues for teaching preschool children to throw are to step with the opposite foot, throw hard, and to turn the opposite side of the body toward the target. These three cues are introduced one at a time.

The more often a cue is stressed, the more likely the children are to improve their skills (Sanders, 1992), and the movement will soon become automatic. Preschool children who learn cues for each skill will be more capable movers in elementary school.

Assessment

> Systematic assessment is based on knowledge of developmental characteristics and ongoing observations in children as they participate in activities. This information is used to individualize instruction, plan objective-oriented lessons, identify children with special needs, communicate with parents, and evaluate the program's effectiveness. (NASPE, 1992, p. 10)

Photo courtesy of the authors

As children's skills and interests change, adults adjust the program to further accommodate each growing child

Table 3.

Movement concepts in physical education for young children

Space Awareness	**Body Awareness**
Personal Space	**Whole Body**
Self space	Front/back
Place in space	Sides
General Space	**Body Parts**
Middle of	Hands/head
Sides of	Feet/knees/toes
Boundaries of	Fingers/elbows
Directions	Shoulders/hips
Up/down	Stomach/eyes
Forward/backward	Mouth/neck
Right/left	Face/chin/ears
Sideways	Nose/ankles/wrist
Level	**Actions**
High/medium/low	Moving/still
Size	Weight on feet
Big/small	Weight on other parts
Pathways	Balancing
Straight/curved	**Body Shapes**
Angular/twisted	Wide/narrow
Figure eight	Round/twisted
Zigzag	
Shapes	
Round/square	
Triangular	
Rectangular	
Effort/Quality	**Relationships**
Time	**Space Words**
Fast/slow	Under/over
Faster/slower	On/off
Sudden/sustained	Around/through
Force	Between/among
Heavy/light	Near/far
Strong/weak	**Contact**
Hard/soft	Touching/not touching
Harsh/gentle	Together/apart
Flow	**People**
Bound/free	By yourself/with people
Stopping/going	Leading/following
Jerky/smooth	Mirroring/matching
	Unison/contrast

Teachers in developmentally appropriate programs continually and thoroughly assess children's progress. As children's skills and interests change, adults adjust the program to further accommodate each growing child (Grace & Shores, 1992). NASPE developed physical education benchmarks for students from kindergarten through the 12th grade. These benchmarks (see Table 5) are reasonable skill and knowledge outcomes that students would expect to achieve as a result of participating in a quality physical education program (NASPE, 1990).

How do teachers use these benchmarks to see if the children are progressing? The criteria for assessing physical skills are not unlike the criteria used to assess the social, emotional, and mental development of young children. The Southern Early Childhood Association (Grace & Shores, 1992) established these criteria that can be used as a foundation for assessing the physical skills of children.

1. **Assessment must be valid.** It must provide information related to the goals and objectives of a program.

2. **Assessment must encompass the whole child.** Programs must have goals and assessment procedures which relate to children's physical, social, emotional, and mental development.

3. **Assessment must involve repeated observations.** Repeated observations help teachers to find patterns of behaviors and avoid quick decisions.

4. **Assessment must be continuous.** Each child should be compared to his or her own individual course of development over time, rather than to average behavior for a group.

5. **Assessment must use a variety of methods.** Gathering a wide variety of information from different sources permits informed and professional decisions.

An assessment portfolio is a collection of a child's work which demonstrates the child's efforts, progress,

Table 4.

Example cues for selected skill themes

Catch
Use large colorful balls to help in tracking
Emphasize catching with the hands
Use a ball on a string for a more consistent toss
Use soft textured balls
If ball is above the waist, keep thumbs together
If ball is below the waist, hold pinkies together
Keep eyes on the ball [as it comes] into hands

Throw
Use visual aids (footprints or tape on floor) to help in the stepping position
Use large targets
Emphasize using opposition
Step, turn toward the target, throw hard

Kick
Use large targets
Use soft textured balls
Keep eye on the ball
Step beside the ball
Kick hard

Balance
Encourage alternate foot stepping
Begin walking by holding onto a rope or hoop
Gradually move to balance beam
Increase height of balance beam as children improve
Look straight ahead, move slowly, balance before taking next step

Spatial Awareness (Personal and general space)
Learn how to move, dodge, and stop
Keep head up when moving
Look left and right
Watch where you are going

Jump (Vertical and distance)
Two feet take off and two feet land
Maintain balance
As arms go up, feet come off the floor
Jump as high or as far as possible
Use arms for balance

Strike
Have ball on tee or suspended on string
Place ball at child's waist level
Bat should have large hitting surface and small handle (one-liter plastic bottles make good bats)
Step toward target, keep eye on ball, swing level and hard

and achievements over time (Grace & Shores, 1992). The portfolio can be made up of a variety of different assessment tools such as work samples, screening tests, rating scales, checklists, and systematic observations of the child's performance or behavior. When this collection of information is put together for each child, families and teachers can get an accurate picture of children's learning.

Table 5.

Benchmarks for kindergarten physical education

- Demonstrates competency in many movement forms and proficiency in a few movement forms
- Applies movement concepts and principles to the learning and development of motor skills
- Exhibits a physically active lifestyle
- Achieves and maintains a health-enhancing level of physical fitness
- Demonstrates responsible personal and social behavior in physical activity setting
- Demonstrates understanding and respect for differences among people in physical activity setting
- Understands that physical activity provides the opportunity for enjoyment, challenge, self expression and social interaction

Table 6 illustrates a checklist that might be used by teachers to see if kindergarten children are achieving the NASPE benchmarks.

Another tool to record children's progress is the video camera (see Reynolds & Milner in this issue). Videotape children individually as they perform a number of skills such as running, jumping, throwing, catching, and striking. Bring families into the assessment and learning process by viewing and discussing the video with them.

Teachers who continue to improve their professional practices help ensure that children will continue to have positive attitudes about physical education, and all learning, in the future.

References

American Public Health Association, & American Academy of Pediatrics. (1992). *Caring for our children: National health and safety performance standards: Guidelines for out-of-home child care programs.* Washington, DC, and Elk Grove Village, IL: Authors.

Bredekamp, S., & Copple, C. (Eds.). (1997). *Developmentally appropriate practice in early childhood programs* (Rev. ed.). Washington, DC: National Association for the Education of Young Children.

Gallahue, D.L. (1995). Transforming physical education curriculum. In Bredekamp, S. & Rosegrant, T. (Eds.), *Reaching potentials: Transforming early childhood curriculum and assessment* (pp. 125–137). Washington DC: National Association for the Education of Young Children.

Gallahue, D.L., & Ozmun, J.C. (1995). *Understanding motor development: Infant, children, adolescents, adults.* Dubuque, IA: W.C. Brown & Benchmark.

Grace, C., & Shores, E. (1992). *The portfolio and its use: Developmentally appropriate assessment of young children.* Little Rock: Southern Early Childhood Association.

Photo courtesy of the authors

Incorporate instructional strategies that maximize opportunities for learning and success for all children.

Graham, G., Holt/Hale, S., & Parker, M. (1993). *Children moving: A reflective approach to teaching physical education.* Palo Alto, CA: Mayfield.

Kruger, H., & Kruger, J. (1989). *The preschool teacher's guide to movement education.* Baltimore: Gerstung.

National Association for Sport and Physical Education (NASPE). (1990). *Definition of the physically educated person. Report of the NASPE Outcomes Committee.* Reston, VA: American Association for Health, Physical Education, Recreation, and Dance (AAHPERD).

NASPE. (1992). *Developmentally appropriate physical education practices for children. A position statement of the Council on Physical Education for Children of NASPE.* Reston, VA: AAHPERD.

Sanders, S.W. (1992). *Designing preschool movement programs.* Champaign, IL: Human Kinetics.

Stephen W. Sanders, Ed.D., is Assistant Professor of Health and Human Performance at Auburn University in Auburn, Alabama.

Bill Yongue, Ed.D., is Assistant Professor, Department of Health, Physical Education, and Recreation at Florida International University, Miami.

Table 6.

Sample checklist for physical education benchmarks

Child's name______________________________

Date ___________________________________

Check the appropriate column
Demonstrated = D   Not Demonstrated = ND

Skill	D	ND
Kicks a stationary ball using a smooth, continuous running approach prior to the kick	____	____
Rolls sideways without hesitating or stopping	____	____
Makes both large and small body shapes while traveling	____	____
Walks and runs using a mature motor pattern	____	____
Tosses a ball and catches it before it bounces twice	____	____

What Role Should Technology Play in Young Children's Learning?

Susan W. Haugland

We face an important crossroads regarding the role of computers in young children's lives. Over the past 10 years, significant improvements have been made in technology. Whether we use technology with young children—and if so, how—is a critical issue facing early childhood educators and parents.

Computers and children—Starting at the right age

Many of my colleagues (Elkind 1998; Hohman 1998) and I do not recommend computer use for children younger than three. Computers simply do not match their learning style. Children younger than age three learn through their bodies: their eyes, ears, mouths, hands, and legs. While they may return over and over again to an activity, they are full of movement, changing focus frequently.

Photo courtesy of Robertson's Creative Photography.

Furthermore, computers are not a good choice for the developmental skills these children are learning to master: crawling, walking, babbling, talking, toilet training, and making friends, to name just a few. Children under three are active doers, gaining control of their bodies and making things happen in a fascinating world of possibilities. They are busy manipulating a wide variety of objects, such as digging in the sandbox or finger painting with pudding, and in the process learning about themselves and their environment. Frequently it is a challenge for adults just to keep up with them!

Thus, it is my recommendation that computers be introduced to young children when they are about three years of age.

Developmentally appropriate computer activities

Developmentally appropriate ways we use computers with threes and fours are different from the ways we use computers in kindergarten and the primary grades. Unfortunately, computers are used all too often in ways that are developmentally inappropriate.

__Susan W. Haugland__ is a professor emeritus in child development at Southeast Missouri State University and the president of K.I.D.S. & Computers, Inc., which provides teacher training and children's computer classes, evaluates software, publishes software evaluation on a website and in a newsletter, and sponsors the Developmental Software Awards yearly.

From *Young Children,* November 1999, pp. 26-31. © 1999 by the National Association for the Education of Young Children (NAEYC). Reprinted by permission.

In 1995 a comprehensive federal study, *Teachers and Technology: Making the Connection* (Congress 1995), found that while "schools are steadily increasing their access to new technologies . . . most teachers use these technologies in traditional ways, including drills in basic skills and instructional games" (p. 103). Clements (1994) makes a similar point, noting, "Children use mostly drill and practice software; their teachers state that their goal for using computers is to increase basic skills rather than to develop problem-solving or creative skills. . . . What we as early childhood educators are presently doing most often with computers is what research and NAEYC guidelines say we should be doing least often" (p. 33).

It is my recommendation that computers be introduced to young children when they are about three years of age, no younger.

Photo courtesy of Robertson's Creative Photography.

Using computers with young children should be a process of exploration and discovery for both teacher and child. What teachers tend to do most (drill and practice) is the opposite of what is recommended: encouraging children to solve problems and be creative. Enjoy the computer together!

Thus it should come as no surprise that computer use by children is often attacked based upon whether computers really increase learning and if we can justify the cost of technology (Oppenheimer 1997; Healy 1998). As Papert (1998) explains, computers are being criticized because of *how* they are being used. Computers are at their "weakest doing a job that is not what [they] can do most powerfully" (p. 3). Papert stresses that computers have an impact on children when they provide concrete experiences, children have free access, children and teachers learn together, peer tutoring is encouraged, children control the learning experience, and the computers are used to teach powerful ideas. (For a more detailed description of developmentally appropriate and inappropriate computer experiences, see *Young Children and Technology: A World of Discovery* [Haugland & Wright 1997].)

Parents support computers in the classroom

In contrast to the critics of children using computers, most parents believe that computers can have a positive effect on children's learning, as dramatically illustrated in a national study done by the Milken Exchange on Education Technology and Peter D. Hart (1999). When asked to rate the importance of computers for learning, 87% of parents in the study gave computers a strong rating. "The perception that computers are important in education does not vary much by occupation, income, or education, though fully 91% of [the] African American [parents in the study] think that computers will make a significant difference in the quality of [their children's] education" [Milken Exchange & Hart 1999).

Photo courtesy of Robertson's Creative Photography.

The computer center should be just one more activity center in a classroom filled with enticing learning centers. The teacher can supervise from a distance or move over to assist a child in the same way that she keeps an eye on everything going on in a free-choice classroom, stepping in to teach or guide as needed.

In 1996 NAEYC published the "NAEYC Position Statement: Technology and Young Children—Ages Three through Eight." The position statement provides important guidelines regarding appropriate use of technology with young children. Yet, many teachers still struggle: Should I use computers with young children? Do computers teach children important cognitive, physical, language, social, and emotional skills? What is my role in the computer-integrated classroom?

Models for computer integration

It is important to realize that using computers with young children is a process of exploration and discovery for both you and the children. How you use computers the first year in your classroom will probably be very different from how you use them five years later.

I would like to share with you one model for using computers with three- and four-year-olds and another for children five to eight. These models are just one approach; there are alternative methods. But these models may provide a vision of how technology can offer unique opportunities for you to enhance children's development.

Developmentally appropriate ways we use computers with threes and fours are different from the ways we use computers in kindergarten and the primary grades.

Computers and preschoolers

Children three and four years of age are developmentally ready to explore computers, and most early childhood educators see the computer center as a valuable activity center for learning.

Why include a computer center for children this young? Because research has shown that three- and four-year-old children who use computers with supporting activities that reinforce the major objectives of the programs have significantly greater developmental gains when compared to children without computer experiences in similar classrooms—gains in intelligence (mean score increases were 6 points), nonverbal skills, structural knowledge, long-term memory, manual dexterity, verbal skills, problem solving, abstraction, and conceptual skills (Haugland 1992).

Unfortunately, all too often computers are used in ways that are developmentally *in*appropriate.

From September through April the children in the study used developmentally appropriate software whenever they desired. The computers were given no more importance than any other activity in the classroom. Some children were more fascinated by the computers than others. Yet even children who rarely used the computers visited with children using the computers, sometimes standing behind them to discuss a program, solve problems cooperatively, or just watch the action!

Timing is crucial. Give children plenty of time to experiment and explore. Young children are really comfortable clicking various options to see what is going to happen next. Intervene when children appear frustrated or nothing seems to be happening. Frequently, just a quick word or two, even from across the room, reminds children what they need to do next to reach their desired goal. Providing children with minimal help teaches them they can operate the computer successfully. In addition, because the teacher observes what children are doing, he can ask probing questions or propose problems to enhance and expand children's computer experiences.

Locating the Computer Center in the Environment

In an ideal classroom the computer center is in a visible location. The monitors are situated so that they can be seen from throughout the classroom (Haugland 1997). Children interact with those using the computers, although they may be working in another center. All of this stimulates peer mentoring, social interaction, language development, and cooperative play. In addition, a highly visible computer center enables you as the teacher to supervise the computer center without leaving the area of the classroom in which you are teaching. You need move to the computer center only when it is necessary to assist children, or you can ask a child who is not busy if she is willing to help.

Computers for kindergartners and early primary children

As children enter kindergarten and the primary grades, it is important that they continue to have a computer center with a library of developmentally appropriate software. Children need opportunities to make choices about some of their computer experiences. In addition, you as a kindergarten or primary-grade teacher will use the computer for more directed activities that match your learning objectives. For example, to enhance keyboard and language skills, children can compose a letter to a friend or relative using the template provided in Claris Works for Kids (Claris Works 1997).

In another example, you may ask children to work in small groups using Scholastic's Magic School Bus

As we prepare to enter the twenty-first century (in less than two months!), we probably should make our peace with the fact that computers will be in early childhood classrooms —and learn to use them wisely.

Explores the Rainforest (1997) to compare two of the seven ecozones in the program by listing how they are alike and different. Using Kids' Desk: Internet Safe (1998), other small groups can investigate these two ecozones on Internet websites selected by the teacher. The groups then merge to share their discoveries and write a report on the ecozones, illustrating each with pictures drawn by members of the group or downloaded from the Internet sites.

Through exploring computer experiences, these children build memory skills, learn how to seek out information, use knowledge until they have a clear understanding from multiple sources, and integrate their knowledge of how each ecosystem functions. In the process they learn to delegate responsibility, interact with others, problem solve, and cooperate to reach a goal.

Benefits. What are the benefits of providing computers to kindergarten and primary-grade children? The answer to this question varies depending upon the kind of computer experiences offered and how frequently children have access to computers.

The potential gains for kindergarten and primary children are tremendous, including improved motor skills, enhanced mathematical thinking, increased creativity, higher scores on tests of critical thinking and problem solving, higher levels of what Nastasi and Clements (1994) term *effectance motivation* (believing they can change or affect their environment), and increased scores on standardized language assessments.

In addition, computers enhance children's self-concept, and children demonstrate increased levels of spoken communication and cooperation. Children share leadership roles more frequently and develop positive attitudes toward learning (Clements 1994; Cardelle-Elawar & Wetzel 1995; Adams 1996; Denning & Smith 1997; Haugland & Wright 1997; Matthews 1997).

Photo courtesy of Robertson's Creative Photography.

Some children are more fascinated than others by computers. Yet even children who rarely use the computers may visit with children using them, sometimes standing behind them to discuss a program, help solve a problem, or just watch the action. Teachers can encourage social interaction, conversation, cooperative play, and peer teaching.

Making the connection

Research has clearly demonstrated that computers provide children with some unique and important avenues for learning. As adults committed to the development of young children, finding ways to connect children to computers is an essential goal for all centers and schools.

How children connect with computers, and the goals for children's use of computers, need to come from the teachers, parents, and administrators working in your center or school. Early childhood programs serve diverse populations and have different schedules, curriculums, staffing patterns, resources, and so on. Goals and the steps that centers or schools take to integrate computers into their classrooms may be completely different but equally successful. An important first step, however, is providing the interest and increasing the knowledge of administrators, teachers, and parents.

Enlisting support from the school community

As we all know, teachers are busy—supervising children, developing lesson plans, arranging activities, implementing activities in the classroom. Yet all teachers, no matter what their philosophy, share a common goal: to do what is best for every child in their classroom. I believe that administrators, teachers, and parents, when they recognize the dramatic learning opportunities computers can provide young children and the unique developmental gains children demonstrate from computer exposure, will not be able to turn their backs on this valuable learning resource.

It is not easy to implement a totally new tool for learning. For computers to be used successfully, teachers must be open to learning (Papert 1998). Teachers then will need help in ac-

Scheduling Computer Study Group Meetings

This may be one of your most difficult challenges. Ask everyone who has expressed an interest to indicate times they are available. The most likely options are noon meetings, early afternoon meetings, potluck dinners (with child care provided), or evening meetings. To be successful, match the most individuals possible with their meeting preferences. Personally contact those who cannot meet at that time, and see if they can rearrange their schedule. If not, ask if you can recruit them for a specific project at a later date. How will the children be supervised during the meetings? Recruit parent volunteers who may not want to serve on the study group but would assist during the meeting. Remind all participants several days before each meeting. Nothing lowers teacher and parent morale faster than poor attendance.

quiring computers, learning how to use them effectively with children, and discovering how to integrate them into their classrooms.

A viable beginning is for teachers, administrators, and parents to share magazine, journal, and newspaper articles they have seen regarding children using computers. Administrators can then survey, determining which teachers, parents have an interest in using computers. With directors, principals, teachers, and parents working together, you can make it happen!

Photo courtesy of Robertson's Creative Photography.

Only a few teachers in a small number of schools have been trained to maximize technology use in classrooms. Teachers need practical experience, workshops, models, mentors, and supervisory follow-up to develop confidence and to learn strategies for integrating computers into their curriculum.

A recent report reveals that only a few teachers in a relatively small number of schools have been trained to maximize technology use in classrooms (Gatewood & Conrad 1997). Teacher training is essential for computers to be an effective teaching tool. In fact, due to this key connection, some schools make teacher training their first step before computers are even purchased. Training opportunities enable teachers to build skills and confidence and learn strategies to integrate computers into their curriculum.

Assessing each teacher's comfort level and current computer skills is an important and continuing aspect of the training process. Equally important, training should include not only how to use the technology, but how to effectively integrate these tools into the existing curriculum.

Epstein (1993) identifies four critical components of training: practical experience, workshops, models and mentors, and supervisory follow-up. In your school or center, a valuable introduction to computers is learning how to turn on a computer and how all the wires behind the computers are attached. This builds confidence that teachers can handle the computer and replace a wire if one falls out.

Setting up a computer study group

Organize a study group of all the individuals at your school or center who have expressed interest in children using computers.

A good beginning for your first meeting is to review integrating computers into your school or center. Summarize the benefits of using computers with young children, then discuss goals for the year. It is important that the study group be involved in determining the goals and that they be realistic, taking into consideration the cost of computers, the time required for teacher training, and so forth.

Probably your first goal will be obtaining computers. Don't let the group become overwhelmed! Start with one or two classrooms, and then expand from there. Remember, the ratio of computers to young children is important—at most one to seven, preferably one to five. If you cannot meet this ratio with the resources you have available, it is far better to use a set of computers in a classroom for a month, quarter, or semester, and then rotate them to another classroom. Equal access for children who are in the classroom is essential. Furthermore, even the most talented teacher will have difficulty integrating computers into her classroom with only one computer.

Seek out mentors in your community who can provide guidance to the study group. These mentors might be teachers currently using computers, an instructor or a professor at a college, or leaders in business. While business members may not have expertise using computers with children, they may have some innovative, terrific ideas for fundraising.

Brainstorm possible fundraisers that might be successful in your particular program and community. Explore the possibility of obtaining used computers from doctors, dentists, businesses. (One word of caution: make sure the computer has the capacity to run software that is currently being marketed for young children.)

Consider compensating parents who participate in the study group or volunteer to supervise the children with a small fee reduction or stipend based upon the hours they contribute. This serves two purposes: it emphasizes the importance of integrating computers, and it confirms to your parents that their time and contributions are valuable.

Teacher training

The next step in the process is teacher training. Computers will have little impact on schools or children's learning without the commitment of teachers and parents.

Giving teachers computer experience

Now the fun begins! Give teachers software that is developmentally appropriate for their classrooms and let them explore, experience, and discover. Many teachers will be very hesitant at first, but I have found that nothing is as effective as hands-on experience. It dissolves the fear teachers have of technology, exposes them to a variety of unique learning opportunities, and most of all, they have fun! Within 15 minutes, my training sessions are full of interaction, excitement, and laughter!

It will probably take several sessions to review some of the software that is developmentally appropriate for their classrooms. As teachers explore software and build skills, give them opportunities to mentor other teachers who are having difficulty with a program they have already explored. It is essential for the environment to be accepting and for everyone to feel free to explore ideas, raise questions, and discuss concerns or problems.

After teachers have explored the software, outline the potential learning objectives of the programs and activities they could use to integrate particular software in their classroom. Even if they do not yet have computers, this will provide teachers with wonderful resources to discuss with parents whose children have computer exposure at home.

Workshops, mentors, follow-up

Workshops integrate the developmental theory and research regarding computer use with hands-on experiences. Understanding theory and research strengthens teachers' knowledge, their commitment, and their confidence in communicating with parents. Visiting other programs that have integrated computers with young children also can be an extremely valuable learning experience, providing a clear, first-hand picture of how computers are being used successfully.

Mentors are also important. Mentors provide teachers with affirmation, support, and new possibilities for using computers in their classrooms. They can be faculty from a community college or university, or they may be teachers currently using computers in their classrooms.

Ultimately, principals or directors are essential to the success of teacher training and computer integration. Administrators must have realistic expectations and goals.

It is unrealistic, for example, to expect that teachers, after initial training, no matter how extensive, will integrate technology into their total curriculum and use it for assessment. Rather, each teacher and the administrator should meet and establish realistic goals for the children and classroom. The goals should be revisited every four to six months, and the need for additional hardware, software, or training reassessed.

As the teachers implement technology in the classroom, their vision of the role of technology in the teaching and learning process will undoubtedly change. Administrators need to continually support teachers in their quest to discover how technology can best enhance their children's learning.

Summary

Using computers with young children is a journey. It begins with being receptive to learning about a unique new resource that provides children significant opportunities for growth and learning. The path then leads to obtaining computers, providing teachers with hands-on computer experiences, sharing knowledge of research and teaching strategies, and hopefully finding mentors to aid in the process. From that point on, the journey travels in different directions as teachers create unique ways to use computers with young children. Ideally, this last part of the journey never ends as teachers continue to search for and implement new ideas and products that can enhance young children's learning.

References

Adams, P. 1996. Hypermedia in the classroom using earth and science CD-ROMs. *Journal of Computers in Mathematics and Science Teaching* 15 (1/2): 19–34.

Cardelle-Elawar, M., & K. Wetzel. 1995. Students and computers as partners in developing students' problem-solving skills. *Journal of Research on Computing in Education* 27 (4): 378–401.

Claris works. 1997. Claris Works for kids. [Computer software]. Santa Clara, CA: Author.

Clements, D. 1994. The uniqueness of the computer as a learning tool: Insights from research. In *Young children: Active learners in a technological age,* eds. J. Wright & D. Shade. Washington, DC: NAEYC.

Denning, R., & P. Smith. 1997. Cooperative learning and technology. *Journal of Computers in Mathematics and Science Teaching* 16 (2/3): 177–200.

Elkind, D. 1998. Computers for infants and young children. *Child Care Information Exchange* 123: 44–46.

Epstein, A. 1993. *Training for quality.* Ypsilanti, MI: High/Scope Press.

Gatewood, T., & S. Conrad. 1997. Is your school's technology up to date? A practical guide for assessing technology in elementary schools. *Childhood Education* 73 (4): 249–51.

Haugland, S. 1992. Effects of computer software on preschool children's developmental gains. *Journal of Computing in Childhood Education* 2 (2): 3–15.

Haugland, S. 1997. Computers in early childhood classrooms. *Early Childhood News* 9 (4): 6–18.

Haugland, S., & J. Wright. 1997. *Young children and technology: A world of discovery.* New York: Allyn & Bacon.

Healy, J. M. 1998. *Failure to connect: How computers affect our children's minds—For better and worse.* New York: Simon & Schuster.

Hohman, C. 1988. Evaluating and selecting software for children. *Child Care Information Exchange* 123: 60–62.

Kids' Desk: Internet safe. 1998. [Computer software]. Redmond, WA: Edmark.

Matthews, K. 1997. A comparison of the influence of interactive CD-ROM storybooks and traditional print storybooks on reading comprehension. *Journal of Computing in Education* 29 (3): 263–73.

Milken Exchange on Education Technology & P. D. Hart. 1999. "Public opinion poll, 1998." Available online at: www.milkenexchange.org/publications

Nastasi, B. K., & D. H. Clements. 1994. Effectance motivation, perceived scholastic competence, and higher-order thinking in two cooperative computer environments. *Journal of Educational Computing Research* 10: 241–67.

National Association for the Education of Young Children. 1996. NAEYC position statement: Technology and young children—Ages three through eight. *Young Children* 51 (6) 11–16.

Oppenheimer, T. 1997. The computers delusion. *Atlantic Monthly* 280: 45–62.

Papert, S. 1998, September 1. Technology in schools: To support the system or render it obsolete? Milken Exchange on Education Technology. [Online serial]. Available at: www.milkenexchange.org/feature/papert.html

Scholastic. 1997. Magic School Bus explores the rainforest. [Computer software]. Redmond, WA: Microsoft.

U.S. Congress, Office of Technology Assessment. 1995. *Teachers and technology: Making the connection.* OTA-EHR-616. Washington, DC: Government Printing Office.

Unit 6

Unit Selections

36. **Learning to Go with the Grain of the Brain,** John Abbott and Terence Ryan
37. **Almost a Million Children in School before Kindergergarten: Who Is Responsible for Early Childhood Services?** Richard M. Clifford, Diane M. Early, and Tynette W. Hills
38. **Why Students Lose When "Tougher Standards" Win: A Conversation with Alfie Kohn,** John O'Neil and Carol Tell
39. **Achieving Excellence in Education,** Barbara Bowman
40. **Early Learning, Later Success: The Abecedarian Study,** *Frank Porter Graham Child Study Center*

Key Points to Consider

- How does the method that children use to learn differ from traditional classroom practice?
- What types of preschool services do schools in your community offer?
- Should common standards for all students be adopted across the nation?
- Name five characteristics of excellent early childhood programs.
- How early should intervention begin for children of poverty in order to make a significant difference in their school success later?

Links

www.dushkin.com/online/

31. **Awesome Library for Teachers**
    http://www.neat-schoolhouse.org/teacher.html
32. **EdWeb/Andy Carvin**
    http://edweb.cnidr.org
33. **Future of Children**
    http://www.futureofchildren.org
34. **National Institute on the Education of At-Risk Students**
    http://www.ed.gov/offices/OERI/At-Risk/
35. **Prospects: The Congressionally Mandated Study of Educational Growth and Opportunity**
    http://www.ed.gov/pubs/Prospects/index.html

These sites are annotated on pages 4 and 5.

Trends

An intriguing look at how young children learn is the lead article of this unit on trends. Scientists are changing their assumptions about human learning as they come to understand that the brain is an adaptable organism. The problem is that our theories of educational practice are not changing fast enough to keep up with new information on the way the brain processes information. This is the premise of "Learning to Go with the Grain of the Brain." Passive learning is no longer sufficient. The focus of pedagogy must be on helping children learn-by-doing in order for them to become masters of a wide range of skills.

It's appropriate that the next article looks at the increasing involvement of schools in preschool programs. More and more, the onus will be on schools to teach very young children effectively. Currently, the types of programs offered by school districts are extremely broad and they vary in quality and depth. "Almost a Million Children in School before Kindergarten: Who Is Responsible for Early Childhood Services?" is a timely look at both positive and negative implications. The authors propose that a national commission be created to bring continuity to the patchwork of services that exists in school districts across the nation.

Consistent standards is the topic of "Why Students Lose When 'Tougher Standards' Win: A Conversation with Alfie Kohn." This is a frank discussion of the problems of raising the bar for higher standards without attending to pedagogy. For young children, the result may not be a deeper understanding of concepts, but passive testing, more homework, and rote learning. It's a danger that Kohn believes is inherent in the national push to toughen standards.

To Barbara Bowman, high standards in early childhood education are intrinsically linked to developmentally appropriate practice. In "Achieving Excellence in Education," she thoughtfully defines 10 characteristics of excellent programs. The fundamental themes underlying her principles are balance, individualizing, and diversity. To achieve excellence, all aspects of a program from planning to curriculum to guidance to assessment would reflect those developmental themes.

The Abecedarian study is major proof of the effects of excellence in education. "Early Learning, Later Success: The Abecedarian Study" is a summary of preliminary outcomes of an early childhood educational intervention for poor children. Long-term results of this program are startling. Not only was the children's cognitive development greatly enhanced, enabling them to succeed in school, but they also successfully adapted in adulthood. The most significant policy implication of the study is that high-quality early childhood education improves academic achievement and social adjustment even into early adulthood. The Abecedarian model is a developmentally appropriate, individualized program with particular emphasis on language. It is a prime example of excellence in education.

What is becoming increasingly clear as we move into the new millennium is the importance of links between children's brain functioning and effective learning techniques. We cannot afford to waste the valuable early years of children by using ineffective and inappropriate practices. Our task is to continually apply new information about how children learn and grow to our teaching and caregiving.

Learning to Go with the Grain of the Brain

By John Abbott and Terence Ryan

IF YOUNG PEOPLE ARE TO BE EQUIPPED EFFECTIVELY TO MEET THE CHALLENGES OF THE 21ST CENTURY, IT IS SURELY PRUDENT TO SEEK OUT THE VERY BEST UNDERSTANDINGS FROM CURRENT SCIENTIFIC RESEARCH INTO THE NATURE OF HOW HUMANS LEARN BEFORE CONSIDERING FURTHER REFORM OF THE EDUCATION SYSTEM.

An analogy; humans have been eating and using their brains since the beginning of time. We think we know how to do this—it is all a matter of common sense. Yet, with the breakthroughs in the understanding of diet in the last 30 years, we are eating better and now live longer. That analogy is useful when we look at the brain and the opportunities that now present themselves to expand its capabilities. We are now in a position to understand the brain's adaptive functions—learning—far better.

Researchers in the 1990s have uncovered massive evidence in the cognitive sciences, and in neurobiology, evolutionary biology, evolutionary psychology, and even archaeology and anthropology, which shows us in great detail how it is that humans actually learn. We now can see why learning is much more than just the flip-side of good teaching and schooling. Much of this evidence confirms what many people have always intuitively thought; learning involves far more than schooling. People are quick to recognize that many successful public figures were either school failures or removed themselves from formal schooling at an early date. Conversely many successful people in school seemed to have disappeared without a trace. Why? Not surprisingly, long-term studies show that the greatest predictors of success at university are:

1. the quantity and quality of the discussion in the child's home before entering school;
2. the amount of independent reading, regardless of subject matter, which the child does;
3. the clarity of value systems as understood and practised;
4. strong positive peer group pressure; and
5. the primary school. Further down the list is the secondary school. Formal schooling is only part of what fires up the inquisitiveness in a child's mind.

Children's learning is the most natural and innate of human skills; humans are born to learn—we are better at that than any other species. Brain imaging technologies enable researchers to literally watch learning occur as specific patterns of brain activity within the brain light up on a computer screen. The unprecedented clarity this technology reveals about brain function is causing scientists to revise many of their earlier assumptions about how individual learning takes place. These findings have undermined the behaviourist metaphor of the brain as a blank slate waiting for information. The brain is now seen as a far more flexible, self-adjusting, biological metaphor—the brain as a living, unique, ever-changing organism that grows and reshapes itself in response to challenge, with elements that wither through lack of use. The evidence now emerging about learning and brain development has spawned a movement towards edu-

John Abbott is President of The 21st Century Learning Initiative. He has been both teacher and principal and introduced Britain's first fully-computerized classroom. Director of the Education 2000 Trust since 1985, he has been involved in the development of techniques and environments that enable young people to have confidence in their ability to become life-long learners. In 1997 he was invited by Mikhail Gorbachev to join the State of the World Forum.

Terence Ryan is Senior Researcher at The 21st Century Learning Initiative.

First published in *Education Canada,* Vol. 39, No. 1, Spring 1999, pp. 8-11. Permission to reprint granted by the authors and the Canadian Education Association.

cational practice which confirms that thinking skills (meta-cognition), as well as significant aspects of intelligence, are learnable.

The prestigious Santa Fe Institute noted in a 1995 collection of essays, *The Mind, the Brain and Complex Adaptive Systems,* the mismatch between emerging learning theory and dominant educational practice, "The method people naturally employ to acquire knowledge is largely unsupported by traditional classroom practice. The human mind is better equipped to gather information about the world by operating within it than by reading about it, hearing lectures on it, or studying abstract models of it."

These new understandings about human learning and the brain question the long-term effectiveness of plans among many governments to place even more reliance on the role of the school and the classroom in young people's learning.

Most school reform movements have been within the existing paradigm of pupils/teachers/schools—what we need now is out-of-the-box thinking which starts by focusing on the brain's ability to learn and how we become more effective humans. Only then can we think about how to develop and nurture appropriate learning environments.

We are, who we are, in large part because of our species' evolutionary experience over millions of years. Those experiences are firmly encapsulated in all of our brains, with each of us carrying all those predispositions that previous generations found useful to their survival. The work of the Dartmouth cognitive neuroscientist, Michael Gazzaniga, shows that life is largely about discovering what is already built into our brains. He warns that, "All the ways that human societies try to change minds and to change how humans truly interact with the environment are doomed to fail. Indeed, societies fail when they preach at their populations. They tend to succeed when they allow each individual to discover what millions of years of evolution have already bestowed upon mind and body."

As children get older, their **learning** must be integrated into the broader life of the community with **real tasks** for young people to do, and real responsibilities for them to shoulder.

Evolution, we now understand, has provided humans with a powerful tool kit of predispositions that go a long way in explaining our ability to learn language, co-operate successfully in groups, think across problems, plan for the future, and how to empathize with others. Predispositions provide individuals with a whole range of skills that enable them to relate flexibly to their environment. Yet, because for most of human history man tended to live in relatively small groups, these skills have to be developed collaboratively as very few people ever possess all these attributes. The speed with which our predispositions evolve seems to be incredibly slow, and it is thought there have been no major changes in the last 30,000 years.

By melding neurological discoveries in an evolutionary framework, researchers can see how, within a single generation, the influences of millions of years of evolution mingle with the priorities of a particular culture. The *Harvard Business Review* stated graphically in late 1998, "You can take man out of the Stone Age, but you can't take the Stone Age out of man." We are enormously empowered by an array of evolved predispositions which enable us to adapt to vastly different sorts of circumstances, yet these evolved predispositions inhibit us as well.

We have to be cautious to devise learning environments that take such predispositions beyond "what comes naturally,"—in doing this we must go with the grain of the brain.

That "grain" we can now begin to understand far better. The relationship between nature and nurture is well summarized by the English professor of psychobiology Henry Plotkin in his 1996 book *Evolution in Mind.* Plotkin notes, "Nature has itself evolved. Nurture can only be fully understood in light of historical causes. Nature has nurture." This goes a long way towards explaining just why humans learn the way they do.

Harvard's Howard Gardner uses his theory of multiple intelligences to show that, deep within our minds, we have multiple survival strategies that include an ability to look at any situation from a number of different perspectives. Link this with the emerging understanding of how the neural structures of the brain grow, and we begin to get an understanding of how these different forms of intelligence enable each of us "to make sense of our environments in very different ways." These "different ways" are critical to our species survival, and help provide insight into the origins of creativity. The balance between emotion and logic, the role of intuition, and the relationship between intrinsic and extrinsic motivation are all part of the "complex adaptive system" that best describes the brain's ability to deal with the messiness of ordinary everyday life situations.

Now, consider what we know about the brain and effective learning in light of the many systems developed over the past 150 years to organize individuals within an industrial economy. Prosperity meant organizing people into factories where their broadly-based skills were not needed and, very quickly in support of this, school systems were built which emphasized functional transactional skills that only utilized a small proportion of each individual brain. Such underused brains had to find their satisfaction elsewhere, and factory owners were quick to replace intrinsic motivation with extrinsic reward. Our present "crisis in schools" relates partly to the collapse of the old factory system and the recognition that successful workers now have to have more than just basic skills and an amenable attitude, which is largely what was required of their parents and grandparents.

Things are now very different. Author Daniel Yergin, winner of the Pulitzer Prize, recently observed, "Companies are being forced to think differently. . . . That means fostering a culture that encourages alertness, responsiveness, and flexibility, and the speeding up of the cycle time of processes and decisions. In the aftermath of re-engineering and restructuring, competitive forces now demand a rediscovery of employees and of the knowledge they command. . . . The high-rise pyramids of hierarchical corporate structures are being transformed into the low-rise of the flatter organization—less bureaucracy, more teamwork, and a greater dispersion of responsibility, information and decision making." In short, we need people who are competent problem-solvers, creative, flexible and personally responsible for their welfare and the welfare of those in their family and neighborhood.

Research from the evolutionary sciences show that these collaborative higher order skills and attitudes are indeed largely innate. Thus, with continuous and progressive stimulation at an early age (as would have been the case in pre-industrial times) they quickly develop. Despite six, eight or ten generations of such limited demands being placed on our sense-making skills, our genetic inheritance has not yet been modified a jot. Children are still born with latent predispositions, as it were, equipping them to take on the world. During much of this century, formal schooling has struggled to provide appropriate simulation of real-life situations. It has met inevitably with only limited success. For those who have been able to succeed in abstract terms, there are as many for whom schooling has been a disaster because they are more practically orientated. Industrial society had no place for children in the world of adult affairs—children were seen to be in the way. So we are stuck with a system which has progressively turned childhood into an extended virtual holiday; in reality we have trivialized adolescence by denying adolescents the opportunity of learning from their own experiences, and making them good processors of information provided by other people.

However, it is only very recently that researchers have come to understand this. Learning theory in the late 19th and early 20th centuries was generally behaviourist—people needed rewards to do tasks; our brains were blank sheets awaiting instruction; and intelligence was dimly thought of as being completely innate and inherited. As England and its territories developed an education system for the masses (initially as much to keep children off the streets as to give them useful skills), it rapidly came to reflect the industrial factory model. When universities were asked to advise on the curriculum, they did so by suggesting a highly reductionist model of learning. The study of learning was a strictly academic affair to such early educational experts. They measured what happened in classrooms when people performed abstract tasks, but they hardly ever deigned to study the calculating ability of an apprentice working on the job such as Benjamin Franklin, or a street trader on the Whitechapel Road in the East End of London.

This late 19th century compromise between the scientific understandings of the day, the needs of industry and the desire to give all children basic skills, increased productivity and raised standards of living significantly. But this came at a cost. With so much of their latent predispositions untapped by the daily routine of instruction, many children became deeply frustrated. Instead of the daily challenge of making sense of their environment, they now waited to be told what to do and how to do it.

Societies now stand at a very exciting time in human history—at an evolutionary crossroads. Will we be able to capitalize on these understandings and reverse what is now seen as an upside down and inside out system of education?

Everything that we understand about our intellectual development suggests that below the age of seven or eight, particularly below the age of three, we are heavily dependent on external encouragement and stimulation to develop the brain in ways survival skills (the ability to collaborate and see across issues) can be learned. In today's society, the functional skills of reading, writing, and numeracy are survival skills. If they are not learned at an early stage, learning them later on is far more difficult. Every youngster needs to make great demands on adults in order to master these basic survival skills. Although adults may

> These new understandings about **human learning** and the brain question the long-term effectiveness of plans among many governments to place even more reliance on the role of the school and the classroom in **young people's** learning.

be ambivalent about their roles as parents and caregivers, good parenting is utterly essential to a child if his or her mental faculties and social skills are to develop.

When they move into puberty, the natural tendency of young people is to reverse their dependency on adults. They want to be in control; not because they want to be bloody minded, but because all the hormonal changes going on within are pressing them to show they can now use what they learnt earlier to become fully functional, independent people. If they are not equipped with basic survival skills, adolescents are ill-prepared to deal with the physiological changes of adolescence and end up mentally, emotionally and socially adrift.

Now, consider the current model of schooling. In the elementary schools of many countries, class size is largest when children are very young. When children's predispositions are at their most fertile, we place them in classes of 30 or more. However, in secondary school we decrease class size—which clashes with the increasing desire of adolescents at about 14 or 15, to be independent. Many, for the most natural reasons, get completely turned off by schooling at this stage because it simply does not seem real in comparison to the emotionally-charged environments they experience away from school with their peers.

To remedy this upside down and inside out model of learning, we've got to go back to the way the brain developed through continuous interaction with its environment before the introduction of the industrial model of schooling interrupted the natural flow of learning. Such a brain-friendly model of learning would be based on a set of arrangements that mirrors, as far as possible, the biological process involved in weaning. It requires the development of a pedagogy that emphasises the young child's mastery of a range of skills, and that child's embryonic but growing ability to take responsibility for directing their own work and realizing that they'll be doing this for a lifetime. As early as possible, the system must aim to get the child to be a worker. It is no longer enough for them to simply be recipients. As children get older, their learning must be integrated into the broader life of the community with real tasks for young people to do, and real responsibilities for them to shoulder.

Elementary schools should provide classes for five-year-olds of no more than ten or 12. Teachers should construct learning programs that combine—in the child's mind as well as theirs—an understanding of both content and process in ways which make children's thinking visible to themselves. This will significantly change the role of teachers, making it essential for them to model the very techniques of good learning that children need to acquire. Although good teachers will remain essential, successful learning requires more than just teacher, chalk and talk. As a policy, investment in the technologies of learning should increase with the child's age.

Let's briefly turn to the inside out part of the current model of learning. Young people spend no more than 20% of their waking hours between the ages of five and 18 in a classroom. However, within the community at large, an increasing number of people have many professional skills and attitudes to share with young people. For example, many individuals who have taken early retirement would be interested in sharing expertise and help young people's learning. These are the people adolescents need to be able to relate to—almost surrogate grandparents. The human resources of the community need to be recruited to work with young people.

If current education budgets were not increased but we began the formal education of young children in classes of ten or 12, we might think classes of 40 our more would be required in secondary school. But that need not be the case. If schools do their job properly and children get intensive support in the earliest years, it would actually be better for adolescents, probably before the age of 16, to have little more than half their classes formally taught. It would be more helpful to them if they learnt to work on their own, and accessed the rich learning resources that schools and community mentors would then be able to provide. Too much instruction makes adolescents too dependent on the teacher and the classroom.

We now have it within our power to construct models of learning, at no greater cost than at present, which go with the grain of the brain while at the same time reconnecting adults and children outside the formal setting of a school.

The 21st Century Learning Initiative is a transnational program aiming to synthesize the best of research and development into the nature of human learning, and examining the implications of this for education, work and the development of communities worldwide.

For more information and resources, please refer to the Initiative's web site at http://www.21learn.org

The 21st Century Learning Initiative 11739 Bowman Green Drive Reston, VA 20190-3501 Ph: (703) 787-4020 Fax: (703) 787-4024 info@21learn.org

Almost a Million Children in School before Kindergarten: Who Is Responsible for Early Childhood Services?

Richard M. Clifford, Diane M. Early, and Tynette W. Hills

Richard M. Clifford, Ph.D., is an investigator and fellow at the Frank Porter Graham Child Development Center and codirector of the National Center for Early Development and Learning, University of North Carolina at Chapel Hill. He is immediate past president of NAEYC and conducts research on quality assessment and policy in early childhood education.

Diane M. Early, Ph.D., is an investigator with the National Center for Early Development and Learning, Frank Porter Graham Child Development Center. Diane is involved in several studies addressing the public school's role in prekindergarten education, as well as studies of quality and teacher preparation in early childhood settings.

Tynette W Hills, Ed.D., is a project consultant to the National Center for Early Development and Learning, Frank Porter Graham Child Development Center. She served many years as director of early childhood education, New Jersey Department of Education, and presently consults on issues of program planning, assessment, and policy for child care centers, school districts, state agencies, and organizations.

This research was supported under the Educational Research and Development Center Program, PR/Award Number R307A60004, as administered by the Office of Educational Research and Improvement, US Department of Education.

Schools and school districts are becoming increasingly involved in providing services to children and families prior to entry into formal school at the customary kindergarten entry age. Data are scarce on the role of public schools in the education of prekindergarten-age children; even the most basic information about these services is lacking. The goal of this article is to provide the best information currently available on the types of programs offered and the children served by or through local and state education agencies.

What types of preschool services do schools offer?

A number of federal programs fund schools to provide preschool services. Perhaps best known of these programs are the extensive services provided to preschool-age children with disabilities and their families under the individuals with Disabilities Education Act (IDEA). These services are provided by the schools themselves or by other agencies under contractual arrangements with the school districts.

Less well known is the fact that school systems themselves constitute many Head Start grantees and delegate agencies. Some of these Head Start programs are located in school facilities and some work cooperatively with other

From *Young Children,* September 1999, pp. 48-51.

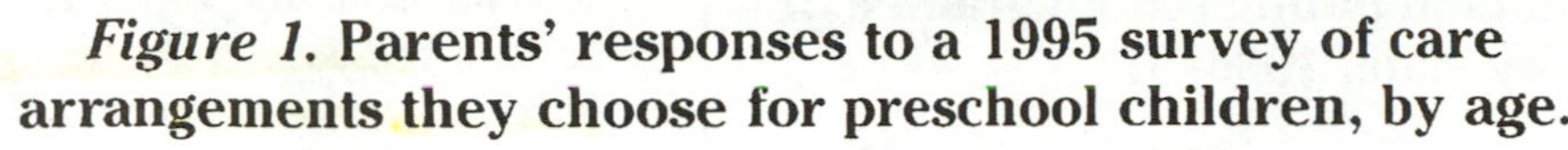

Figure 1. **Parents' responses to a 1995 survey of care arrangements they choose for preschool children, by age.**

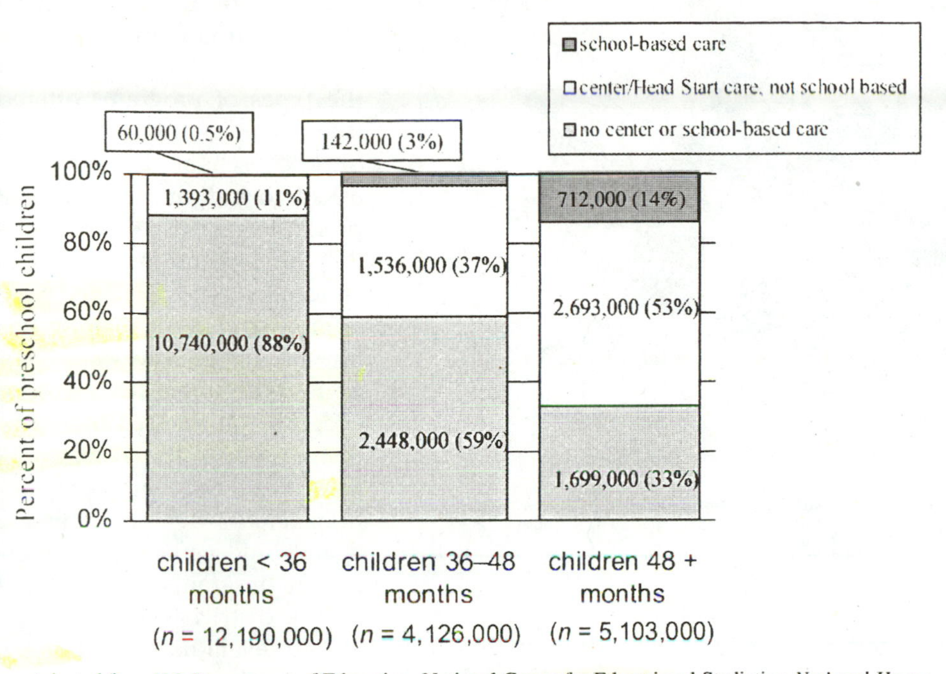

Adapted from U.S. Department of Education. National Center for Educational Stadistics. *National Household Education Survey of 1995* (Washington. DC: Author, 1996).

community agencies to operate programs in nonschool settings but under the auspices of the local school board.

Other preschool programs in schools are funded through Title I of the Elementary and Secondary Education Act. These programs are based in high-poverty schools and serve children who are at a high risk of later failing school. Because Title I program plans are made at the local school and school system level, little information is routinely gathered about the extent and nature of these efforts.

In addition to federally funded preschool programs, there are numerous state-funded initiatives. These are run either through the state's education agency or through another agency in conjunction with the state's department of education. Some efforts to document these programs have been made in the past few years. The Families and Work Institute conducted a recent review of prekindergarten programs funded by states (Mitchell, Ripple, & Chanana 1998) and found that 39 states provide funding for some prekindergarten programming. Only 7 of the 39 limit that funding to public schools. However, in all states that fund prekindergarten programs, school districts are eligible to offer the programs.

The National Center for Children in Poverty survey of states (Knitzer & Page 1998) found that 34 states report that they support statewide, comprehensive programs for preschoolers and in many cases have expanded their initiatives since 1996. The center found that schools and school districts are beginning to exert influence in developing a vision for an early childhood system.

States seem to be shifting increasingly toward a community-oriented approach, providing funds to communities and allowing those at the local level to make decisions about the use of the funds. The Children's Defense Fund reports that in recent years there has been a substantial expansion of state prekindergarten programs and of states' efforts to provide comprehensive programs and linkages with

Figure 2. **Public school districts' responses to a 1993–94 survey of preschool programs they offer, by program type and administering agency.**

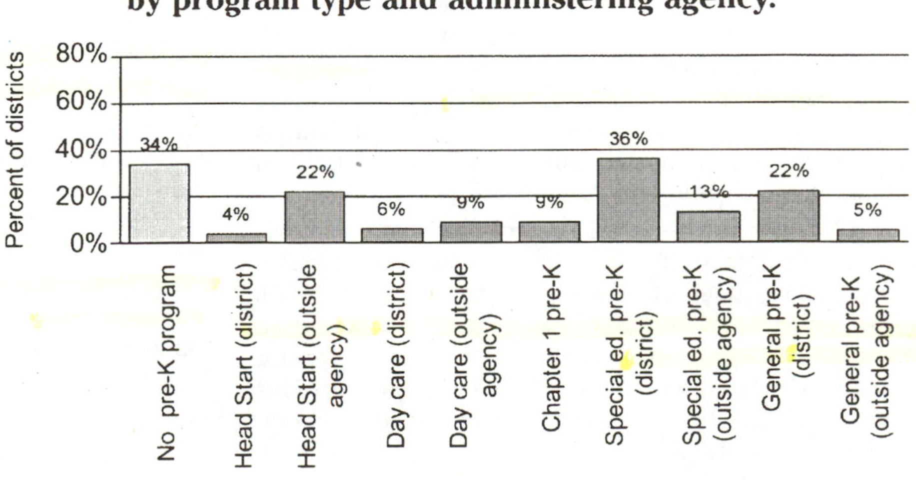

Adapted from the Teacher Demand and Shortage Questionnaire for public school districts (LEAs). U.S. Department of Education. National Center for Educational Statistics. *Schools and Staffing Survey: 1993–94* (Washington, DC: Author, 1994).

***Figure 3.* Percent of Head Start slots in public school grantee or delegate programs, by state, 1996–97.**

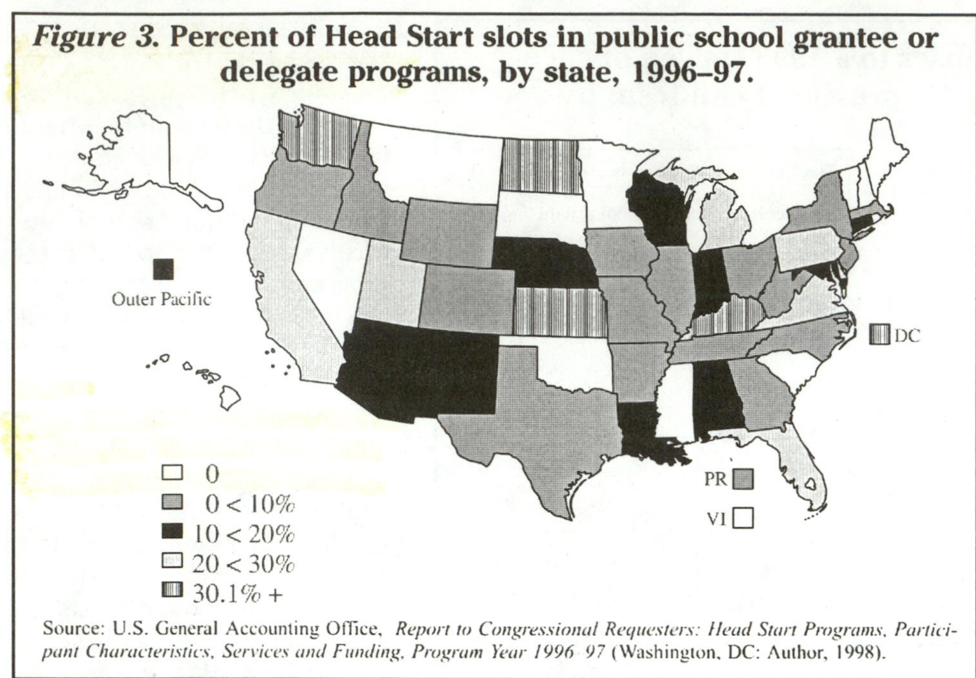

Source: U.S. General Accounting Office, *Report to Congressional Requesters: Head Start Programs, Participant Characteristics, Services and Funding, Program Year 1996–97* (Washington, DC: Author, 1998).

Head Start (Blank & Adams 1997). Researchers at the Yale Bush Center (Ripple et al. 1999) summarized state efforts to provide prekindergarten education and found that the extent and quality of services vary widely among states.

Overall it is clear that schools play a major role in the education of children before the typical age of entry into kindergarten, but information on the nature of school involvement and the extent of services available is lacking.

Who are the prekindergarten children served by schools?

As a first step in attempting to get a fuller picture of the role that schools and school districts now play in the education of three- and four-year-olds, we turned to the U.S. Department of Education's National Center for Educational Statistics (NCES) NCES collects information on all aspects of education in the United States, including a limited amount of information on prekindergarten children.

Two NCES surveys contain useful information on this topic. Using data from the *National Household Education Survey of 1995* (Department of Education NCES 1996), we estimate that some 900,000 prekindergarten children were served in programs at public elementary, junior high, and senior high schools in 1995 (see Figure 1). This number includes both children who attended a school-based program as their main form of child care and children who attended a part-day program at a school and spent the rest of their time with their parents or in another nonschoolbased setting. Most of these children were four or five years old.

Data from the other NCES survey, the *Schools and Staffing Survey: 1993–94* (SASS) (Department of Education NCES 1994), support this estimate and give us some idea about the types of programs offered (see Figure 2). During the fall of 1993, school districts were asked to indicate the types of prekindergarten programs they offered and the number of children served. Most districts offered some type of program for prekindergarten-age children, with special education programs administered by the district being the most common. Head Start programs administered by an outside agency and general prekindergarten programs administered by the district were also common. Information from this survey indicates that more than 866,000 children were being served in these programs nationwide in late 1993. Districts reported that 101,518 prekindergarten students were receiving services through Title I programs, indicating that roughly one in nine prekindergarten children in schools was supported through Title I funds.

Because SASS also reports on participation in the National School Lunch Program, it provides some information on the economic levels of the families of children served in these school-based prekindergarten programs. Children from families whose income is 185% of the poverty level or less are eligible for free or reduced-price lunches at school. Districts reported that 307,012 prekindergarten applicants were approved for the National School Lunch Program, indicating that more than one-third of prekindergarten children in public schools in 1993 were poor or near poor (Department of Education NCES 1994).

Additional information on school-based prekindergarten services was available from the Head Start Bureau and the U.S. General Accounting Office (GAO 1998). From data provided by these agencies, we learned that a substantial number of Head Start programs are operated by schools, with four states (Kansas, Kentucky, North Dakota, and Washington) and the District of Columbia having more than 30% of their Head Start slots in public school grantee or delegate programs (Figure 3).

By examining data collected in 1997 by the GAO, we estimated the numbers of children served in school-based programs and the funding provided to support services for these children. Assuming equal response rates for school- and nonschool-based programs, we estimate that approximately 23% of all Head Start programs are related to a public or private school, with the schools as Head Start grantees or as agencies delegated to provide Head Start services by grantee agencies. Responding public and private school-based programs reported serving nearly 100,000 children with funding at a level of just over $400 million.

Given that roughly 14% of the programs did not respond to the GAO survey, the true numbers of children served and the funding are probably somewhat higher. These estimates appear to be in line with Head Start's report to Congress for 1995–97, which indicates that 29% of its facilities were in schools and 19% of Head Start grantees and delegate agencies were public schools (Department of Health and Human Services 1998).

Each year the U.S. Department of Education is required to issue a report to Congress on implementation of the IDEA. For the 1995–96 school year, the department reported that nearly 300,000 three- and four-year-old children with disabilities received early intervention services (Department of Education 1997, A-15) It is not known how many of these children were actually served in schools. Moreover, because the intent of Congress is that children with disabilities be served in inclusive programs to the greatest extent possible, many such children are counted in the previous reports of children in other programs. However, the fact that the schools have accepted responsibility for providing services to such a large number of preschoolers with disabilities is significant.

What are the implications for the field of early childhood?

In summary, it is clear that school systems are a major source of services to children younger than the traditional kindergarten entry age. Schools constitute a major new force in the early childhood field, a force whose presence has both positive and negative implications for the field.

On the positive side, schools bring a strong tradition of service to all children. A hallmark of public education in the United States has been universal access. There is evidence that schools can bring the same level of standards they apply to other grades to the prekindergarten arena. Ripple and colleagues (1999) report that standards for state-funded prekindergarten programs in many states are quite high. For instance, in as many as 15 states, teachers in state-funded prekindergartens must have at least a teaching certificate or bachelor's degree. Most of these programs are based in the public schools. Bryant, Peisner-Feinberg, and Clifford (1993) found that all prekindergarten teachers in North Carolina classrooms had at least a bachelor's degree and that class size and adult-child ratios generally met NAEYC recommendations.

Schools represent a strong potential ally in securing revenue for early childhood programming. Current expenditures for elementary and secondary education in the United States are estimated at $244.1 billion for 1995 (Department of Education NCES 1997). A rather modest increase in this figure could result in a huge new investment in early childhood services. Furthermore, the education establishment has a great deal of leverage when it comes to seeking funding and setting standards for services.

On the negative side, school officials have been reluctant historically to incorporate into their domain services to children below kindergarten entry age—a position sometimes supported by public opinion regarding the appropriate role of the elementary and secondary education system. Schools have been slow to meet the needs of families for services beyond the traditional school day (usually about 6.5 hours per day) and school year (usually about 9 months). Today most families with children three to four years of age need full-day (at least 8 hours per day) and full-year services.

As schools develop expanded services, they face a number of critical issues: Will they be able to deliver the full range of services? Will they be able to adapt to the current market-based approach to delivery of services? Will schools dominate the market and force a shift in services in the private sector toward serving even younger children, as happened when schools expanded the availability of kindergarten services?

There are some hopeful signs. As reported by the Children's Defense Fund, the Families and Work Institute, and the National Center for Children in Poverty, many state prekindergarten initiatives are attempting to integrate services from all of the major sectors into a more unified system. Perhaps the most successful early example is the Georgia Preschool Program. In this program the state of Georgia provided services to more than 61,000 four-year-olds in the last school year. The program is open to a wide range of providers, including Head Start agencies, private for-profit and nonprofit child care centers and preschools, as well as public schools. The program has incorporated many private providers into the system. At the same time, the program has raised the standard of services and compensation for early childhood professionals in the state (see www.osr.state.ga.us).

In addition to Georgia, a number of other states also are making major strides toward developing mechanisms for local-level collaborative decisionmaking regarding the provision of services.

Conclusion

The expanded involvement of schools requires a comprehensive review of the relative roles of the various levels of government in financing, regulating, and delivering services. We propose the creation of a National Commission on Early Childhood Services to examine the issue of how the United States as a country will serve its youngest citizens. Until there is agreement on the basic issues of who has responsibility for governing early childhood services, who has responsibility for financing these services, and how to best take advantage of the rich resources for serving children in this country, many families will continue to be faced with a patchwork of services, and many children will spend their early years in settings of unknown quality.

References

Blank, H., & C. Adams. 1997. *State developments in child care and early education, 1997.* Washington, DC: Children's Defense Fund.

Bryant, D.M., E.S. Peisner-Feinberg, & R.M. Clifford. 1993. *Evaluation of public preschool programs in North Carolina. Final report.* Chapel Hill: Carolina Policy Studies Program, Frank Porter Graham Child Development Center, University of North Carolina.

Knitzer, J., & S. Page. 1998. *Map and track: State initiatives for young children and families.* New York: National Center for Children in Poverty, Columbia University.

Mitchell, A., C. Ripple, & N. Chanana. 1998. *Prekindergarten programs funded by the states: Essential elements for policy makers.* New York: Families and Work Institute.

Ripple, C.H., WS. Gilliam, N. Chanana, & E. Zigler. 1999. Will fifty cooks spoil the broth? The debate over intrusting Head Start to the states. *American Psychologist* 54: 327–43.

U.S. Department of Education. 1997. *Nineteenth annual report to Congress on the implementation of the Individuals with Disabilities Education Act.* Washington, DC: Author.

U.S. Department of Education. National Center for Educational Statistics. 1994. *Schools and Staffing Survey: 1993–94.* Washington, DC: Author. CD-Rom.

U.S. Department of Education. National Center for Educational Statistics. 1996. *National Household Education Survey of 1995—Adult education/early childhood program participation.* Washington, DC: Author. CD-Rom.

U.S. Department of Education. National Center for Educational Statistics. 1997. *Projections of education statistics to 2007* (NCES 97-382). Washington, DC: Author.

U.S. Department of Health and Human Services. 1998. *Fiscal year 1997 biennial report to Congress on the status of children in Head Start programs.* Washington, DC: Author.

U.S. General Accounting Office. 1998. *Head Start programs. Participant characteristics, services and funding* (GAO/HESHS-9865). Washington, DC: Author.

Why Students Lose When "Tougher Standards" Win

A Conversation with Alfie Kohn

If students are to help design their own learning experiences and if teachers are to be free to develop a curriculum on the basis of their students' needs, schools must buck the "Tougher Standards" movement, author Alfie Kohn says.

John O'Neil and Carol Tell

This issue of* Educational Leadership *focuses on how teachers can shape instruction to meet the unique needs of learners. At present, though, there is an even stronger trend toward creating common standards for all students. Are these common standards incompatible with the ideals of personalized learning?

The current approach taken by the proponents of Tougher Standards is incompatible with personalized learning and with the interests of kids at the margins, and, ultimately, I think it is incompatible with excellence.

The content standards begin, "All students will be able to. . . " so that even before you look at the expectations, you notice that the standards are uniform. The message here seems to be that individual differences either don't exist or are illegitimate and should be ignored. This wording willfully disregards the fact that not all kids learn at the same pace or should be expected to do so.

Most standards are highly specific. Often they consist of hundreds of detailed items, facts, and subskills that students have to know. Harold Howe II, the former U.S. Commissioner of Education, was once asked what national standards should be like if they had to be issued. He summarized half a century's worth of wisdom in four words: "As vague as possible." The more narrow and rigid the requirements are, the less responsive educators can be to what distinguishes one circumstance from another, or your child from mine.

Does that mean that you would only support content standards if they weren't precise about common outcomes for all students?

We need to make several distinctions here. "Horizontal" standards offer guidelines for shifting how teach-

From *Educational Leadership,* Vol. 57, No. 1, September 1999, pp. 18-22. Reprinted with permission of the Association for Supervision and Curriculum Development.

ing and learning happen in classrooms. All students deserve the chance to do meaningful problem solving in math class rather than to be turned into human calculators, and to learn to read and write by doing real reading and writing rather than to be forced to plod through skills devoid of context. Standards that move instruction in those directions are terrific—as long as they're not just shoved down teachers' throats, of course.

What I object to are "vertical" standards: the mindless, macho talk about "raising the bar" in which the pedagogy remains the same but we do it longer or harder or give more tests.

Another distinction has to do with the student's age. Some specificity is appropriate if we're talking about what we can expect from students by the time they graduate from high school. But it's entirely different to talk about what all kids must know before leaving the 2nd grade. That is outrageous from a developmental perspective. Even at the high school level, though, broad guidelines of intellectual competence are more helpful than the list of facts and skills that are showing up on high-stakes exams: You recite the right details about the Industrial Revolution, or distinguish correctly between xylem and phloem, or else you can't graduate.

The primary effect of requirements like these won't be to make schools excellent but to force a whole lot of kids to drop out. We'll end up denying diplomas to those who can't or won't commit to temporary memory a bunch of facts that very few adults know by heart. And the Tougher Standards contingent is applying the same thinking to elementary schools by forcing more and more kids to repeat a grade if they don't pass a test—never mind whether the test is reasonable, never mind *why* they're having trouble, and never mind research that shows retention to be a disaster for the students.

A lot of horrible practices are justified in the name of "rigor" or "challenge." People talk about "rigorous" but often what they really mean is "onerous," with schools turned into fact factories. This doesn't help kids become critical, creative thinkers or lifelong learners. In fact, the more we cave in to demands for Tougher Standards, the less schools are able to reach those more ambitious goals.

But plenty of good teachers are innovative, yet their students score well on whatever test you can point to.

The extent to which that happens depends on the nature of the test. The more we define "raising standards" as raising scores on norm-referenced, skills-based, multiple-choice tests, the more we try to fill passive vessels full of facts instead of helping kids engage with ideas. If we use more meaningful, open-ended performance-based exams, then we can maintain some decent teaching in the classroom. However, we may still be increasing the test designers' authority to decide what gets taught. The worst possible combination is a basic-skills, fill-in-the-blank test *and* a high-stakes environment where people are pressured into raising the scores.

"Learning doesn't take place at a district or a state level; it takes place in a classroom."

Only someone who knows nothing about teaching and learning could support such practices. The best teachers understand the need to involve students in designing their own projects, allowing them to develop a style of, and a proficiency at, intellectual exploration. Teachers need the flexibility to take unexpected detours. In one math class I visited, for example, students ended up taking an entire period to debate the definition of a pyramid. Fortunately, that teacher could be flexible enough to allow this sort of student-driven, in-depth learning because those kids didn't have to take a standardized test.

That's why I say that the Tougher Standards and accountability movement is squeezing the life out of schools. I'm finding example after example of teachers who, at best, have to carve out portions of their week to prep kids for horrible tests before they can get back to the real learning. And sometimes the real learning never happens. Kids are being deprived of recess, are having to stay longer at school during the day, are having more and more homework piled on them. The result isn't a deeper understanding of ideas or a commitment to continue pursuing learning. Quite the opposite.

What is an appropriate role for testing in schools and in classrooms?

It's legitimate to collect information—carefully and only occasionally—about a student's level of understanding and improvement, using meaningful measures. The purpose is to enhance the quality of students' learning—without undermining their *interest* in learning.

For starters, any test must be open-ended so that students can generate options and explain their answers, as opposed to filling in ovals. And the content of the examination has to reflect what we value, what we honor in our society—the kinds of things that we think people really need to know. This is obviously not the case right now because very few of us as adults could pass a lot of these high school proficiency tests.

Learning doesn't take place at a district or state level; it takes place in a classroom. Therefore, the assessment should be focused on students' learning over time by the person in the best position to judge the quality of that learning. There's an inherent problem with any one-shot test that's designed and then scored by somebody far away.

So you see quite a bit of usefulness for assessment constructed by teachers to meet their needs, but very little usefulness for district-mandated tests, state tests, nationally normed tests, and so on?

Right, although I would add that a teacher-designed—and perhaps externally validated—assessment doesn't meet only the teacher's needs. If it's done right, it also meets the needs of parents and citizens to make sure that the teachers and schools are doing a decent job. Parents want to be reassured that the teacher's judgment is reasonable and that, in the face of largely exaggerated press reports about the failure of our schools, our kids are being well educated.

Of course, the best way to find out what's going on in the school is to visit and look around: watch whether kids are grappling with complex ideas, as opposed to being hunched over worksheets. If kids come home babbling excitedly about something they've been doing in class and just figured out, that's a powerful signal that something is going right.

What do you see when you visit classrooms where teachers are personalizing the curriculum?

The kind of teaching that responds to different interests, talents, and proclivities of different children rarely takes place in a classroom where the teacher is in the front of the room disgorging information and covering a preset curriculum. In many traditional classrooms, the only difference between one kid and another is how fast each moves up a single, adult-constructed ladder. Real responsiveness to individual differences entails maximizing kids' participation in deciding—not just alone, but with one another—what they're going to explore and how and when and with whom and why. And then the students will play a big role in figuring out how to assess the success of what they've been up to.

Personalization itself looks different in different settings and for different ages, but roughly speaking, the strategies described as constructivist, holistic, collaborative, and learner-centered provide the possibility of learning that is responsive to what distinguishes one kid from another. It doesn't guarantee it, however. One can imagine a version of cooperative learning, or a hands-on lesson, that was "one-size-fits-all." Traditionalists have indignantly insisted that all kids don't necessarily learn best with a given progressive method. My response is, first, that a lot more kids learn better by doing something than by listening, by having some choice rather than none. Second, many of these critics seem to be born-again supporters of specialized instruction. They've long supported classrooms that are the opposite of responsive to individual differences.

> **"The more narrow and rigid the requirements are, the less responsive educators can be to what distinguishes one circumstance from another, or your child from mine."**

You've been quite critical of traditional classrooms. Many commentators, though, feel that schools are too interested in nontraditional techniques, that educators tend to pick up every fad.

It's interesting that only progressive practices are labeled *fads* even though that epithet would seem to be at least as appropriate for the latest version of, say, explicit phonics-based instruction, where kids can read only stories that match the skills lesson.

For my new book, I combed the literature to see what's really going on in schools, to see whether there's any truth to the conservative claim that a monolithic "educationist" establishment is driving good old traditional practice underground and turning our schools into progressive experiments. My conclusion, based on research and my own visits to schools all over the country, is that this claim is so audacious as to be downright comical. Across the grade levels and the disciplines, American schools are stultifyingly traditional, far more similar to what they were like 30 years ago than they are different.

Most students still spend the day with kids their own age. Most schools still use awards assemblies and letter or number grades. Most classes, especially in high school, continue to use textbooks. Most kids still have little to say about what they're being taught. Most math teaching is still about skills more than about understanding. Whole Language remains the exception rather than the rule; a recent survey found that most primary-grade teachers, despite paying lip service to a balanced approach, continue to teach discrete phonics skills to all kids, even to the majority who could learn in other ways. In short, progressive practice, despite its powerful research backing, continues to be present in only a tiny minority of classrooms around the country.

This assessment, by the way, comports with that of most serious scholars, including John Goodlad and Larry Cuban. But notice its significance. If traditionalists are right that our schools are in trouble, it's hard to argue that progressive practices are responsible if those practices are actually quite rare. In fact, the argument is turned on its head. If students aren't achieving the way we'd like, if they lack a disposition to learn, it may be precisely *because* schools continue to be so traditional. Indeed, that's exactly what the latest international mathematics comparisons suggest: Our kids are at a comparative disadvantage because the "back to basics" folks have won.

Have you rethought your theory of motivation, discussed in **Punished by Rewards,** *now that you're a parent?*

The research demonstrates that people who do something to get a reward tend to do it less well and typically lose interest in the task itself. Everything I've seen in my own house is consistent with those data. I will admit that as a dad, I have a fresh appreciation of how tempting it is to use carrots, stickers, and other implements of control on children who just won't go to bed when you want them to. But my view hasn't changed at all about the wisdom of trying to resist that temptation. It takes a lot less time and skill and courage to promise a child a sticker if she brushes her teeth or to give her a "time out" if she acts up or to tell her, "Because I said so." But my wife and I are constantly finding reasons to reaffirm that, ultimately, it makes more sense to work *with* our daughter than to do things *to* her.

That also includes resisting the temptation to constantly fling judgments at her, including positive judgments. If anything, now that I'm a parent it's even harder for me to listen to what has become a verbal tic for a lot of adults: "Good job!" Every time parents and teachers praise kids, they're telling them how to feel about what they did, stealing from them the opportunity to reflect on what they've done themselves and take genuine pride in it. My experience as a parent confirms that what kids really need from us is unconditional support, acknowledgment, encouragement, and, occasionally, informational feedback. What they do *not* need is an adult following them around saying, in effect, "You've met *my* standards, and I will dole out approval based on your continuing to do so."

> **"I'm talking here about letting people—even small people—learn to make decisions about their own lives."**

In **Beyond Discipline,** *you write that the more we manage students, the more difficult it is for them to become sophisticated thinkers. Although teachers often fear losing control in a classroom, the opposite of control is not necessarily chaos.*

Exactly: This false dichotomy is routinely used to justify unnecessary control over students. After I wrote *Punished by Rewards,* it became increasingly clear to me that underlying the particulars of grades or praise or timeouts is the fundamental issue of how willing we are as adults to share some of our authority with students. It's hard to ask kids how we might solve a problem together because then we no longer have unilateral control over them. And that is frightening. It carries with it a whiff of something utterly unfamiliar and terrifying to most Americans: democracy.

I'm talking here about letting people—even small people—learn to make decisions about their own lives. Kids who are told what to do all day aren't developing socially or ethically the way they could be, just as kids are not developing intellectually in a classroom driven backward by demands for Tougher Standards.

Over the years, you've articulated a very coherent view of what schools could be. Through the course of your own education, how did you come to the views about things like control in the classroom, appropriate curriculum, and so on?

Well, there's no single cause. My education was an uninterrupted exercise in low-level control with relatively few opportunities to experience real quality learning until I got to college.

In elementary school, I was a good student, but I was also a rebel. Once, in 5th grade, when a teacher gave us some busywork to do, I thought I might as well call it what it was, so I neatly headed my paper with my name, the date, and the word "busywork." This did not go over well. In a way, I've been rebelling against that stuff ever since.

But that doesn't mean I had a clear sense of how learning happens or what teaching could be like—even when I became a teacher. I did stuff that makes me cringe in retrospect. What I've learned about teaching and learning has been from watching teachers more talented than I, from reading the work of thoughtful educators, and from reviewing and thinking about research. I test these ideas out in various ways, and people are often kind enough to challenge my thinking. Which is only fair, considering that's what I'm doing for them.

Alfie Kohn is the author of *The Schools Our Children Deserve: Moving Beyond Traditional Classrooms and "Tougher Standards"* (Boston: Houghton Mifflin, 1999). He is currently setting up a grassroots network of people opposed to the Tougher Standards movement (Web site: www.alfiekohn.org). **John O'Neil** (e-mail: joneil@ascd.org) is Contributing Editor and **Carol Tell** (e-mail: ctell@ascd.org) is Associate Editor of *Educational Leadership*.

Achieving Excellence in Education

By Barbara Bowman, Erikson Institute

What I would like to do is to point out some of the characteristics of excellent programs and give you some examples of how these principles can be used in practice.

Principle #1: Excellent programs use developmental principles to help them plan. As I am sure many of you know, the National Association for the Education of Young Children recommended that practices used in preschool/primary programs be developmentally appropriate. There has been considerable contention about what is meant by developmentally appropriate. Some people seem to think that developmentally appropriate means that you can't teach preschoolers letters or numbers, or kindergartners to write, or give children information about the world, or expect them to pay attention to the teacher. They think it means children should not do anything they don't want to do, and should play all day. Indeed, some people seem to think it is harmful to intentionally and explicitly give children information that will help them be school successful. I believe this is the wrong way to interpret developmentally appropriate. I think that developmentally appropriate simply means we organize programs that fit in with how children learn and develop.

We know that a developmental principle is that learning builds on itself. If we want to teach children to read we don't start when they are two with an alphabet chart. They do not yet know what words are and that symbols (letters) can stand for them. Instead, we may start with symbols—like drawing pictures and identifying logos and the McDonalds' arches. Then we might teach the letters in the child's own name and gradually extend to the names of his or her friends. At each step along the way we would want to make sure that children have the background they need to learn what we want to teach. Excellent programs also incorporate new knowledge about child development. It is unfortunate that developmental principles do not stay the same over time. New research is constantly feeding us new information about how children learn and grow. I suppose it natural for us to wish things could stay the same and so we often try to depend on older principles for practice and ignore what we are learning. But this is a mistake.

Each child needs a different type of help to learn in the same program.

For instance, we have only recently learned from neurobiologists just how important early childhood is to how the brain functions. The brain accomplishes most of its growth during the first 4 or 5 years of life and pretty much completes its growth by age 10. And, the kinds of environments young children have beginning at conception—play an enormous role in shaping how the brain develops. In other words, the quality of care and education children get during early childhood periods can either support healthy development or seriously compromise it.

Language development is a good example of new information that may affect our teaching practices. For example, in taking pictures of the brain while it is working, neurobiologists have shown us that young children learn languages with a different part of the brain and more easily than do older children and adults. This means we need to reassess our practice of focusing exclusively on first or home language with young children before introducing a second one. It is likely that if we want children to know more than one language well, we should introduce them in early childhood. As new information comes it is sometimes hard to decide which we should incorporate into our practice. And certainly we want to be careful that we don't fall for quick fixes and scatterbrained ideas with no substance. It seems to me that at teacher conferences such as this we have a chance to hear about new things and to think about how these affect our work.

From *Center for Early Education at Rutgers Vol. 1, Issue 2,* March 1999, pp. 1-7.

The quality of children's relationships with their preschool and kindergarten teachers predicts how well they will adapt and learn the following year.

Principle #2: Developmental principles are not the same as recipes for practice. Principles provide a framework for thinking about practice; they don't determine the practice itself. One principle of practice is that novelty attracts attention of young children. For instance, infants pay attention to novel sounds, visions, and touches. They will attend most closely to things they do not expect or which are perceptually exciting. However, stimuli continuing over time are of less and less interest. We use this principle when we play peek-a-boo, when we make noises with rattles, when we tickle tummies—all of which can command the baby's attention. But the principle does not tell us if, with a particular child on a particular day, we should play peek-a-boo, or shake the rattle, or tickle a tummy or do something else that is novel and perceptual. Practice responds to principles, but there may be a number of practices that reflect the same principle.

For instance, a literacy principle is that young children who have an opportunity to understand uses of written language through meaningful activity learn to read better and faster than those who do not; Most of our programs will respond to this principle by making good books, like *Make Way for Ducklings*, available for children to look at. But it is equally valid to make books out of old magazines, to generate stories and pictures on a computer, or to use photographs to make books. For instance, a good story book like *Make Way for Ducklings* may be inappropriate if children are not allowed to hold the book and study its pictures and print. In a school that is short of funds and cannot afford the wear and tear of children's handling on good books, homemade books made from magazines might be much more appropriate. What this means is that each practice must be looked at for whether it is meaningful and needed for particular children, not whether the practice itself is good or bad.

Principle #3: Excellent programs pay attention to children's maturation and the pace of development in planning programs. Some things we want children to learn depend on maturation. You can't run until you can walk, you can't read until you can talk, you can't remember until your brain is organized for memory.

What task children of different ages should learn depends to some extent on the demands of the environment in which the child lives. I lived for many years in a small town in southern Iran and used to go stay with the tribes. I was astonished to see 4-year-old boys herding sheep quite competently with only the guidance of a 10-year-old. The 4-year-olds were not allowed, however, to work with the camels because they were "too young." Similarly, 6-year-old girls often carried little babies while their mothers worked, but mothers checked frequently on the babies' well being and coached young girls about the proper care. These children had learned what was expected of them by watching their elders and through explicit instruction and were well able to master the tasks assigned to them. So, when we say age is a factor we are not saying that we know exactly what 4-year-old children all over the world can learn. We are saying that developmentally appropriate learning pays attention to how old children are in relationship to the tasks we want them to perform.

Principle #4: Excellent programs individualize children's care and education. Some of children's growth and development is guided by their biological predisposition. Temperament—shyness, low tolerance for frustration, sociability—for instance, have been found to be a relatively stable characteristic and do determine, to some extent, how children will interact with the environment. Thus, when children come to schools and centers, some hide behind their moms, some walk in and say to the first child they meet, "Will you be my friend?" and some pick up a block and crown anyone who doesn't do what they want. We need to understand that these differences in how children handle the same environment are not just attempts to frustrate the teachers. Each child needs a different type of help to learn in the same program.

Not only do children have different styles of development, they don't develop evenly over 12 months or over even 5 years. The new research on growth has shown that children may grow as much as a half an inch a day and have other days when they do not grow at all. Some children will learn to walk at 9 months, others at 15 months. Whether they start at 9 or 15 months has little to do with how well they will walk at age 3. Fast learners slow down and slow learners speed up and we cannot tell in advance what pattern individual children will have. What does this mean for those of us who work with young children? First, it means diversity is normal. We will not get all children to do the same things at the same time, or learn to do them in the same way, no matter how hard we try. What we can do is to make sure that opportunities to learn are always available so that chil-

> ***Many of the differences between children from diverse groups represent similar developmental competence.***

dren who are maturing at different rates, or who have different temperaments, or past experience, have the opportunity to learn in the environments we set up.

Principle #5: Excellent early childhood programs pay attention to cultural similarities and differences by connecting what children already know with what we want them to learn. This is a particularly important developmental principle for young children who do not come from the cultural mainstream. I mean children from economically depressed families. I mean children of color—African American, Native American, Hispanic, and Asian children. These groups often have different ideas about appropriate developmental goals and educational objectives than those traditional in early education. Unfortunately, professionals often dismiss the perspectives of culturally different peoples as uninformed. What appears on the surface to be a debate between those who know a lot about child development and those who do not, is, in reality, a debate between individuals who hold different values about the purposes of schooling, what counts as legitimate knowledge, and presumably, the nature of the good life and the just society. Many of the differences between children from diverse groups represent similar developmental competence. Thus, African American children who speak Black English are just as smart as those that speak standard English; Native American children who don't look adults in the eye are just as respectful as white children who do; Hispanic parents who are reluctant to come to school meetings love their children just as much as the parents who come. Asian parents who always want their children close by them, who want them to be dependent on the family, are just as concerned about them as mainstream American parents are who want their children to be independent. They just see the world differently.

Children who come from different groups will have learned different things and we cannot judge the behavior of children who come from one group by the behavior of children from another. For example, when we use criteria for performance derived from middle class white children and apply them to poor children, we find the poor children do not seem as competent as their peers do. Yet it may well be that they simply have not had the same opportunities to learn the same things. Attributing all differences in performance to developmental inadequacy reinforces the deficit hypothesis encouraging us to believe many children cannot learn because they have not learned what we expect. Does this mean that children from some culture groups should not be asked to learn the center or school's curriculum because it does not match their culture? Of course not. We should not assume that because a child has learned one culture that he or she is unable to learn another or that they have different rules of development. Poor children, minority group children learn by the same developmental rules as all other children. They need to construct their own knowledge to be active learners, to be interested and motivated to learn, to have teachers who they love and admire and who they love and respect. But they also need bridging between what they already know and what we want them to know. How should we bridge? There are no standard answers like we should always teach African American kids like this, or we should always teach Spanish speaking kids like that. In a multicultural society bridging requires knowledge, understanding, compromise, and the merging of beliefs, attitudes, and perspectives, so, as a community we create a new consensus and respect each other's differences.

Principle #6: Excellent programs pay attention to relationships. I'm sure you have all seen the pictures and read about the Romanian orphanage children who did not receive personalized human attention during their early months. Many of these children fail to develop normal intelligence, motor skills, and social interaction patterns. Parents, because their relationship with their children is an ongoing and consistent one, are likely to be the most influential relationships in children's lives. This is why good quality early childhood programs support parents so that they can do their jobs better. That's why we make the school or center welcoming to parents, provide opportunities for parents to learn about child development. We provide a sympathetic ear for parents and find other resources for them when they are needed. Teachers' and caregivers' relationships with children are also important. A number of studies have pointed out that teachers and caregivers also make a difference in how children develop. For instance, the quality of children's relationships with their preschool and kindergarten teachers predicts how well they will adapt and learn the following year.

We also have evidence that some children, whose parents are unable to provide the quality of relationships they need, are able to do so with their teachers and caregivers. What this research means is that people other than parents, are powerful influences on the development of young children. We've all seen examples of this principle—children who make it despite the fact that they grow up in neglectful or abusive homes, or without adequate support and guidance, or

Making sure children are ready for school means teachers must think through carefully what to teach and how to teach it.

with developmental disturbances and disabilities, or in families over stressed by divorce, unemployment, and death. And they usually make it because there are other people—relatives, neighbors, friends, but often their teachers and caregivers, give them the support, guidance, and high regard necessary for every child to grow and develop well.

What lessons should we learn from our understanding children's need for meaningful relationships? Teachers and caregivers need to build a trusting relationship with parents. For children to learn well in schools and centers their parents must trust us and convey that trust to their children. Parents who send their children to schools and centers with confidence in the people who will be teaching them, give their children a leg up on learning. Secondly, it means for those of us who plan programs and provide services to children and families, we must make sure that every child in our centers and schools finds committed and responsive adults, ready to be involved in a meaningful relationship.

Principle #7: Excellent programs provide a balanced curriculum. One of the raging arguments in education over the past 25 years has been between teaching young children basic skills—the nuts and bolts of academics—or to focus on intellectual skills, such as opportunities to think for oneself, to be creative, to solve problems. In reading, the conflict has been between teaching phonics, which emphasizes decoding and teaching, or whole language, which emphasizes understanding and thinking. A similar conflict in math and science has focused on either direct instruction or discovery methods as the alternatives. A recent report from the National Research Council on the Prevention of Reading Difficulties contended that it is time to end what they call the reading wars between phonics and whole language. Children need both. They need to know phonics and how to decode, but they also need to be able to take meaning from their reading—that is to understand what the words they read mean and to tie these meanings to other things that they already know or can know. In other words they need to think, and connect, and learn as well as to sound out and to spell.

Another example is in math. The National Council of Teachers of Mathematics has recommended that we teach children the principle of measurement. Some teachers have understood this to mean that children should measure with rulers and tape measures if they do not know their numbers, since those are the tools we associate with measuring. But if children are still unable to read the numbers on the stick or tape, these tools become relatively useless. What do we do? In excellent schools we see young children measuring with their shoes, their fingers, pieces of string, long blocks using hatch marks to indicate "how many," thus learning a far more intellectually important idea about measuring, that is, any uniform size tool can be used to measure.

We can say the same thing about all of the disciplines we want children to learn. Children who know their number facts can think more easily about number problems. Children who have learned to categorize animals can think about the nature of their work more efficiently. Children who know that words are written with an alphabet tied to sounds can understand the uses of reading and writing. We do not need to protect children from academic knowledge like counting, and the alphabets, or categorizing elements in our world, if we encourage or provide opportunities for them to use them to think with. An intellectually challenging program provides both the opportunities to learn the basic skills and the reasons and uses for them in thinking.

A challenging curriculum is one that provides opportunities for children to know about the world, to learn specific skills, and to use those skills to better understand and think about the world around them.

A challenging curriculum, then, is one that provides opportunities for children to know about the world, to learn specific skills, and to use those skills to better understand and think about the world around them. It is also one that commands the interest and attention of children so that learning is exciting and worthy of hard work.

The world is full of things to construct knowledge about. If we lived in Alaska, we would point out to our children the many different types of snow and which ones work well for igloos. Since this is not important here, we rarely call children's attention to different types of snow, we do not plan experiences for them that focus on how sticky, or granular, or wet snow is, nor do we make opportunities for children to construct play igloos. In the U.S. it is important to learn how to read. But, just as it is not inevitable that all children will notice and understand the building qualities of different types of snow, it is not inevitable that all children will construct for themselves the relationship between the alphabet and reading. Most children need to have this relationship pointed out to them, just as Eskimo children need the qualities of snow pointed out to them. Children must learn that reading has meaning, that letters tell adults what to read; that letters and sounds of words map or match to one another; that letters are configured differently from one another, each with a different sound. They must know the meaning of a large number of words and be able to identify the sequence of sounds in a word in order to match them with particular letters. Children need all of these pieces of the puzzle to construct reading for themselves.

Children are not likely to learn these things from just singing the alphabet song. I am not saying that it will harm children to sing the alphabet song, I am saying that it is not enough. I am saying that children also need information that permits them to construct the "meaning" of reading so that they will have an easier time learning the mechanics of the decoding process when they get to school. The same is true for math. Rote counting permits familiarity with the invariant order of the numbers, but children also need to understand one-to-one relationships, that all things can be counted and described with numbers, that parts may be deconstructed from wholes and reconstructed, that there are many different ways to use numbers (addresses, bus numbers, etc.), and that the counting system is orderly. These are the things that adults need to point out and value if children are going to struggle to understand them.

Principle #8: Excellent programs make learning enjoyable. There is one other aspect of an excellent curriculum I want to mention. That is, it engages children's interest and encourages them to want to know more. It balances what adults know children will need to know, with what children want to know, so that learning is a pleasurable activity that lasts a lifetime. This means that teachers need to expend as much energy on making lessons (basic skills or thinking and problems solving), interesting, rewarding, and personally satisfying.

Teaching children these things does not need to be drudgery, with children passively listening to lectures by teachers or doing the same lessons over and over until they get it. I do not know why so many teachers think that if we want children to be school successful we should teach them the same things in preschool that they are supposed to learn in first grade. So, we often find 4-year-olds who do not yet like and understand stories, being force-fed with phonics. In a developmentally appropriate classroom, the teacher plans the environment and activities so that children can understand all of the ideas that underlie the complex concepts in reading and math. She makes sure that the readiness lessons that children need to be successful in school are there to be learned in an interesting and useful way. Making sure children are ready for school means teachers must think through carefully what to teach and how to teach it. I often suggest to preschool teachers to consult with kindergarten teachers, not so they can teach the kindergarten curriculum, but so they can prepare children to learn it easily. Careful planning is the most important thing preschool teachers can do to make school subjects like reading and math so enjoyable children will go to school eager for more.

An excellent curriculum engages children's interest and encourages them to want to know more.

Principle #9: Excellent programs do not use lockstep curricula. Children are not like cars on an assembly line. We cannot stamp out a standard model child using standardized curricula and practices. Back-to-basics with work sheets and basic drill and practice will no more ensure that every child learns than leaving children alone to learn only what they want. Does this mean that there are no group expectations? Absolutely not, what it means is that we help children in different ways meet our expectations, leaving room for individual differences.

Principle #10: Excellent programs assess children's development and learning. When we have selected a curriculum, the next most important activity is figuring out how to assess children's learning to see if our practices are having the desired effect.

But there are some problems with assessment. You remember my principle of individual differences and that development does not unfold in lockstep fashion. A recent study done on 2-year-olds is a case in point. Many of the children who knew as few as 8 words when they were 2 years old were perfectly normal in their language development at age 4. If we assess at age 2 we might decide these 8-word 2-year-olds were

We must pay attention to developmental principles—not as laws but as starting points for our thinking.

language-delayed and institute all kinds of unnecessary interventions. The most important aspect of assessment is that it continues over time and shows the direction of development rather than making diagnoses on the basis of a snapshot in time. Being delayed in language development at age 2 does not predict language delay at age 4. Timing of our assessments of children is terribly important and we must be extremely careful about making predictions for the future on the basis of what a child can do today.

My favorite story about the diversity of children of the same age and assessment occurred in a kindergarten program I was the consultant for. The teacher was convinced that the worksheets she had the children doing were teaching them to be ready for first grade. One day when I was visiting, all of the children were coloring a worksheet of the letter "s" that had pictures of a sock and a sailboat on the page. All the children had correctly circled the S as distinct from C and Z and all had successfully written six S's. I asked four children what they were doing. One child said, "It's an alphabet" but didn't think the pictures had anything to do with it. One said, "It is an s and sock and sail start with it." Another child didn't know the name or the sound of the letter but identified the pictures as "a stocking and a boat." The last child said, *"Yo no se."*

Standardized tests and screening instruments are often used to test whether children are learning from the curriculum, but these are rather like the worksheet, you don't always know what children understand by what you ask. Further, young children's performance of these instruments can be affected by their emotional state, by their interests, by their understanding or the meaning of the tests, so tests are less reliable and valid for young children than they are for older ones. An excellent early childhood program has ongoing assessment of what children actually are able to do and know and does not depend solely on one-shot evidence. Portfolios, check lists, student self-assessment, projects, and anecdotal notes can all be used effectively to mark how different children learn, the pacing of their learning, and the results of using different interventions when learning does not occur. Teachers need tools to monitor change as children move toward mastery of the curriculum. The responsibility rests on the teacher to ensure that children are learning what is being taught.

My message for this morning is that we must pay attention to developmental principles—not as laws but as starting points for our thinking. I have called your attention to the developmental importance of relationships between teachers/caregivers and children, to the fit between children's learning styles and our curriculum, to adapting group goals and objectives to individual and cultural differences. But, I have also said that there is no foolproof blueprint of practices that are tied to these principles. In fact, each program, each teacher must work out the best way to apply developmental principles to particular children in particular settings. Which, of course, is not easy.

10 Guiding Principles for Excellence

Excellent programs

- use developmental principles to help them plan.
- acknowledge that developmental principles are not the same as recipes for practice.
- attend to children's maturation and pace of development.
- individualize children's care and education.
- accommodate cultural similarities and differences by connecting what children do know with what we want them to learn.
- pay attention to relationships.
- provide a balanced curriculum.
- make learning enjoyable by engaging children's interest and encouraging them to want to know more.
- do not use lockstep curricula: children are not cars on an assembly line.
- assess children's development and learning.

Early Learning, Later Success: The Abecedarian Study

Early Childhood Educational Intervention for Poor Children

Executive Summary

Frank Porter Graham Child Development Center
(University of North Carolina at Chapel Hill)

Background

- Poverty in early childhood has long-lasting negative consequences for cognitive development and academic outcomes, as shown by numerous studies. Comparisons among different groups of school children find that poor children fare worse academically than those raised in more advantageous circumstances. Poor children begin to lag behind in the earliest school years, suggesting that they enter school not adequately prepared for success.[1]
- In an effort to overcome the negative academic odds for poor children, early childhood education has been provided both in rigorous, University-based model programs and at the state and national levels. Such endeavors were generally based on the theory that providing early intellectual stimulation would enhance cognitive development, thereby allowing children to enter school better prepared to learn. This should in turn increase the probability of early school success, lead to later scholastic success, and eventually, result in vocational achievement and successful social adaptation in adulthood.
- Unfortunately, few early childhood programs have been sufficiently well controlled to permit scientists to evaluate the extent to which long-term outcomes are attributable to the program itself. Low numbers of participants or high attrition among samples reduced confidence in findings from some University-based programs. Many state and local programs lacked the degree of scientific control necessary for firm conclusions.
- From pooled long-term results of other early childhood programs, investigators concluded that such programs were associated with reductions in the degree to which treated children were placed in special education and retained in grade during the public school years.[2] Short-term gains in cognitive development were also found along with boosts in academic performance. However, both kinds of gains tended to erode 3 to 6 years after participants entered school.

Originally published by the *Frank Porter Graham Child Development Center,* October 1999, pp. 1-3.

- The Abecedarian Project differed from most other early childhood programs in that: 1) it began in early infancy whereas other programs began at age 2 or older, and 2) treated children had five years of exposure to early education in a high quality child care setting whereas most other programs were of shorter duration.

The Abecedarian Project

- The Abecedarian Project was a carefully controlled study in which 57 infants from low-income families were randomly assigned to receive early intervention in a high quality child care setting and 54 were in a non-treated control group. This degree of scientific control gives investigators greater confidence that differences between the treated and untreated individuals can be attributed to the intervention itself, rather than to differences among treated and untreated families.
- The treated children received full-time educational intervention in a high-quality childcare setting from infancy through age 5. Each child had an individualized prescription of educational activities consisting of "games" that were incorporated into his or her day. These activities addressed social, emotional, and cognitive development but gave particular emphasis to language.
- The treated and untreated children were initially comparable with respect to scores on infant mental and motor tests. However, from the age of 18 months and through the completion of the child care program, children in the intervention group had significantly higher scores on mental tests than children in the control group. Follow-up cognitive assessments completed at ages 12 and 15 years showed that the intervention group continued to have higher average scores on mental tests. The treatment/control group gap narrowed but the trajectories did not converge. Effect sizes remained moderate.
- Treated children scored significantly higher on tests of reading and math from the primary grades through middle adolescence. Effect sizes for reading were large; those for math were large to moderate.
- The investigators have now completed a young-adult follow-up assessment of study participants. At age 21, cognitive functioning, academic skills, educational attainment, employment, parenthood, and social adjustment were measured. One-hundred-four of the original 111 infants (53 from the intervention group and 51 controls) were assessed.

Major Findings of the Young Adult Follow-Up Study

- Young adults who received early educational intervention had significantly higher mental test scores from toddlerhood through age 21 than did untreated controls. Averaged over the age span tested, the mental test score effect size for treatment was moderate and considered educationally meaningful.
- Enhanced language skills in the children appears to have mediated the effects of early intervention on mental test performance (i.e., cognitive skills).
- Reading achievement scores were consistently higher for individuals with early intervention. Treatment effect sizes remained large from primary school through age 21. Enhanced cognitive skills appeared to mediate treatment effects on reading achievement.
- Mathematics achievement showed a pattern similar to that for reading, with treated individuals earning higher scores. Effect sizes were medium in contrast to the large effects for reading. Again, enhanced cognitive functioning appeared to mediate treatment effects.
- Those with treatment were significantly more likely still to be in school at age 21—40% of the intervention group compared with 20% of the control group.
- A significant difference was also found for the percent of young adults who ever attended a four-year college. About 35% of the young adults in the intervention group had either graduated from or were at the time of the assessment attending a four-year college or university. In contrast, only about 14% in the control group had done so.
- Young adults in the intervention group were, on average, one year older (19.1 years) when their first child was born compared with those in the control group (17.7 years), although the youngest individuals in both groups were comparable in age when their first child was born.
- Employment rates were higher (65%) for the treatment group than for the control group (50%), although the trend was not statistically significant.

Policy Implications

- The importance of high quality, educational childcare from early infancy is now clear. The Abecedarian study provides scientific evidence that early childhood education significantly improves the scholastic success and educational attainments of poor children even into early adulthood.
- The Abecedarian study began treatment in early infancy, emphasizing the importance of providing

a learning environment for children from the very beginning of life. Every child deserves a good start in an environment that is safe, healthy, emotionally supportive, and cognitively stimulating. Welfare reform means that, more than ever, poverty children will need early childcare. The educational stimulus value of these early caregiving years must not be wasted.

- Childcare officials should be aware of the importance of quality care beginning in infancy.
- Quality care requires sufficient well-trained staff to ensure that every child receives the kind of appropriate, individualized attention provided by the Abecedarian model.
- Future research should concentrate on identifying the specific learning techniques most effective for all groups and types of young children.
- More and more of America's children will need out of home care. This is especially true for poor children. We must not lose this opportunity to provide them the early learning experiences that will increase their chances for later success

1. Alexander, K. L., & Entwisle, D. R. (1988). Achievement in the first 2 years of school: Patterns and processes. *Monographs of the Society for Research in Child Development, 53* (Serial No. 218).
2. Lazar, I., Darlington, R., Murray, H., Royce, J., & Snipper, A. (1982). Lasting effects of early education: A report from the consortium for longitudinal studies. *Monographs of the Society for Research in Child Development, 47* (Serial No. 195).

Index

I

J

K

L

M

N

O

P

AE Article Review Form

We encourage you to photocopy and use this page as a tool to assess how the articles in ***Annual Editions*** expand on the information in your textbook. By reflecting on the articles you will gain enhanced text information. You can also access this useful form on a product's book support Web site at ***http://www.dushkin.com/online/.***

NAME: DATE:

TITLE AND NUMBER OF ARTICLE:

BRIEFLY STATE THE MAIN IDEA OF THIS ARTICLE:

LIST THREE IMPORTANT FACTS THAT THE AUTHOR USES TO SUPPORT THE MAIN IDEA:

WHAT INFORMATION OR IDEAS DISCUSSED IN THIS ARTICLE ARE ALSO DISCUSSED IN YOUR TEXTBOOK OR OTHER READINGS THAT YOU HAVE DONE? LIST THE TEXTBOOK CHAPTERS AND PAGE NUMBERS:

LIST ANY EXAMPLES OF BIAS OR FAULTY REASONING THAT YOU FOUND IN THE ARTICLE:

LIST ANY NEW TERMS/CONCEPTS THAT WERE DISCUSSED IN THE ARTICLE, AND WRITE A SHORT DEFINITION:

ANNUAL EDITIONS revisions depend on two major opinion sources: one is our Advisory Board, listed in the front of this volume, which works with us in scanning the thousands of articles published in the public press each year; the other is you—the person actually using the book. Please help us and the users of the next edition by completing the prepaid article rating form on this page and returning it to us. Thank you for your help!

We Want Your Advice

ANNUAL EDITIONS: Early Childhood Education 00/01

ARTICLE RATING FORM

Here is an opportunity for you to have direct input into the next revision of this volume. We would like you to rate each of the 40 articles listed below, using the following scale:

1. Excellent: should definitely be retained
2. Above average: should probably be retained
3. Below average: should probably be deleted
4. Poor: should definitely be deleted

Your ratings will play a vital part in the next revision. So please mail this prepaid form to us just as soon as you complete it. Thanks for your help!

RATING	ARTICLE
	1. Starting Early: The Why and How of Preschool Education
	2. What Makes Good Early Childhood Teachers?
	3. A Child Shall Lead Us
	4. Mysteries of the Brain
	5. Using Early Chilhood Brain Development Research
	6. Do Working Parents Make the Grade?
	7. Fetal Psychology
	8. Children's Prenatal Exposure to Drugs: Implications for Early Childhood Educators
	9. Baby Talk
	10. Boys Will Be Boys
	11. The Education of Hispanics in Early Childhood: Of Roots and Wings
	12. The Petite Elite
	13. Simply Sensational Spaces: A Multi-"S" Approach to Toddler Environments
	14. Don't Shut Fathers Out
	15. A Case for Developmental Continuity in a Bilingual K-2 Setting
	16. Homework Doesn't Help
	17. Make or Break
	18. Playtime Is Cancelled
	19. "But What's Wrong with Letter Grades?" Responding to Parents' Questions about Alternative Assessment
	20. From Philosophy to Practice in Inclusive Early Childhood Programs
	21. Emergent Literacy in an Early Childhood Classroom: Center Learning to Support the Child with Special Needs

RATING	ARTICLE
	22. Inclusion of Young Children with Special Needs in Early Childhood Education: The Research Base
	23. The Why and Wherefore
	24. Teaching Peace Concepts to Children
	25. Television Violence and Its Effects on Young Children
	26. Fostering Intrinsic Motivation in Early Childhood Classrooms
	27. Adverse Effects of Witnessing Violence
	28. Play As Curriculum
	29. Why Curriculum Matters in Early Childhood Education
	30. Isn't That Cute? Transforming the Cute Curriculum into Authentic Learning
	31. Productive Questions: Tools for Supporting Constructivist Learning
	32. Beginning to Implement the Reggio Philosophy
	33. Documenting Children's Learning
	34. Challenging Movement Experiences for Young Children
	35. What Role Should Technology Play in Young Children's Learning?
	36. Learning to Go with the Grain of the Brain
	37. Almost a Million Children in School before Kindergarten: Who Is Responsible for Early Childhood Services?
	38. Why Students Lose When "Tougher Standards" Win: A Conversation with Alfie Kohn
	39. Achieving Excellence in Education
	40. Early Learning, Later Success: The Abecedarian Study

(Continued on next page)

ANNUAL EDITIONS: EARLY CHILDHOOD EDUCATION 00/01

BUSINESS REPLY MAIL
FIRST-CLASS MAIL PERMIT NO. 84 GUILFORD CT

POSTAGE WILL BE PAID BY ADDRESSEE

Dushkin/McGraw-Hill
Sluice Dock
Guilford, CT 06437-9989

ABOUT YOU

Name | Date

Are you a teacher? ☐ A student? ☐

Your school's name

Department

Address | City | State | Zip

School telephone #

YOUR COMMENTS ARE IMPORTANT TO US !

Please fill in the following information:

For which course did you use this book?

Did you use a text with this *ANNUAL EDITION*? ☐ yes ☐ no

What was the title of the text?

What are your general reactions to the *Annual Editions* concept?

Have you read any particular articles recently that you think should be included in the next edition?

Are there any articles you feel should be replaced in the next edition? Why?

Are there any World Wide Web sites you feel should be included in the next edition? Please annotate.

May we contact you for editorial input? ☐ yes ☐ no

May we quote your comments? ☐ yes ☐ no